They Left It All Behind

New Imago: Series in Theoretical, Clinical, and Applied Psychoanalysis

Series Editor

Jon Mills, Adler Graduate Professional School, Toronto

New Imago: Series in Theoretical, Clinical, and Applied Psychoanalysis is a scholarly and professional publishing imprint devoted to all aspects of psychoanalytic inquiry and research in theoretical, clinical, philosophical, and applied psychoanalysis. It is inclusive in focus, hence fostering a spirit of plurality, respect, and tolerance across the psychoanalytic domain. The series aspires to promote open and thoughtful dialogue across disciplinary and interdisciplinary fields in mental health, the humanities, and the social and behavioral sciences. It furthermore wishes to advance psychoanalytic thought and extend its applications to serve greater society, diverse cultures, and the public at large. The editorial board is comprised of the most noted and celebrated analysts, scholars, and academics in the English speaking world and is representative of every major school in the history of psychoanalytic thought.

Titles in the Series

They Left It All Behind

Trauma, Loss, and Memory among Eastern European Jewish Immigrants and Their Children

Hannah Hahn

ROWMAN & LITTLEFIELD
Lanham • Boulder • New York • London

Published by Rowman & Littlefield
An imprint of The Rowman & Littlefield Publishing Group, Inc.
4501 Forbes Boulevard, Suite 200, Lanham, Maryland 20706
www.rowman.com

6 Tinworth Street, London SE11 5AL

British Library Cataloguing in Publication Information Available

Library of Congress Control Number: 2019949310

∞ ™ The paper used in this publication meets the minimum requirements of American
National Standard for Information Sciences Permanence of Paper for Printed Library
Materials, ANSI/NISO Z39.48-1992.

For my grandparents,
Ida Zigman Asch, William Asch,
Helen Hoffman Hahn, and Phillip Hahn

And my parents,
Marion Hahn and Jack Hahn

Contents

Foreword

In the Shadow of the Shtetl

For Eastern European Jews, there is the shadow of the shtetl. In retrospect, shtetl life can conjure up images of community and togetherness, extended family, and the bustle of communitarian life. With its assigned roles, strict religious observance, culture of interdependency, and panoptical quality of living in a tight-knit community, the shtetl promised to provide a clear structure for an industrious and observant life. The tight-knit nature of the community, however, could also be stifling for freer spirits, and this, as well as the grinding poverty and persistent discrimination both in shtetls and in urban communities, offered a powerful impetus for East European Jews to flee. The clustering of Jews in shtetls and urban enclaves also marked their communities as distinct and created vulnerability to anti-Semitic attacks. The annihilatory pogroms that originated in Tsarist Russia in the late 1800s were an early terrifying and egregious example that created a culture of pervasive fear during the period under discussion here. For the people featured in this book—descendants of East European shtetl dwellers and their counterparts in urban enclaves—the shadows are ever-present, and Hannah Hahn devotes her inquiry to shining light on these shadows and the ways in which the ghostly lineages of the flight from the shtetls continue to echo through the lives of their descendants; some of the turn-of-the-century immigrants fled involuntarily—and often under severe duress—to whatever safe haven they might find. Others fled, in the grand tradition of economic migrants, in simple hopes of a better life. A very large number of these migrants landed in New York City, and their descendants continue to leave an indelible mark on the intellectual, cultural, and commercial life of their adopted city and country.

The story is more complicated, of course. For all involuntary migrants, there are cumulative layers of trauma. As the stories in this book reveal, the origin trauma that triggered flight from shtetls, communities, and nations was profoundly traumatic for many of the fleeing East European Jews. Some survivors had narrow escapes from mass murder, rape, and incarceration; others witnessed the annihilation of their loved ones. Families were wrenched apart as some stayed behind and others were scattered in a Jewish diaspora across the globe. Many had also lived lives of grinding poverty in the shtetls, and they had endured generations of anti-Semitic attacks—both of which, no doubt, left deep scars.

Then there was the trauma of the passage. Apart from the arbitrariness of the destinations to which people were forced to flee, there was the immensely difficult passage across the ocean, especially for the many who suffered severe privation while traveling in steerage. For survivors who arrived at Ellis Island with exalted hope and undying gratitude, the harshness of the new immigrant experience was a slap in the face. Many of those arriving in New York, for example, struggled with the awfulness of tenement life, lack of fluency in English, lack of local cultural knowledge, unemployment and poverty, labor exploitation, cultural estrangement, and anti-Semitic prejudice against their language, religion, and customs.

Finally, hovering in the background is the shadow that we have come to know as the Holocaust. The descendants of these original East European Jewish migrants continue to live in the shadow of the Holocaust. While the original migrants could not have anticipated the culminating act of Hitler's Final Solution, which sought to exterminate all Jews, their children and their children's children have had to live with the terrible knowledge and the abject consequences of this mass genocide, and the shadow of this event no doubt colors their recollections and interpretations of earlier events. They have also lived with the knowledge that their survival was assured only because of the sacrifices entailed in the earlier flight of their parents and grandparents from the shtetls and urban enclaves of Jewish Europe. A great many of their cousins who had stayed behind, and who had survived waves of anti-Semitism and genocidal pogroms, were not so fortunate when the Nazis put their genocidal plan into action—creating further cascades of un-fathomable loss for those who survived.

Those early migrants are no longer with us, and Hannah Hahn, acting here as psychocultural historian, seeks to exhume the lingering effects of these cumulative traumas by sitting with a small sample of their descendants and piecing together a narrative that might suggest the intergenerational line-ages that have shaped their emotional lives and ways of being. "Sitting with" may sound like a fairly companionable and even innocuous task. However, one of the most robust findings in studies of the intergenerational conse-quences of trauma is that silence serves as a very powerful agent of transmission. As Davoine and Gaudillière (2004) noted in the epigraph to their book *History beyond Trauma*, "Whereof one cannot speak, thereof one cannot stay silent," thereby suggesting that trauma that cannot be spoken will find other modes of expression. Hahn goes in depth into the mechanism of silence and pays close attention to the gaps, silences, and moments of *nescience*—what Christopher Bollas (1987) calls *unthought knowns*—that so profoundly shape our subjectivity. Some years ago, in my book *The Subject of Childhood* (2009), I reported on my difficulty in engaging my own beloved mother in a conversation about the legacy of the emotional and material privations that I was dimly aware were part of her history:

> I gained further insight into the power of shame in creating walls of secrecy when I decided last year to interview my mother about her early life experiences. The anxiety I experienced at the prospect of asking her was surely indicative that I was aware of the taboo of ambient ghosts. My mother consented, but then she grew agitated. "There wouldn't be any point in me talking to you," she said, "because I couldn't tell you the bad things. They are too awful. I wouldn't want anyone to know them." She was not persuaded by my argument that it would be helpful to me in understanding myself and understanding how I came to be. Her argument appeared to be partly composed of a suggestion that such painful memories are best forgotten, and partly that revelation of abject memories could only perpetuate shame. . . . What surprised me most, I think, was that the memories that were shameful to her were not for the most part memories of particular traumas, but simply memories of the everyday abjection of severe poverty. She reminisced about the fact that her sister and she shared one good frock, and therefore alternated days attending school, despite the fact that both loved learning intensely. She spoke repeatedly of the daily humiliations of rural poverty, repeatedly prefacing her remarks with "You won't believe this" or "I can't believe we had it that hard." (O'Loughlin, 2009, pp. 54–55)

Later conversations with my mom's sister left me in no doubt that my mother had indeed spared me—and perhaps herself—from reckoning with the more unspeakable traumas of her childhood.

The work that is embodied in this book is one of piecing together a story partly from narrated fragments; partly from suffering inscribed on the body; and partly from the gaps, fissures, and lacunae that are suggestive of unspoken—and perhaps unspeakable—suffering that transmits from generation to generation largely through the working of silence. This silence, as Lawrence Langer noted in *Holocaust Testimonies: The Ruins of Memory* (1993), is to be received sympathetically, not pathologized or condemned. Sometimes, even for succeeding generations, the risk of looking back and seeking truth is clearly dangerous and risks re-traumatization. The reward of speaking, however, as the material in this book illustrates, is a possibility of symbolizing experience and receiving permission to re-story experience and to move on with a narrative no longer held in thrall to a frozen past. At a minimum, the material in this book offers an opportunity to bear witness and to walk the road, if only for a moment, with those who have fashioned lives built on the great losses, great idealism, and tremendous sacrifice of their forebears. The testimony also raises important questions about the workings of resilience and the capacity of penurious, culturally dislocated, and sometimes trauma-tized migrants to create the conditions for their own material success and to create ladders to professional success for their children. Hannah Hahn bears witness to her own family's sacrifice here. She also bears witness to the sacrifices of the East Europeans Jews that constitute her community of ori-gin. In doing so, she invites us to join her in this act of witnessing, asking us to accompany her in the humbling but deeply human act of witnessing the capacity of the human spirit to remember and the capacity of humans to go on despite the great privations inflicted on them by other people. Fundamen-tally, bearing witness is an act of remembering and hope in a painful world.

Michael O'Loughlin
Adelphi University

Preface

They Left It All Behind

"My grandparents were part of the great wave of Jewish immigration from Eastern Europe that occurred between 1881 and 1924. I knew all four, and three lived well into my adulthood; as an adult, I spent a good deal of time with my mother's parents. Yet I understood little about their subjective experiences as immigrants. As a young child growing up in a gentile, working-class suburb, surrounded by Catholic neighbors, I felt some shame about the visits by the 'funny little Jewish people' from my extended family" (Hahn, 2015, p. 179). They talked strangely, and their European table manners seemed uncouth. My first-generation American parents highly valued proper speech, and I privately wondered if perhaps there was something wrong with the people unable to speak as I was taught. I secretly pondered the possibility that they might be retarded. As I became an adult, I began to feel guilty thinking about my grandparents' lack of opportunities and the poverty they had endured compared to all that I had been given. They had sacrificed, I felt, so that I could have the riches of an American life. On some level, I realized that they were "little" because indeed they had been malnourished. Yet none of this was spoken about.

This work was born in the summer of 2007, while I was reading Weinberg's *The World of Our Mothers* (1988), based on oral histories of Eastern European Jewish immigrant women. One day I realized that I too wished to be able to interview these immigrants. Weinberg's informants, like my four grandparents, arrived in America before 1924, when legislation effectively ended immigration for all but a few Eastern and Southern Europeans. As I thought about my wish to do this work, I realized that—even though I was both a psychologist and a psychoanalyst—my family and I knew little about my grandparents' subjective lives as immigrants. On some level, I probably wanted to do this work because I wished to meet people like my grandparents, perhaps to experience at first hand what I imagined was the richness of their backgrounds, and certainly I missed my grandparents; I even missed their "strange" accents. Since almost every person from my grandparents' generation by then had died, I decided to interview the immigrants' children, people from my parents' generation.

The birth of this book on that summer day was unusual for me. The inspiration for it happened inside of a few minutes; it had almost chosen me rather than the other way around, and I did not consider myself a person to whom long-term interests "happened." I had up to that time been only somewhat interested in Jewish themes. Later that summer, I visited Paris and Prague, spending time in Paris's Musee d'Art et d'Histoire du Judaisme and Prague's Jewish quarter. Upon my return, I began background research and consulted with another psychologist about interview questions.

As I started to formulate my study, I wanted to understand what my grandparents had never spoken about: what was it like subjectively to be an immigrant? I was struck by the enormity of what this generation had done. What was it like to come from a country so far away, to leave everything that you knew? Some of the immigrants had left their families and come alone: what was it like to know that you would almost certainly never see your family again? What was it like to live in a country in which the language, the ways of life, and the physical surroundings were new? I knew that I would only be able to find approximate answers to these questions, as they would be refracted through the lenses of the immigrants' children's eyes. I was also curious about the psychological lives of the adult children, who both absorbed the difficulties of their parents' lives and navigated the path to becoming Americans.

With my research training as a psychologist, I constructed an interview that would enable me to answer my questions with data. But where was the psychoanalyst in me, the person who would look at my own motives for undertaking this ambitious endeavor? I did not realize for some time that, as much as this was an objective research project, it was also a personal journey: it would help me to explain concerns about my own family.

Gradually I began to think about the denial that shrouded my grandparents' stories and that was implicitly reinforced by my parents. This denial, which we can also think about as disavowal or silence, was, as I found out as I began looking for research participants, widespread among the immigrant generation. More often than not, the immigrants' children knew little about what their parents had gone through in Eastern Europe or during their transition to America. Because of the silence surrounding the histories of so many, this book grew into an attempt to flesh out the empty spaces left in the personal narratives passed down by many of the immigrants, as well as in their children's accounts. I think of this as the re-creation of lost memory. In other words, for the many people who knew little about the objective and subjective lives of immigrant forebears, this book attempts to provide an idea of the memories that were lost. It may also prompt some people to explore the puzzling parts of their families' lives.

As I began to interview people, I realized how prevalent trauma was for their immigrant parents. Since most arrived after World War I and its brutal aftermath, many had been affected by the violence and upheaval of that period. But their children were also affected, and gradually the intergenerational transmission of trauma became one of the book's main topics. In my own family, my maternal grandmother endured violence and war, and my paternal grandmother's entire family was killed in the Holocaust; both grandmothers were motherless at early ages. Three of my grandparents had been so extremely poor and hungry that this in itself could be considered a form of trauma. Although as a young person I knew some of this as disembodied facts, even as an adult I knew none of it in a real way. Nor was I taught in Hebrew School about the pogroms (officially tolerated massacres) that were widespread.

It is indeed difficult to think about the trauma suffered by those that we love. I imagine that my parents, though they certainly cared about my grandparents, were too close to their parents' suffering to truly work out how they had been affected by it. Because we have the perspective of distance, it falls to us in the third and successive generations to begin to make sense of our families' painful stories.

Over the course of four-and-one-half years, I interviewed twenty-two adult children of Eastern European Jewish immigrants whose parents arrived by 1930. I spoke with each person for five to six hours, conducting semi-structured psychohistory interviews. Life stories of these individuals—which recount and make psychological sense of what they told me—constitute the backbone of this book. I asked during interviews about immigrant parents' subjective experiences when immigrating and about adapting to America. And I asked about the children's early memories and whether they had wished to have lives different than their parents'. A central question was whether their parents had missed home or the people they left there.

I analyzed the interviews through my perspective as a psychoanalyst. My task was both to convey the textures of individuals' lives and to make inferences about the subjective realities of both the immigrants and their children. A central perspective was intergenerational: what were the psychological influences of the immigrants' lives on their children? In a broad sense, my purpose in writing this book was to describe the influence of historical events on the lives of the immigrants and their children.

Chapter 1 begins with my surprise that, when I asked whether their parents missed home or family, many said, in effect, no: "They left it all be-

hind." In other words, there was nothing for them to miss. This was a disavowal of loss, and it very often was a result of trauma. I describe the history
of the Eastern European Jews in the nineteenth and early twentieth centuries
to shed light on the trauma of persecution, pogroms, and poverty.

Chapter 2 explores trauma among the immigrants and its intergenerational transmission to their children, as well as different ways in which parents
communicated about trauma to their children. Immigrant life during the period of transition to the U.S. is one topic of chapter 3, and the chapter also
treats loss. We know from the historical record that, despite the trauma that
many of the immigrants suffered, most of them actually were homesick for
the Old Country. Nevertheless, only a small number of immigrants' children
told me that their parents truly missed either the families left behind or the
Old Country itself.

Chapters 4 and 5 explore the childhoods and adulthoods of interviewees.
For some, memories of happy parts of childhood stand out alongside the
impact of their parents' difficulties; for others, the effects of parental trauma
overshadow normal spontaneity and play. Parents wanted their children to
have better lives than their own, and children often wanted to repay their
parents' sacrifices by excelling. In thinking about my interviewees as adults,
I was struck by their resilience despite the trauma passed on by parents. They
found ways of remaining connected to their parents' pasts while becoming
successful Americans.

How did trauma and loss affect what we know about our histories? In the
concluding chapter, I discuss how trauma influenced the transmission of
memory, as well as other reasons that information and the complexity of
emotions were lost between the generations. Because of the children's painful emotions about their parents' losses or traumatic histories, they had their
own sometimes defensive interpretations of parents' pasts; some needed to
avoid knowing too much.

Just as my grandparents did a century ago, today huge numbers of people
seek to immigrate to the U.S. in search of better lives. More than one million
legal immigrants came to the U.S. in 2016, many because of traumatic conditions at home; all had to cope with the losses of migration. As I write in 2019,
thousands of Central Americans, unprotected by their own governments, flee
the terror of gang violence. Hoping to enter the U.S., their trauma is only
increased because American immigration policy criminalizes them and separates them from their families (Allen, 2019). This book's exploration of the
legacies of trauma and loss for immigrants of the past and their children can
help us to understand how to aid the immigrants of the twenty-first century.

Acknowledgments

My warmest thanks go to the many people who provided professional support and personal encouragement as I completed this book. I owe my greatest debt to my husband, William C. Tucker. He encouraged me unconditionally, listened with interest as I developed themes, and provided editorial skills. Over the long period of the book's realization, he sacrificed my company, and he kept our household going after his retirement. There are two others without whom this book would not have become a reality. Eva Fogelman, a psychologist specializing in the Holocaust, helped greatly in constructing the interview questionnaire and provided much guidance and support during data collection and initial stages of the writing process. Professor Michael O'Loughlin of Adelphi University believed in this work, contributed professional advice, answered countless questions, and encouraged me every step of the way. He also read drafts of parts of the manuscript and helpfully wrote the book's foreword. Another person, my daughter Hayley, also deserves mention: being a mother to Hayley taught me firsthand about connection and secure attachment, and she helped me to enjoy life even in the midst of completing this book.

There are several other people to whom I owe the greatest of debts. David Lobenstine generously and enthusiastically helped me with writing suggestions, championed many of my early ideas, and heartened me during early phases of the work. Joyce Rosenberg believed in my work and encouraged me during the long final months it took to complete this book. Her energy and tireless work were priceless. Two colleagues contributed professional nurture: Amy Schaffer generously read the drafts of every chapter, and Nirit Pisano found time in her busy life to read parts of the manuscript; I am very grateful for their perceptive comments.

And most importantly, I am grateful to the men and women who shared their family memories and their own stories with me. They gave willingly of their time and allowed me glimpses both of the world of the immigrants and their own personal lives. Because they shared memories that were sometimes painful, they deserve my deepest appreiation.

I would like to thank Joyce Slochower and her writing group for their help in honing ideas found in the book's first half. Karen Starr and her writing group were helpful at a later stage in the book's development. Jill Salberg provided perceptive comments on the book's first chapter. Other psychoanalysts whose interest was helpful were Arnie Richards, Darlene Ehrenberg, Haydee Faimberg, and Eve Golden. Sydney Stahl Weinberg's book *The World of Our Mothers* inspired me to begin interviewing the immigrants' children.

Two Barnard students, Shoshana Oster and Perin Avari, provided energetic and willing assistance with library research and editing tasks. I very much appreciate their help. And thank you to all those who provided the book's photographs.

Finally and very importantly, I would like to thank Jon Mills for accepting this book in the New Imago Series. Alison Pavan and Katie O'Brien, past editors at Rowman & Littlefield, deserve thanks. And I so much appreciate the work of Mark Kerr, Courtney Packard, and Lara Hahn, my excellent current editors at Rowman & Littlefield.

Introduction

My mother's father was generally silent. At home he seemed to be a broken man, usually sleeping on the couch in the afternoon, both to escape his wife, my grandmother, and because he worked as a waiter at night. He broke his silences either during fights with my grandmother (usually instigated by her) or, during the other infrequent times that he spoke, with the refrain "only in America." But "only in America" was largely inexplicable to us as children. Looking back now, it seemed to mean: "Feh, America! What happens here is no good!" This makes sense when we realize that surely, with his heavy accent, he did not quite fit in in America. Furthermore, as a waiter rather than a small business owner, he was not considered successful even among his fellow immigrants.

Yet if life for him in America was not good, at the same time he could not have truly missed the Old Country. Indeed, in the U.S. he spat when he walked past a church, as he had been taught to do because of the anti-Semitism of Eastern Europe. Thus "only in America" was a highly ambivalent refrain, and we knew this because we understood that our grandfather said this with an ironic undertone. Our grandfather's irony suggested much that was left unsaid. We grew up with his silence, strange phrases, and irony, but we knew very little about his feelings. To this day, I know only a bit about his life experiences.

This grandfather was one of the many immigrants who communicated little to his children and grandchildren about his experiences. His silence is an example of how in many families a great deal about the past was lost between the generations. For my grandfather, "only in America" seemed to mean not only that America was no good, but "Feh. Nothing has been any good!" That is, his existence as a boy in Russia and his subsequent life in New York had been difficult. Looked at in another way, however, we realize that my grandfather's "home" in Russia was not a place to which he could have returned; this was typical for those who emigrated after 1903 (Matt, 2011; Sarna, 1981).[1] "Home" by its nature could no longer be home. Certainly, many of my grandfather's experiences in Eastern Europe would have been terrible.

My father's father was only a bit more communicative than my mother's father. According to Cowan and Cowan, "many of our grandparents . . . were actually uncommunicative with their own children, were tight, closed off" (1996, p. xviii). In my study, I specifically recruited interviewees who *had* at least one parent who spoke to their children about their experiences of immigration and/or their early years in America. But despite this, quite a number of the people I interviewed had at least one parent, usually a father, who said very little about the past. A few of these fathers died before their children reached the age when they might have initiated conversations about the past. Yet the frequency of uncommunicativeness about the past is evident.

Poverty, discrimination, or pogroms (officially tolerated massacres) had a devastating impact on the lives of the Eastern European Jews in the late nineteenth and early twentieth centuries. To our questions about such pasts, immigrants might have responded with a non-answer like: "What is there to talk about?" Silence was one frequent response to a past so difficult that often immigrants wanted to forget it. Yet partly because my grandparents did not speak about it, before I began my research, I did not fully understand the overwhelming difficulties of the immigrants' lives.

With two mostly silent grandfathers, it is perhaps no wonder that as an adult I wanted to know more about the immigrant generation. And it seems natural to begin a study of the subjective aspects of immigration, of the transition to a new country and a new way of life, with the question: "What did it feel like to be uprooted?" After all, my grandparents' generation had left behind an entire mode of living.

The Eastern European Jewish migration to America that occurred roughly between the years of 1881 and 1924 is termed the "third migration," distinguishing it from the first, or Sephardic migration, which began in 1654 and lasted through the American Revolution, and from the second, or German-Jewish migration, which spanned 1820 to 1880 (Diner, n.d.; Zollman, n.d.).[2] When I began my research into this wave of immigration, almost every one of the immigrants had died, and consequently I decided to interview the immigrants' children, individuals from my parents' generation. I would be recounting the psychological experiences of the immigrants as seen through the lens of their children's eyes. While much has been written about the immigrant generation—though from a historical rather than a psychological point of view—the voices of their children were generally eclipsed. Here I give voice to that generation also. As I would come to understand, the children were profoundly influenced by their parents' difficult lives as immigrants. Conserving these narratives is important not only for the historical and psychological information they provide but also because they are rich and fascinating accounts in themselves.

I interviewed twenty-two men and women for this book, each of whom had two parents who immigrated to the U.S. between 1881 and 1924. Understanding the influence of historical circumstances on the individual psyche is important to this study. For example, how did living through a pogrom affect a person? What was it like to go from a rural environment to a teeming city? And how did the experience of immigrant parents affect their children's psychological lives? Through much of the book, my emphasis is intergenerational.

Throughout the book, life stories bring alive the interviewees' narratives; these are in-depth psychological portraits. Occasionally, shorter accounts of an interviewee's life, which I call vignettes, appear. Because some interviewees' lives are featured in more than one chapter, and to help the reader keep track of names, a dramatis personae precedes each chapter.

When I began asking my interviewees about their parents' experiences of being uprooted, I expected that—if parents emigrated from a place in which traditional Jewish culture remained—I would hear that their parents missed either people left at home or the old ways of life. Like most of those from my generation, I imagined traditional Jewish Eastern Europe as a place of communal orientation and vibrancy, where people were known to one another and communal ties meant that individuals were looked after (Ewen, 1985; Kassow, 2007a; Shandler, 2014). As the opening song of "Fiddler on the Roof" tells us, the shtetl was the locus of tradition; we imagine that religion provided some comfort and that its rules gave life structure. One only has to open the pages of *Life Is with People* (Zborowski & Herzog, 1952) to be instructed in the richness of this traditional way of life.[3] Furthermore, I knew from the memoir literature (e.g., Calof, 1995; Cohen, 1995; Reisman, 2006) that for most, leaving Eastern Europe was painful and that, once in the U.S., many found the transition extremely difficult. As one immigrant told her daughter: "If I would ever know what I was going to go through, if papa had spread dollars all across the Atlantic Ocean, I would never have gone to America" (Weinberg, 1988, p. 107).

I was surprised, however. As I completed my first several interviews, although some of my interviewees said their parents missed family or what had once been home, I heard many statements like: "My father wanted to leave it all behind" or "My mother said she ran away and [had] only bad memories of it." I began to think about the effects of anti-Semitic violence and extreme poverty on the immigrants and their adult children. These were tales of trauma.

The psychological impact of trauma—the result of anti-Semitic persecution, pogroms, war, and extreme poverty—and the intergenerational transmission of this trauma became a main focus of the book. I have included a brief history of Jewish life in Eastern Europe: the Jews' precarious economic circumstances, their increasing persecution within the Russian Empire, and the chaotic maelstrom of World War I and its aftermath. This provides the context that explains the trauma of my interviewees' parents.

Immigration to America was often destabilizing, and I wanted to learn how the Eastern European Jews experienced the early weeks, months, and years after arrival in the U.S. A few parents, according to their children, were homesick and intensely missed either their families or their lives in Eastern Europe; a small number were unable to recover from this. Their stories and the impact of their difficulties on their children are described.

As I conducted the interviews, I became increasingly interested in the lives of my interviewees both as children and as adults. Because this interest developed fully only when I was well into the interviewing process, I have in-depth information on fewer of the immigrants' children's lives. Yet in a real way this book represents the children's stories. I wanted both to preserve their histories and to explain how they were affected by the repercussions of trauma and loss. I felt that it was crucial to make this part of my narrative.

While children felt the hardships and anxieties of their parents' lives, the ability to have better lives was for them perhaps the redemption of their parents' losses. It was extremely important to do one's best, to move up the socioeconomic ladder, and to become American. The adult children indeed flourished. Yet despite their real resilience, many of them were profoundly affected by their parents' loss and trauma.

Why was so much left unsaid in the transmission of immigrants' memories to their children? Trauma was just one of many reasons. Often nuances of emotion and complexity of information were lost between the generations. Adult children sometimes interpreted their parents' painful pasts in ways that would minimize their own difficult feelings.

Because my goal was to understand the influence of history on the individual, I also explored historical context. Learning about the conditions faced by new immigrants to America helps us to understand how they fared psychologically. The pressures and opportunities that the immigrants' sons and daughters encountered provide a background to our appreciation of their childhoods and adulthoods. The children wanted both to succeed in school and to integrate into the American world. The affluence of postwar America and the options open to Jews beginning in the 1960s contributed to their success as adults. Jews felt increasingly at home in the U.S.

RESEARCH APPROACH

As I began this research, my goals were to explore the immigrants' psychological, or subjective, lives and to find out what it was like to be a child of these immigrants. My interviews centered on these questions (a copy of the interview is found in appendix A). However, the focus shifted as my work proceeded. Many of the immigrant parents had experienced trauma before they left their homelands, and a few had experienced migration trauma.

Twelve women and ten men were interviewed for this work. Although the third wave of immigration effectively ended with the restrictive Immigration Act of 1924,[4] a few individuals belonging to this group arrived after 1924, which the law allowed when close family members were already U.S. citizens. Each of my interviewees' parents arrived by 1930. The majority of those I interviewed were in their eighties, several were in their seventies, and a small number were younger or older. All were cognitively intact. Most were retired, and their former professions included medical doctors, lawyers, scientists, teachers, and social workers; thus they were educated and articulate. Because of their high educational levels and socioeconomic status, overall they are not representative of second-generation American Jews.

Participants were located through synagogues, a Jewish senior service program, YIVO's online newsletter (the YIVO Institute for Jewish Research), a psychoanalytic institute's listserv, and acquaintances. All lived in the greater New York metropolitan area. I screened interviewees during an initial brief telephone conversation.

I conducted each interview, which consisted of two two- to three-hour sessions, and thus I spent approximately five to six hours with each person. The semistructured questionnaires I administered contained both open-ended and specific questions. I asked the same set of questions of each participant, but people were able to elaborate on questions in their own ways. Analogously, I was free to follow up on their responses based on what they said, and my freedom to respond this way is a hallmark of interpretive research (Addison, 1989). Interviews were recorded for backup purposes.

After each interview session, I recorded my psychological reactions to and "clinical" impressions of the individual. For example, how did the person react to me and to the interview questions? Was he or she open, evasive, in denial, or anxious?

In analyzing the interview information, I used my clinical skills and intuitions to understand the psychological influences on each participant. I then constructed what I call life stories based on my understanding of each. Interviewees varied greatly in their own level of psychological insight, and the psychological sophistication of the life story I formed varied in part because of this. The underlying theory of human development that informed how I thought about each person is described in the theoretical section that follows.

For confidentiality reasons, I changed the names of interviewees and their parents, as well as the places my interviewees were born and live currently. In addition, I did not specify where in Eastern Europe their parents were born.

Appendix B contains a more detailed account of the research.

THEORETICAL APPROACHES: A SUMMARY

Several groups of theoretical ideas are important to this book, and this "thumbnail" summary aims at helping to familiarize the reader with them. My understanding of psychoanalytic theory—my overall way of thinking—informed the life stories I constructed, and I describe this first.

The psychoanalyst is formed by her theory. Over my many years of study and thinking about patients, I found that the theory I had learned became so implicit and ingrained that its presence was sometimes barely remembered. Nevertheless, I realized that I applied the same gestalt of ideas to those I interviewed for this book as I do in thinking about my patients. In simplified and broad terms, my theory is that the individual develops primarily in the context of past and present interpersonal relationships; present relationships build on the pattern of past relationships. When early relationships provide emotional and physical protection and security—I think of this as responsive parenting or attunement—the person develops in a healthy manner. On the other hand, when a parent is extremely anxious, preoccupied, or otherwise not able to be responsive to a child because of his or her own psychological issues or real-world challenges, the child will be insecure and develop various coping mechanisms, or defenses.

My professional development, during which I studied relational psychoanalysis, attachment theory, and research on mother-infant interactions, provided the background through which I now understand both healthy psychological growth and the individual who is psychologically compromised. Mother-infant research, such as Stern's (e.g., 1985) or Beebe and Lachmann's (e.g., 2002) split-screen studies of affective attunement, demonstrates that babies react positively when caretakers are responsive to an infant's cues; they pull away or shut down, however, when a parent is overly stimulating. Such research has informed trauma studies, as well as our general understanding of human development. Specifically, a parent who has been severely traumatized will experience moments of dissociation, leading to distance and withdrawal in the dyadic relationship; alternatively, the parent may become extremely anxious and hypervigilant, leading to fear in the relationship (Markese, 2012, p. 204). Both possibilities lead to difficulties in parent-infant emotional regulation.

In my work with patients and those I interviewed for this study, I have tried to understand how each was affected by early patterns of interaction with parents and how each might have modified these patterns throughout their lives. How did each transform early influences as he or she developed into the adult I met? Of course, with both adult patients and interviewees, I am inferring backward from adulthood to childhood, and this caveat must be kept firmly in mind; our hypotheses cannot be proven. Yet we continue to try to answer these questions. With those I interviewed, how did immigrant parents' persecutions, hardships, and expectations influence their children as they developed into adults?

I note in the course of this book that there are interviewees whom I believe to be securely or insecurely attached. When I use these terms, I have particularly strong hypotheses about their development. Interviewees whom I considered to be securely attached were those who I believed had responsive and attuned parents, while those who I thought were insecure had parents who did not seem attuned, usually because of their own trauma.

THE INTERGENERATIONAL TRANSMISSION OF TRAUMA AND LOSS

As I spoke with many of my interviewees, I understood that these were people who were impacted by their parents' trauma. By definition trauma overwhelms the ego, and consequently, the horror of past traumatic events is dissociated so that the trauma survivor can go on living. Because trauma is incomprehensible, it cannot be thought through or processed; yet, even though it cannot be consciously held in mind, it lives on in some way. When trauma is transmitted intergenerationally, the parent's past becomes the child's present. This may be manifest, for example, in a repetitive fantasy about a traumatic part of a parent's history that involuntarily intrudes on the day-to-day life of the adult child. Or a traumatic event from the parent's past may be without thought acted out in the child's present life.

Relational psychoanalysis proposes a complementary theory. Trauma is passed on intergenerationally through the parent's momentary dissociations or absences, which mark overwhelming affect states (Halasz, 2012). The infant or child registers these frozen moments or brief states of blankness in the attachment relationship (Salberg, 2017a). Alternatively, dysregulated states of too much emotion, even anger, may represent the parent's trauma. Thus parental trauma may manifest as too much or too little affect. The parent who is briefly affectively compromised will at those moments be inaccessible to soothe or contain the child. Instead it is the child who must regulate the parent's emotional state. In this model, what is passed on is not a "clear transmission of something," a reenactment, but is a consequence of the dysregulated affective states that evoke the child's fantasies of the parent's secret trauma (Salberg, 2017a, p. 94).

Immigrants suffered different kinds of trauma—and some suffered more than one. They endured the trauma of violence, but also of prolonged fear (for example, of pogroms) and grinding poverty; these could prove traumatic because they caused deep psychic distress. One interviewee, whom I called David, described his mother's childhood using the words: "the pain, no money, constant fear, starvation, disease." David was not referring to a terrible event that he described as traumatic. Nevertheless, both his mother and David seemed to feel that her experiences were traumatic. In the pages that follow, I will write about the concepts of large-T trauma and small-t trauma, which refer to catastrophic trauma and adverse life events, respectively (EMDR Institute, n.d.; Marich, n.d.). Both types of trauma can cause psychic distress. Some of the small-t trauma we're familiar with include verbal abuse, medical crises, and racial or ethnic discrimination.

Some of the parents of my interviewees were affected by both the trauma just discussed and their experiences during migration—and migration very often caused its own type of trauma. The deep stresses of migration might then be passed on intergenerationally.

That everything was unfamiliar in America—language, food, and customs—meant it was disorganizing and difficult to be here (e.g., Akhtar, 2011). But because America was the "Golden Land," what problems or losses could the immigrant admit to and what, therefore, could be related to one's own children? America was often idealized in the eyes of immigrant parents and children alike (e.g., Garza-Guerrero, 1974). If America was glorified, then Eastern Europe might be devalued. Or the opposite might happen: immigrants might disparage America and see home through rose-colored glasses.

Immigrants' sense of identity was rooted in their former homes, and thus migration meant that the sense of self was at risk in America; this was very emotionally stressful (Ainslee, Harlem, Tummala-Narra, Barbanel, & Ruth, 2013). The parts of oneself associated with America might be idealized, and the parts of oneself associated with the Old Country might be too easily discarded, or vice versa.

Because of persecution in Eastern Europe, Jews who had emigrated could not return home after 1903 (Matt, 2011; Sarna, 1981), and they generally had a strong desire to become Americanized. They had to keep their eyes on the future, as they might risk depression if they looked back (Boulanger, 2004). Consequently, some couldn't permit themselves to mourn what they had left; as mourning the past was often unacceptable among Eastern European Jews, this very important aspect of adjusting to a new country was often foreclosed.

Just as Eastern European Jews did a century ago, the people who immigrate to America today to escape violence and poverty hope for better lives for their families. The percentage of immigrants in the U.S. is steadily rising (Lopez, Bialik, & Radford, 2018). Therefore, understanding the immigrant experience is becoming increasingly essential for psychotherapists and humanitarians alike. As we know, poverty or trauma often precipitates immigration, and except for young children, almost all immigrants in one way or another endure feelings of loss and cultural dislocation. Strikingly, of the 1.18 million people admitted to the U.S. legally in 2016, 13 percent (153,400) were refugees and/or asylum seekers (U.S. Department of Homeland Security, 2017); many of them were fleeing trauma. Consequently, psychotherapists are faced with the fact that a huge number of immigrants living in the U.S. are coping with the aftereffects of terror.

Because immigrants and immigrants' children will constitute an increasing percentage of our psychotherapy practices, we must keep our clinical "ears" open to hearing the particular reverberations of loss and/or trauma important for each patient. To be sure, this book does not directly consider current immigration to the U.S. But its insights into trauma, loss, and their intergenerational transmission will help the reader to be sensitive to issues salient to a vulnerable part of our population.

My grandfather's uncommunicative nature, disguised by his ironic repetition of "only in America," illustrates the frequent silence surrounding the immigrants' personal histories. Silence, denial, or disavowal might have many reasons. For some it was a reaction to trauma. My maternal grandmother was one of the many immigrants who suffered trauma during World War I and the civil wars that followed it. During the war—when she, like many other Eastern European Jews, was a refugee—several members of her family died needlessly, including her mother. After the war, she returned to her partially destroyed city, living in an unheated room; forced to scramble for food, she was often unbelievably hungry. Most of this I learned only years after my grandmother's death, when researching this book.

So that I could understand the pasts of the immigrants, I specifically sought adult children whose parents *had* communicated about their lives. By listening to and recording the children's stories about their families, I hoped to help flesh out the memories that were lost by the immigrants' disavowal or silence. Because it was the children who narrated these tales, it was important also to understand and explain the impact their parents' histories had on them.

In the pages that follow, I will tell you, the reader, both what I learned from the immigrants' children and what I inferred as a psychoanalyst. This was in part a personal journey. My grandparents—like so many others who came to America from different ethnic and religious groups—fled persecution and poverty. In my family, as perhaps in yours, their grim circumstances were thought of as ordinary. Through life stories, I will focus on the immigrants' and their children's psychological lives and on intergenerational influences; we will think about what they experienced in historical context. Trauma such as my grandmother suffered will sometimes hold center stage; sometimes my focus will be loss and its disavowal.

NOTES

1. After the Kishinev pogrom of 1903, many Jews realized that they could no longer return to live in Eastern Europe. Until then, return migration was common for Jews, as it was for their gentile neighbors (Matt, 2011).

2. The Sephardic Jews traced their ancestry to Spain and Portugal. The first Sephardic Jews came to New Amsterdam from Brazil in 1654, and a second group arrived from Holland shortly afterward (Sachar, 1992).

3. This widely read book was found to contain many errors, "some of them howlers" (Zipperstein, 2010). The coauthor and main intellectual behind *Life Is with People*, Mark Zborowski, had earlier, before emigrating to the U.S., been a member of the Soviet secret police. According to Zipperstein, he influenced the committee behind the book's writing "with more authority than knowledge."

4. The Immigration Act of 1924 was also called the Johnson-Reed Act. It restricted the number of immigrants allowed to enter the U.S. through a national origins quota, and its effect was to greatly limit immigration from Southern and Eastern Europe (Anbinder, 2016).

Dramatis Personae

In order of first appearance:

Benjamin: For his parents in Eastern Europe, the risk of death was ever-present. Their passage to the U.S. was paid as a wedding present.
Mother: Minna. Father: Saul.
(Chapter 1)

Seymour: His mother saw nightmares around her as a child during World War I. His father's entire family was killed in the Holocaust, and Seymour repeatedly re-experienced this event as a repetition of the past.
Mother: Sadie. Father: Amos.
(Chapters 1, 2, and 5)

Barbara: Her parents experienced terrible poverty in Eastern Europe; as adults, all talking was fighting. Barbara felt unloved and neglected as a child.
Mother: Bella. Father: Joe.
(Chapters 1, 2, and 4)

Irene: Irene called Eastern Europe a "bad place with bad memories for the Jews." Her mother was mentally ill and physically abusive. Building Jewish community was important to Irene as an adult.
Mother: Letty. Father: Leo.
(Chapters 1 and 5)

Norman: His father, who missed his family terribly, was at first a cowboy in the U.S. Norman grew up in abject poverty, but he denied his childhood of deprivation.
Mother: Gitel. Father: Abe.

(Chapters 1, 3, and 4)

Elaine: Her mother came to the U.S. alone and later overwhelmed her daughter with her feelings of loneliness. She never wanted to set foot in Poland again. Elaine as an adult had a fulfilling life.
Mother: Chaya. Father: Frank.
(Chapters 2 and 3)

David: He "grew up in the shadow of the shtetl." Although he deeply felt the pain of his mother's childhood of fear and starvation, he as an adult seemed determined to enjoy his life.
Mother: Pearl. Father: Philip.
(Chapters 2 and 4)

Stanley: His mother "felt the bullets whizzing by" during World War I, and his family became wealthy in the U.S. Stanley absorbed his mother's anxiety.
Mother: Liba. Father: Chaim.
(Chapter 2)

Aaron: His mother as an adolescent discovered the body of her own father, who had been murdered in a pogrom. Growing up, he was expected to be "the best, the first."
Mother: Estelle. Father: Max.
(Chapters 2 and 4)

Ruth: Her mother came from an impoverished background that was full of fear. Her enactment of her mother's family's procedure during pogroms represented an embodied ghost of her mother's past.
Mother: Devorah. Father: Harry
(Chapter 2)

Helen: Her mother came to the U.S. alone but intended to return to her shtetl. She was "distraught beyond words" when World War I made communication with her family impossible.
Mother: Rivka. Father: Ray.
(Chapter 3)

Frances: Her mother lived a "gay, cosmopolitan life" before emigration. She was never satisfied with life in the U.S., where she was miserable and lonely; she, consequently, was never nurturing to Frances.
Mother: Anna. Father: Louis.
(Chapter 3)

Susan: Susan's mother was nostalgic for life in Eastern Europe, despite a life of "drudgery" and dangerous anti-Semitism. Susan found her mother's nostalgia exasperating.

Mother: Raisa. Father: Milt.

(Chapter 3)

Miriam: Her mother, after a period of homesickness, was a determined and dominant entrepreneur, who "made it here for everybody."

Mother: Trudy.

(Chapter 3)

Louise: Louise was like a child of Holocaust survivors because of her father's experience. Her mother, because of World War I trauma, was "terrified as a person." Louise felt that her job was to repair her damaged parents.

Mother: Edith. Father: Beryl.

(Chapters 3 and 4)

Dorothy: Her happy household turned unhappy when her father became ill and later died. Her mother, who had suffered trauma in Eastern Europe, could not provide for her emotional needs.

Mother: Dina. Father: Harold.

(Chapters 4 and 5)

Sarah: Sarah immigrated at age six with her mother. She minimized her mother's losses, saying: she "took it in stride. This is how it was." She herself lost her father as a young adult.

Mother: Blume. Father: Avram.

(Chapter 5)

Chapter One

They Left It All Behind and the Disavowal of Loss

DRAMATIS PERSONAE

In order of appearance:

Benjamin: For his parents in Eastern Europe, the risk of death was ever-present. Their passage to the U.S. was paid as a wedding present.
    Mother: Minna
    Father: Saul

Seymour: His mother saw nightmares around her as a child during World War I. His father's entire family were killed in the Holocaust, and Seymour repeatedly reexperienced this event as a repetition of the past.
    Mother: Sadie
    Father: Amos

Irene: Irene called Eastern Europe a "bad place with bad memories for the Jews." Her mother was mentally ill and physically abusive. Building Jewish community was important to Irene as an adult.
    Mother: Letty
    Father: Leo

Barbara: Her parents experienced terrible poverty in Eastern Europe; as adults, all talking was fighting. Barbara felt unloved and neglected as a child.
    Mother: Bella
    Father: Joe

Norman: His father, who missed his family terribly, was at first a cowboy in the U.S. Norman grew up in abject poverty, but he denied his childhood of deprivation.

Mother: Gitel

Father: Abe

My father's father was born in a tiny village in a rural area; he and his extremely poor family lived surrounded by the natural world. A stream ran in front of the family's house in which the women washed clothes, and the children played in the bushes. The family had animals with which they were in contact constantly. That my grandfather "ice skated," rags covering his feet in order to protect his only pair of shoes, was part of the family lore.

At age seventeen, because he could not have survived economically at home, he immigrated to New York City. The teeming, filthy streets and the dark rooms of its tenements and sweatshops must have felt like the antithesis of his former life in the natural world. As an older man in New York, he was lucky enough to live near a park, but this was very different from his early contact with nature. Occasionally in his later life, he had the opportunity to walk in actual woods, and he would eat wild berries. We were scandalized: we would exclaim, "Don't you know that those might be poison?" But from his life in Eastern Europe, he may have known far better than we did how to tell a poisonous berry from an edible one.

My grandfather must have missed his early life surrounded by the natural world. Yet no one spoke about this while he was alive, and I have never heard family speak of it since. No one ever talked about what our immigrant grandparents had lost. Our grandparents could not have stayed where they were. After all, almost every single one would have been killed by the Nazis had they stayed. Yes, they had been uprooted, but, in the words of one immigrant's child, "you had to think about priorities." You couldn't think about what might have been.

None of my four grandparents spoke about their lives as immigrants. Indeed, many who had made the long journey from the Old World to America rarely spoke about their experiences. Even in talking to their own children, the immigrant generation tended to be uncommunicative, "tight," or "closed off" (Cowan & Cowan, 1996, p. xviii). In particular, they rarely spoke about their subjective experiences.

Perhaps one reason for the immigrants' silence was the difficulty of acknowledging what they had lost. Each of my grandparents came to America to survive, but in leaving Eastern Europe, each also lost a way of life. They left behind loved ones and the places where they had been born. My father's mother was parted forever from her beloved father and all of her siblings,

Barbara's great-grandfather in Eastern Europe. His picture suggests the extreme poverty of many immigrants. He came to the U.S. in the 1870s but returned to the Old Country, where he died. *Courtesy of anonymous interviewee Barbara.*

each of whom later perished in the Holocaust. And while my father's father joined siblings already in America, he left his parents and two siblings behind.

Each of my grandparents left the places they had known since birth. We rarely think about how difficult this must have been. Perhaps silence was one thing that helped them cope. It may be that, in order to go on with their lives, it was necessary to keep under wraps what was too difficult to think or talk about.

I began my research to try to understand the psychological lives of the immigrants. One essential question I had was: what had the immigrants experienced during their geographical and emotional journeys between Eastern Europe and America? To learn about this, I began by asking immigrants' adult children what they knew of their parents' feelings about having been uprooted. What was it like for their parents to leave family, friends, acquaintances, and community? What was it like to leave the physical geography of home, to know they would never again see the familiar streets and buildings or the rocks and bushes they had always known? And I had another type of question. I wondered how many felt not only out of place but also displaced in America. How many of the immigrants had been resilient and how many had felt overwhelmed by the process of emigrating? Individuals made enormous sacrifices to leave their old lives and build new ones in America. What were the psychological consequences of having done this?

I could find answers to my questions only by asking the immigrants' adult children. Thus everything I was to learn would be mediated by the perceptions of the second generation.

To begin my research, I needed to find immigrants' children who knew about their parents' pasts. But because so many of the immigrants had spoken little to their own children about either their lives in Eastern Europe or their early years in America, I spoke to many second-generation individuals who knew too little to be able to participate in my project. Thus I was directly confronted by the all-too-common, though not universal, silence of the immigrants.

As I proceeded with my research, I discovered that other authors had written about the theme of silence and denial in the narratives of Eastern European Jewish immigrants. Roger Cohen (2015, p. 16) wrote about his family's "habits of silence"; the past of the "shtetl, pogroms, and penury" were to be kept secret (p. 26). For his family, such things were better kept quiet if its members were to assimilate and become successful. Furthermore, researchers Neil Cowan and Ruth Schwartz Cowan, as mentioned above, who interviewed one hundred Jews born between 1895 and 1915, found that this generation could be uncommunicative. And Nancy K. Miller (2011) after her father's death was confronted by the mysterious mementos of his Eastern European Jewish forebears. Her father had never spoken about them, and she followed various leads, ending up in Kishinev, the site of terrifying pogroms. These writers seemed to be drawing a parallel between silence or denial and the poverty, persecution, and pogroms because of which the immigrants fled Europe. Could it be that the immigrants' silence or denial was not just due to unacknowledged loss but might also be associated with trauma? As I proceeded with my own work, I began to understand that the subjective experiences of the immigrants were complex and multifaceted.

Before beginning my interviews, I expected that—if you emigrated from a shtetl, a tiny village, or even a small city in which traditional Jewish culture remained strong—there must have been much that you missed both about people and the old way of life. I assumed that in studying immigrants' feelings about being uprooted I would hear about a sense of longing or loss. I knew that immigrants felt strong ties to home, that their "sense of uprootedness was keen" (Weinberg, 1988, p. 67). Moreover, I had been influenced by immigrants' statements such as this one, quoted by Elizabeth Ewen: a female immigrant, describing her first year in New York said, "I didn't smile for a long time. Why? Because this was a different country. Everybody was for himself, and there was always money, money, money; rush, rush, rush" (Ewen, 1985, p. 62). In America, according to Ewen, first-generation women mourned the loss of sunshine in the tenements of New York City, which she believed was a "metaphor that described feelings of alienation and unfamiliarity."

From preliminary research, not only had I learned about immigrants' experiences of alienation and the difficulty of breaking away from home, but I had also encountered another kind of literature. These were scholarly and fictional works depicting the shtetl as a place of community orientation and emotional warmth. I call this characterization of Eastern European Jewish life the "romantic" view of the shtetl. For example, *Life Is with People* (Zborowski & Herzog, 1952), a well-known retrospective anthropological study of Eastern European Jewish life published in 1952, popularizes this perception of the shtetl. "A celebration of a lost world" and supposedly a scholarly study, it presented the shtetl as timeless and warm, an "idyll" (Kirshenblatt-Gimblett, 1995, p. 1; Livingston, 1986, p. 1).

Although I suspect that many people of my generation grew up with this romantic or idealized perception of the shtetl, it does not represent the reality of Jewish life in Eastern Europe. Instead it is a product of post-Holocaust reconstruction. On one hand this "imagined" view of the shtetl as a "paradigmatic locus of communality" (Shandler, 2014, p. 44) does have a basis in fact: in the actual shtetl, an ethos of mutual responsibility was important. Communal ties and communal responsibility were necessary in the dangerous world in which Jews were an oppressed minority, and the collective needs of the community took precedence above all else (Ewen, 1985, p. 46). Shopkeepers and peddlers assisted one another without expecting to be repaid immediately and "food was . . . shared within the community" (p. 47). But it is only in the romantic or imagined view of the shtetl that it was a harmonious, warm community (Kassow, 2007a). According to Kassow (2007a, p. 8), the "shtetl could be a cruel place." Those who were uneducated, poor, or performed menial jobs were constantly reminded of their low status, and shtetl society could be judgmental and harsh.

As I began my research, I did not yet know that my vision of Jewish life in Eastern Europe was in part a product of the post-Holocaust remembered shtetl. Furthermore, in part because of the silence of my grandparents' generation, I did not know the extent of the pogroms that decimated Jewish life in Russia. Indeed I had been taught by my father that the traditional Jewish life was a rich and wonderful one. My father may have had a factual basis for viewing the shtetl in this way. His parents were from Galicia, where, in contrast to Russia, there were no organized pogroms though there was anti-Semitism.[1] While my grandfather's family had been the poorest of the poor, I believe it was a loving family. And although my father's mother had suffered in many ways, her family was middle-class when she was young, and she looked up to *her* father because of his piety. And perhaps I wanted to believe that my Eastern European Jewish heritage represented something to be missed.[2] Perhaps I needed to trust that a place had existed where people were "good" and cared for everyone in their community; this was lacking in the suburban, gentile suburb where I grew up. For all these reasons, I believed I would learn from my interviews about immigrants' sense of longing and loss. My preconceptions about this have been tempered by listening to my interviewees.

THEY LEFT IT ALL BEHIND

The theme that I call "they left it all behind" began to emerge as I conducted many of my earlier interviews. It is highlighted in the words of one interviewee, Elizabeth, speaking about her father: "[He] wanted to leave it all behind. [He didn't] want any part of it. It was a new beginning." She continued, "Both parents agreed that they would never set foot in Europe again. They had had it."

More often than not, the immigrants' children denied that their parents missed their former homes and said, in effect, that their parents wanted to "leave it all behind" and would never want to even visit. Thus this was an important phenomenon, and I will try to explain its differing meanings in the lives of my interviewees and their parents.

Some individuals, in contrast, did speak about their parents' longing for the Old Country or said they missed the family they had left; some depicted this in heartbreaking ways. However, the majority of my interviewees had at least one parent who, they believed, never again wanted to set foot in their homeland, and about one quarter said that both their parents were "done with" Eastern Europe. In just a few instances, a child believed that the same parent both experienced some type of loss *and* wanted to leave it behind.

Some parents who adamantly wanted to "leave it all behind" were Elaine's mother and Benjamin's parents. Elaine's mother never wanted to go back. She hated being Polish and refused to speak Polish in the U.S. Her intense feelings were associated with the terrible anti-Semitic violence in her home city and with the poverty and difficult living conditions her family had faced after her father's death. Benjamin's parents had both left a world where the risk of death was ever-present, and both feared gentiles. Indeed, Benjamin's father always limped after being hit by a gentile nobleman. When asked whether she wanted to visit her hometown, Benjamin's mother said: "No, I ran away and I have only bad memories of it."

Many parents fled anti-Semitic violence, discrimination, and poverty, and often their children believed that they were glad to "leave it all behind." In a number of interviews, the children reported that their parents said they wanted nothing to do with their Eastern European homes. Often, however, it was the children themselves who stated that their parents were "done with" Eastern Europe. For example, Ruth said her mother had had a "very hard life" and suffered a "lot of fear" in Eastern Europe; there was nothing to miss about her life there, emphasized Ruth. Her mother grew up in a small city in which the family feared pogroms at the hands of the "whimsically ruthless" Russian soldiers; they were "very deprived" economically. As a young adult, Ruth's mother endured the privations of World War I, living with her family in the forest in a shack in a lumber camp. Ruth's father endured forced labor during the war and consequently suffered a lifelong injury.

These were tales of trauma. Most often those who told me that their parents were "done with" Eastern Europe were reacting to the anti-Semitic violence, discrimination, or extreme poverty faced by their parents. Some immigrants who had experienced trauma needed to deny the possibility of positive memories about their childhood homes. They could not acknowledge the loss of a place where they and those they loved were treated terribly. I call this the disavowal of loss. Others—perhaps too young when oppression and terror took over their lives to have any happy memories of home—felt only hatred for Eastern Europe (Cowan & Cowan, 1996). Because of trauma, they simply wanted to leave it all behind. Still others, like my father's father, who experienced extreme poverty rather than violence, might have found it difficult to speak, or in some cases even to think, about what they lost in leaving Eastern Europe. For many of the immigrants, and for their children who told me their stories, loss and trauma were interrelated themes underlying the immigrant narrative.

LIFE STORIES AND VIGNETTES

The stories my interviewees told about their parents provide a window into the lives of Jewish people in early-twentieth-century Eastern Europe. The five stories that follow show the difficult emotions associated with leaving the Old Country. Two are in-depth narratives of interviewees who stated that their parents wanted to leave their former homes behind. In both I detail what I learned of their parents' experiences, as well as my understanding of how my interviewees were affected by the knowledge of all their parents endured. Three shorter vignettes follow: in them it is the adult children's interpretation that their parents were "done with" Eastern Europe. Trauma stands out in each of these five narratives; in the last the trauma is the small-t trauma of prolonged poverty and fear of pogroms.

Benjamin

Benjamin's parents were among those who wanted to "leave it all behind."

"No, I ran away and I have only bad memories of it," his mother asserted when Benjamin asked whether she wanted to visit her birthplace. According to Benjamin, his parents had left a world in which the risk of death was ever-present.

Benjamin was a very intelligent professional in his eighties who still worked part-time in his own office. His extremely rational, even-toned approach was notable, and the lack of emotion in his delivery contrasted with the theme of the dangerous world from which his parents had escaped. Benjamin's account was knowledgeable and detailed, and to use his own word for himself, he was "bookish" and probably introverted. At this point in his life—because of difficulty hearing and getting around—Benjamin seemed to have little social life. I sensed that his life was somewhat diminished, and I wondered about the possibility of some current depression. Benjamin had two grown children and lived with his wife in their Manhattan apartment.

Benjamin's parents, Minna and Saul, born shortly before 1900, were a few years apart in age. His mother came from a market town in the Ukraine, and his father's early life was spent in the countryside near his mother's shtetl. Anti-Semitism was prevalent; it was "the rule," according to Benjamin, and his parents always feared the gentiles. Theirs was a "precarious life"; his parents never themselves experienced pogroms, but his mother's family always feared them. When rumors of pogroms circulated, his mother and her siblings were sent away to relatives who lived far away in the woods.

Benjamin's parents married in 1919, when the Ukraine was a "chaotic" and dangerous place. After World War I, violence between the anti-Semitic White Army and the Communist Reds raged, and pogroms grew more frequent. Consequently, the fear of gentiles was more intense than during Benjamin's parents' childhoods before the war. Benjamin said his parents, who arrived in the U.S. in 1921, emigrated because their lives were in danger.

Benjamin's mother grew up in a shtetl that featured a major market; peasants came to it from great distances to exhibit and sell their wares and buy city goods. His mother's father was a glazier who not only had his own store but would also go to the farms of neighboring gentiles to fix glass. When she was young, his mother was taught to cut glass. Once, as a girl, his mother was tending her father's store alone when soldiers arrived. They joked about how a little girl was repairing lanterns. They were nice to her, said Benjamin, because they needed something, but we would imagine that she was frightened. Benjamin's father's family, who lived in a rural area nearby, bought and sold grain and perhaps horses, dealing regularly with the gentile peasants.

During the turbulent civil war that followed World War I, a townsman returned from New York to encourage and assist people with emigration. Afterward, relatives made a "group decision" that his parents would emigrate—they were "selected" to leave. The couple's own parents, as wedding presents, provided money for their passage.[3] Benjamin's parents escaped illicitly across the Dniester River to Rumania by paying someone with a rowboat. There the couple waited for a year until they were able to receive immigration papers. Benjamin said his parents' decision to uproot themselves was a choice: "they could easily have stayed," as did their brothers and sisters. Yet Benjamin repeatedly contradicted his own assertion, stating that his parents emigrated because their lives were in danger.

Upon arrival in New York, Benjamin's parents were met by his father's sister, Rochel. Her first task was to help them both to acclimate to the strange new world of America and find work. After some time, they established a little grocery store and lived in the back. Like other immigrants, they "eked out a living" from the store; "every penny counted." Benjamin's father awoke six days a week at 5 a.m. to get deliveries. Benjamin was born after his parents had lived in New York for four years, and he had a brother eight years younger. The family ate meals in the back of the store, getting up from their dinners mid-meal if a customer came in.

Benjamin's mother, he said, was friendly, outgoing, practical, realistic, and "completely unneurotic." His father, in contrast, was taciturn, reserved, and probably introverted (and, Benjamin thought, probably had a more difficult time adjusting to the U.S. than did his mother). A strict person, his father expected rules about behavior to be followed. While his mother was calm, his father was abrupt, a commander or director, and could be angry. He was not happy about his life: "it was not a glorious existence." Benjamin's father worked extremely hard to make a living for his family. At age forty his father became sick with a heart condition, and he died when Benjamin was only twenty-two.

What sustained Benjamin's parents during their years of struggle, he believed, was their connection with others from their shtetl. They belonged to its Jewish hometown society, called a *landsmanshaft*. They socialized with friends from their town, and "in a sense they continued the shtetl here." His mother spoke to him often about her family and neighbors from home, and

Benjamin met friends from their shtetl at *landsmanshaft* meetings; their shtetl was here, Benjamin explained. Thus, although his parents did not want to return, they experienced some sense of continuity with what had been home, and Benjamin too felt this.

Benjamin spoke about his parents' uprooting in a nuanced way. He said that their descriptions of their shtetl were, for the most part, negative, and he believed that neither parent wanted to see Russia again; he repeated that they left "because of a risk of death." "My parents escaped a terrible place," he said, a place where "getting a piece of bread" was a "big deal." But he also stated that although "it was a miserable life," it was not true that they had "only bad memories of their lives there." His mother, for example, experienced a rich interpersonal life as a young person in their shtetl. Indeed Benjamin said that his mother "pined" for her brothers and sisters whom she had to leave. Acknowledging the losses of emigration along with the gain, he said his mother experienced "joy at leaving the mess behind" but "sadness at leaving her family." Benjamin believed his parents did not want to forget their previous lives in Eastern Europe entirely, only to put their terrible memories behind them; this supports the idea that their lives at home had positive aspects along with the trauma and difficulties.

When Benjamin was an adult with a successful career, he asked his mother whether she would like to visit the place that had once been home. It was at this time that she said she had run away and had only bad memories; her statement reflects the trauma she had experienced. Despite such statements and despite the truly terrible events they had lived through, Benjamin's parents remained connected to their shtetl through their *landsmanshaft* and relationships in New York City.

I was interested in Benjamin's mother's descriptions of the positive aspects of migration. Because there was "no hope for the Jews" there, "they wanted to uproot themselves." "There was a better life," and his mother "wanted to get it." She had heard about America's "freedom" and wanted the "opportunity" that America represented for her as-yet-unborn children.

During World War II, Benjamin was drafted. His parents were "very frightened" that he might experience the same trauma they had, and thus they were fearful at the prospect of his going to Europe. Benjamin reassured them both before and after leaving for Europe and explained to them that the U.S. Army was not anti-Semitic.[4]

After the war, Benjamin, with the help of the GI Bill, attended an Ivy League graduate school, where he socialized with the other "New York guys." Afterward, he became a successful professional. He married, had two children, and participated in the cultural life of New York City.

As I considered Benjamin's narrative about the persecution and poverty his parents endured, I wondered why he referred to his father's limp—the result of his having been hit by a gentile nobleman—only once. The injury,

Benjamin explained, occurred when the man's horses had been galloping fast through town. Benjamin rationalized that, rather than resulting specifically from anti-Semitism, this was instead the result of "a superior not caring" about the lives of other people. Benjamin's rationalization may have been his own way of defending against the knowledge of the terrible injustice and physical pain his father had suffered. Yet to me, his father's injury constituted an overt reminder that "the risk of death was ever-present" in the chaos that followed World War I.

Idealization seemed to constitute an important defense for Benjamin as he dealt with his knowledge of his parents' trauma and loss. He described his childhood as "very happy," recalling it with "fondness and joy" as a time of closeness. His family did have some good times together when he was young. From our perspective, however, his childhood was not ideal. His unhappy father was often abrupt and sometimes angry, and he often enough directed his anger at Benjamin; Benjamin's mother, however, was a calming influence. Furthermore, the struggle to make a living during the Depression was extremely stressful. I believe that, in describing his childhood in an idealized way, Benjamin must have, consciously or not, been comparing the safety of his childhood to his parents' dangerous early lives.

Moreover, Benjamin idealized his mother. He never said a negative thing about her, describing her as "calm," "friendly," and "completely unneurotic." In addition, during a discussion of his younger brother, Benjamin said that the two of them felt "devotion, obligation, and thanks" toward both their parents. I suspect that both Benjamin's gratitude and his inability to be negative were associated with his feeling that his parents had sacrificed so that he could succeed. Benjamin's parents had left everything and everyone they knew so their as-yet-unborn children could prosper in America.

Benjamin knew full well that his parents had endured traumatic events, in addition to poverty and day-to-day discrimination, in Eastern Europe. He also knew that his mother "pined" for the siblings she would never again see. Thus Benjamin's mother, like many other immigrants, experienced profound loss, along with the relief and many gains of having escaped poverty and persecution. I believe his mother's statement that she ran away from her hometown and had only bad memories of it represents a disavowal of the very real connection she felt. Because home became a place of trauma, she needed to disavow the loss she must have suffered in leaving.

Seymour

Seymour's mother, Sadie, never wanted to see Poland again, and thus she too wanted to leave it all behind. The outbreak of World War I must have shattered her life; she was only nine when it began, and she "saw nightmares" occurring around her. After the war, in 1919, she fled Poland with her mother and siblings. I believe that for her, leaving it all behind had a different meaning than it had for Benjamin's parents. Because Sadie was so young when the war began, she may not have had the same early attachment to Eastern Europe that Benjamin's parents did.

Seymour was a brightly cheerful, intelligent, intellectual, and slightly built professional in his seventies whose energy and agility made him seem younger than his age. The intensity of his manner, regardless of whom he was speaking to, made him seem at times not quite in tune with others. Seymour was active in leftist politics. He had had three children in middle age and took an active interest in their lives. He and his wife lived in a not unattractively crowded Brooklyn apartment.

Sadie was, in fact, Seymour's stepmother, although he always called her his mother; his biological mother died in childbirth when he was twenty-six months old, along with her baby. Sadie had come from a tiny village in a rural area, where the family earned a living using an ox-drawn grinding wheel; they ground grain and crushed oil-bearing seeds, keeping as their only profit whatever was left in the wheel. The family lived in poverty. Sadie's father had emigrated to America when she was very young. As a small child, she was sent alone into the countryside to buy milk and eggs from the Polish peasants; at that time it was safe for a child to travel among the gentiles.

All this changed, however, after World War I broke out. Anti-Semitism increased, and invading armies would take over towns, directing soldiers to seize whatever they needed. Sadie's family was already very poor when German soldiers confiscated the family's food for their own use. Seymour's grandmother, determined to feed her family, tried to hide food under her house floorboards; she was imprisoned when this was discovered. In this dire situation, Sadie and her siblings were forced to beg or otherwise find food on their own. Somehow they also had to find enough food to bring to their mother in jail. Two traumatic visual images from this terrible time were passed on to Seymour by his mother. While traveling on a train to Warsaw, his mother saw an old Jewish man having his "jaw chopped off." This was her childhood perception of a gentile ruffian cutting off the Jewish man's beard in order to humiliate him and drawing blood as he did so.[5] The second image was of Sadie herself holding a baby brother who had just died of cholera; she was then still a child.[6]

Sadie and her family finally escaped Eastern Europe in the midst of the civil war and pogroms that followed World War I. At the time, Seymour's grandfather, already in America, was planning to return to his village, as he thought America was *treif* (unkosher). However, the family wrote him saying that if he did return, they would pass him as they fled in the opposite direction.

It is hard to imagine the traumatic impact on Sadie of seeing the Germans confiscating the family's small amount of food, then watching her own mother jailed over an attempt to save the family's food, and finally being forced to beg for food herself. What did she feel, still a child herself, holding her baby brother as he died of cholera? Seymour believed that his mother's temperament made her very tough and well-suited to endure. Yet the ongoing traumatic situation must have affected her deeply. Seymour explained that his aunt, in contrast, the oldest in the family and probably temperamentally more sensitive, suffered long-term effects of the trauma they endured. As an adult, she seemed "scarred," both a "bitter, anxious human being" and "sour and negative."

While Sadie never wanted to see Poland again, Seymour's father, Amos, came to this country alone and probably missed his family.[7] Amos had come from a Russian city, where his family was middle-class and educated—they owned a piano. His middle-class status did not protect Amos from terrible experiences, however. When still a child during World War I, a German soldier capriciously bayonetted his beautiful white pet dog in his presence. In the civil war that followed World War I, their city was at the mercy of anti-Semitic White Russian Army soldiers; Seymour described them as drunks and thieves. When soldiers tried to rob his grandfather's dry goods store, Amos, then fifteen or sixteen years old, successfully resisted them but probably rightfully feared that they would return to retaliate. Consequently, he fled the country alone, working his way to the port of Hamburg, where he embarked for America. Although he had some cousins in New York City, he had no close relatives in America and largely made his way on his own. Seymour felt that his father missed his family, despite the fact it was something he never mentioned.

While Amos did not witness the amount of violence in Eastern Europe that Sadie did, he did suffer the cumulative effects of the trauma experienced over the course of his lifetime. Seymour said his father was able to cope with the traumas of seeing his dog killed, of precipitously fleeing his home and family, and then, in 1939, of the death of his beloved and beautiful first wife. I would add that it must have been overwhelming to be forced to leave home and family without the ability to properly say good-bye or to mourn. Moreover, Amos endured the stress of working very hard to establish himself in America. Seymour said that despite all this—and despite the loss of his wife—when he himself was growing up, his father remained a cheerful and even jovial person. In 1947, however, what Seymour described as the "coup de grace" occurred. His father received a letter from the Red Cross describing the deaths during the Holocaust of his immediate family. According to Seymour, his father, as a consequence, became permanently withdrawn and removed; probably deeply depressed, he remained a shell of his former self until his death in 1958 (he was also beginning to suffer from Parkinson's disease). Seymour himself was only ten years old when his father received this blow. Seymour said that afterward he felt deprived of a father and sensed that he could never again turn to his father for advice or companionship.

Seymour told me his mother's feeling of hate for Poland had been solidified by the Holocaust; afterward, she called Poland the "cursed land." Seymour believed that, if not for the Holocaust, her feelings about Poland might not have been negative in every way.

Seymour psychologically reacted to the impact of his parents' trauma and losses in several ways. He felt intensely the effects of his father's shock and withdrawal after reading the letter from the Red Cross; not until Seymour entered high school several years afterward did he begin again to enjoy his own life. Seymour's description of the bleak few years before he started high school contrasts with the anger he felt as an adolescent. He explained that the combination of both his parents' stories led him at an "early age" to see the world as an "awful" place. This realization "fed" an angry attitude, and Seymour—a slight adolescent growing up in the tough and often enough anti-Semitic streets of Brooklyn—"determined" never to be a "victim." He taped a kitchen knife to his wrist, and ready to take down anyone who threatened him, he projected a scary unpredictability.

Idealization seemed to constitute an important defense for Seymour, as it did for Benjamin, in dealing with his knowledge of his parents' agony and loss. Because the adults in Seymour's life were coping with their own trauma, they were, it seems, emotionally unavailable to help Seymour deal with his own difficulties, and he described some insensitive interactions with his parents during his early childhood. Nevertheless, Seymour idealized this time of his life, stating that he "grew up surrounded by love." Seymour also seemed to idealize his rather tough stepmother, emphasizing her "moral attributes and positive disposition," as well as her relationship with his father. They *never* fought (his emphasis), he said, and they had an "intense affectional relationship." Seymour's idealization of his parents was, I believe, his attempt to protect these people, who had both suffered so much and sacrificed to give him a good life, from any negative opinions of them. Seymour's own cheerfulness as an adult, which might have been an identification with the joviality his father lost when Seymour was ten, might have also been the manifestation of an instinct to cut himself off from his own feelings, from his knowledge of his parents' pain and trauma.

Sadie, like Benjamin's parents, wanted to "leave it all behind"; she never wanted to see Poland again. I suspect, however, that while Benjamin's mother's statements about home represented a disavowal of her connection to her shtetl, Sadie's experience was different. Because Sadie was only nine when her life turned hellish at the start of World War I, she had few positive feelings about home and few reasons to cultivate an attachment to a home that had never nurtured her. Perhaps this was one reason that, unlike Benjamin's parents, Sadie was not a member of a *landsmanshaft*. Because Benjamin's parents were several years older than she, and thus were teenagers before the difficulties of World War I began, they remembered good times as well as bad in Eastern Europe. To Sadie, Poland was the "cursed land." Because of the trauma she suffered there, she simply wanted to leave it behind.

A number of memoirs of Eastern European Jewish immigrants suggest that life at home had been so terrifyingly full of anti-Semitic violence and privation that their writers experienced no conscious loss when they immigrated to the U.S. For example, Rose Soskin, echoing my interviewees' words, wrote: "We went to this country and left everything behind and that's it. You know I would never want to go back there either. I'm not lonely for anything that I left behind, but she [her mother] missed them so we used to go to the *Semiatycze verein*" (the hometown society for their town) (Soskin, 1976, p. 43). Soskin had been about the same age as Sadie when World War I upended her life. Soskin, who arrived in the U.S. at age seventeen, notes that her mother—who had deep ties to Eastern Europe—missed home. Thus many who emigrated when young might have truly left it all behind; they might have been more likely than those who were older and had more positive memories and more ties to the Old Country to relatively unambivalently leave it behind.

Cowan and Cowan in *Our Parents' Lives* (1996) corroborate the idea that the young might have more easily left it behind, and they contrast the experiences of children and their parents.

> Many Jews . . . must have departed from their homelands in Eastern Europe with . . . hatred in their hearts . . . a hatred born of harassment, oppression, and terror. . . . The children, carried along by their parents' decisions, left—insofar as they can now remember their feelings about it—with fear and loathing. The adults were more ambivalent. The Old Country, after all, was home: the place in which they had been raised, the place where beloved relatives still lived. Happy memories—before the pogroms, before the trouble started—were just as plentiful as unhappy ones. (pp. 36-37)

Benjamin's narrative combines the themes of loss and trauma. His mother so much missed the siblings[8] she had left behind in the Ukraine, and she must also have missed her parents. She needed to put this loss behind her as she left her birthplace to get to the "better life" that she would find in America. The traumatic situation at home meant she needed to choose America. Seymour's narrative about his mother, in contrast, highlights trauma rather than loss. His mother did not leave family behind in Poland: when she arrived, she joined her father and two siblings who were already in America; she was accompanied on her journey by her mother and her remaining siblings. There was little choice for Sadie and the family members with whom she came to

America. Because of the trauma at home, like Rose Soskin, she left everything behind and that's it.

Irene

Irene herself characterized Eastern Europe as a "bad place with bad memories for the Jews"; her parents' former home should "fade into obscurity" for
the Jews, she added. Irene carried the dreadful knowledge of what her parents, and her father in particular, had endured in Eastern Europe. Her parents
had not overtly stated that they were "done with" the places that had been
home. It was her belief, however, that her father simply had no use for his
former home. Although in later life her father was able to travel, "he never
wanted to go back," and Irene believed that her mother felt similarly. In fact,
she said, neither of her parents were interested in Russian or Polish as a
language or culture.

Irene was a warm, animated, welcoming woman in her eighties, whose
liveliness made her seem younger than her age. She was knowledgeable
about Judaism and had been both professionally and personally active in the
Jewish community. Her parents' traumatic histories in Eastern Europe illustrate why she felt they wanted to leave it all behind. Her mother, who arrived
in 1921 at age fifteen, was the youngest of seventeen children; her family had
been extremely poor in Eastern Europe. Irene knew little about her mother's
life there, but one shocking bit of family history had survived. No one had
been able to care for seventeen children, and indeed two of the children had
wandered off, fallen in the river, and died. In her mother's family no one
wanted to dwell on the past, Irene said.

Irene's father, Leo, also from a poor family, had as an older man dictated
a memoir about his life in Eastern Europe. Because he did not talk much
about his early life during Irene's childhood, she learned about the extreme
difficulties Leo had faced only when she translated his Yiddish memoir into
English. Leo's father died very young, leaving Irene's grandmother and the
seven surviving children to support themselves. Leo at age ten-and-a-half
very much wanted to contribute to the family, and he found a job in a local
glass factory. When he was thirteen, however, their formerly peaceful
shtetl—which harbored both traditional and enlightened ideas—was virtually
destroyed by the retreating Russian army during World War I. After robbing
and beating the Jewish residents, the Russians, with only fifteen minutes
notice, ordered them to evacuate their shtetl, then laid it waste and set it on
fire. Leo, his family, and the other shtetl inhabitants lived in the open fields
until they were allowed to return to the "ravaged streets and houses" of their
town. From this time on, Leo and his family were war refugees, forced to
leave their shtetl for other towns and living under the German occupation.
Leo, by dint of his wit and resourcefulness, helped his family to survive as

they were forced to move around. Leo was beaten and endured a bout of dysentery during these years. In addition, the family watched helplessly as a sister perished due to the absence of medical care. Family members were often extremely hungry and at times feared attack by the anti-Semitic peasants. Leo arrived in New York in 1923 at age twenty-one, after having spent a couple of very difficult years in Palestine.

Irene, understanding the grim experiences that her parents had survived, stated that "uprooting" had been a "good thing" for her family. There had been "no good old times" for them, and she felt it was no wonder that they, consequently, wanted to let their memories fade. Nevertheless, when I read the transcribed version of her father's memoir, I could feel the affection he held for his shtetl, which had been a vibrant place before World War I.

Although it was probably true that her father did not want to revisit his birthplace, it was Irene who emphasized that Eastern Europe had been a "bad place with bad memories" for her family. She was unable to talk about the positive feelings her father had about his shtetl. Because of her own feelings about the trauma that her family had endured in Eastern Europe, she had to disavow any sense of loss that her parents might have experienced in leaving. This was her own way of managing the painful reality of her parents' trauma and loss.

Barbara

Barbara also disavowed any losses that her parents might have experienced as a consequence of immigration. She adamantly stated that "there was nothing in Europe that [her parents] had lost." Barbara had good reasons for her contention, as her parents had indeed lived through appalling times before they had arrived in the U.S. Nevertheless, her parents actually did have some connection to their Eastern European pasts, and thus Barbara had difficulty holding these contradictory ideas in mind. Barbara herself was a shy, quiet woman in her fifties, whose long, curly hair and long but muted dresses retained a 1960s feel. She worked as a freelance artist and teacher. Her parents, several years apart in age, had each come from small shtetlekh at age thirteen, joining their fathers who were already in America. Barbara conveyed that as young children, both her parents' families suffered grinding poverty, living in houses with dirt floors and greased paper for windows. The family of Barbara's father, Joe, was so poor that he and his younger brother resorted to petty thievery to obtain food. The family of Barbara's mother, Bella, grew up with even more poverty and fear than did her father's; theirs was a "fragile existence." In Bella's family, Barbara said, there was "nothing to cook." Because of this, when there *was* food to cook, Bella's mother was unable to cook well. The possibility of pogroms hung over Barbara's mother's family when her mother was a tiny child. When German soldiers came through their shtetl during World War I, Barbara's grandmother, to protect them from possible rape, hid her older daughters in pickle or apple barrels (Bella was at that time too young to be raped).

Barbara's maternal grandmother was a peddler selling needles and ribbons. Left with no money during World War I and forced to support her children, she would regularly bake seven loaves of bread for her children and then leave the children alone for the week while she traveled as a peddler. The trauma of Bella's childhood is epitomized in the following event that took place during one of the peddling trips. When she was returning home to her village through the woods, gentile boys in a tree overhead dropped a beehive onto Bella's mother for sport; badly stung, she was found and carried back to their village.

Barbara vehemently stated that what her parents had left behind was "pogroms, fear, and starvation." At another point during the interview, referring to her mother, Bella, Barbara interjected: "That's what she left behind . . . having her sisters hidden in barrels." While Barbara's identification with her parents' trauma meant that she viewed their pasts as too painful for them to miss, she nevertheless depicted her parents as having important ties to their Eastern European community. Her parents were members of her father's *landsmanshaft*, attending the society's weekly dances. Bella once won first prize at the society's beauty pageant. During Barbara's childhood summers, thirty-five years after her parents had left home, they joined other immigrants from her father's town in dancing and singing along the boardwalk near their neighborhood. Furthermore, her parents joined a weekly card game that included immigrants they had known in Eastern Europe. Barbara added that family members were "nostalgic" for what they had left: "They would have liked to have gone back and seen it."

Norman

The theme of connection to the past versus disavowal takes an interesting turn in Norman's account. Notably, his mother's family *did* retain a connection to the past, frequently talking about it among themselves but not to their children: family members spoke about their experiences as children. They referred to their village as *der haym* (literally "the home"). Using this term with me, Norman immediately stated that "they didn't think of it as home because every single immigrant was glad [that] they came [to the U.S.]." Norman's mother, Gitel, who emigrated before World War I, came from a very poor shtetl, which was threatened by pogroms.

Norman himself as a child was not only uninterested in hearing about *der haym* but reported a "disdain" for learning about his family's previous life. Indeed, he stated that he was "divorced from it." When asked about this, he said that this was so in actuality for the very reason that his family "hated it."

Norman said, "I couldn't find any connection" with the language or the culture; it was "as if they wanted to tell me about China." He also expressed, "Now I want to know."

While I believe that Gitel and her family hated Russia and did not desire to revisit it, at the same time I feel that they—as they often revisited this life among themselves—must have felt very much connected to it. Norman himself felt a need to think that Gitel had "left it all behind," but Gitel herself may not have felt this. It was Norman who dampened the connection to the past. Had I been able to interview Gitel myself, it is possible that there may have been aspects of life in the Old Country that she missed.

Norman's very immediate contradiction of the hint of missing life in Eastern Europe is repeated in a strikingly similar way in an oral history written by a child of immigrants from my father's family. Discussing the frequent visits of family members to his parents' apartment, he says:

> And what did they talk about?[9] . . . The conversation always came around to the "home": the old country and the shtetle[10] were always referred to as "home." The actual expression was "inderheim" [sic] or at home. This despite the fact that they were all, without exception, glad that they had left the poor primitive life of Galicia and would not have wanted to spend a week there. After 60 or 70 years in America they still referred to the miserable shtetle as "home" without at all meaning it. Such is the power of habit and convention. (Stopper, 1983, p. 2)

Norman's mother's life of privation in Eastern Europe, with the threat of pogroms in the background, was one of great difficulty. Similarly, I am sure that the parents and extended family of my father's relative also suffered poverty and privation before leaving the "poor primitive life of Galicia." Both Norman and my father's family member believed that life *in der haym* had nothing positive to be remembered. They seemed unable to come to terms with the contradiction between the lives of poverty and threatened danger that their parents had left and the idea that this life, nevertheless, may have held a great deal that was meaningful to them.

JEWISH LIFE IN EASTERN EUROPE: A PRECARIOUS LIFE

Now that I have presented some life stories containing trauma, we need to learn about the historical reality underlying what the children knew. We think of traditional Eastern European Jewish life as unchanging, but all societies are transforming. Particularly during the second half of the nineteenth and the beginning of the twentieth centuries, Jewish life was evolving rapidly, spurred on by economic and social changes. Discrimination and poverty increased and anti-Semitism rose during this time; impoverishment and heightened persecution spurred mass migration. Between 1881 and 1924, more than 2,500,000 Jews left their homes in Eastern Europe, seeking a better life in America (Soyer, 1997; Weinberg, 1988).

In 1880, almost six million Jews lived within the Russian Empire, Austria-Hungary (Galicia and Bukovina), and Rumania (Epstein, 2007; Meltzer, 1974; Rischin, 1970; Weinberg, 1988). The majority lived within the Russian Pale of Settlement, the territories of the Russian Empire to which they had been confined by Tsar Alexander I (Meltzer, 1974; Epstein, 2007; Weinberg, 1988).

Understanding the exact geography of Jewish Eastern Europe is complicated, as much of what was considered Poland ("Congress Poland") was acquired by the Russian Empire in the eighteenth century, and Jews in this part of Russia and those under Austro-Hungarian rule considered themselves Polish Jews. Furthermore, national boundaries changed drastically at the close of World War I. In this section I will be referring to the Jews of Eastern Europe in general, except when I specify otherwise; the persecution of Russian Jews is also included. A second section briefly describes life for both Austro-Hungarian (Galician) and Rumanian Jews; political and economic conditions for them differed somewhat from those of Russian Jews.

Despite variations among regions, the Jews of Eastern Europe shared a way of life, religious ties, and the Yiddish language (Howe, 1976). Before the late nineteenth century, most Jews were town dwellers—the word "shtetl" refers to a town—although some lived in smaller villages or tiny rural settlements (Kassow, 2010; Shandler, 2014; Weinberg, 1988). The shtetl was small enough, often several thousand people, that it was a "face to face community": almost everyone was known by name or nickname (Kassow, 2007a, p. 7; Kassow, 2007b, p. 125). Jews differed from their gentile neighbors in religion, language, culture, and occupation.

Eastern Europe in the late nineteenth century.

Jews often constituted a majority in a shtetl, and religion permeated the day-to-day life of shtetl inhabitants. However, the shtetl was in no way an exclusively Jewish world (Kassow, 2007a). It functioned as a market town for the surrounding agricultural population and served as a link with larger city markets (Soyer, 1997). On the weekly market day, Jews and peasants mixed and were connected by personal as well as economic links (Kassow, 2007a, pp. 3–4).

Living conditions for the majority of Jews were primitive even in the larger towns (Weinberg, 1988, p. 4). Houses had earthen floors and roofs might be thatched. Mud puddles in yards hosted roaming pigs. Sanitation was rudimentary, and disease spread quickly (Kassow, 2007a; Weinberg, 1988, p. 4).

Jews generally made a living in the "crevices of a backward agricultural economy," according to Howe (1976, p. 10). Often forbidden to own land, they were traders or artisans, and many had to improvise a living. In villages, Jews worked as innkeepers, millers, distillers, and blacksmiths (Shandler, 2014). Jews in towns might have shops or tiny stands, and many were tailors, carpenters, shoemakers, bakers, tinsmiths, carters, or water carriers (Kassow, 2007a; Shandler, 2014). Much of this work was seasonal, and consequently making a living was frequently precarious.

Widespread discrimination contributed to the poverty of the majority of Jews in Eastern Europe. However, individual Jews ranged from very poor to very wealthy (Shandler, 2014). Some were well-to-do contractors, wholesale brokers, or entrepreneurs (Kassow, 2007a, p. 2). Higher-income families might buy or sell grain or logs, and Jews commonly oversaw farms or estates for gentiles (Shandler, 2014; Zborowski & Herzog, 1952).

While poverty was one constant, a second was fear (Sorin, 1992); this was particularly true as conditions worsened in the second half of the nineteenth century. Jews were seen as outsiders (Weisser, 1989) and "free game to all, from school children to government officials" (Sorin, 1992, p. 13). Shtetl Jews were isolated, persecuted, and intimidated; in this atmosphere, the need to minimize risk was ever-present (Weisser, 1989).

A story some of my father's cousins told me revealed the dangers of everyday life. My great-grandfather, returning through the woods, perhaps after a trip to the city to sell milk, was beset by Russians hooligans. They threatened to tie him to his wagon, then have his horse drag him to his death. He protested, "No, if you're going to kill me, don't do it this way—just kill me now." Shamed or frightened, the men fled.

The role of religion was paramount in Eastern European Jewish culture (Howe, 1976, p. 8). Here "God was a living force, a Presence" (p. 11). Blessings thanking God made every daily task holy, and ritual governed everything from the way a chicken was to be killed to the way that shoes were put on in the morning (Howe, 1976, p. 13; Rischin, 1970).

A great strength of shtetl life was its system of communal responsibility (Sorin, 1992). The Jewish community council, or *kehillah*, run by the wealthy and learned, dispensed charity (Kassow, 2007a; Sorin, 1992). The kehillah maintained orphanages and schools for the needy, and its various associations played an important role in shtetl society. They included the burial society, as well as groups that provided dowries for poor girls, visited the sick, and distributed charity to the poor (Kassow, 2010).

Despite these organizations, the shtetl was not a peaceful community, and much was problematic. Schools, especially for poor children, were frequently terrible. Dirt and squalor were common, as were devastating fires. During the spring and fall, the unpaved streets were full of mud, while in the summer the shtetl smelled of raw sewage and horse manure. Individuals of low status were often treated poorly, and societal judgment could be harsh (Kassow, 2007a).

Changes in Eastern European Jewish Life

The "premodern and preindustrial" world of the Jews I have described was sometimes seen as stable but was actually changing throughout the nineteenth century (Dawidowicz, 1982, p. 8; Sorin, 1992). Particularly during the second half of the century, Jewish life was affected greatly by economic changes and the "new social and political thought" (Sorin, 1992, p. 20).

The Haskalah, the "Jewish offshoot" of the European Enlightenment, introduced secular education to the traditional world of Eastern Europe (Dawidowicz, 1982, p. 11). Proponents of the Haskalah developed a rational conception of Jewish theological beliefs (Etkes, 2010). These modern thoughts were introduced to members of the middle classes, and in cities with upper-middle-class Jewish populations, some synagogue services began to be modernized (Dawidowicz, 1982; Weinberg, 1988).

Conscription posed another challenge to traditional life. Each country drafted Jews according to its own draconian rules (Epstein, 2007). In Russia, beginning in 1827, Jewish boys were drafted into preparatory military training at the age of twelve. Army service might last twenty-five years, and once in the army, Jewish boys faced tremendous pressure to convert and assimilate (Sorin, 1997). In some cases, Jewish boys who refused conversion were "dragged into churches to undergo forced conversion" (Epstein, 2007, p. 6). Because the *kehillah* was charged with recruiting the boys for the authorities, conscription threatened the "fabric of Jewish communal life" (Lederhendler, 1989, p. 64). Although in Russia the draft laws were modified in 1855, easing some of the pressure, the role the communal elite played in conscription alienated shtetl Jews from them (Soyer, 1997, p. 17).

During the nineteenth century, economic conditions became increasingly difficult due to population increases, industrialization, and increased discrimination (Shandler, 2014). The number of Jewish people rose dramatically between 1800 and 1900 because of high fertility and low mortality rates (Alroey, 2011; Dawidowicz, 1982; Rischin, 1970; Sorin, 1992). Furthermore, the old peasant-based economies of Eastern Europe were changing. The beginnings of industrialization and the newly built railroads diminished the economic role of the area's market towns, and traditional Jewish middle-class occupations declined, including running inns, mills, taverns, and estates

(Rischin, 1970, p. 24). Many Jews became artisans and petty traders. At the same time, the construction of factories meant less work for skilled Jewish workers (Rischin, 1970).

The economic situation for gentiles was also unstable, and that had consequences for the Jews. In Russia, where there was an atmosphere of pervasive economic fear, the "government sought to deflect peasant anger away from political leadership and so sought a scapegoat" (Epstein, 2007, p. 3; Sorin, 1992). In the 1860s and 1870s, even before the organized pogroms began, Jews were often attacked.

Increasing economic pressures forced Jews throughout Eastern Europe to move so they could make a living; this changed the geography of where they lived (Shandler, 2014; Sorin, 1997, p. 23). Jews moved from village to town to city (Rischin, 1970, p. 24), and urban centers quickly formed. Warsaw, which had 3,500 Jewish residents in 1781, had 219,000, comprising one-third of its population, by 1891 (Rischin, 1970, p. 24; Sorin, 1992).

In tsarist Russia, conditions became dire as economic restrictions of the 1870s were followed by the pogroms and the tyrannous May Laws of the 1880s. Organized pogroms began soon after the assassination of Tsar Alexander II in March of 1881, for which a Jewish woman had been an accessory (Dawidowicz, 1982; Sorin, 1997).[11] Jews became scapegoats as the government fostered charges that they "were responsible for the misfortunes of the nation" (Dawidowicz, 1982, p. 13; Sorin, 1997, p. 32). The first organized pogrom took place in Elizavetgrad in April of 1881, followed by thirty additional attacks in three days (Epstein, 2007, p. 9).[12] In 1881 alone, twenty thousand Jewish homes were demolished; women were raped and children savagely attacked (Dawidowicz, 1982, p. 13; Epstein, 2007, p. 9).

The following description of the 1905 Kiev pogrom was written in a letter to the Jewish Territorial Organization in the hope that publicity would encourage international aid for Russian Jewish emigration.[13]

Shouts outside, screams in the homes, in the basements, in the attics, in the caves. The screams of children and infants, the sound of women fainting, the groans of the dying, and the breaking of the bones of old people thrown from the upper floors deafen the air of Kiev! Infants and children are being torn up, ripped in half, and thrown to the dogs! They are slicing open the stomachs of pregnant women, cutting out organs from healthy people, and flaying them with iron combs. If the heavens don't explode at the sound of the cries, they must be made of iron and brass! If the earth doesn't shudder at the sound of the wails, then it is a bloody earth, a wasteland full of the fire of the inferno!

Oh! All the property of the Jews has been plundered! The damage totals fifty million. All the merchants and shopkeepers in the city have been left naked and destitute, with only the shirts on their backs. Starvation is rampant in the city.

. . . It is hair-raising to see the hooligans wielding axes and picks, knives and swords to chop off the heads of men, women, and children! . . . The army,

police, and hooligans get special pleasure from hearing a Jew or Jewess
screaming, "Help!" (Letter 27, Alroey, 2011, p. 139)

Pogroms caused widespread fear, destroyed businesses, ruined credit, and
cost thousands of workers their jobs (Cowan & Cowan, 1996, p. 34).

This first wave of pogroms was followed by the discriminatory May
Laws of 1882, enacted to protect the Russian population from Jewish economic control (Epstein, 2007, p. 11). Over time these laws were increasingly
restrictive. One prohibited Jews from living in villages with less than ten
thousand residents (Epstein, 2007, p. 11) and led to the expulsion of a half-
million Jews from rural areas (Sorin, 1992, p. 22). Jews were forced to move
to already overcrowded cities, creating a disastrous situation (Sachar, 2005,
p. 201). Quotas restricted Jewish attendance at gymnasia and universities and
limited the number of Jews allowed to be doctors and lawyers. In 1891,
thousands of better-off Jews were expelled from Moscow, St. Petersburg,
and Kiev (Rischin, 1962). In 1897, more than a hundred thousand Jews were
forced to abandon their livelihoods as innkeepers and tavern keepers when
the government took over the liquor monopoly, previously largely a Jewish
occupation (Rischin, 1962; Weinberg, 1988). The Jews of Russia were re-
duced to penury. Although pogroms had stopped in 1884, between 1903 and
1906 they resumed, including the Kishinev pogrom of 1903. In Zhitomer,
Kiev, Bialystock, and Odessa, hundreds of people were killed, robbed, raped,
and mutilated (Sorin, 1997, p. 34); these pogroms "involved much more
violence and murder" than the earlier ones.

The Kishinev pogrom marked a turning point after which the U.S. Jewish
community provided assistance (Sorin, 1992, pp. 34, 203; see also Zipperstein, 2018). The pogrom grew out of a blood libel charge, and for months
afterward the Russian government and the Orthodox Church incited anti-
Semitism, culminating during the Easter holiday. Fifty Jews were killed and
nearly five hundred were injured during the three-day riots. Rape and pillage
were rampant, and many hundreds of homes and businesses were destroyed.

During this grim time, Jews tried to find new forms of employment (Rischin, 1970). As the continuing growth of factories threatened the income of
Jewish artisans in the 1880s, Jews began to both work in and own small
factories. They also worked as carpenters, plumbers, and locksmiths and at
unskilled jobs such as stone breakers and water carriers.

In the 1870s, women began working as seamstresses at home. By the
1890s, young women were leaving home to work in small factories. However, neither Jews' new occupations nor the fact that all family members were
working saved many families from poverty (Weinberg, 1988, p. 53).[14] Frequently, even middle-class families had little money. In Russia by the end of
the nineteenth century, 40 percent of the Jews depended on charity (Sachar,

2005). Furthermore, in Galicia one-third of all Jews were reported to be on the "edge of starvation" (Weinberg, 1988, p. 43).

By the late 1890s, the Jewish world in Eastern Europe had changed in many ways. By 1898, about half of all Jews lived in urban areas (Weinberg, 1988, p. 53). The oppression and dislocation of Jews gave rise to anger that in turn contributed to the growth of socialism, labor unions, and Zionism, particularly among the young (Sorin, 1992). Strikes and unionization efforts began in Eastern Europe during the 1890s (Sorin, 1997). Zionism grew after the pogroms of 1881 and 1882 (Rischin, 1970; Sorin, 1992). By the turn of the century, socialism, Zionism, and various combinations of the two had grown into a "ferment" among young people from Russia, Poland, and Rumania and had spread to shtetls and villages (Howe, 1976, p. 15).

In this atmosphere, there was movement away from traditional Jewish life (Soyer, 1997; Howe, 1976; Weinberg, 1988). Not only did the "young intelligentsia" and city dwellers begin to secularize, but even in small shtetlekh a few people tried to "reconcile a degree of secularism with religious tradition" (Weinberg, 1988, p. 57).

Austro-Hungarian and Rumanian Jews

Although the cultures of Austro-Hungarian and Rumanian Jews were similar to those of Russian Jews, their political and economic situations differed to some degree (Rischin, 1970). Most of the Austro-Hungarian Jews lived in the eastern province of Galicia and a few lived in Bukovina.

In Austria-Hungary, Jews did not suffer from the pogroms and government restrictions that Russian Jews did (Bartal, 2005). In fact, in 1868 Austro-Hungarian Jews were granted equal rights and integrated into the political system. The poverty Jews suffered in Austria-Hungary, however, was perhaps even worse than in Russia (Rischin, 1970). This was due in part to poorly developed industry and undeveloped natural resources. As in Russia, changes brought by industrialization increased the Jews' poverty, and many lost their ways of making a living (Rischin, 1970). Thousands of Jews starved to death in Austria-Hungary annually, and in the 1880s, 60 percent of its Jews were supported by charity (Sorin, 1992).

In Galicia, anti-Semitism increased in the 1890s. "The Catholic clergy pursued a systematic and intensive campaign of anti-Semitism and hatred" (Manekin, 2010; Masserman & Baker, 1932, p. 233). Jewish workers were barred from some industries, a Catholic convocation initiated an economic boycott of Jews, and restrictions on university admissions were instituted (Manekin, 2010). In June 1898, peasant mobs attacked Jewish neighborhoods in central and western Galicia.

Most of the Jews of Rumania, where they constituted only 4.5 percent of the population, lived in the province of Moldavia (Sachar, 2005, p. 204;

Volovici, 2010). Under the Rumanian Constitution of 1866, Jews were denied civil rights, and they were discriminated against by anti-Semitic political groups (Volovici, 2010). Violence and local pogroms sometimes occurred. In 1886 and 1887, the government instituted "draconian limits" on Jewish economic opportunities (Soyer, 1997, p. 26). They were progressively excluded from various occupations (Masserman & Baker, 1932, p. 233), could not attend schools, and were unable to live in villages (Rischin, 1970).

Despite this discrimination, Rumanian Jews were able to advance economically, and while most were extremely poor, a few became merchants, bankers, physicians, and lawyers. However, in 1899, during a significant economic depression, the Rumanian legislature denounced the Jews. They were expelled from many areas, and the government not only tolerated but encouraged pogroms (Sachar, 2005; Sorin, 1992). After 1899, a high proportion of Rumanian Jews immigrated to America (Rischin, 1970), starting with "fusgayers," young people who set out by foot for the embarkation point of Hamburg (Sorin, 1992; Soyer, 1997).

Immigration to America

Starting in the early 1880s, Jews in Eastern Europe saw no possibility that the future at home would be better for themselves or their children (Anbinder, 2016, p. 309). Emigration from Russia and Austria-Hungary had actually begun in the 1860s and 1870s with the increasing poverty and, in Russia, the ominously increasing anti-Semitism (Sachar, 1992, p. 117). Books and articles about America were disseminated, and reports from relatives already in America extolled its benefits.

The dream of going to America spread to cities and small towns alike (Sorin, 1992). Mary Antin, who emigrated with her family at age thirteen in 1894, explained the excitement of emigration:

> "America" was in everybody's mouth. Business men talked of it over their accounts; the market women made up their quarrels that they might discuss it from stall to stall; people who had relatives in the famous land went around reading their letters for the enlightenment of less fortunate folks . . . children played at emigrating; old folks shook their sage heads over the evening fire, and prophesied no good for those who braved the terrors of the sea and the foreign goal beyond it:—all talked of it, but scarcely anybody knew one true fact about this magic land. (1985, pp. 11–12)

"It is a beautiful country, the land of freedom," wrote one immigrant in a letter. "Wherever [a Jew] wants to move he can go, whatever he wants to accomplish he can attain" (Anbinder, 2016, pp. 309–310). Another immigrant wrote of the "guarantees of individual freedom, freedom of conscience, and security of all property."

Motivations for emigration were complex; poverty and discrimination were not always the primary reasons. The "restless energy of young people discontented with their lot" and the hope bred in them by ideologies such as Bundist Socialism and Zionism led many to leave (Dawidowicz, 1982, p. 17; Sorin, 1992, p. 36). Several of my interviewees mentioned the narrowness of shtetl life as a factor in their fathers' decisions to emigrate, and it is described in this immigrant memoir: "The small town felt narrow to me, and I wanted to go somewhere else," wrote Aaron Domnitz, who came from Belarus in 1906. "Even my parents asked me to go abroad. The mood in general was to emigrate" (Domnitz, 2006, p. 135; also cited in Anbinder, 2016, p. 312).

Males sometimes mentioned the adventure of immigration (Ravage, 1917, p. 3): "Those days everybody's dream in the old country was to go to America. . . . We heard about better living. . . . I figured, I have a trade, I have a chance more or less to see the world. I was young." Avoiding conscription, which posed real danger, was a common reason for men, as was the desire to improve their economic situations (Weinberg, 1988, p. 18).

Girls emigrated to send back money for their families but sometimes too in the hope of getting an education or finding a husband (Epstein, 2007; Weinberg, 1988). Sometimes young women left to escape the prospect of being married off against their will to undesirable men (Anbinder, 2016).

Although the young often immigrated to America on their own, families frequently immigrated together (Epstein, 2007: Soyer, 1977).[15] Those who left tended to be "poorer than those who stayed behind" (Dawidowicz, 1982; Weinberg, 1988, p. 76). "Chain migration" was common: families who were less well-off economically generally sent a father, older brother, or sister to America first to earn money to bring over the others (Weinberg, 1988).

My paternal grandfather was preceded to America by two older brothers and an older sister in the early years of the twentieth century; moreover, my maternal grandmother's father and an older brother left for America before World War I. Like many of those I write about, my grandmother and the rest of her family were trapped in Eastern Europe by World War I.

For Russian Jews, the pogroms and May Laws were sometimes the "final push" toward the decision to leave; immigration spiked following the pogroms of 1881 and those of 1903 to 1905 (Anbinder, 2016; Sachar, 1992). Nevertheless, the desire to leave was more often motivated by economic reasons (Alroey, 2011; Anbinder, 2016; Epstein, 2007, p. 13; Sorin, 1992). Alroey (2011) argues persuasively that emigration was more often a response to economic hardship than to pogroms, citing several sources and various data that show, for example, higher rates of emigration from places like Galicia that did not suffer pogroms, as well as higher rates of emigration from regions that were worse off financially (Alroey's data covers the years 1905–1914).[16] This was also true for prerevolutionary Russia (Sorin, 1992, p. 35).

The immigration process itself was often extremely stressful. Emigrants were occasionally arrested and jailed, as Jews might lack passports or have fake ones (Anbinder, 2016). Emigrants frequently required the help of a professional smuggler to cross the Austro-Hungarian or German border, and delousing at the port city might be a "bewildering shock" (p. 323). The ocean voyage in steerage was characterized by seasickness, "crowding," "indignities," and "pandemonium" (p. 324).

Immigration to the U.S. was cut off by World War I and then resumed in 1918. However, the number of immigrants decreased in 1921 because of the Emergency Quota Act, and the U.S. virtually shut the doors to Eastern European Jewish immigrants—as well as other Eastern and Southern Europeans—with its Immigration Act of 1924, also called the Johnson-Reed Act (Anbinder, 2016; Cohen & Soyer, 2006; Weinberg, 1988). Between 1881 and 1914, about 2.1 million Eastern European Jews (approximately one-third the total inhabitants) immigrated to the U.S. About 1.6 million came from tsarist Russia; 400,000 came from came from Austria-Hungary, largely from Galicia; and about 80,000 Jews came from Rumania (Anbinder, 2016; Soyer, 1997).

World War I and the Catastrophic Civil Wars

World War I and its aftermath were a horrific disaster for the Jews of the Russian Pale and Galicia. According to Winter (2015, p. 3), "The impact of the 1914–1918 conflict was so great as to constitute a crisis in Jewish life and thought." For individual human beings, the war changed not only their concept of the "external world but of the moral world as well" (Benjamin, 1968, as cited in Winter, 2015). The magnitude of this catastrophe explains why some of the parents of those I interviewed left it all behind with alacrity.

The military movements across the region during World War I disrupted the lives of all people, Jews and Christians alike (Engel, 2010). For Jews, however, the war's impact was significantly worse because of the virulent anti-Semitism of the tsarist government (Engel, 2010; Sorin, 1992; Weinberg, 1988).

In 1915, as the enemy approached, the Jewish population living in Russian border areas—suspected of treachery by the tsarist government—was forced to leave. Jews traveled on foot and sometimes in freight cars; some slept in open fields for weeks (Engel, 2010; Sachar, 2005). Because many of the able-bodied men were serving in the army, it was the women, the children, the aged, and the infirm who composed the legions of refugees (Sachar, 2005). Girls were routinely raped (Weinberg, 1988). Sachar (2005) stated that an estimated 60,000 to 80,000 Jews died of starvation or exposure during the 1915 expulsion. However, Winter (2015) wrote that the retreating Russian soldiers murdered as many as 250,000 Jews. He stated, "This massive pogrom . . . was a catastrophe on a completely different scale from that suffered in Kishinev and elsewhere a decade before" (p. 9).

More than half a million Jews were expelled between March and September of 1915 (Engel, 2010). The entire Jewish population of northern Lithuania and much of the Latvian Jewish population were among those displaced. Often, after they were forced to leave home, their property was looted or destroyed.

In 1914 and 1915, Russian armies also wreaked havoc upon the Jews of Galicia and Bukovina (Engel, 2010). Not only did they use the same tactics as they did within the Russian Empire, but the Russians also imposed huge levies on the Jewish population to support their troops. The 1914 Russian invasion led to the flight of between 200,000 and perhaps 450,000 Jews from areas that seemed likely to be captured. In addition, the Russian commanders ordered the deportation of more than 50,000 Jews deep into the Russian interior.

The war created an economic disaster: shortages of all types of goods, harvest failures, famine, and unprecedented inflation destroyed the savings and ways of life of individuals in Central and Eastern Europe (Winter, 2015, p. 6).[17] In occupied areas, unsanitary conditions fostered the spread of cholera. (The cholera epidemic plays a part in Seymour's story, and it affected Irene's father.)

Toward the end of the war, tensions between Jews and non-Jews in Eastern Europe increased amid suspicions that Jews were Bolshevik agents (Engel, 2010). Food shortages were blamed on the Jews. During the war's last year, food became more scarce amid German grain confiscations. Because Jews were important in the grain trade, peasant anger over German grain levies and the food shortage in general was deflected onto the Jews.

Beginning in November 1918, the withdrawal of German and Austrian armies resulted in a breakdown of authority (Engel, 2010). Jews were caught in the crossfire of subsequent conflicts, as soldiers fought over recently occupied areas (Engel, 2010). Between 1918 and 1921, "pogroms and mass pillage" affected every Jewish city and town in the Ukraine (Sachar, 2005, p. 320; Sorin, 1992). Tens of thousands of Jews were mutilated, raped, or murdered, and half a million were left impoverished. For Jews, "the war after the war was as bad as the 1914–1918 conflict itself" (Winter, 2015, p. 15).

According to Sachar (2005, p. 322), the horror of World War I and its aftermath in the Ukraine represented the most profound catastrophe until the Holocaust. Both the war and subsequent civil wars "tore apart vast areas of Jewish settlement in Eastern Europe" (Winter, 2015, p. 17). Many Jews were never able to recover economically. Furthermore, war refugees and deportees often found it difficult or impossible to return home. As mentioned above, it is the legacy of this terrible period that caused many of my interviewees to state that their parents never wanted to set foot in Eastern Europe again.

For those Jews who survived World War I and the ensuing massacres and economic ruin, emigration was of the utmost importance (Sachar, 1992). Consequently, in 1920, some 190,000 Jewish immigrants reached the U.S. By 1920, however, as anti-immigration sentiment in the U.S. reached a peak, immigration to the U.S. dropped to 53,000 in 1921 and fell even more sharply in 1922.

History and Psychology

Understanding the traumatic circumstances faced by Eastern European Jews and those who emigrated helps to explain the tremendous psychic damage they suffered. According to Weisser (1989, p. 62), poverty and upheaval meant shtetl Jews' "perception of life was circumscribed by the immediacy of risk, causing decisions to be made carefully, deliberately, and fearfully." Recollections of shtetl life, he wrote, were characterized by a sense of limitation and insecurity. Others believed, however, that the psychological damage caused by long-term victimization and the fear of pogroms was more devastating than poverty was: "The knowledge that in the full light of day . . . a crowd of the lowest rabble may burst into your house, plundering and murdering, destroying all that you have toiled for . . . the knowledge that it is useless to struggle because behind the pogromists armed force is ranged against you—such knowledge paralyzes the energy of the people" (Dillingham, 1911, p. 279).

In general, wrote Cowan and Cowan (1996, pp. 30–31), "the immigrants' sense of themselves" was from birth "wrapped up" with the "sense of being victimized by Christian indifference and brutality," with the sense that neighbors who are your friends today can become "mortal enemies" tomorrow. One immigrant wrote that during World War I, Cossacks invaded his town; his father was walking down the street and a Cossack "kicked him in the face and knocked out every one of his teeth," then pulled off his father's boots and coat and rode away (p. 31). Commenting about the Jews' powerlessness, the man continued: "There was no appeal from that." The Jews had "no standing, no recourse." Women were regularly raped by soldiers, and one woman wrote: "It was dangerous just to be."

The pogroms that occurred between 1919 and 1921 were marked by unimaginable "mass slaughter" (Weisser, 1989, p. 67). The psychic damage caused by an atmosphere in which "atrocities" included "almost every type of torture and violence that humans could suffer at the hands of other 'humans'" can only be imagined when we realize that some survivors, for the remainder of their lives, suffered each night from nightmares (Cowan & Cowan, 1996). The terror of this period can be seen in the following passage: a female emigrant who survived these years found herself wavering in her resolve to embark on the voyage to America. Her mother "insisted," saying,

"Not here. You cannot stay here. The Russian earth is soaked in blood, and one is never certain of what new events may bring" (Fox, 2006, p. 226).

The Jews' experience of coming to America was different from that of other immigrant groups. As we have seen, Jewish immigrants and their children were affected by the persecution and fear they experienced in the Old Country. Consequently, wrote Cowan and Cowan (1996, p. 36), the immigrants' children, whether born in Europe or the U.S., spent their early years in the "shadow of the pogroms, in the shadow of fear, oppression, and terror"; this shadow "distorted" their "essential understanding of themselves." Moreover, Eastern European Jews constituted the one group of American "immigrants whose movement away from their homeland resulted from a conscious policy of extermination and expulsion" (Weisser, 1989, p. 25). Individuals from other European countries might return to their homelands to retire; departure from home was often not thought of as permanent (Matt, 2011). For Jewish immigrants, however, this was not true. After World War I and the postwar pogroms, they knew from their moment of arrival that the Old Country "was no longer a safety valve in case things did not work out as planned" (p. 26).

From 1881 until the outbreak of World War I in 1914, more than one-third of Eastern Europe's Jews crossed the ocean (Rischin, 1970; see also Sorin, 1992). Over 90 percent journeyed to the U.S., while a small minority of students went to Palestine (Epstein, 2007), and other Jews emigrated to destinations such as South America. The distressing conditions that precipitated immigration influenced individuals psychologically. What were the subjective reasons that caused many of the immigrants' children to say, in effect, that their parents wanted to "leave it all behind"?

CONCLUSIONS: TRAUMA AND THE AMBIGUITY OF LOSS

When asked about their parents' feelings about being uprooted, only some of the immigrants' children I spoke to replied that their parents missed family or home. The majority told me about the anti-Semitic violence and poverty that made their parents relieved to escape Eastern Europe. I was trying to understand how historical circumstances influenced the subjective lives of the immigrants and their children. As I began my research, however, several phenomena had occluded my understanding of the historical facts that influenced the Jewish immigrants. First was the widespread silence of the immigrants themselves. Often they did not talk either about the victimization they had faced or about their daily lives in Eastern Europe; as we shall see, often trauma led to dissociation or reticence. In addition, they may have felt that their children's lives were so different that they would not have understood.

Second was the silence of history: the effects of World War I and the ensuing massacres of the Jews were not well studied by historians, and they had receded from the "consciousness of a public that wanted to forget" them (Weisser, 1989, p. 68; Winter, 2015). Finally, was the commonly held romantic view of the shtetl, which viewed it as a place of spiritual life and community orientation.

The historical record suggests that, despite discrimination and violence, Eastern European Jewish immigrants generally felt the loss of their former homes (Ewen, 1985; Howe, 1976; Matt, 2011; Menes, 1972). Matt (2011, p. 145) writes that Jews often felt extremely homesick. Until the Kishinev pogrom of 1903 and the subsequent violence against Jews, Jews longed to return to Eastern Europe, and many did so (Matt, 2011, p. 147).[18] Even in the 1920s, when the tragedy of World War I and its aftermath made life intolerable for so many, Jews continued to feel homesick. In 1921, one Polish immigrant wrote, "We Jewish immigrants from Bialystok suffer from an acute homesickness" (Matt, 2011, p. 147).

What do we make then of many of the immigrants' children insisting that their parents "left it all behind"? Many indeed might have come from backgrounds so deprived or violent that they felt there was nothing to miss. Indeed, violence affected the parents of many of those I interviewed. The majority of the parents emigrated after the scourge of World War I and its violent aftermath; Seymour's, Benjamin's, and Irene's interviews reflect this reality. It is true that many of those whose parents reportedly stated that they never wanted to go back had survived World War I; moreover, some who themselves believed that their parents could not have missed anything in Eastern Europe also had parents who had lived through the war and its aftermath. In addition, extreme poverty affected many. Letters written by Eastern European Jews on the brink of emigration for economic reasons depict the desperation of those who found it impossible to support their families (Alroey, 2011); Barbara's story of her parents portrays this kind of intense poverty. Thus, even though migration and displacement were difficult, some may have been glad to be "done with" Eastern Europe. For them, leaving it all behind may have made sense after the terrible things they experienced.

In fact, because the majority of the parents of those I interviewed arrived after the 1914–1921 conflict in Eastern Europe, these immigrants comprise a special subset of those who arrived in the 1881–1924 wave of emigration. Many of these immigrants experienced not only violence but also unbelievable hunger and terror. To repeat a statement quoted earlier made by the mother of an immigrant: "You cannot stay here. The Russian earth is soaked in blood, and one is never certain of what new events may bring" (Fox, 2006, p. 226).

Nevertheless, I suspect that while some immigrants might have actually felt that there was nothing to miss, for most immigrants the reality must have been more complex. One can be homesick even when leaving a country of violence and hardship. For example, David's mother, presented in the next chapter, experienced fire, acute hunger, and serious disease as a child in Russia, yet she not only did not want to emigrate but many years later felt nostalgia for her home. And an article in the *Dallas Morning News* of 1906 was entitled "Homesick Russian Jews: Refugees who Yearn for the Land of Persecution" (Matt, 2011, p. 146). According to the article, "not even the news of massacres at home" cured those whose homesickness made them apply for help in returning to the Old Country.

For the immigrants, America was a new world with a vastly different way of life from the one they had left. Displacement and loss were real and painful feelings for them. In the face of the loss they must have felt, some newly arrived immigrant parents may have used denial as a coping technique. They would not allow themselves to miss their families or familiar surroundings for fear that doing so would hinder them from "making it."

This notion in itself is a complex one. In fact, the immigrants were in actuality abjured by those in authority to forget the past and assimilate (Matt, 2011). For example, officials at the United Hebrew Charities and writers of advice books regarded homesickness as a weakness. In addition, the "Bintel Brief," a widely read advice column in the popular Yiddish daily *Forward* newspaper, encouraged homesick readers to try to overcome their emotions and adapt; if they did so, they would "in time" be able to bring their parents to America (Matt, 2011, p. 169; Metzker, 1971, p. 114). Jewish immigrant leaders encouraged adaptability after the Kishinev pogroms, as those who returned to Eastern Europe faced the possibility of death. Thus the disavowal of loss was an adaptive stance.

Not only did immigrants receive the message from others that homesickness must be suppressed, but, in addition, psychological forces encouraged its repudiation. Jill Salberg (2005, p. 436), discussing her immigrant grandparents, wrote: "For them America, the *Goldene Medina* ("Golden Land"), promised a better life, and to harbor longings for the past was unthinkable. Thus, what they had left behind couldn't be mourned." Because there was no future for the Jews in Eastern Europe, the immigrants had to look forward, to leave it all behind; they simply could not let themselves miss what they couldn't have.

While migration was ultimately an individual decision, Jewish emigration to America was in many ways a collective decision, a movement (Howe, 1976). So many, particularly among the young, followed the lead of both peers and advisors in emigrating. The collective nature of this migration discouraged allowing oneself to miss family or home.

Silence was one form of disavowing loss, and it might serve to keep unacceptable feelings under wraps. And disavowing loss in the face of trauma makes sense. Often the immigrants and their children seemed unable to think that one could miss the place where oneself or one's loved ones were treated unspeakably. For an immigrant to say, I never want to go back there—or for an immigrant's child to say, there was nothing that my parent could have missed—is a way of simplifying something that was painful and complex. It was better for immigrants and their children to repudiate the loss and to say, as Elizabeth did: my father "wanted to leave it all behind" or "Both parents agreed that they would never set foot in Europe again."

The majority of those I interviewed said in one way or another that their parents were "done with" life in Eastern Europe. We know from memoirs and history, however, that homesickness was common. The truth may be that parents' feelings about leaving home may not have been transmitted to children. Parents may have believed that their American children simply would not understand their painful decisions about migration or their feelings about home.

Immigrant parents escaped the trauma of anti-Semitic violence and unremitting poverty but left behind family and lost everything that had been familiar. Barbara's parents had escaped a life that was indeed dangerous; it was a "fragile experience," yet they were nostalgic for the past. For Benjamin's parents, "the risk of death was ever-present," but they had experienced good times along with the bad. And the fact was that had their parents not left Eastern Europe, all would have been killed in the Holocaust. The losses that the immigrants faced would have seemed ambiguous to their children. In disavowing their parents' losses, the children simplified the complicated calculus of managing their own feelings about what their parents had been through. Like Irene, they could say, Eastern Europe was a "bad place" that should "fade into obscurity" for the Jews.

In many cases "they left it all behind" may have been the children's own interpretation, helping them to avoid thinking or knowing too much about their parents' traumatic histories or about the losses of migration. For example, it was Norman, rather than his mother, who said he could not imagine that his mother missed anything. And the immigrant autobiography written by a family member of mine made a similar assumption. Some children simply could not understand the importance of their parents' ties to the Old Country. After all, from the children's point of view, Eastern Europe was such a terrible place and America was so much better in every way. In general, for both parents and children, not thinking too much about the past was an important coping strategy in allowing them to move forward in order to build a new life in America (Bar-On & Gilad, 1994).

Had I been able to interview the parents themselves, many might have expressed more nuanced points of view about their pasts than those described by their children. For example, Benjamin's mother, discussed above, carried only "bad memories" of her town, but at the same time she "pined" for the siblings she would never see again. Because she and many other immigrants experienced profound loss, along with the relief of having escaped poverty and persecution, we can speak of the ambiguity of their losses.

For these immigrants, complicating the difficulty of leaving everything familiar was, of course, the reality that the majority had to leave Eastern Europe. Thus one of the problems their children faced in speaking about their parents was the ambiguity of the immigrants' losses. The concept of the ambiguity of loss describes the complex sets of feelings that arose from the combinations of trauma and loss each immigrant suffered (L. Robinson, personal communication, January 19, 2012).[19] Children's feelings were complicated because their parents faced a complex balance of gains and losses as they immigrated. The children's own feelings about this were often painful and difficult to comprehend.

Additional examples of the ambiguity of loss come from the memoir literature. For example, Bertha Fox (2006, p. 230) arrived in 1923 after massive trauma, but she went on to marry a "fine man" and to have two sons of whom she was proud. Yet in 1942 she wrote, "I am the only one in my family saved from death by coming to America" (p. 230). She was unable, for many reasons, to bring other families to the U.S. She hoped that in the future "our Jewish duty will be to multiply ourselves and replace the gruesome numbers of victims with new lives." Chaim Kusnetz (Cohen & Soyer, 2006), who, like Fox, survived the famine and violence of the post–World War I era, had different ambivalent feelings. In the U.S., he realized that he had a good life to all external appearances; he had a devoted wife, a pretty little daughter, a steady job, and enough money. Yet he wrote about his subjective feelings of alienation, emptiness, and loneliness.

Many of the immigrants' children were coping with the knowledge of their parents' sacrifices—their parents had emigrated so their children would have better lives than their own. They felt the burden of what their parents had suffered. We will learn more about the legacy for the children of their parents' trauma in the next chapter, before going on to explore the consequences of uprooting and loss for parents and children in chapter 3.

NOTES

1. Pogroms in Galicia occurred during World War I and its aftermath but rarely occurred before.

2. Mark Naison (2002, p. 143) wrote that residents of Crown Heights in the 1950s "seemed determined to shield their children from the weight of history." He added that a "communal code of silence" sought to protect their children from the knowledge of the Depression, the Holocaust, and tragedy so that they would grow up "feeling that the world was fundamentally benign." Perhaps some of my own innocence of what my grandparents' generation suffered

was due to a similar reaction by my own parents and the Jewish educators who taught me at our local Sunday School.

3. This differs greatly from the many parents who were devastated at the idea of never again seeing their children and therefore resisted the idea that they wanted to emigrate. It reflects the danger of the post–World War I years.

4. Benjamin did experience minor anti-Semitism in the army, such as anti-Semitic remarks from other soldiers.

5. Forcibly cutting off a Jewish man's beard was a form of persecution, and it was done by the Nazis. The Mishnah—a written redaction of Jewish oral law—prohibits using a razor on a man's beard. Consequently, all Orthodox Jewish men had beards and forcibly cutting off this symbol was humiliating.

6. They also saw a German soldier killed in front of their home.

7. Both because he probably missed his family and because he fled a middle-class life (he was working class in America), Amos's story was different from those who left it all behind. However, his story was crucial in understanding Seymour.

8. She was joined in the U.S. by only one of her several siblings.

9. I omitted a sentence here. The full passage reads: "And what did they talk about? Why about the old country: the parents and relatives they had left behind—never to see again."

10. *Shtetle* was his spelling for *shtetele*, which means small town in Yiddish.

11. At first the assassination was blamed on the terrorists who had committed it and who were then hanged. It was afterward that the Russian government "blamed the Jews for all of Russia's troubles" (Dawidowicz, 1982, p. 13). "Government circulars focused on 'the harm caused the Christian population by the activity of the Jews with their tribal exclusiveness . . . religious fanaticism and exploitation,' and declared that 'the people in the Ukriane suffer most of all from the Jews. Who takes the land, the woods, the taverns from out of your hands? The Jews. The Jew curses you, cheats you, drinks your blood'" (Sorin, 1992, p. 32).

12. The Russian government did not explicitly encourage the violent actions of the mobs against the Jews. However, by encouraging scapegoating, it had implicitly encouraged pogroms, and in not punishing the "pogrom activitists," "its officials were egregiously negligent, even culpable" (Sachar, 2005, p. 199).

13. Israel Zangwill of the Jewish Territorial Organization led a search for a country to which Jews could safely move until conditions were ready for the Jews to immigrate to Palestine (Alroey, 2011).

14. A "few manufacturers and financiers were able to take advantage of the changing economy to become wealthy" (Soyer, 1997, p. 22).

15. A large proportion of those who immigrated to the U.S. from other ethnic groups returned to their countries of origin. However, after 1905, only 5 to 8 percent of Eastern European Jews returned (e.g., Sorin, 1992).

16. See also Soyer (1997, p. 26), who says that in Russia "the terror of pogroms played less of a role in influencing migration patterns than did government measures that directly affected the Jewish economy." In fact, Jewish emigration to America from Eastern Europe had begun in the 1870s, before the pogroms.

17. My paternal grandmother's formerly middle-class family suddenly did not have enough food, and my great-grandfather told my grandmother and her sister that they would have to leave home for Vienna in order to get jobs. Previously it would have been unthinkable for educated, middle-class Jewish girls to have been sent to work (in fact, my grandmother was only able to find a job in an envelope factory; in letters home, she was forced to lie about this, as her father would have been shocked that she had not found a more genteel position).

18. Matt cites Jonathan Sarna's article, "The Myth of No Return: Jewish Return Migration to Eastern Europe, 1881–1914." *American Jewish History* 71 (1981): 256–68. In addition, she cites a March 10, 1906, *Dallas Morning News* article, "Homesick Russian Jews: Refugees who Long for the Land of Persecution."

19. In Boss's (1999) *Ambiguous Loss: Learning to Live with Unresolved Grief* (Cambridge, MA: Harvard University Press), the idea of the ambiguous losses of immigrants is mentioned. Although immigrants of one hundred years ago severed ties to family members back home, the author—who was descended from these immigrants—did not know whether the people she had

never met were really her family; similarly, because homesickness was part of her family's life, she never knew "where home really was" (p. 1). Boss's idea of ambiguous loss is somewhat different from my concept of the ambiguity of loss.

Chapter Two

Communicating about the Past and Trauma

DRAMATIS PERSONAE

In order of appearance:

Elaine: Her mother came to the U.S. alone and later overwhelmed her daughter with her feelings of loneliness. She never wanted to set foot in Poland again. Elaine as an adult had a fulfilling life.
 Mother: Chaya
 Father: Frank

Seymour: His mother saw nightmares around her as a child during World War I. His father's entire family were killed in the Holocaust, and Seymour repeatedly re-experienced this event as a repetition of the past.
 Mother: Sadie
 Father: Amos

Barbara: Her parents experienced terrible poverty in Eastern Europe; as adults, all talking was fighting. Barbara felt unloved and neglected as a child.
 Mother: Bella
 Father: Joe

David: He "grew up in the shadow of the shtetl." Although he deeply felt the pain of his mother's childhood of fear and starvation, he as an adult seemed determined to enjoy his life.
 Mother: Pearl
 Father: Philip

Stanley: His mother "felt the bullets whizzing by" during World War I, and his family became wealthy in the U.S. Stanley absorbed his mother's anxiety.
   Mother: Liba
   Father: Chaim

Aaron: His mother as an adolescent discovered the body of her own father, who had been murdered in a pogrom. Growing up, he was expected to be "the best, the first."
   Mother: Estelle
   Father: Max

Ruth: Her mother came from an impoverished background that was full of fear. Her enactment of her mother's family's procedure during pogroms represented an embodied ghost of her mother's past.
   Mother: Devorah
   Father: Harry

As I listened to my interviewees speak, I realized that the denial that characterized my grandparents' stories might have been connected to the various kinds of trauma in their histories. My maternal grandmother endured violence and war, and both my grandmothers lost their mothers when young. The intense hunger three of my grandparents suffered could in itself be considered a form of trauma. But how my grandparents communicated about their traumatic pasts differed. Because I based my research on what the immigrants told their children and how the children experienced what they heard, it is essential to know how the parents spoke to their children.

There were great variations in the ways immigrants described their pasts and the ways they transmitted traumatic experiences to their sons and daughters. "They told us kids nothing. They wanted to make a marked transition to the U.S. and dump all that stuff. 'We're here. Let's forget that,'" said Jacob, a highly intelligent and curious scientist. He knew only a few details about his family's life in Europe and was unable to speculate about his parents' psychological transition to the U.S. He conveyed to me that, for his family, survival was paramount and, consequently, there was no room for thoughts of happiness. Jacob's experience was typical in that many parents, particularly fathers, said very little about their lives in the Old Country and their subjective experiences upon arrival in America.[1]

Rose, an astute professional woman in her sixties, had a different experience. She seemed overwhelmed by her parents' massive sense of loss and trauma, and she felt they communicated about the past in opposite ways. Her mother, Leah, spoke in detail and repetitively about her own mother's frightening experiences during World War I. Displaced with her young children, including Leah, she courageously chose to live with them in an isolated barn rather than with sick families. In contrast, Rose's father never once spoke of his experiences. As a teenager, Rose begged her father to tell her at least one story; he told her about a recurrent traumatic experience from his childhood. Each day when he and the other Jewish boys from his village walked to school, they formed a circle with one boy walking inside the circle. They were stoned by gentile boys, but the boy in the middle was protected. Rose sensed that this was the least troubling of the experiences her father might have told her.

Rose's father seemed to be trying to protect both her and himself from the experience of trauma by not speaking about it. Moreover, Rose let me know that she wanted to separate herself from her parents' terrible communications. Her father's silence was reminiscent of the silence of Holocaust survivors. For them, "the impossibility of speaking" was the only way to deal with unspeakable horror (Kaplan, 1995; Laub, 1992, p. 65).

Elaine's story also shows the impact an immigrant parent's trauma could have on a child. Elaine was an educated, retired professional in her seventies, who was agreeable and open during her interview. Her mother, like Rose's, spoke a great deal about the past, describing in detail the family she had left behind in Europe. In fact, she flooded Elaine with her stories of loneliness and trauma. Elaine's father, however, was silent about much of his past.

Elaine began her interview with "My mother had a very, very hard time," suggesting the intense impact of her mother's suffering on her. Elaine's mother, Chaya, arrived in the U.S. at about age twenty without any immediate family members. Because she missed her family, she cried herself to sleep nightly for a couple of years. She had expected to work and save money so her mother and siblings could follow her to New York. However, because of changed U.S. laws limiting immigration, they were forced to immigrate to South America, thousands of miles away. To compensate for this separation, Chaya told Elaine, an only child, so many stories about her own sisters and brothers that Elaine felt that she actually knew her mother's family. By speaking so much about her family, Chaya kept them psychologically alive; she flooded her child with her loneliness and sadness.

Chaya also told her daughter about her father's early death from cancer and about anti-Semitic violence, including a pogrom, that took place in her mother's small city. Although she made clear to Elaine its traumatic impact on her—it also made her hate everything Polish—she actually said very little about the pogrom itself. Elaine felt her mother's hate deeply. Significantly, the dreadful feelings of loss and emptiness Chaya experienced during her early years in New York may have been intensified by the trauma she suffered before her arrival.

Elaine felt overwhelmed by her mother's feelings. "I could feel my mother's sadness as a young child," she said, and she believed that her mother never completely escaped from it. Sitting with Elaine, who appeared to be fulfilled and well-adjusted, I had a sense of absence and flatness when she spoke about her mother. Elaine was profoundly affected emotionally and, I thought, traumatized by her mother's feelings of loss.

Elaine's father spoke little about his experiences. He was a frustrated man, a musician who worked by day in a belt factory and wished for more education. Although she did not know any details, Elaine believed that there were "difficulties" in his family and his past was "too painful" for him to talk about. He seemed less resilient than her mother.

Elaine's absence and flatness represent the ghost of the immense sadness that she took in from her mother and also suggest her father's silent suffering (O'Loughlin, 2009). Her mother, having no one else at hand, seemed to unwittingly have chosen Elaine as the child listener who could cure her (Kaplan, 1995; O'Loughlin, 2009). Yet trying to assess the overall effects on Elaine of her parents' trauma is complicated. It appeared possible that, during Elaine's later childhood, her mother might have in part recovered from her loneliness—in fact, contact with her mother's family increased at that time. Furthermore, Elaine reported that her mother was social and had a loving marriage. Elaine appeared to have been securely attached (Main, Kaplan, & Cassidy, 1985) and generally treated sensitively by her parents. This, together with her open attitude during the interview, suggests that she had been partially able to work through her parents' painful communications. Although I believe that her parents' traumas had reverberations in her present life, Elaine's resilience is attested to by the fact she has a generally fulfilling life (Pisano, 2012, p. 40).

Many immigrant parents, like Elaine's and Rose's fathers, spoke little about their pasts. Although there were many reasons for silence, in a number of cases their reluctance to speak represented an attempt to protect their children from memories that were too raw. Most often it was fathers who were silent.

Some fathers who were silent—like Benjamin's father, who limped because he had been hit by a gentile nobleman—had indeed been traumatized. Some, like Rose's father, communicated their trauma wordlessly (Kaplan, 1995; Laub, 1992). Two of the parents described here, including Elaine's mother, had a different method of dealing with traumatic memories and losses: they spoke in detail or overwhelmed their children with what had occurred.

Overall, many of the immigrants experienced some trauma in Eastern Europe or during the immigration process that was transmitted intergenerationally. The severity of its impact on the children varied widely, but most of them proved resilient and successful. In the remainder of this chapter, I will discuss trauma and its intergenerational transmission, first theoretically and then as it is seen in several of my interviewees' life stories. As we know, trauma may lead to psychological disruption. Parents who have suffered trauma may have momentary or frequent difficulty in attunement to their infants, breakdowns in empathy, or other types of relational impairment. Some of the immigrants' children, like Elaine, were able to work through their intergenerational trauma. For others, trauma was too overwhelming to allow processing and, consequently, intrusions or repetitions of the past might occur.

INTERGENERATIONAL TRANSMISSION OF TRAUMA: THEORY

The parents of many of those I interviewed suffered firsthand from the victimization to which the Jews were subjected. Persecution, of course, varied over different geographical areas and different time periods, but until 1918 the majority of the Jews of Eastern Europe were subjects of the Russian Empire.[2] Briefly what happened in Russia was as follows. A wave of pogroms between 1881 and 1884 was followed by the discriminatory May Laws. The Kishinev Pogrom of 1903 was the beginning of another three years of pogroms, and throughout the first decade of the twentieth century, Russian Jews suffered "constant abuse and intimidation" (Weisser, 1989, p. 67). Many of the parents of those I interviewed endured World War I and the "mass slaughter and destruction" that followed the war; therefore, trauma was common (Weisser, 1989, p. 67).

Yet even many of those Jews who themselves did not live through violent persecution—such as the Austro-Hungarian Jews, who, in general, were not subject to pogroms—endured "little t" trauma. The everyday bullying to which Jews were subject in Eastern Europe caused shame and humiliation. Moreover, the wrenching poverty and extreme hunger that were common took their toll over time. Most of the more than two million Eastern European Jews who immigrated to America did so before the massive disruption of World War I, and probably the majority of these Jews left because of economic conditions rather than pogroms. Nevertheless, most had been "trapped" by the grinding "poverty of daily life"; they were perceived as an "alien population" by the Christian majority (Weisser, 1989, p. 69). Jews knew they had no future in Eastern Europe. According to Weisser (1989, p. 69), the consequences of surviving under such debilitating conditions led to a survival strategy that entailed fear of change and the necessity of weighing every decision against the "possibility of failure."

Some writers discuss "large T" versus "small t" trauma. "Large T" trauma refers to events such as war, predatory violence, sexual abuse, or terrorism, which cause "such horror and threat" that they may "temporarily or permanently alter" individuals' coping ability (van der Kolk, 2000, par. 1). "Small t" trauma, while not threatening to life or physical safety, are instead "ego-threatening"; they can cause helplessness and may have a cumulative effect (EMDR Institute, n.d.). "Small t" trauma can include ongoing poverty, daily discrimination, or abrupt relocation.

The accumulation of "little t" trauma is important in considering the lives of the pre-1930 migrants. While individuals like Norman's mother or Barbara's parents might not have personally experienced pogroms or World War I violence, the accumulation over time of severe stress during their lives as young people had an ongoing crippling effect.

The concept of the intergenerational transmission of trauma, while part and parcel of Holocaust dialogue, is generally not discussed in connection with the 1881–1924 wave of Eastern European Jewish immigration. In this chapter, I present several of the immigrants' children's stories in which their parents' trauma plays a part. While continuing to consider the different ways in which parents spoke to their children, I will concentrate both on telling the children's stories and understanding how their parents' trauma affected the children's lives. First, however, I will present a striking example of transmitted trauma, followed by theory about how trauma is communicated intergenerationally. Much of the literature I draw on in discussing theory was conceived using Holocaust experiences and Holocaust survivors as examples.

Seymour (discussed in the previous chapter) regularly experiences an intrusion of the past in which he relives his father's trauma. During weekly Sabbath services, Seymour, like many Jews, closes his eyes to recite the prayer called the "Shema." When he does so, he is visited by a variation on what he called the following "vision."

> He is a little boy standing near the edge of a ditch, when an older naked woman—he assumes that this is his father's mother—links arms with him; together they will be shot (and there the vision ends, before the bullets hit them).

Thus, each week, Seymour experiences inside himself the death of his grandmother at the hands of the Nazis, as well as the terror that he too may be killed in this way.

This ghost of the past illustrates the influence of historical events on the individual psyche. As mentioned, Seymour's father's entire family was killed during World War II, and his father and in turn Seymour were profoundly influenced by this. In his weekly fantasy, we see that the historical events of the Holocaust survive in him as an individual.

How does intergenerational transmission occur? We are burdened with un-spoken ghostly transmissions passed on by people in our pasts, writes Frosh (2013). Because they are not talked about, they are reenacted. Consequently, we often repeat the past without remembering or working it through. That is, through uncanny processes, the invisible and inaudible past is preserved through unwilling repetitions (Faimberg, 2005; O'Loughlin, 2013).

In focusing now on how trauma is transmitted from individual parents to children, I will describe parents who "cannot recall" or "will not speak" of what has happened to them, a frequent occurrence in families of Holocaust survivors (Pisano, 2012, p. 25). By definition, trauma is incomprehensible; it overwhelms the individual's capacity to cope. After a massively traumatic event, because the mind cannot encompass the horrific event, dissociation occurs. In other words, to protect himself from overwhelming affect, there is a disconnection in the person's consciousness, memories, identity, or actions (Pisano, 2012, p. 24). Because the trauma has been dissociated and is not consciously available, there is, in effect, no self to observe or witness the trauma (Kaplan, 1995; Pisano, 2012). As a corollary, there are no words to convey the massively traumatic event, and for that reason, it can neither be symbolized nor worked through. By its very nature, massive trauma cannot be processed.

In the aftermath of a traumatic event, the dissociated truth of the terror lives on as an "unthought known," in other words, something in some way known yet unable to be thought about (Davoine & Gaudillière, 2004; Pisano, 2012).[3] Often it leaves its mark on the body (Rogers, 2006; van der Kolk, 2014). To go on with life, the survivor of massive trauma represses or "cuts out" his experiences and never looks back (Pisano, 2012, p. 21; see also Davoine & Gaudillière, 2004). Frequently, the survivor remains silent, hoping to "grow back into a whole human being," and silence helps her to preserve her remaining bits of sanity (Kaplan, 1995, p. 218).

When traumatized parents cannot make conscious contact with their dis-sociated memories of the event, they nevertheless often find a way to show what cannot be spoken (Davoine & Gaudillière, 2004). How they transmit the otherwise unrecognized trauma by showing it—often to their children, who exist as witnesses—can be described at the dyadic parent-child level. Traumatized parents experience momentary dissociations or absences, which are markers of overwhelming emotional states (Halasz, 2012, p. 149) and represent the scars of terror. These moments of altered affect state or silence are noticed by the infant or child. For example, note Davoine and Gaudillière (2004), if a nursing infant's mother receives an alarming communication—in the past a telegram and today an e-mail or text—the baby registers that her expression and heartbeat have changed. Alternatively, when the parent of an older child momentarily re-registers the traumatic past, the child feels the "changes from a familiar soft, reactive face to a frozen one," from a "gentle musical voice to a robotic one," or a "warm lingering hug to a quick pat on the head" (Halasz, 2012, p. 152). When children sense these subtle affective changes, they wonder about their meaning (Pisano, 2012). On some level they divine that their parents are "hiding some terrible secret" (Kaplan, 1995, p. 219).

Kaplan gives this example of a child learning about her parent's past:

> A policeman approaches on the street; the mother has a panic attack. She clutches the child's hand tightly and stands as still as a statue. Nothing is said, but the child registers the mother's reactions and knows "something" is wrong. The child comes to know that existence is precarious. (Kaplan, 1995, p. 231; also cited in Pisano, 2012, pp. 27–28)

While the parents of my interviewees often would not speak of what happened to them, in other cases traumatic events *were* spoken about, sometimes only rarely and sometimes often and in detail. Rogers (2006) emphasizes that even in families in which appalling events were talked about, something unsayable remained. That is, just because mothers and occasionally fathers were able to put shockingly traumatic events into words does not mean these events were comprehensible. The magnitude and horror of the trauma were difficult to capture in words. That is, when talking about these events to their children, years later, "the words available" to them "miss the point" (Fink, 1999, p. 86; as cited in Pisano, 2012, p. 24). The unsayable element of a parent's history remains a potent and uncanny presence in the child's or adult's life.

Some of my interviewees as children began to ask about their parents' stories (Kaplan, 1995). "A parent's silence and secrecy actually stimulate the child's need and desire to uncover his past," writes Kaplan (1995, p. 227). Interviewees whose parents *did* speak about the past might also become curious about their parents' narratives. However, because of the "unspeakable" portions of traumatized parents' histories, whether my interviewees as children actively inquired or not, they were left with gaps instead of narratives at the incomprehensible parts (O'Loughlin, 2013, p. 61). Experience that is "unthought and unnamed" by a parent—manifested by an absence or a frozen moment—leads to a ghost or intrusion of the past for the adult child, a disguised reminder (p. 61). The trauma may be represented as an uncanny event (O'Loughlin, 2013, p. 58). For instance, a descendent of the Irish Great Hunger might experience the compulsive need to feed others at a soup kitchen.

Of the adult children I interviewed, some were left with a destructive repetition of the past. Others, however, had worked through the trauma and carried a more benign type of ghost, such as a compulsive need to know about Jewish history. Elaine's mother was able to talk about the sadness and loneliness of her migration; consequently, Elaine's was a more benign type of ghost. In contrast, other parents suffered events such as their own parents' violent deaths or continued exposure to war, about which they could not speak. The experience was unnamed and perhaps unthought by a parent (O'Loughlin, 2013). In these instances, repetitions or reenactments like Seymour's might occur.

An even more extreme type of transmission is described by Judith Kestenberg, herself a refugee from 1930s Europe. Kestenberg, writing about Holocaust survivors, gave the name "transposition" to the unconscious process of transmission of massive trauma, by which—especially when the parent is unable to feel anything—the "past reality of the parent intrudes into the present psychological reality of the child" (Kaplan, 1995, p. 224). Transposition works through projective identification; the child, sensing that the parent freezes at a particular moment, not only intuits that something is wrong but also uncannily absorbs her parent's trauma as her own. Her unconscious hope is to cure her parent. In a strange reversal of time between parent and child, the child unwittingly becomes the subject of the parent's suffering. It becomes her role to devote a "lifetime to working through" the psychological "devastation" of the past, which she and the parent now share; she does this by reenacting the parent's trauma (Pisano, 2012, p. 26). Thus she gives "up her own right to exist in the present" (Kaplan, 1995, p. 224).

According to Kaplan (1995, p. 224), transposition is "more awesome" than other varieties of intergenerational transmission because the child's ongoing existence is wholly devoted to healing the parent's unspoken wounds.

> An example of transposition is the daughter of Holocaust survivors who develops an unconscious fantasy that she has been selected by her mother to perform a special mission. She, and she alone, can repair her mother's trauma by sacrificing her own desires and longings. She becomes obese, thus effectively concealing her beauty under layers of fat. Or she starves herself until her body is transformed into the body of a concentration camp survivor. (Kaplan, 1995, pp. 226–227; also cited in Pisano, 2012, p. 26)

Some of those I interviewed felt themselves to be intimately connected to their parents' suffering. Similarly to those subject to transposition, they might unconsciously wish to care for and heal their traumatized parents. A small number had the "hunger for pain" that we encounter in children of Holocaust survivors (Pisano, 2012, p. 184).

The psychological effects of unmetabolized trauma led to uncontrolled anger and unpredictability in some parents (Lieberman, 2014, p. 278; as cited in Salberg, 2017a, p. 90) and states of fear or emptiness in others (Salberg, 2017a). Because trauma affects the parent-child bond, an immigrant parent whose trauma was unprocessed might be impaired in his ability to be attuned to or empathic with his infant or child.

Under what conditions are the recipients of intergenerational trauma resilient? In general, adult children who are securely attached will be more resilient. Those who had sensitive, responsive parents, leading to secure attachment status, could more easily work through trauma passed down to them (Cyrulnik, 2007).[4] These parents had at least partly worked through their own trauma. Moreover, those children who are able to talk about what they know have more of a chance of working through trauma than those who are unaware of or unable to speak about the secrets of their parents' pasts. According to Cyrulnik (2007, p. 9), those who have the "day to day emotional support of those around" them, as well as the understanding of larger societal groups, are more able to heal from intergenerational trauma.

Parents of my interviewees might suffer from two general categories of trauma. Migration trauma, when the act of emigration itself proved traumatic, affected Elaine's mother. The trauma of violence, extreme poverty, or anti-Semitic discrimination affected Rose's father as well as Benjamin's and Seymour's parents.

It is important to note that many people experience catastrophic experiences but do not suffer the lasting effects of trauma (van der Kolk, 2000). Both the content of traumatic events and individual personality traits influence someone's likelihood of developing psychological sequelae of trauma (van der Kolk, 2000; van der Kolk, McFarlane, & Weisaeth, 1996).

Seymour's vision illustrates intergenerational transmission. A piece of his father's past is lodged inside Seymour; it lives inside him in a visceral way. By reliving it every week, he not only keeps it alive, but he also lives out something for his father, something that destroyed his father. Seymour's vision reenacts that which cannot be processed because of its unspeakable nature; it is, consequently, repeated rather than worked through. As Frosh remarks, what provokes the most suffering must be kept alive (Frosh, 2013; citing Derrida, 1986, p. xxxv).

As a child, Seymour heard noises in his parents' bedroom at night, and when he inquired, his mother told him that his father had nightmares during which he lashed out as if to hit someone. Seymour explained that, because his father in the past was powerless to help save his family, he, Seymour, in his fantasy took his grandmother's arm in order to comfort her. He did this for his father, to help his father. Seymour's vision illustrates how past becomes present when trauma is transmitted intergenerationally.

LIFE STORIES

Barbara and David both dealt with parental trauma, but their life stories contrast. Barbara's parents' anger and unpredictability suggest unmetabolized trauma, and their disturbed communication was complicated by Barbara's mother's severe depression. The terrible circumstances they had endured were put into words, but the affect conveyed meant that they were beyond comprehension. Barbara as a child identified with her parents in an unconscious attempt to cure them.

While David's mother suffered trauma as a child, his father came from a calm home; his father's calm presence in David's life was helpful. As an adult, David felt pained by his mother's past, but he was able to separate from it and to enjoy his life.

Barbara

Barbara's parents, like Elaine's mother, communicated a great deal about the past, and Barbara seemed to have been overwhelmed by her parents' traumatic recollections. During her interview, Barbara related many extremely painful memories, both about her parents' lives and about growing up with her parents. It was not only the content of Barbara's parents' reminiscences that proved problematic. Their emotionally uncontained communication style during Barbara's childhood was very difficult for her; most talking consisted of yelling. This suggests the unprocessed nature of her parents' traumatic experiences.

Barbara, described briefly in chapter 1, appeared to be, more intensely than Elaine, the recipient of family trauma. Indeed, the circumstances of Barbara's parents' lives did appear to be more disturbing than what we know about Elaine's mother's background. Furthermore, Barbara did not enjoy the secure love during childhood that Elaine did. Barbara's parents, because of their own psychological issues, were able to pay little attention to her emotional needs, and as a child she felt both unloved and disadvantaged. One similarity to Elaine's story jumped out at me, however. Communication style changed around the issue of pogroms; when Barbara asked her mother about pogroms, her question was met by silence.

Barbara, perhaps as a way to receive nurturance from the parents who were able to give her little emotional support, actively encouraged them to tell her the stories of their lives; she "egged them on." Indeed, she seemed closely identified with them and seemed to connect around the issue of their deprivation. When I asked if her parents had lost anything in leaving their Eastern European homes, she emotionally replied that they had left behind "pogroms, fear, and starvation." Barbara's vehemence here reflected her emotional identification with her parents' pain.

Barbara herself was a shy and quiet woman in her fifties. She lived in a book-filled apartment and was married with a college-aged daughter. Her usually quiet style contrasted with the flashes of emotion that punctuated her interview when she felt strongly.

As mentioned, both her parents came from small *shtetlech* in areas that changed hands between Russia and Poland. Her father, Joe, was born in 1907 and her mother, Bella, in 1913. Both arrived in America with their mothers and siblings at age thirteen; their fathers were already in New York. The reader will remember that both parents as children lived in extreme poverty. Speaking about her father, Barbara stated that he had a "sense of escaping tsarist Russia," though the tsar was gone when he emigrated in 1920. Joe and his younger brother narrowly escaped being "kidnapped" into the tsar's army by running to freedom when the soldiers who had seized them momentarily turned away. Barbara's father's family lacked even the money to send him to *cheder* (school for teaching Hebrew), which was very unusual; this was so because during World War I, when communication was cut off, money from relatives in the U.S. could not reach Russia.[5] Because they needed food, Joe and his younger brother stole cherries from the local priest's orchard and climbed trees in a forest to take eggs from birds' nests. Getting caught (Barbara reported that her father was shot at by the priest) was worth it to have this extra food.

As described, Barbara's mother's family grew up with even more poverty and fear than did her father's. In Bella's family, there was "nothing to cook." Because of this, when there *was* food to cook, Bella's mother was unable to cook well. As a child, Bella's job was to draw water from the well, which she did several times a day; during the winter, the ground around the well was icy, making a difficult job dangerous.

In a telling detail about family communication, during Barbara's childhood, her parents, talking about their poverty, would "battle" about the cow owned by her father's family in Eastern Europe. Joe would say, "We had a cow; when it died, we cried and mourned for it like a family member because afterward we had nothing to eat." Bella would fling back: "You at least had a cow." The extreme deprivation of Bella's childhood underlies this anecdote of marital discord.

In her interview, when Barbara and I spoke about her mother's sisters being hidden to protect them from rape during pogroms, Barbara interjected: "That's what she left behind . . . having her sisters hidden in barrels."[6] Barbara reported the following related event, which occurred when she was an adult. Visiting an exhibit of photographs of Jewish Poland with her parents, they entered a room filled with photographs of a pogrom. In some photographs, women with no clothing stared "blankly" in the "aftermaths of terrible rapes." Bella seemed both fascinated and disturbed by this exhibit. When Barbara asked her mother whether she had experience with anything similar, her mother refused to speak about it.[7]

In Eastern Europe, Barbara's father, Joe, had "no sense that life was going to add up to anything." Upon arriving in New York City at age thirteen with his mother and siblings, Joe was reunited with his own father. He was re-

Barbara's mother, Bella; Bella's parents; and her siblings in 1925. The picture is a composite—Bella's father, top center, was then in New York, while the others were in Eastern Europe. Top right, Bella's sister, who never emigrated, was killed in the Holocaust. *Courtesy of anonymous interviewee Barbara.*

quired to attend school but was ashamed at being put in a class with second-grade "babies." Although he hoped to become a druggist, this required additional schooling, and he fell asleep in night school after working during the daytime. He became apprenticed to a butcher and was eventually able to successfully support his family with his butchering business, even taking his own father into the business.

Barbara reported that each of her parents, upon their arrival in the U.S., perceived America—with its riches to which they were unaccustomed—as a paradise. They believed that if they worked hard, they would do well. Soon after Joe arrived, he had to learn to ride a bicycle to work as a telegraph delivery boy, and Barbara reported that riding the bike was fun for him. Her mother as a teenager was tall, thin, and admired for her beauty; according to Barbara, she had the freedom to have fun here that she would not have had in Russia. Sadly, Bella was extremely disappointed when she, along with her mother and sisters, was reunited with her father upon arrival in New York City. Bella had no actual memories of her father, who had left Eastern Europe when she was very young; she did, however, have romantic dreams of what he would be like. The man she met at Ellis Island, unfortunately, was a "short, funny-looking man." A second disappointment was that Barbara's grandmother did not enjoy being reunited with her husband after so many years; the two had no relationship, and the marriage remained an unhappy one.

Negative feelings and discord characterized the family's life in the U.S. While Bella completed one year of school in the U.S., graduating from the eighth grade, her two older sisters were sent immediately to work in factories, and they resented that their father had lied about their ages so they could work. They felt that their father was cheap and bad-tempered. In this unhappy family, they also resented and were jealous of their pretty younger sister, Barbara's mother.

According to Barbara, her parents' marriage did not begin well. Her mother was only eighteen when they married, and while her father actively chose her mother, her mother merely settled for her father. She had been urged by others to marry this successful butcher, who by then already owned a car. Bella disdained even the way her husband proposed marriage: he placed the engagement ring inside a piece of stuffed cabbage she was eating for dinner. Bella had wanted to become an actress and dancer. Instead she became pregnant quickly and gave birth to a sickly infant. Because she was angry at her husband for having burdened her with a sick baby, she cut off her hair, which her husband liked. Bella felt cheated by becoming a mother at such a young age; throughout her life, she continued to resent that she had lacked the opportunity to, in Barbara's words, "grow up and find herself."

Bella probably was never adequately nurtured herself. Her own mother—struggling to eke out a living for her children and coping with pogroms and fear—would have had little energy for her, particularly as she was at the younger end of several children. Thus Bella had no model for how to nurture her own children and instead mightily resented giving up her own life to care for babies.

Barbara was her parents' fourth child and second daughter; she was born when her mother was thirty-nine and her father forty-six. Barbara felt that it was difficult to grow up with older, immigrant parents. They were mistaken for grandparents, and, furthermore, she was ashamed of their accents and lack of education. Most difficult, however, was that Barbara felt stigmatized and disadvantaged in school because her parents "didn't seem to know things that other parents knew." Indeed, she was laughed at because, for example, her knee socks always fell down. Their elastic had worn out; the other parents, she said, knew "the trick" of holding up socks with rubber bands. In school she was "reprimanded" because papers fell out of her loose-leaf notebook; her parents failed to buy her reinforcements for loose-leaf papers so that this wouldn't happen. Moreover, Barbara's parents never purchased Scotch tape or a ruler for her. She needed Scotch tape in order to properly paste current events articles into a scrapbook, and so she instead used Band-Aids.

Barbara stated that her care was handed over to her sister, Ellen, who was thirteen years older; she was Ellen's "toy," and when Ellen left home to get married, Barbara felt abandoned. No one explained to Barbara, then eight years old, why her sister had left or that she was not planning to return. When Barbara complained to her mother that she was bored, Bella (perhaps angrily) responded, "Go bang your head against the wall." Barbara reported that her early childhood, before her sister and brother left, was noisy, full of yelling and laughing; she was mercilessly teased by her brother Allen. She stated that she was often locked out of her sister's room, her brother's room, and, on Sundays, her parents' room. This may have led to feelings of shame at her neediness and lack of importance to family members; perhaps it added to her painful shame about being laughed at in school.

A year after Barbara's sister married and subsequently moved to California, one brother enlisted in the navy and a second brother joined her sister on the West Coast. Bella felt abandoned and ashamed—what terrible thing had she done to cause her children to leave her? She became so depressed that she cried constantly, talked about dying, and went to bed. Bella consulted a psychiatrist for a time but found therapy to be "nonsense." Bella never fully recovered from the episode, and she subsequently took amphetamines in order to lose weight. When Barbara was in junior high school, her mother experienced mood swings and yelled for no reason.

Barbara's parents' dysfunction exhibited itself in a number of ways. Most importantly, according to Barbara, they fought about literally everything. Her father, Joe, became aware only in old age that "people don't like it when you yell at them." Joe treated Bella, who was seven years younger, as his child; he made the rules. In fact, Bella acted childishly and temperamentally. She had to wheedle money out of her husband for extra expenses or luxuries. Barbara's depressed mother retained until the end of her life the feeling that she had wasted her life, that she had been cheated of the opportunity to make something of herself. Barbara's father seems to have been significantly better functioning psychologically than Bella, and at the end of his life, Joe was content and perhaps even proud of his achievements as a successful butcher. Yet, at the same time, Joe carried feelings of sadness at his lack of education and status; he seemed to feel some sense of shame as he compared his achievements to those of David Sarnoff, the president of RCA (the Radio Corporation of America), who had immigrated from the same shtetl.

Bella responded to her childhood hunger by "swallowing food before she chewed it." Perhaps histrionic, Bella, according to Barbara, was passionate, romantic, and dramatic, a good storyteller who exaggerated for effect. She was easily angered but would be fine soon after an angry outburst. In contrast, Joe was quiet. He worked hard and came home late—cold, tired, and in a bad mood. While he did not anger easily, he often held a grudge and sometimes stopped talking for several days. When Barbara was a young child, she often felt that he was like a stranger.

Barbara's development was profoundly influenced not only by her shame in school and her shame about her immigrant parents with their accents, but also by her parents' fighting. When, during elementary school, her father tried to teach her some Yiddish words, her mother furiously yelled, "You want her to be a greenhorn?" Joe wanted to send her to a yeshiva (traditional Jewish school), but Bella said no; "she wanted me to be an American girl," explained Barbara. While her family thought that she would go to college, unlike most adolescents of her generation, she was not pushed to do so.[8] Perhaps the most important fact about Barbara's adolescence was that she became very ill for a semester beginning when she was sixteen; she suffered from mononucleosis, hepatitis, and gallstones.[9] She was hospitalized in excruciating pain and felt sad and frightened, as she never knew when the illness would recur. Barbara did not fully recover for ten years, echoing her mother's lack of full recovery from her depression some years earlier. Interestingly, her mother quit a part-time job to care for Barbara during her illness, and Barbara stated that she was "grieved" that her deprived mother had to give something up for her. Thus Barbara felt connected to her mother's deprivation. My hypothesis is that Barbara's long illness represented the "ghost" or reenactment of her mother's depression. When Barbara should have been blossoming into adolescence and young adulthood, her body held her back, and she was deprived of this period of her life, just as her mother had been deprived of so many opportunities.

The trauma Barbara's parents suffered was conveyed in words. However, the magnitude of, for example, their near-starvation as children or her grandmother being cruelly attacked by gentile boys with bees meant that the horror of these situations was unsayable; it was beyond words. Barbara keenly felt these traumatic aspects of her parents' young lives and her unconscious response was, I believe, to attempt to care for them and to cure them. Her connection to and identification with their suffering was in service to her wish to care for them. That she "egged them on" to tell her stories about their pasts demonstrates the "hunger for pain" characteristic of children of trauma survivors (Pisano, 2012, p. 184).

One complicating factor in the psychological makeup of Barbara's family was Bella's severe depressive illness. Her depression during Barbara's childhood was preceded by her angry response to her sickly first child's birth. Cutting off her own hair to punish both her husband and herself seemed to have been a self-destructive and disturbed reaction. Bella seemed to have been particularly vulnerable to the effects of her childhood trauma, and her mental health may have been worse because of it.

By her own account, Barbara was the neglected and unloved child of a depressed and depleted mother and an angry, tired father. She stated that her parents had had no "emotional energy" for her during her childhood, and this is certainly substantiated by their failure to purchase basic school supplies for her. Barbara was also deeply affected by her parents' trauma. Indeed, I could feel almost palpable reverberations of this trauma during her interview. Not only had she deeply felt the pain of her parents' childhood deprivation and fear, as well as their adult frustration, but her parents' uncontrolled and chaotic communication during her childhood flooded her with feelings that she was unable to process. She continued to endure their pain when—perhaps in an effort to "heal" them—she elicited their harrowing stories. By doing so, she kept alive inside herself these pieces of her parents' pasts. Indeed, Barbara's parents had taken "up residence" in her psyche, where they continued to cast a shadow (Fraiberg et al., 1975, p. 165; as cited in Pisano, 2012, p. 25).

David

"I grew up in the shadow of the shtetl," David told me. His mother, Pearl, talked "all the time" about her experiences prior to emigration. David was born a full seventeen years after his mother's arrival in the U.S. in 1921, and the darkness of the shtetl's shadow for both him and his mother becomes evident when we realize that, so many years after Pearl's arrival, she transmitted her traumatic feelings to him.

David himself was a small, courteous, dapper, and sprightly man in his seventies; an intelligent and cultured man, he had retired from a successful career in the public sector. Despite being deeply affected by his mother's pain, he had a tremendous "joie de vivre" and seemed to be optimistic. He spoke a great deal, with great precision and knowledge, seeming to want to preserve all his memories. While he had a calm demeanor, his very detailed presentation seemed to reflect a deeper anxiety.

David seemed both pained by the terrible knowledge of Pearl's childhood experiences and personally connected to her suffering. He represented Pearl's childhood experience in these words: "the pain, no money, constant fear, starvation, disease." Pearl began her life in 1908 in a tiny *dorf* (village), where her family of nine lived in poverty in a two-room house with dirt floors. Her father was a blacksmith. By 1913, no longer able to make a living, he immigrated to America, where he believed that he could get a good job; his intention was to return to Eastern Europe in the future. Pearl's family was stranded in Eastern Europe without her father throughout World War I and its aftermath.

When she was a young child, Pearl was injured in a fire, which scarred her ankle. She later contracted typhoid fever. To get more food, Pearl stole potatoes from a gentile's yard. Her mother's arrest, however, was perhaps the most frightening event in Pearl's childhood of privation and calamity. This occurred when the Russian army tried to conscript her fourteen-year-old brother. Determined to avert this, Pearl's mother "picked up the kids" and left; the family then hid under a piece of canvas. Soldiers discovered them and threatened to arrest Pearl's mother if she did not allow her son's conscription. In fact, Pearl's mother was arrested and jailed when she stood her ground. Pearl remembered bringing her mother potatoes in jail. Having her mother in jail was "horrifying," said David. We can also imagine the entire family's terror at being discovered and threatened by the Russian soldiers. A final note on Pearl's traumatic childhood experiences is that, when the family emigrated and arrived at Ellis Island, a doctor stated that the children were bloated from malnutrition.

Pearl was able to immigrate with her mother and siblings to the U.S. in 1921; she was then thirteen. Her father, already in New York, sent for his family after he realized there was no future for the Jews in Eastern Europe. At that time, Pearl didn't want to leave what she knew as home. She was the only one of her siblings who wanted to remain in the Old Country. In New York, Pearl sometimes wept that she wanted to go home, although she *did* realize later this had been a "foolish" attitude. Throughout her life, while Pearl never wanted to return to visit because of her painful memories, she also remained nostalgic; she had "strong, evocative childhood memories" of home, which David said were "sweet." Her feelings of missing home were mixed with bitterness about what had happened to her.

David told me, "I know too much." Indeed, he was subjected to hearing his mother Pearl talk "all the time" about the past. Moreover, he learned much of what he knew by listening to his mother and his father's mother conversing. From his account, Pearl did not treat David directly as a confidante, yet he was not protected against information that could be overwhelming to a child. Indeed, as a ten-year-old child after the Holocaust, he heard more than he could bear. When a young woman who had survived the Holocaust came to visit, David was doing his homework as the young woman explained that the reason that she had survived was because she was a sex object; she had been repeatedly raped. Furthermore, she stated that, after the war, in order to avenge her parents' deaths, she told the Russians who exactly had shot them. David told me that he had felt burdened by this knowledge; he believed that his mother inappropriately allowed him to remain in the room to hear about this. One effect of his mother's traumatic past was that it left her at times unable to be attuned enough to her son's needs to ensure that he would be protected against information he was too young to bear.

David's father, Philip—who arrived in New York at age fifteen with his mother and siblings—had very different pre-emigration experiences than did Pearl. Although poor, Philip had not been as poor as Pearl, and his childhood was not unhappy. A calm person, Philip spoke infrequently about his life in Eastern Europe but would answer questions when asked. Because David described his father as calm, I asked him whether his father had given him the sense that life would turn out "OK." David's reply to me was yes. Elaborating, he said that his father's favorite expression was "The sky isn't falling" (in Yiddish: *Himmel falt nischt*). No matter how terrible things were, Philip would say in English, "It will work out."

Philip's mother, considered an old maid in Eastern Europe at age twenty, was trained to become a chef so she would be able to support herself. A competent woman, she was proud of her profession. After working as a chef, she was married off to an older widower with four children, and she then cared for his children. The couple had three children together, including Philip. In 1911 or 1912, Philip's father, David's grandfather, immigrated to America, taking with him his oldest two children. As a child Philip liked socializing on the street in their Russian shtetl, hanging out with the fire brigade. He remembered the White and Red Armies coming and going through the town during the Russian Revolution. As he told it, although their arrival was frightening, everything was fine after they left. Philip did not remember significant anti-Semitism. Philip's capable mother supported the family as a chef, and she created a calm household after her husband departed for America.[10] When, in 1921, David's grandfather sent for his family, fifteen-year-old Philip eagerly looked forward to emigrating. In New York, Philip was happy both to be reunited with his father and to take advantage of American opportunities. David explained later that his father did not speak much about the past but not because he was unable to think about it. When asked, Philip's attitude was "matter of fact"; he would say, "This is what it was."

David's parents were married in 1928, and they had two daughters, nine and five years older than David, in the early 1930s. Philip worked in a series of small businesses, ending up in the family seltzer delivery business. The Depression, however, changed everything for Pearl and Philip: it "destroyed" their "optimism," said David. Philip was not able to "provide for his family" and felt "emasculated." And for Pearl, the Depression was another trauma from which she "never recovered." She became extremely frugal, and David felt that his mother's financial anxiety was "terrifically sad." Unlike Pearl, however, Philip "took tremendous satisfaction" in the fact that the family's finances eventually stabilized.

David was born in 1938, near the Depression's end. As a child he felt "secure, comfortable, and safe." David's sisters were both protective of him, and one of his early memories was of his father driving up to their home with a tricycle for him. When David was eighteen, his father became ill and unable to work. David feared then that he might be called on to support the family and be unable to attend college, but instead his mother returned to work. Philip lived until David was thirty-one. Two or three years afterward, his oldest sister died of cancer. Both his father's debilitating illness and his sister's tragic early death affected David deeply.

The influence on David of his mother's traumatic past was, I think, somewhat tempered by his father's attitude of calm acceptance: the sky isn't falling. David's father had matter-of-factly left the past "somehow in the past." David was aware that he himself was perhaps overly attached both to his mother's traumatic past and to other painful aspects of family history. Yet what made him resilient was, in part, his ability to be aware of his own over-concern. Twelve years before David's birth, his father's father had died an "awful death" from colon cancer. Reflecting on this during the interview, David asked, "Why am I burdened by how my grandfather died?" He was haunted by this piece of the past. Yet the fact that he was able to ask this suggests that David was grappling with understanding his obsession with the past. After asking this during the interview, David then said that he did not know "why he was attracted" to researching his Jewish past. My hypothesis about David is that his dogged concentration on his past was a way of working through the trauma that had been passed on to him, of lessening for himself the darkness of the shtetl's shadow.

Although David was indeed connected to his mother's pain, he was aware that he was overly preoccupied with it. Unlike Barbara, however, he had not been flooded by his mother's trauma; he was in many ways able to process the trauma that had been passed on to him. In contrast to Barbara's chaotic home—in which she was locked out and neglected and in which communication consisted of angry yelling—David described a safe and loving home.

His parents, who had a good relationship, generally spoke rather than yelled. I hypothesized that David's mother received a feeling of security from her own family, which enabled her both to be more resilient than Barbara's mother and to be, with some exceptions, a responsive mother to David.

David remained deeply pained by the trauma of his mother's past. Nevertheless, he and I agreed that he was a "very self-actualized person." In his forties—while continuing his career in the public sector—David both enrolled in a doctoral program in Jewish studies and participated in a research program at a secular Jewish educational institution. Because of unexpected career opportunities, David did not complete his doctorate; nevertheless, his studies enriched his life. At the time of his interview, he had been creatively retired for several years. David was very involved in various pursuits, lecturing on Jewish themes and running a small and active cultural business. While deeply feeling his family's painful past, David at the same time seemed determined to enjoy the present.

Stanley's mother was silent about the World War I trauma to which she was subjected, and its effects were transmitted wordlessly to Stanley. Overall, however, she was able to create a stable and comfortable life during Stanley's childhood; I believe she was able to remain emotionally alive in important ways (Salberg, 2017a). Stanley's career was very successful, although he had many anxieties as an adult.

Stanley

Stanley was an intelligent and intellectual but slightly odd person. He spoke in a sort of British-accented, affected manner, yet at the same time he was also warm and welcoming. He was in his eighties and had a loving, attentive wife and two children. A professional who had earned a very good living, he lived in a beautiful apartment and still worked part time in his office, despite having had serious health problems about ten years previously.

Stanley's mother, Liba, had been traumatized during World War I and spoke little about her life in Eastern Europe in general or about the specific traumatic events she had endured. An otherwise extremely competent woman, she had a serious episode of hysteria when Stanley was eighteen years old; as an adult Stanley had pockets of anxiety, as well as periods of depression, that seemed to affect his functioning in significant but circumscribed ways. Stanley's mother, I believe, communicated her anxiety to Stanley both implicitly and explicitly.

Liba was born into a family of upper-middle-class merchants in a Russian shtetl in 1893. In contrast, Stanley's father, Chaim, a few years older than his wife, was a penniless scholar from a small nearby city; descended from a long line of rabbis, he himself was the son of a rabbi who had died at a young age. As a young man, Stanley's father traveled to Germany, where he became educated as a medicinal chemist. Chaim was the first in his family to break away from the traditional Eastern European Orthodox existence. After Stanley's parents were introduced by a matchmaker and married in 1910, Liba gave birth to a daughter. Three years later, Chaim migrated to England, where he did well financially as a medicinal chemist.

Because Stanley's father was then working in England, his parents were separated when World War I began. The war brought Austrian troops to their shtetl, and Liba, her young daughter, and her own parents fled eastward further into Russia. As they did so, they could "feel the bullets whiz by," said Stanley. After the war, Liba, her parents, and her daughter, then nine, immigrated to New York, and sometime after their arrival in 1920, Stanley's father joined them. The experience of war never left Liba or her daughter Esther. That this family had money, both in Europe and in America, did not spare them the trauma of war.

Chaim's business gave the family a very comfortable life in New York City. Stanley's clothes came from the best stores, and the family had a maid; they had books in Hebrew and Yiddish, friends and family, and maintained an Orthodox though not fanatical way of life. When he was a child, their home, according to Stanley, was a "geographical transplant" of Eastern Europe, and in some ways his parents were psychologically still in the Old Country. Stanley described his mother as "very competent." Though she was never comfortable speaking English, Liba made all the family investment decisions. Stanley as a child felt secure, comfortable, and privileged in every way.

Although this wealthy Orthodox family had a maid during his childhood, Stanley told me that—because his mother was particular about preparing for *Shabbos* (the Sabbath)—she wouldn't allow the gentile maid to scrub the floor. He said, "She scrubbed on her hands and knees the floor." In saying this, Stanley's impeccable English used Yiddish syntax, a verbal remnant of the past suddenly inserting itself into our interview.

Paradoxically, Stanley's parents in New York "kept the Yiddish way of life almost forever," while talking very little about their lives in Eastern Europe. Their attitude about their former lives in Eastern Europe seemed to have been: "That was Europe. It was in the past. It was gone." Stanley knew that pogroms had occurred in his parents' area but also that neither had direct experience of them; his parents did not talk much about this. Stanley believed his mother did not miss her shtetl and, for Liba, coming to the U.S. was a fresh beginning. My thought is that, because of World War I, Liba experienced a rent in her middle-class existence; consequently, she never wanted to look back. On the other hand, Stanley had some inkling that Chaim missed friends, family, and the culture of Eastern Europe.

Several traumatic situations affected Stanley's family. About six years before Stanley was born, his mother gave birth to a baby boy who had a heart condition and did not survive. Stanley said this "left its mark on my mother and me." Because of that, "I was her golden child." Two years later, another sister, Helen, was born. The family's traumatic war experiences continued to affect Stanley's older sister, Esther. Always "profoundly anxious," according to Stanley, she never seemed to recover. Over the course of the interview, Stanley repeatedly referred to Esther's anxiety.

During his childhood, Stanley was not only secure and privileged; he was also watched over and protected. His mother was very anxious about her children's well-being and particularly about that of her only surviving son. Stanley believed that Liba would have thought: "This is my little boy, and I need to keep him intact." His use of the word "intact" implies that in his imagination, his mother feared that he could physically break apart. Stanley was not allowed to go swimming or skiing, to play baseball or touch football, or to go away on trips. Unfortunately, when Stanley was ten years old, he developed a high fever, and Esther's husband, a doctor, diagnosed scarlet fever. Liba, panicked, exclaimed in Yiddish: "Get a doctor in here." In her terror, she did not realize that a doctor was already in the room. Stanley remembered Liba pinching her face in anxiety during his illness.

Liba suffered a short breakdown when Stanley was eighteen. She began screaming in hysteria and went to bed; her screaming lasted for several hours, during which Chaim sat with her. "Something overwhelmed her," explained Stanley. He continued, "Something was eating at her that she usually coped with." Stanley mentioned that his sister Helen often overwhelmed their mother; she was "willful" and "rebellious," an apostate in this Orthodox family. It is probable that it was not only Liba's trouble with Stanley's sister but also Liba's memories of her own terribly traumatic experiences during the war that came back to so destabilize her.

Stanley felt that, despite her "profound" anxiety, Liba was overall a strong woman. On the whole, she was stable, friendly, and a person to whom relatives and friends looked for advice. She had "common sense" and great self-confidence, and "she knew what she was about." In fact, said Stanley, she was president of her *landsmanshaft*.[11] As mentioned, she was the parent who made all the family's sound investment decisions, and she "called the shots" in most areas of the family's life.

A terrible part of Stanley's life was his father's early death. Chaim had an ulcer, and by age fifty, he also developed high blood pressure. About nine years later, when Stanley was twenty or twenty-one, his father died of a stroke. Stanley said that in his father's hospital room at the moment of his death, he reacted by falling to the ground. Chaim's death was a "dirty trick," said Stanley, and he repeated twice during the interview that he felt deprived of a mature relationship with his father. From his description, it seems possible that Stanley suffered a depression of significant duration after his father's death; he continued to feel vulnerable when he began his professional education about a year later. Stanley's sorrow about the loss of his father encouraged him years later to try to talk frequently with his own son. Stanley said, however, that Chaim never would have communicated with him a great deal had he survived since Stanley was becoming an American and his father held onto his old-world identity.

This family suffered from both family and historical trauma; surely the two interacted and their impacts were passed on intergenerationally. We can imagine that as a sick ten-year-old, Stanley saw and internalized the look of terror in his mother's eyes that would have accompanied her pinching her face. Thus her trauma was communicated implicitly. While we assume that in the 1930s most mothers would likely have been anxious to hear that their child had scarlet fever, this mother might have felt haunted; the memories of losing an infant son and being shot at during World War I—when her first child, her parents, or she herself might have died—were traumatic pieces of her past.

Stanley, like his mother, reported intense anxiety about the well-being of his own children; he feared that each could get hit by a car or become ill, and he also worried about his wife. He always needed to know when his wife was due home, and he feared that she could be injured when driving (in reality, he said, she did drive too fast). He added, "I circumscribe my own activity" because of anxiety.

Stanley had a fruitful and lucrative career despite being the recipient of intergenerational trauma. Neither of his sisters, however, did well in life. His older sister, Esther, had not only experienced the terror of war, but she also encountered personal tragedy. Strikingly beautiful and also amusing, she was only able to stay at college for one year. After marrying a doctor and suffering a series of miscarriages, she lost a child at birth. Subsequently, said Stanley, she was never again "quite right psychologically." She did, he said, continue to very much adore him. In the 1980s, at about age seventy, Esther died of stomach cancer that Stanley believed was not properly treated.

Stanley's sister Helen, born safely in America, was rebellious and perhaps also manipulative. She left college because she was in love with a boy who was much less intelligent than she; their father cried at Helen's "shotgun wedding." Because Helen's husband could not make an adequate living, she played the piano in nightclubs, which one imagines would have shocked this respectable Orthodox family. That Helen was not able to live a balanced life suggests that she too, like both Esther and Stanley, had unconsciously absorbed her mother's trauma.

Stanley was well aware of his mother's anxieties about her children; indeed, she did not permit him to play as other children did. Liba, however, communicated her trauma about the terrors of World War I implicitly; she did not speak much about her experiences. Stanley hypothesized that Liba did not want to burden her children and therefore refrained from talking about her fears. The panic engendered by being shot at, especially while caring for a young daughter, must have been impossible to capture in words; because it could not be fully symbolized, Liba's terror was transmitted wordlessly. Liba, I believe, had areas of dissociation associated with the unprocessed aspects of her war trauma. This would have at times made it difficult for her to empathetically attune to her children, and on occasion each of them must have experienced their mother's overwhelming anxiety (Halasz, 2012; Pisano, 2012). That Liba's two daughters were emotionally compromised suggests the truth of this hypothesis. Stanley, however, as the adored son, probably experienced his controlling and overprotective though loving mother as more responsive and less intrusive than did his sisters; sons are, in general, allowed by their mothers to be more separate than daughters (Chodorow, 1978).

Liba suffered from a combination of family, or individual, trauma and the historical trauma of violence. Stanley's anxieties about both his family and his own safety repeat his mother's; his periods of depression may be related to the early death of his father. Yet Stanley's mother was in many ways stable, and his father—because he had been in England—had not been directly impacted by World War I. Moreover, as a child Stanley knew that he was loved and protected. Consequently, Stanley had many areas of healthy functioning. Although in adulthood he had symptoms that I believe resulted from his mother's transmitted trauma, the stability of his early life enabled him to be successful and fulfilled.

Aaron's and Ruth's mothers were both badly traumatized in Eastern Europe. Absence or deadness seemed to characterize attachment relationships between the mothers of both and their children. Aaron's mother was unable to be empathic with him, yet in his eighties, Aaron remained preoccupied with her. Ruth's cut-off quality suggested silence, and during her interview, she enacted a repetitive piece of her mother's past, her childhood experience of pogroms.

Aaron

Aaron was a retired successful ophthalmologist in his eighties who was still involved in his profession. Married with two children and a loving wife, he lived in an attractive house decorated with art and family photos. Although he was flattering and courtly with me, he was at the same time somewhat formidable. He seemed not entirely at ease either with himself or with me, and he suggested that, although people think of him as "nice," part of him was not nice, as he was "too self-concerned." He talked in so much detail with me that he appeared to need my attention. Over the course of three interviews, he talked and talked and then, guarding his time carefully, ended each one promptly at the scheduled moment.

Aaron stated, "My mother has never died for me"; not a day in his life passed during which his thoughts were not occupied by his mother, Estelle, who had died thirty years prior to our interview. Aaron felt that his focus on his mother amounted to an obsession. The intensity of his thoughts about Estelle suggested to me the possibility of the intergenerational transmission of trauma. Estelle's father had been killed in a pogrom in their Eastern European town. After the pogrom, Estelle, then a teenager, found her father's dead body in the basement, where Jews had been hiding. [12] Despite her devastation, Estelle took charge of her family's affairs after her father's murder, as her own mother was ineffectual.

In some cases, the children of traumatized parents unconsciously attempt to cure the parent's trauma, and it seems possible that Aaron's disengaged mother had "taken up residence" in his psyche; perhaps Aaron needed to devote his life to working out the trauma that she had suffered (Fraiberg et al., 1975, p. 165; as cited in Pisano, 2012, p. 25). Kaplan (1995, p. 224) explains this psychological phenomenon as originating in the child's need to be "close to the parent," "to be at one with the parent," and in the mother's empathic failures. When a traumatized mother repeatedly exposes her child to "experiences that are . . . beyond his emotional capacities," he realizes that he must both "protect himself" and protect and "care for" his mother (p. 225): "He must become his parent's bridge to life." It is this dynamic that may explain Aaron's obsession with his mother; it is similar to Barbara's unconscious effort to heal her parents by enduring their pain.

Supporting the hypothesis of the intergenerational transmission of trauma was Estelle's silence about the past. She never talked about her life in Eastern Europe—she was "very here and now"—and neither did she speak about the murder of her father. Aaron stated that he did not know how he found out about this traumatic event—"he just knew." From Aaron's description of his mother's relationship to her life in the Old Country, it seems possible that she dissociated her memories of it. Not only did Estelle never talk about the Old Country, but Aaron said, "I know nothing about her feelings" about it, as there was "no evidence," no "reference to" his mother's feelings about the Old Country.

Estelle's silence suggests that she communicated the trauma that she experienced wordlessly. During Aaron's infancy, it is likely that, because of her trauma, she experienced moments of dissociation, which Aaron registered. Aaron in turn intuited that something was psychically wrong, and he experienced his mother's dissociations as gaps or absences.

Aaron himself over time surely consciously registered the enormity of how his grandfather died. He made the unusual statement: "The terror was from pogroms, not the Holocaust," adding that the Holocaust was actually the *end* of the process of "slaughtering" the Jews (his emphasis). [13]

Aaron's parents had interesting pasts. His mother's educated family had a comfortable upper-middle-class life in their large Eastern European town. Her father, somewhat assimilated, headed a well-regarded bookkeeping school that was attended by both Jews and gentiles. The gentiles who completed this school's program were able to be admitted to the University of Kiev. Estelle completed high school, which meant she was well-educated. In contrast, Aaron's father, Max, was a poor orphan who as a young child was placed with the family of a Communist tailor. Aaron reported that his father was made a Communist Party member at age seven; at that time he began conducting errands for the party. When the Revolution occurred, Max became a soldier in the Red Army, rising to be a lieutenant and political commissar. Thus this poor orphan became an important man, accorded high status in their town; after World War I he was made the head of a leather factory.

The war brought privation for Aaron's mother and the residents of her city. To save herself and her family, she married Max, then a high-ranking but uneducated Communist soldier; Estelle's family's status was much higher than her husband's. Their marriage was one of expedience, a "business arrangement," according to Aaron. Because Aaron's father procured salt to be used at their wedding celebration, he was accused by the Communists of "economic crimes" and court-martialed. To escape punishment, Max fled Russia with Estelle; accompanied by her sisters and her mother, they immigrated to a large middle-American city where some of her siblings already lived.

Max's experiences as an important party member and a lieutenant constituted the apogee of his life. In the U.S., he was only a poor laundry owner; later he owned a dry-cleaning store. As he felt "diminished" in the U.S., for the remainder of his life, Aaron's father talked extensively and obsessively about the Old Country. Although Max never stated this outright, Aaron believed that he missed the Old Country. Aaron described his father's personality as "distant," "self-centered," and "not interpersonally sensitive." He also worked all the time.

Aaron's first response when I inquired about his earliest memories of childhood was of getting lost during a trip to the beach with his mother; he was then less than five years old, and Aaron was "scared to death." Describing this as a "*real* experience" (his emphasis), he said that to this day he was still afraid of getting lost: "I have to know where I'm going." He felt that this experience had contributed to his anxiety about "not doing the right thing and screwing up." Adding that his mother was "*not* overprotective" (his emphasis)—and that "she was burdened with other things"—Aaron reported a second instance of his mother's failure to protect him. He ran across the street and was hit by a motorcycle, suffering a broken clavicle. "She shouldn't have let me get out," he said.

Writing about the intergenerational transmission of trauma in families of Holocaust survivors, Louise Kaplan (1995, p. 226) says, "Because of his [the parent's] own terrors of being found and caught," "when the little child experiments with running away from the parent, the parent may be oblivious to the child's wish to be found and caught." Thus the "parent looks away from the child's playful drama and lets him get lost." It seems possible that Estelle, having herself survived pogroms and massive unrest in Russia during her adolescence, unconsciously enacted with her son a piece of her own past traumas. Moreover, it is possible that—because the day-to-day financial survival of Aaron's family during the Depression was a constant stressor—Aaron's burdened mother could not properly attend to her son's safety.

Failures of parental ability to be empathically attuned to their children are important in the experiences of traumatized parents and their children. A mother who is unconsciously preoccupied with her own trauma will be disengaged and misattuned (Halasz, 2012; Kaplan, 1995; Pisano, 2012; van der Kolk, 2014). Estelle—who had to cope not only with her father's murder and her shock at having discovered his body, but also with the strain of guiding her family through the remaining years of the war—would have had many reasons for being disengaged and misattuned. An understandably disengaged mother can easily lose her child or allow his exposure to danger. The relational impairment that can result from exposure to trauma is illustrated in Estelle's failure of empathy.

Aaron's parents arrived in the U.S. in 1922. For many years afterward, supporting the family "totally preoccupied" his parents, although his father continued to be interested in Communism and world politics. "Just getting through life" was a struggle, "making things work," and there were constant strains around money. For his parents, "no category called fulfilling yourself" existed, explained Aaron. His parents not only wanted Aaron and his older brother to be educated and successful, but to be the best, to be first.

Fighting was Aaron's poorly matched parents' usual mode of communication, and they fought "all the time" and about everything; if his father "said it was Tuesday, his mother knew it wasn't." I can imagine that, given the massive trauma that Estelle had endured, her emotions were dysregulated and uncontrolled, and this could have been one reason for the constant conflict. Furthermore, Estelle was critical by nature, and she looked down on her husband because she felt he did not earn enough money.

Estelle was "strikingly good-looking, well-dressed," and "charismatic"; "Everyone looked at her," said Aaron. He also admitted that she was "not self-aware." Paradoxically, Aaron stated that his mother—who to me seemed misattuned to his needs—was "so focused" on him and his older brother. Aaron explained that his mother ensured that her sons were both well-dressed and excellently educated. Aaron resented that he was treated as the "non-preferred son." Although both sons worked in the same high-status profession, his mother introduced them to others as "my [older] son the doctor, and this is Aaron, my son the truck driver"; Estelle repeatedly belittled Aaron. He felt hurt and disappointed by his mother's poor treatment of him; it was obvious to everyone that his mother favored his brother, Aaron said.

Davoine and Gaudillière (2004), in their ground-breaking book about the intergenerational transmission of trauma, wrote that because survivors of trauma are unable to feel, they can make "horrific decisions" about their own children; for example, they may expose them to danger. This inability to feel tends to be disguised as "hypernormality," and, accordingly, "indifference passes for wisdom" and "insensitivity to those close to them" passes for "devotion to distant causes." (That Aaron's mother was the family member who took charge suggests that she was seen as wise.) It is possible that Estelle's insensitivity to his feelings was associated with a necessary inability to feel, which had its roots in her traumatic experiences in Eastern Europe.

Aaron suffered psychologically in a number of ways. As a child, he felt truly lonely and alone, and he never felt comfortable forming friendships. I imagine that emptiness marked his childhood years, given that his mother was preoccupied and psychologically neglectful, his father was distant, and the two were constant fighting. Currently, Aaron has a tendency toward depression and negativity; I don't have a "sunny disposition," he remarked.

Aaron did not like some aspects of his personality, including the fact that he wanted to have all the attention for himself. He described himself as "piggish" and "too aggressive," explaining, "I raise my voice too quickly." His obsessional, overly detailed speaking style with me suggested both a need for control and an avoidance of painful feelings. Throughout his adult life, Aaron felt left out, that he "didn't belong," and that he was an outsider and peripheral. He experienced this both in the gentile world and to some degree also with other Jews. Aaron described feeling that "I'm not part of *them*" (his emphasis). These experiences were associated with growing up feeling that he did not belong in the gentile world. But they also derived from being the son who didn't belong in his own family; not only was he the "second son," but he also felt alone within his nuclear family. His parents demanded that his educational and career performance be the best, and he consequently feared "screwing up." He seemed to have suffered significantly from his fear of "not doing the right thing." By confiding in me that "my bluster is external," Aaron indicated that his persona belied his inner anxiety.

Aaron's discomfort with himself and others suggested that he was insecurely attached. Yet he was strikingly obsessed with the unempathic mother with whom his insecure attachment originated. His obsession with his mother was captured in these words: "She was my mother. I want her to be happy." Even thirty years after her death, his mother occupied such a huge space in his psyche that he referred to her in the present tense. I believe that Aaron's focus on his mother had to do with his need to cure the trauma that his mother had unconsciously transmitted to him. Interestingly, Aaron's obsession with his mother was not only an emotional problem, but also functioned as a spur to his noteworthy professional accomplishments. As he explained to me, he now thinks, "Look what I did, Ma!"

In Aaron's family, trauma was communicated in part through the dysregulated affect of his parents' continual fighting. His mother's failure of empathy, a consequence of her trauma, stands out in Aaron's story. Yet in what he told me about his life, Aaron revealed no obvious repetitions of trauma. Assuming that he had not omitted a portion of his story (and I have no reason to believe that he hid anything from me), this aspect of psychological health was at least in part due to the considerable self-healing in which he had engaged. My assumption was that indeed Aaron had been able to process some of the trauma transmitted to him. Despite Aaron's discomfort with himself and his feeling of perpetually being on the outside, he stated that he felt "fortunate." Not only did he have a fulfilling career, but his personal life had many positive aspects; he appeared to have a loving wife, and he enjoyed his relationships with his children, who themselves were successful.

Ruth

Ruth's mother, Devorah, came from an impoverished, deprived background that was "very hard" and full of fear. Ruth believed that her mother wanted to "leave it all behind." Ruth herself was an intelligent, musically knowledgeable, beautifully dressed woman in her eighties, who lived in a well-appointed suburban Long Island apartment and had three children. Her husband had been very successful financially, and Ruth had held important volunteer positions. Her warm, expansive stance on the telephone contrasted with what seemed to be a difficulty connecting to me or to her own feelings during the interview. She seemed psychologically opaque and often flat, and her husband noted her characteristic "stiff upper lip" when talking about her family. I believe that Ruth cut off her emotions in the face of the unsayable family traumatic memories evoked by the interview.

Ruth's mother, Devorah, was the third of four children born in the 1890s in a tiny village; the family lived in a house with a dirt floor. Devorah's mother died in childbirth when Devorah was two years old. After her mother's death, her father took the children to live next door to relatives in a nearby city. They were very poor, and Devorah began working at age ten, selling sundries at a little street stand. Because she was motherless, Ruth said Devorah "raised herself." Devorah did not talk a great deal about her life in the Old Country. Devorah, however, "talked enough" about pogroms at the hands of "whimsically ruthless" Russian soldiers. Indeed, during her interview, Ruth acted out for me Devorah's family's procedure for hiding her younger sister during pogroms. Using the doors of her own dining room as an example, Ruth demonstrated how Devorah's family hid her younger sister behind two open doors while soldiers searched inside the house. The horrifying danger of this experience must have been truly traumatic. Strikingly, this terrifying piece of her mother's history was alive in Ruth, and Ruth's animation at that moment in the interview contrasted with her flatness and attempts to defend against negative affect.

Ruth's understanding of the pogroms her mother's family feared was this: "they just happened," but there could be no sense of "why and when" one would occur. "You couldn't say, 'If I behave, they won't come.'" This was "true of all subjected peoples," she continued; the Jews had been "purely victims." Ruth could be emphatic when moved.

Devorah and her family had survived not only pogroms but also war. During World War I, everyone from their city was displaced, and her father, who worked in the lumber business, took the family to live in a lumber camp in the forest. Ruth reported that a family member died on the trip out of the forest after the war. Devorah's future husband, Harry, did forced labor during the war as a woodsman, and he suffered a permanent injury as a result.

Devorah lived a "very deprived" life in Eastern Europe, Ruth felt. "There was nothing about" her mother's life in the "Old Country that would have made her homesick," she declared. "What was there to miss" about this "very hard" and frightening life? "They were slaves and peons," she added, referring to Jewish life in Eastern Europe.

Ruth also described her mother's frustrated wish for an education. Devorah had a "great desire to learn" and consequently begged her father to send her to school. Devorah's older sister, however, said this was not fair, and her sister was sent to school instead. When she did not like school and quit attending, the tuition money was lost, and consequently Devorah's opportunity for an education was gone. Devorah was "mad all her life" about this.

In 1921, Devorah and Harry, by then married, immigrated to New York City with Devorah's father and a baby son. Arriving in the U.S. was frightening. Harry had been so seasick on the voyage that, upon arrival, he failed the requisite medical exam. He was detained at Ellis Island for ten days while authorities decided whether or not he was to be returned to Europe. Her mother "must have been terrified out of her mind during those ten days," said Ruth. Fortunately, Harry recovered and was allowed to stay.

In New York, they joined extended family, and Ruth, their third child, was born in 1926. The family's hardship continued during their early years in the U.S. They lived a "hand to mouth, rough" existence and were aided economically by extended family members. Harry at first worked at a chicken market and then for a series of store owners; when he assisted a butcher, his pay was so low that Ruth's mother had only five cents to use to purchase rolls for her sons' lunches. Eventually, Harry and Devorah ran a series of stores together, first a butcher shop, then a candy store, and for a time a liquor store; the candy store was what lasted. Ruth stated that for her parents the candy store was "slave labor."

Ruth emphasized the fear, difficulty, and poverty of her mother's life as a child and young adult in Eastern Europe. As an adult, Devorah was closed off and very private: she "tended to keep her mouth shut," and although close to family members, she "didn't love a million people." My picture of Devorah was of a woman who had been traumatized by her fear of pogroms and motherless childhood. Devorah was also a "backing off kind of person" and, therefore, although ashamed of her inability to write English properly, was unable to ask others for help with it. Ruth described her mother's general strategy for dealing with life this way: "My mother was a coper." "You dealt with what you were dealt and moved on." Ruth, in fact, repeated this formula about her mother's coping three times; the deprivations of her tough life had taken their toll. Ruth related an anecdote about Devorah that suggested the lasting effect of her early maternal loss: once when elderly, she awoke from anesthesia very agitated and calling for her own dead mother. I hypothesized that Ruth's closed-mouth, motherless mother was insecurely attached, and— though mother and daughter were close—Devorah passed on her insecure attachment to Ruth.

Ruth's own distance and remote presentation with me was reminiscent of how I imagined her mother. Her flatness and cut-off quality suggested silence and absence. Moreover, her enactment of her mother's family's procedure during pogroms represented psychic trauma that had never been absorbed or processed; thus it was an embodied ghost of her mother's past, a transmission of traumatic memory (Coles, 2011; O'Loughlin, 2013).

The hypothesis of Ruth as a recipient of trauma is supported by her use of denial, dissociation, and compartmentalization throughout the interview. For example, in describing her childhood, she said: "It was a difficult life; I didn't give it much thought." She said things like "I can't read [my parents'] minds." Of the difficulty of having parents who were always working, she said, "I tucked it away into whatever little compartment till it needed to be looked at."

Ruth evaded my psychological questions, and indeed I felt frozen out and foolish when asking them. I wondered whether, because Ruth seemed to dissociate her painful inner life, her inability to answer my questions made her feel inadequate, and she then projected that feeling into me. Tellingly, when I asked about her parents' courtship, Ruth responded, "I know nothing about it, and I never asked." Ruth as a child was not touched, hugged, or kissed. And as an adult, rather than depending on others emotionally, her style was to keep her own counsel, to make judgments without consulting others. Rather than "asking," her process was to "hear," "see," "absorb," and then "do."

While Ruth's mother was very private, her father, Harry, who was outgoing, loved discussion. In their store, Harry argued about politics with family and customers alike; his three children enjoyed baiting him in arguments. Ruth's father was, like her mother, frustrated with his relatively poor English; however, as he was more open, he would ask customers in the store for help with tasks such as writing an English letter. Harry was also more expansive than Devorah, and he enjoyed gift giving. Education was important in this family; Ruth's parents read several newspapers daily, the children were given music lessons, and Ruth never doubted that she would attend college.

While Ruth was growing up, her family spent its entire life in the store. Her mother opened the store at six a.m. and her father closed it at midnight. Although it was a social atmosphere, it had some hateful associations for Ruth; the smell of ice cream, which she ate daily in the candy store, disgusted her as an adult, and, in fact, she refused to voluntarily eat ice cream until the age of fifty-five. A source of pain for Ruth when she was growing up was that all family interactions took place in the store. Nothing was private. Not only did they eat dinner and complete homework in the back of the store, but "anything that you said or that was told to you" was public. For example, Harry would sign and publicly comment on Ruth's report card in the store. Later in life Ruth realized how exposed this had made her feel. Yet through her parents' determination and their hard work in the store, her parents achieved their goal of sending their three children to college.

Ruth's parents' lives were shadowed by trauma. Devorah lost her mother at age two and endured poverty and pogroms, as well as prolonged displacement during World War I. Harry suffered a permanent injury during the war. In the U.S., Ruth's family struggled economically. Though Ruth's mother was able to put some of her experience of pogroms into words, its terror suggests that the resulting trauma was unprocessed and "unsayable." I imagine that both because of the effects of her unprocessed trauma and because she was motherless, Devorah during Ruth's early years had difficulty being well-enough attuned to her young daughter. Thus the relational impairment resulting from trauma was, I believe, passed on to Ruth.

Ruth absorbed both her mother's terror of pogroms and the effects of her mother's deprivation. She may have also been scarred by her knowledge of her father's brutal treatment during World War I. Her mother's shut-off quality and Ruth's cut-off remoteness suggest the silence and absence characteristic of traumatized families. Moreover, Ruth's enactment of her mother's history with pogroms represented the intergenerational transmission of traumatic memory (O'Loughlin, 2013). This psychic trauma, because of its unresolved nature, might have been passed on to future generations.

CONCLUSIONS

In this chapter I attempt to delineate the influence of historical trauma on the psychic lives of the immigrants and their children. That many of the Jews who arrived between 1881 and 1924 were affected by trauma is rarely spoken about. This very real trauma was often passed on intergenerationally. In part because of the overwhelming trauma of the Holocaust, the appalling difficulties suffered by the immigrants who arrived in the earlier period were eclipsed. In our collective memory as Americans, Jewish trauma and its intergenerational transmission reside with Holocaust survivors and their descendants.

In formulating my research goals, I originally decided to interview many individuals to provide a more systematic portrait of the psychological lives of immigrants and their children. The presentation of multiple narratives is particularly important when their subject is trauma. The very nature of post-traumatic memory is that gaps or confusions of memory may produce idiosyncratic versions of experience (O'Loughlin, 2018). Thus my recounting of multiple accounts helps us, while comprehending the particularities of experience, to conceive of a broader view of what happened to the immigrants who arrived between 1881 and 1924 and of how their children were affected.

Why was the trauma suffered by the third wave of Jewish immigrants left unacknowledged? One reason—in addition to the dwarfing of this trauma by the incomprehensible scale of the Holocaust—was the secrecy that results from trauma. This secrecy brings us back to the immigrants' silence and denial, which were part of my impetus for beginning this research project.

Silence about the experience of pogroms was extremely common (D. B. Ehrenberg, personal communication, March 14, 2016). Ehrenberg (2004), who grew up in a Jewish Bronx community in the 1950s, writes that her childhood friends never acknowledged among themselves the pogroms experienced by many of their parents. Parents often wished to protect their children from terrible knowledge—and probably often themselves from their own memories—by being silent. As I have mentioned, in choosing interview subjects, I encountered many more whose parents were silent about their pasts than whose parents spoke about their lives in Eastern Europe or their lives shortly after immigration.

The topic of secrecy or silence resulting from the traumatic experiences endured by the third wave of immigrants provokes various thoughts. Aaron, discussed above, whose mother discovered her father's body after his murder during a pogrom, reported that he *did not know* (my emphasis) how he knew this fact; it was not spoken about. Moreover, some immigrants' children and grandchildren believed that their parents refused to allow them to learn the Yiddish that they themselves spoke; the older generation felt this would protect the children from knowledge of the horrifying events to which they might allude (L. Hendelman, personal communication, April 3, 2016). Furthermore, some immigrants were silent because they did not trust their neighbors. In the treacherous Eastern European world that they escaped, they could not know who might betray them, so they instructed their American children to be silent about family matters for fear that neighbors could not be trusted (Ehrenberg, 2004).

The idea that the third wave of Jewish immigrants came to America to begin a new life is not unrelated to their silence about the past in general and about trauma in particular. As we have seen, many wished to leave the past in the past. They were also instructed by people seen as authorities to face the future. For example, the "Bintel Brief"—the advice column published in the Yiddish daily *Forward*—repeatedly emphasized the "emotional imperative" to forget the past (Matt, 2011, p. 168). It was an absolute necessity that immigrants adapt because of the dire conditions for Jews in Eastern Europe; in fact, it would in reality have been dangerous for homesick Jews to return home. A related notion is this one, suggested by Irving Howe: during the beginning of the twentieth century, secular Jewish movements shared the goal of wanting to make Jewish life normal. These movements no longer wanted the Jews to be a "pariah people," subject to both exile and persecution (Howe, 1978, p. 93). Part of wanting to make life normal was adaptation to life in America, which implied leaving the past in the past. That many immigrants were too busy with the work of survival to spend time talking was an additional reason for silence about the past and its trauma. Often immigrants worked from dawn until 10 or 11 p.m. Indeed, life in Eastern Europe had trained many in the art of survival; when disasters occurred, one simply pulled oneself together and moved on to the next thing.

My interviews were conceived of and presented to participants as part of a research project, and thus the goal was to collect information. Yet in interviewing these second-generation recipients of trauma, I found myself in the unexpected position of witnessing the trauma passed on by their parents. The idea of witnessing indicates that a process occurs between narrator and listener during the act of communication. When the narrator begins to talk about trauma, what emerges is a co-constructed narrative (e.g., Goodman, 2012; Laub, 1992; O'Loughlin, 2018). Psychologists writing about Holocaust survivors speak about the potency of witnessing; the presence of the witness is the "essential element for bringing the unspeakable" past traumatic events "into existence" (Goodman, 2012, p. 4). In a safe relationship, it is possible to talk about what has been rarely or never spoken about.[14] In the space between people, description and reflection can help the individual to further process what happened in his family; intense feelings, such as terror, grief, or hatred, can be held and contained.

In the act of imparting information to me, those I interviewed spoke of people and events—and implicitly of emotions about these people and events—about which they had rarely spoken and which, as part of their immediate family's pasts, were very important to them. It is likely that at least some of my interviewees left the interviews with new perspectives on these crucial parts of their pasts. My discussion with Susan (to be described in detail in the next chapter) illustrates this. Susan spoke about the cholera epidemic during her mother's childhood that killed so many of her mother's siblings. In talking to Susan about why her mother did not speak much about the cholera epidemic, I hazarded the guess to her that perhaps this was so because of the traumatic nature of these deaths. Susan agreed with me. My thought was that Susan might never have previously used the word "trauma" when thinking about her mother's experience.[15] I expect, moreover, that our discussion about this and our agreement that her mother's experiences qualified as trauma must have been meaningful to her.

The first witness to the horrific events experienced by a trauma survivor is often her child. Children are acutely able to detect parental emotional absence, or unprocessed experience, which represent the scars of terror. Realizing that she must protect both herself and her parents, the child becomes parentified and unconsciously tries to empathize with and care for her parent (Kaplan, 1995; O'Loughlin, 2013). The child may also realize that her parent is trying to hide a terrible secret (Kaplan, 1995). For example, because of her curiosity, Rose was finally able to get her father to speak about the circle of boys who protected their friends against stoning. But she sensed her father was concealing even more devastating secrets.

Trauma entails a breakdown in empathy; as result, parents' relational capabilities are impaired after suffering trauma (Meyers, 2012, p. 291). It is because of parents' inability to be empathic that their infants attempt to protect and empathize with them (Kaplan, 1995). By doing so, the infant is also protecting herself and ensuring her own survival. In Kaplan's (1995, p. 225) words, "The child learns that he must become his parent's bridge to life." Thus among my interviewees, Barbara, David, Ruth—and in some ways Aaron—strongly identified with their mothers, trying to be close to them and to heal them. We can also see identification strikingly at work in Seymour's recurrent Holocaust fantasy: identifying with his traumatized father in his "vision," he *becomes* his grandmother's son. In taking his grandmother's arm as she is about to be shot, he retrospectively tries to help his now dead father (i.e., past becomes present). A variation on identification or empathy is seen in children like Barbara, and to a lesser extent David, who seem drawn to their parents' pain like moths to a flame.

Related to the breakdown in empathy that accompanies trauma are the disturbed ways that traumatized parents communicate with their children. Elaine and Barbara were flooded with information, and David similarly stated that he "knew too much." Barbara seemed to suffer the most seriously from this. She was overwhelmed with frightening information about her parents' deprivation and fear; perhaps even worse was her parents' uncontrolled and frightening communication with each other, which left Barbara traumatized. Stanley and Aaron coped with a different kind of disturbed communication. Their mothers were unable to speak about the massive trauma to which they were subjected. As Aaron's mother could not process the shock of finding her father's body after a pogrom and Stanley's mother could not process the terror of being shot at while fleeing the bullets of World War I, they passed on their trauma wordlessly. Disturbed communication is also suggested by Ruth's story. Although she stated that her mother *did* speak about a pogrom, the trauma passed on to Ruth was unable to be processed. Ruth's remoteness and cut-off quality, as well as her use of denial, dissociation, and compartmentalization, suggest her mother's serious difficulties in communication.

The breakdown in empathy and the associated impairment in relational capacities that accompany trauma stand out in the stories the immigrants' children told me. In particular, Barbara's and Aaron's mothers were unable to attend to their children's emotional needs. While it is understandable that these mothers would often be overwhelmed by their own concerns, the degree to which they ignored their children is striking (Barbara's mother's emotional illness was a contributing factor in her failure to respond to her daughter's needs). Barbara's parents seemed unable to even notice their daughter's needs, while Aaron's mother allowed him to be exposed to physical danger, and when he was older, she belittled him in front of others. Davoine and Gaudillière (2004, p. 50) describe the inability to be empathic that follows trauma, noting that severe trauma can leave individuals anesthetized, without feeling, and unable to discern what would affect their children's danger and safety or happiness and unhappiness.

The psychological consequences of the trauma suffered by the Eastern European Jewish immigrants who arrived between 1881 and 1924 were pervasive and resulted, for example, in depression, anxiety, and anger or violence at home. Barbara's mother suffered a severe and long-lasting depression, and Stanley's mother experienced episodes of intense anxiety.

Life in my mother's parents' home, permeated by loud arguments, provides another instance of the psychological effects of trauma. My grandmother, who had suffered multiple traumas during World War I, was overburdened as a mother; she was disappointed in my grandfather, who had borne the scars of his own disturbed family. The Depression added to their already considerable problems. There were periods during my mother's early life when, similarly to Barbara's and Aaron's families, all talking was fighting.

I noted previously that secure attachment status is one factor that allowed individuals to partially work through the trauma passed on to them intergenerationally. Secure attachment allows a more ready connection with others and fosters resilience (Cyrulnik, 2007; van der Kolk, 2014). For example, it seemed that Elaine had been sensitively treated by her parents and was securely attached; of those I discussed in this chapter, she was the least severely affected by the parental trauma she internalized. I believe that David also was securely attached, in part because his description of his secure childhood rang true; his two much older sisters were protective of him, and he had other memories of being truly cared for.[16] While David's mother was insensitive in allowing him to be exposed inappropriately to overwhelming knowledge, my assumption is that in other ways she was more responsive. Both Elaine and David were more personable and connected during their interviews than were Barbara, Ruth, or Aaron; the latter three seemed to be insecurely attached.

The type of trauma could influence the ability to work through what had been passed on intergenerationally. I believe that the extreme loneliness and migration trauma suffered by Elaine's mother, though truly debilitating, was different in quality from the types of trauma suffered by the parents of Barbara, Stanley, Ruth, Aaron, or Seymour (chapter 1). Although the distinction was far from clear cut, Elaine's mother's primary trauma was missing family with whom she was still able to correspond; this differed from, for example, hiding one's sister from the Cossacks who might rape her or surviving the experience of bullets whizzing by one's head. Nevertheless, as we will see in the next chapter, migration trauma in an already vulnerable individual might prove to be severely disruptive.

In addition to the trauma that impacted the immigrants discussed in this chapter, these parents were also extremely burdened with trying to survive. For many, the Depression added impossible demands to economic survival. Because the exigencies of earning a living or of keeping a household together took so much of the immigrants' energy, they were doubly unable to be emotionally available to their children.

Jacob, quoted at the beginning of this chapter, said: "They told us kids nothing. They wanted to make a marked transition to the U.S. and dump all that stuff. We're here. Let's forget that." It seems safe to assume that what Jacob's parents wanted to forget in part was the persecution the Jews suffered.

Whether they encountered bullying, poverty, discrimination that robbed them of their livelihoods, or pogroms, the Jews who arrived between 1881 and 1924 experienced widespread and sometimes devastating trauma. The scale of this trauma is rarely discussed, but it had a major impact on the immigrants' children. Before concentrating just on the lives of the children (in chapters 4 and 5)—and investigating the effects of trauma on them—I will explore two other questions. What did immigrants experience during their early days and years in America? What was it like to miss the homes and families to which they could never again return?

NOTES

1. As mentioned, my choice of interview subjects was, in fact, skewed against those whose families told their children nothing about the past. Often an interviewee had one communicative parent and one reticent one.

2. In 1918 the signing of the Treaty of Brest-Litovsk changed national boundaries.

3. The concept of the "unthought known" was originated by Christopher Bollas (1987).

4. Sometimes parental trauma can lead to insensitivity; unresponsive parents will, by definition, have insecurely attached children.

5. Later in life, Barbara's father was perplexed at the fact that there was no money for him to get any Jewish education: he could not even have a Bar Mitzvah. It was additionally confusing because in Barbara's mother's family, which was more impoverished than his, a teacher was hired to tutor the girls.

6. During World War I in Russia, Jews were hastily expelled from their villages amid chaos and brutality. Frequent pogroms accompanied these expulsions.

7. Barbara never found out whether her mother had witnessed rapes as a small child; however, her silence—in contrast to her usual style—is striking. Kaplan (1995) states that silence is a "defining feature" of victims of massive trauma.

8. While Barbara's uncle told her that college was no use for a woman who has kids, her mother supported her desire to go to college. Interestingly, when she was a college student, she wished to move from college dorms into an apartment: her mother "went crazy" because that was not nice: "You'll shame me," her mother exclaimed.

9. Her gallstones were not diagnosed for ten years, which is when she finally recovered fully.

10. Philip's father immigrated to America with his two oldest children, who had caused difficulties for Philip's mother, their stepmother. Thus, according to David, when they left, the family became peaceful.

11. Although Stanley stated that she was president of her *Landsmanshaft*, it is more likely that she was president of the organization's women's auxiliary; these organizations observed the usual gender roles traditional to Jewish society.

12. Although Aaron thought that the pogrom occurred before World War I, my assumption is that it occurred toward the end of the war or in its aftermath, based on Aaron's descriptions and the year of his mother's birth.

13. In fact, Aaron's statement hinted at something in part true: Winter (2015) wrote that the pogroms following World War I indeed paved the way for the Holocaust. Furthermore, the German defeat and its humiliation during the war set the stage for the Holocaust.

14. Indeed, in a couple of my interviews, individuals told me parts of their stories that they had never before spoken about.

15. Susan did consider her aunt, who might have been raped in a pogrom, to have been a trauma victim.

16. In chapter 4, I discuss David's secure attachment.

Chapter Three

Missing the Old Country and Life in America

DRAMATIS PERSONAE

In order of appearance:

Elaine: Her mother came to the U.S. alone and later overwhelmed her daughter with her feelings of loneliness. She never wanted to set foot in Poland again. Elaine as an adult had a fulfilling life.
  Mother: Chaya
  Father: Frank

Helen: Her mother came to the U.S. alone but intended to return to her shtetl. She was "distraught beyond words" when World War I made communication with her family impossible.
  Mother: Chaya
  Father: Ray

Frances: Her mother lived a "gay, cosmopolitan life" before emigration. She was never satisfied with life in the U.S., where she was miserable and lonely; she consequently was never nurturing to Frances.
  Mother: Anna
  Father: Louis

Susan: Susan's mother was nostalgic for life in Eastern Europe, despite a life of "drudgery" and dangerous anti-Semitism. Susan found her mother's nostalgia exasperating.
  Mother: Raisa

Father: Milt

Miriam: Her mother, after a period of homesickness, was a determined and dominant entrepreneur, who "made it here for everybody."
Mother: Trudy

Louise: Louise was like a child of Holocaust survivors because of her father's experience. Her mother, because of World War I trauma, was "terrified as a person." She felt that her job was to repair her damaged parents.
Mother: Edith
Father: Beryl

Norman: His father, who missed his family terribly, was at first a cowboy in the U.S. Norman grew up in abject poverty, but he denied his childhood of deprivation.
Mother: Gitel
Father: Abe

> Why did I come to America,
> And what fortune did I find there?
> Instead, I was forlorn
> Separated from my father and mother,
> So far away from my sisters and brothers.
> —Folk song (Rubin, 1979, p. 346; as cited in Weinberg, 1988, p. 98) [1]

In Anzia Yzierska's short story "Hunger," one young woman laments:

> How I suffered in Savel. I never had enough to eat. I never had shoes on my feet. I had to go barefoot even in the freezing winter. But still I love it. I was born there. I love the houses and the straw roofs, the mud streets, the cows, the chickens and the goats. My heart always hurts me for what is no more. (Yezierska, 1920b, p. 56; as cited in Weinberg, 1988, p. 98)

Despite the trauma many Jews suffered in Eastern Europe, coming to America was difficult. The folk song tells of feeling disconsolate and dejected to be so far from beloved family. And Yzierska's story describes being heartsick at the loss of home in spite of the poverty, hunger, and cold there. Immigration to America was generally destabilizing. It often took years for the immigrant to bridge the gap between Old World and new, to accommodate to the new culture. Adjustment might be particularly difficult for those who arrived with little social support or, alternatively, were psychologically vulnerable before leaving home. Immigration itself was then sometimes traumatic.

How did immigrant parents experience the early months and years after arriving in America? Only a few of the adult children I interviewed knew about the psychological aspects of their parents' emigration. Consequently, to learn about this I turn to memoirs, Yiddish literature, and secondary sources. I also describe the stresses of immigration with the help of the psychoanalytic literature.

The life stories of my interviewees help us understand what it was like to arrive in a completely new place and to leave one's home possibly, even probably, forever. What was it like to miss the family one had left or the old ways of life that could never be recovered?

OLD WORLD TO NEW WORLD: THE TRANSITION

Initial reactions to arriving in America were joyous. Immigrants recall seeing the Statue of Liberty with elation: they had finally reached the country where they would be free from persecution, the land of freedom and opportunity.

The novelist Anzia Yezierska, remembering her own first reactions, wrote:

> Land! Land! Came the joyous shout. America! We're in America! . . . Men fell
> on their knees to pray. Women hugged their babies and wept. Children danced.
> Strangers embraced and kissed like old friends in love. Age-old visions sang
> themselves to me—songs of freedom of an oppressed people. America—
> America. (Yezierska, 1920a, p. 262; as cited in Epstein, 2007)

But once off the boat, disorientation was common. Even for those who came from cities in Eastern Europe, adjusting to life on the Lower East Side was a "quantum leap" (Weinberg, 1988, p. 90). The "sheer size" of New York City, its crowds and noise, were frightening and mind-boggling. While tradition, learning, and religion were markers of respect at home, immigrants faced many difficulties in adapting to a life in which money alone seemed to matter (p. 90). Jews were often even poorer in America than at home, and jobs were demeaning. Homesickness, at least at first, was almost universal.

Rachel Calof (1995, p. 18) wrote in her memoir about the common experience of feeling dazed and confused upon arriving in the metropolis of New York City: "I was simply bewildered by the sights and sounds which assailed my senses. Everything was so strange; the immensity of the city, the manner of the people, the houses, the sounds and smells, all confused and astonished me. It was too much to absorb so quickly." She felt weak and tired by the time she arrived at the boarding house where she was to stay.

New immigrants might be frightened and often confused. On Rose Cohen's first day in America, she was scared to leave her Lower East Side

A new life in America awaits for Sarah's (chapter 5) family. Sarah's father, Avram, and her uncle arriving on the boat from Eastern Europe in 1924. They are in the first row. Avram is almost center, standing to the right of a child. Sarah's uncle is on Avram's right, with a bowtie. Sarah and her mother would not be able to immigrate until 1930. *Courtesy of the family of anonymous interviewee Sarah.*

tenement building (1995). Later she stayed outside, "on the stoop" (p. 71). Here is her reaction a few days later: after hearing in passing a comment about boys having "lost their feet at the sewing machine," which she took literally, she saw a fifteen-year old boy on roller skates (p. 72). Not knowing what roller skates were, she thought that this boy must have lost his feet at a sewing machine, and tears came to her eyes at the thought.

It was common for immigrants to go job hunting after only a couple of days in America, a confusing prospect. The newly arrived Marcus Ravage (1917) tried to look for jobs by getting a child to translate the help wanted advertisements for him. But he wrote, "Half the time I had not the remotest idea of what was wanted. I had been told what a butcher was and what was meant by a grocery-store. But what were shipping clerks, and stock clerks, and bill clerks, and all the other scores of varieties of clerk that were so eagerly sought?" (p. 92).

Immigrants had left behind family and friends and a familiar physical environment, and although often they remained within a Yiddish-speaking milieu, they had to contend with the English language. Homesickness was rampant, and alienation and a sense of displacement were common. The following account of homesickness was published in the "Bintel Brief" (Metzker, 1971), the advice column set up by the *Jewish Daily Forward* specifically to guide new immigrants who had nowhere to turn. The young man who wrote this in 1911 had left home to avoid conscription into the Russian army:

> A long gloomy year, three hundred and sixty-five days, have gone by since I left my home and am alone on the lonely road of life. Oh, my poor dear parents, how saddened they were at my leaving. The leave-taking, their seeing me on my way, was like a silent funeral. . . .
>
> I came to America and became a painter. My great love for Hebrew, for Russian, all of my other knowledge was smeared with paint. During the year that I have been here, I have had some good periods, but I am not happy, because I have no interest in anything. My homesickness and loneliness darken my life.
>
> Ah, home, my beloved home. My heart is heavy for my parents whom I left behind. . . . [He explains that he would return home, but that he would have to be in the army for three years.] I am lonely in my homesickness. (Metzker, 1971, pp. 113–114)

Individuals might feel homesick for years, and sometimes the yearning to see the familiar places, the home where one "was born and raised," lasted a lifetime (Benjamin, 1925–1929; as cited in Matt, 2011, p. 146).

During the nineteenth century, acute homesickness and its symptoms were taken seriously and described by the medical term "nostalgia." According to Matt, in *Homesickness: An American History* (2011, p. 5), many doctors believed that the sufferers "might die" if their nostalgia was untreated. Common symptoms of homesickness included bad dreams; feeling unable to "breathe the American air," to eat, or to sleep; and nervousness or enervation; some people "experienced random pains" (p. 146). There were many Jews who were so homesick that—despite news reports of pogroms in Eastern Europe—they applied for return tickets back home. In 1906, in the wake of several pogroms, the *Dallas Morning News* ran a story titled "Homesick Russian Jews: Refugees Who Yearn for the Land of Persecution" (Matt, 2011, p. 146.)[2]

Beginning in the early twentieth century, homesickness was distinguished from the term "nostalgia" (Matt, 2011). In the pages that follow, I refer to "nostalgia" as a yearning for a "lost era," a "sentimental" or "regretful" memory of the past (Matt, 2011, p. 174; "nostalgia," *Shorter Oxford English Dictionary*, 2007); homesickness is the emotional distress of being away from home.

According to Matt (2011, p. 150), some immigrant men tried to avoid loneliness by emigrating with their wives, rather than sending for them later on, but this "often left their wives desolate." In general, married women were more reluctant to emigrate than were their husbands; they did not want to leave behind older relatives, but they had no choice. Often they "resented the lack of control they had over migration"[3] (see also Weinberg, 1988). Leaving behind family meant male and female immigrants experienced guilt, in addition to loneliness and homesickness (Matt, 2011).

Feelings of displacement, as well as distress at changes in social status, were painful variations on homesickness and loneliness. Harris Rubin, a father of seven and a former Talmud student and teacher, left Russia in 1882 as part of a movement of young Jewish intelligentsia to farm in America. Selected in New York City to work on an upstate farm, where he was well-treated, he felt the emotional pain of having his own world turned topsy-turvy: "It took an iron patience to hold out for the whole summer," he wrote (Rubin, 1983, p. 40). Despite his good employer, he suffered "greatly in the realization that I was only a farm hand and also that in one stroke I had torn myself from my former Jewish roots. This was a torment, a suffering of the spirit." After several months of hard labor, Rubin fainted while working; because he was truly ill, he was put to bed by his employer. "It was then," Rubin wrote, "that I really got a taste of loneliness" (p. 41).

Sholem Asch's short story "Alone in a Strange World" vividly portrays the alienation, confusion, and sheer misery of a shtetl scholar now forced to make a living in the sweatshops of the Lower East Side.[4] Asch's character, here for only seven months, also experienced the hardship and lack of morality that for religious immigrants characterized the New World.

> For more than seven months Meyer has occupied a seat beside a window, opening on a high wall, and has been sewing seams of shirts on a machine. How he ever got there in the first place he does not know to this day. . . . He did not even wonder at the train which races like some fearful beast under ground; on his way to America he had seen so many things, and his mind was so confused, that he would not have been surprised by anything anymore. He did not even think it strange when his relative proposed to him that he take to sewing shirts and when he was seated before a machine. . . .
>
> That he, Meyer, son of Reb Yossele Sochatshover, who was famed throughout the city for his learning and piety and who had been a merchant of parts, should become a shirt-maker like Senderil, the ladies' tailor of their town! (Asch, 1961, pp. 36–37)

Like Harris Rubin, Asch's character, who once had been esteemed as a scholar, felt demeaned to have to work as a common tailor.[5]

When he went to Friday night services with men whom he had known in his shtetl, he felt that the world where each man had his place had been turned upside down. Here a former criminal had metamorphosed into a synagogue official:

> The beadle had been an inept tailor at home. He was nicknamed "Billy-goat" because of his yellowish beard. He had been sent up to Brisk for a robbery one time, and from that time disappeared completely . . . [ellipsis is in text] and here he was in full command of the shul. (Asch, 1961, p. 40)

Homesickness and feelings of displacement were exacerbated by the harshness of life in America, which many found bitterly disappointing (Metzker, 1971, p. 2; Sarna, 1981).[6] Many were worse off economically in America than in Eastern Europe (Matt, 2011).[7] Immigrants commonly worked harder in the U.S. than they had in the Old Country, if they were lucky enough to find work at all (Sarna, 1981). Sweatshop bosses exploited immigrant workers who "worked under the worst conceivable conditions . . . often seven days a week, twelve and even fourteen hours a day, and for miserable wages" (Metzker, 1971, p. 3). Employment was seasonal, and during slack times, "there was no bread, milk, or money for rent." Immigrant families unable to afford their rent were regularly evicted and could be seen gathered on the sidewalks with their few household belongings. "The poverty was oppressive, and more than one newcomer was driven to suicide" (p. 4).[8]

Living conditions for the Jews on the Lower East Side were themselves a cause for misery. Wrote Marcus Ravage (1917, pp. 66–67), "I shall never forget how depressed my heart became as I trudged through these littered streets, with the rows of pushcarts lining the sidewalks and the centers of the thoroughfares, the ill-smelling merchandise, and the deafening noise."[9] Consistent through the literature about and by immigrants are depressing descriptions of the tenement houses, those "monstrous," "crowded," "small, damp," "dirty caves that shut out the sunshine" (Metzker, 1971, p. 3; Ravage, 1917, p. 67). In the short story "The Tenement House," the author describes the "dark, monstrously large six-story building" as being as "gray and unfriendly as a prison, as if some deep melancholy were immured within it" (Kobrin, 1961, p. 27).[10] In addition, the short story "A Wall" describes the "embittered men, pale, despondent women, and languishing children" in a tenement house (Libin, 1961, p. 57). "Sunny rooms are expensive in America; sunlight costs a great deal" (p. 60).[11] Ewen (1985, p. 61) explains the complaints about the replacement of "sunshine with . . . stone and brick" as follows: "Even in Eastern European cities, the woods were a walk away. . . . New York abolished the forests forever." Immigrants compared their "past and present lives" (p. 62): New York, "with its density of people, filthy crowded streets, and small apartments," was the "negation of the previous poor but more natural life."[12] The lack of sunshine and air was particularly depressing: "For many, the loss of sunshine was a metaphor that described feelings of alienation and unfamiliarity, an image of mourning for a world left behind."

The challenges of adjusting to a new country with new customs, new values, and new expectations made poverty and loneliness even less bearable (Weinberg, 1988, p. 93). In America, the drive for status and money replaced the values of traditional Judaism and learning. While in the Old World the "Sabbath was sacred," "*kashruth* [traditional dietary laws] was carefully observed," and the "Jewish holidays were properly celebrated," in the new American strange world, it was necessary to work on the Sabbath and even for men to shave their beards just to get by. It was extremely difficult to observe all the customary rituals (Metzker, 1971, pp. 2–3; Sarna, 1981). Newly arrived immigrants were painfully shocked to be reunited with close relatives who had shed both the outward signs of a pious life and indeed their religious values.

Related to the change from the old religious values to the new economic ones (e.g., Ewen, 1985) was the transition from the importance of the community to individualism. In Eastern Europe, the "collective survival of the shtetl demanded that business be conducted within a framework of mutual aid"; moreover, the "idea of accumulation of money . . . for its own sake was foreign" (Epstein, 2007; Ewen, 1985, pp. 46–47; see also Ravage, 1917). "The competitive nature of American economic life and the emphasis on individual achievement . . . were at odds with the economic interdependence that Jews had in Eastern Europe" (Epstein, 2007, p, 97). [13]

Even the tempo of life changed drastically between the Old World and New. In Eastern Europe, time moved slowly, while America was vigorous, a "hurry up" world (Paver, 1961, p. 93; Shulman, 1976, p. 3), [14] and many new immigrants were disturbed by the relentless rushing of New York. This is illustrated in an exchange between a newly arrived nephew and his New York uncle in Chaver Paver's short story "The Greenhorns":

> "What's this rush? What's their hurry?" [the nephew] demanded angrily. "Each of them, poor fellows, is being rushed-pushed. He may not even stand still on the side-walk." "This is not Tcheremaiyov, Moishe," Uncle Laib instructed him in the customs of the country. "In Tcheremaiyov they walk at ease, come to rest in the middle of the street to consider some matter, to give thought to something. Here, there is no time for thought. If you are going somewhere, keep going or you'll be run down or crushed." (Paver, 1961, p. 92)

The trauma of migration and of adjusting to a wholly new way of life "exacted a high price," leading even to the breakup of families (Weinberg, 1988, p. 110). Because husbands usually came to America first and years later sent for their families, they became Americanized in the intervening years (Epstein, 2007; Weinberg, 1988). When their greenhorn, sometimes prematurely aged, wives arrived, some men no longer wanted anything to do with them. It was not uncommon for men to desert wives and families. Sometimes men, before they could send for their families, took new wives, either for money or because of loneliness (Epstein, 2007: Ravage, 1917). The number of men who deserted their wives was so great that the *Forward*, in conjunction with the National Desertion Bureau, created a special column in 1905 devoted to finding them (Epstein, 2007; Weinberg, 1988).

Many new Jewish immigrants—often young people who had arrived without their families—seemed unmoored in a world they did not understand. In Eastern Europe, not only did most people have built-in social support, but rigid rules governed behavior. In the shtetl, everyone knew everyone else's business and social shaming resulted from flouting convention (Kassow, 2007a). America seemed, in contrast, to be shorn of traditional social controls. Marcus Ravage (1917, p. 79) wrote the following about the recent immigrants he met when he was newly arrived in 1900: "Cut adrift suddenly from their ancient moorings, they were floundering in a sort of moral void. Good manners and good conduct, reverence and religion, had all gone by the board, and the reason was that these things were not American." Of course, it must be kept in mind that Eastern Europe was changing, too. Many people had moved to cities where new ideas and secularization were beginning to take hold.[15]

The "Bintel Brief," the *Forward*'s advice column, was begun in 1906 to give people the "opportunity . . . to pour out their heavy laden hearts" (Cahan's memoir, 1929; cited in Metzker, 1971, p. 7). The "Bintel Brief" letters provide a window into the psychic pain and confusion individuals felt as they attempted to adjust to this baffling world. Many letters were written by lonely and poverty-stricken immigrants who succumbed to temptation and then felt despondent over what they had done; quite a number concerned young immigrant women seduced by the men for whom they worked or with whom they boarded. A female garment-worker wrote a letter after she resisted seduction by the foreman in her shop, then lost her job as a consequence of rebuffing him (p. 67). Another extremely sad letter was from a young woman who had been tricked by a matchmaker into life in a brothel. Rescuing herself after enduring beatings and shame, she could not integrate herself back into a life in which she was respected. And this situation was described by a young woman who was "almost out of [her] mind with worry" (p. 57); her father had died when she was young in Eastern Europe. Presumably to get rid of another mouth to feed, she was sent alone to America by her mother, where she was met by her stepbrother, who married her against her will. She fended off his sexual advances until she had "no more strength to fight him off." It was then that she wrote to the "Bintel Brief" in desperation.

The "Bintel Brief" letters, with their heartfelt pleas for advice, show us how societal and historical circumstances interact with individual lives. Poverty and lack of social support led to circumstances of despair. A fifteen-year-old girl wrote for help after the disintegration of her family; her mother had been rich in Eastern Europe, but she and her family were starving in America, and her mother killed herself from shame when neighbors realized the family's deplorable situation. This happened shortly after the girl's birth, and she was then sent back to relatives in Europe. When they were no longer able to look after her, an aunt newly in America sent for her. Still struggling with poverty, she wrote to the "Bintel Brief" for help in finding her American father. In another example, a poor woman who had received assistance from a childless benefactress was later asked to give up her child to the wealthy woman (p. 103). In the brave new world of America, poverty could and did mean that individuals were lost to their families, were given away as babies, or committed suicide.

Part of the confusion and distress of life in the new world was associated with loss of status and respect. Men worked at jobs far more menial than what they had hoped to find in the U.S. (Epstein, 2007). A chemist was forced to wash dishes in a restaurant (Sarna, 1981); the man of religious learning worked in a sweatshop; and the chairman of the hospital committee sold seltzer from a pushcart (Ravage, 1917). Along with loss of prestige in the transition from Old World to New came economic distress and a lowering of social class. Many Jews who were middle-class in Eastern Europe were lower-class in America. This brought psychic suffering along with the palpable realities of poverty.

"Poverty remained the basic condition of life" for Jewish immigrants throughout the period of immigration, although facilities, amenities, and standards of living improved very slightly throughout the period (Howe, 1976, p. 120).[16] Nevertheless, when many of the parents of my interviewees arrived in 1920 or 1921, wages were glaringly insufficient (Weinberg, 1988).[17] Because fathers, mothers, sons, and daughters needed to work to support the family and because each family member had different working hours, they could not even eat one meal a day together.

PSYCHOANALYSIS AND THE STRESSES OF IMMIGRATION

Leaving for a moment the more concrete challenges of adjusting to a new country, new customs, and new values, I will look more psychoanalytically at the psychological stresses on the individual migrant. This brief section will center on the interrelated ideas of emotional stability; identity—the sense of self and its sameness; and the pain and frustration of mourning the old culture. Migration can have a "destabilizing" effect on one's sense of self (Akhtar, 2011, p. 3). The immigrant Marcus Ravage, who managed to complete college after his arrival in New York in 1900, wrote eloquently about the terrific difficulty of reconciling his old with his new American identity.

> Vowing allegiance to the state is one thing. But renouncing your priceless inherited identity and blending your individual soul with the soul of an alien people is quite another affair. And it is this staggering experience of the spirit—this slipping of his ancient ground from under the immigrant's feet, this commingling of souls toward a new birth, that I have in mind when I speak of becoming an American. To be born in one world and grow to manhood there, to be thrust then into the midst of another with all one's racial heritage, with one's likes and dislikes, aspirations and prejudices, and to be abandoned to the task of adjusting within one's own being the clash of opposed systems of culture, tradition, and social convention—if that is not heroic tragedy, I should like to be told what is. (Ravage, 1917, p. 200)

Ravage felt *abandoned* to the heroically tragic task of adjusting his identity. The effort and strain he found in adjusting to the myriad changes of migration are echoed by the émigré analysts Leon and Rebecca Grinberg (1989, p. 129), who ask, "How much change can an individual tolerate before it works irreparable harm on his identity?"

Identity is at risk in migration because the loss of a sense of place "disrupts the coherence and continuity" of the self (Ainslee et al., 2013, p. 665.) Not only are parents, siblings, children, and broader social networks (p. 664)—on whom we depend for confirmation of our identity—mourned, but the loss of cultural context threatens to be extremely disturbing (Garza-Guerrero, 1974).

One reason for the immigrant's inner disorganization and a related inability to communicate with others is associated with the disruption to place. Relationships with others are embedded in the "cultural and environmental surround" (Gonzalez, 2016). Therefore, when the immigrant loses both the familiar culture and the familiar place, she cannot interact easily with others. Francisco Gonzalez (2016) explains this using Winnicott's (1967) concepts of transitional space and the "inherited tradition" of culture. Gonzalez writes that during infancy, confidence in our world—in the world of people—is built up in connection with our reliable dependence on a caretaker who allows us to trust the environment. The trust in the environment that develops requires the baby's interaction with the "embodied and the material" (p. 26). Therefore, each individual becomes who he or she is in a "distinct actual place" (p. 27); each person's sense of self is "textured by the sense of its place" (p. 28). Gonzalez writes that when we emigrate, we lose "not just language. . . . We also lose the way the words form in our mouths, the smell of a place, the texture of foliage and buildings, whole landscapes of sound, the feel of the air" (pp. 29–30); even the "rhythms of life" differ (Ainslee et al., 2013, p. 664). We lose the "wordless signals . . . the subtleties of manner, . . . customs, comfort foods . . . that are the cultural vernacular" (Hoffman, 1989, cited in Boulanger, 2004, p. 356). When we do not have this sense of the familiar, our disorientation and disorganization interfere with our ability to interact easily with others. For the displaced new immigrant, "the words will not form; the gestures are misunderstood" (Gonzalez, 2016, p. 29). The immigrant who cannot be understood cannot feel that she belongs (Boulanger, 2016).

As mentioned, the "periods of disorganization, pain, and frustration" of migration are in part related to loss of sense of self (Ainslee et al., 2013, p. 665). Harlem (2010, p. 472) states that the exile is someone who can't "'remember' other versions of herself," who can't "bridge" the gap between parts of the self rooted in various times. Boulanger (2004) talks slightly differently about the threat to identity that accompanies migration: loss of contextual continuity means that immigrants experience a chronic absence that they do not want to acknowledge. "They fear being so overwhelmed by feelings of alienation and depression as to be distracted from the business at hand, which is to fit into their adopted culture" (p. 355). If you look back, you will "be desperately" trying to "re-establish continuity," so you "stop identifying with it, look forward, keep planning, keep forging ahead" (p. 357). But if you identify only with the new country, you will cut yourself off from vital parts of the self inadvertently lost in the process of migration. The former alternative, the fear that you will succumb if you do not keep your eyes on the future, is familiar to us as one reason that the Eastern European Jewish immigrants reportedly wanted to "leave it all behind."

Although Ravage (1917) discussed the "opposed" cultures and conventions of old and new worlds as dichotomies, contemporary psychoanalytic writers emphasize the "both/and quality" involved in the immigrant's sense of self (Beltsiou, 2016, p. 4; see also Boulanger, 2004). Beltsiou writes that immigrants "hold the tension between the two worlds inside" themselves; this involves constant "refocusing, automatically keeping both worlds in mind." (Beltsiou, 2016, p. 5; Boulanger, 2016, p. 56). Lobban (2016, p. 71) considers the immigrant's subjective experience as she "attempts to hold two sets of selves," one made of "foreign cloth" and one made in her new environment. What happens to the immigrant's sense of herself if the residents of her new country believe that the foreign parts of herself are inferior? This must have been common for the Eastern European Jewish immigrants—they were believed to be dirty, backward, primitive, and alien. Perceived as the dangerous "other," individuals might often have felt shame associated with the "foreign" and inferior parts of themselves. Eastern European Jewish immigrants faced discrimination even in America, and thus, even in the land of opportunity, they must have felt unsafe. Discrimination is disorganizing to one's sense of self (Ainslee et al., 2013), but Eastern European Jewish immigrants sometimes remarked that what they had faced at home had been so much worse.

Each of the psychoanalytic writers talk about the immense psychological strains of immigration (e.g., Grinberg & Grinberg, 1989; Harlem, 2010; Hollander, 2006; Lobban, 2006). Boulanger (2004, p. 354) likens the stress of migration to the "violence of being torn up by the roots," while Garza-Guerrero (1974, p. 409) writes about how "severely" it threatens identity. According to Bodnar (2004, p. 596), it is the very "experience of living in more than one symbolic world" that may predispose immigrants to "traumatic experience."

Immigration invariably entails mourning what has been left in one's former home, such as "family, friends, language . . . food" and the values and attitudes of one's previous culture (Garza-Guerrero, 1974, p. 409). Akhtar (1999a, p. 102; as cited in Harlem, 2010, p. 471) portrays the immigrant as "moving through a dynamic process in which splits (love-hate; near-far; yesterday-today; yours-mine) are eventually 'mended.'" As part of this process, the immigrant may idealize her former country and devalue her new country, and this process of idealization and devaluation usually oscillates over time so that, for example, it is now the new home that is idealized and the old country that is devalued and vice versa (Hollander, 2006). Aspects of self are idealized or devalued along with the country-of-origin or the country to which the migrant has moved (Harlem, 2010, p. 471). Thus immigrants may suffer when a part of the self has been "lost in transit" (p. 470). Frances's mother, whom I will discuss below, not only idealized the sophisticated German culture that she was forced to leave, but she might also have felt that she had lost her treasured identity as a sophisticated European woman. The solution to the "disjunctive" pain of the migrant is to "build bridges" or to reach the point at which ambivalence is tolerable and normal (Harlem, 2010, p. 470). The process of acclimating to the new country, however, is not "natural, inevitable, or linear," according to Ainslee et al. (2013, p. 667); rather it is dynamic and can have many outcomes, including integration of old and new or rejection of the new culture.

Related to mourning is the depression that may be one of the long-term effects of immigration, since the immigrant can never recover what has been lost (Grinberg, 1978, p. 275, as cited in Akhtar, 2011, p. 9). Helplessness is also part of the trauma of migration. The individual has lost all the protections of home and familiarity (Grinberg & Grinberg, 1989); the mother country and the people one loves are no longer available and perhaps never will be again. The immigrant lives with the "sense of 'chronic absence'" and mourning (Boulanger, 2004, p. 356; as cited in Lobban, 2016, p. 72). "Loneliness and isolation increase the immigrant's" feelings of desolation over what he has lost; he no longer has the support of his familiar social environment in mourning his former world. In other words, the anonymity of immigration increases inner insecurity; the people that one usually relies upon to help one adjust to life's crises have been left in the home country (Grinberg & Grinberg, 1989, p. 90).

We can understand the anxiety and trauma experienced by the Eastern European Jewish immigrants when we remember that most came from a way of life that differed in so many ways from the vast industrial chaos of New York City. This was particularly true for Jews from small villages or towns, but even Jews from Eastern European cities lived a slower-paced life than that of New York. Most of those from towns were steeped in religion and spirituality; they were superstitious and believed in the evil eye (Cowan & Cowan, 1996). While the transition from the Old World to America was for most of the immigrants buffered because they lived and often worked in immigrant neighborhoods, the transition nevertheless engendered enormous psychological strain. Immigrants were unable to understand how much of the world around them worked.

The issue of language magnifies the huge difference between the two worlds. When one begins living in a new language, she experiences a rift in ways of being—we are different people in the two different languages.[18] This is so because language structures "our deepest emotions, longings, and desires" (Beltsiou, 2016, p. 8). Hoffman writes, (2016, p. 212), "In a very real sense, language constitutes our psychic home." The immigrant speaking in her original language may be able to "connect more immediately . . . with the emotions" related to childhood memories (Ainslee et al., 2013, p. 667). Because many of the Eastern European Jewish immigrants spent a good deal of time with immigrant family and neighbors, I suggest that the crisis of language was for them at times lessened. Yet many suffered because of it. Ruth's mother, described in chapter 2, was ashamed of her faulty English. My very intelligent maternal grandmother may have been shy because she was ashamed of her marked accent and poor grammar. Because a person existing in a new language cannot grasp nuances, she may feel stilted or one-dimensional. Furthermore, when she loses her language, she may lose not just everyday words but—like my grandmother—the ability to be outgoing; she may turn from a lively participant to an awkward observer.

Immigrants whose social class was lowered by migration mourned this change. It was not infrequent that Jews could be middle class, or sometimes even prosperous, in Eastern Europe and working class or lower class in America (Weinberg, 1988). Seymour's father and Frances's mother both contended with this, and Frances's mother seemed unable to recover from her fall from her middle-class, "cosmopolitan" life to her new working-class status.

As we have seen, individuals often immigrate because of trauma, and trauma complicates immigration. For example, post-migration mourning is affected by pre-migration trauma; the relief of escaping persecution may mean an immigrant denies the loss of leaving home. Therefore, an immigrant group may be collectively unable to mourn (Volkan, 1997, as cited in Ainslee et al., 2013; see also Ainslee et al., 2013, p. 665). I have referred to this phenomenon among individuals as the disavowal of loss and, in other permutations, the ambiguity of loss. One complication in trying to understand immigrants who have been traumatized is differentiating among the effects of family, or individual, trauma and those of cultural trauma (Bodnar, 2004). Frequently, my interviewees and their immigrant parents were affected by both.

Two authors, Foster (2001) and Hollander (2006), specifically discuss trauma and immigration.[19] Foster's phases of migration during which trauma occurs and Hollander's contributions about trauma and loss that occur in the context of persecutory governments can be used to further understand Eastern European Jewish immigration. The cumulative traumatic events that lead to immigration "constitute an assault on the psyche," wrote Hollander (2006, p. 63). Benjamin's parents' chaotic post–World War I lives, during which "death was ever-present" (chapter 1), and David's mother's pain, fear, starvation, disease, and poverty (chapter 2 and chapter 5) are two of many examples in this book. For Hollander (p. 64), the initial loss is the "loss of life as it once was," before it was "distorted by state persecutions." Formerly comforting landmarks are now "anxiety laden and terrifying." A second set of losses for the refugee is the departure itself. Often—as with Seymour's father, who was forced to leave because he rightfully feared retaliation from the White Russian soldiers—departures represent a "sudden rupture," with little time to say goodbye to family or friends. The long journey to the new country might be traumatic (Foster, 2001, as cited in Ainslee et al., 2013). Border crossings, sometimes with false papers, were often perilous. Helen's mother, described in this chapter, was preyed upon by an older and trusted man. Arrival in the new country might represent a "life crisis" for the already vulnerable refugee, as much of the rest of this chapter shows. Most often there was no parent to help in coping with the strange new country and the accompanying frustration, anxiety, loneliness, and fears (Hollander, 2006, p. 64). Finally, chronic "exploitative living conditions" and lack of support in the new country constitute one more source of trauma (Ainslee et al., 2013; Foster, 2001, p. 156). Hollander (2006) points out that psychological conflict under these extremely difficult circumstances is often somatized, and consequently, over time psychosomatic problems and fatal diseases may result. My maternal grandmother experienced debilitating migraines; many of the immigrant fathers of my interviewees died early, often of cancer or heart disease.

Some final thoughts on both the stresses of immigration and the resolution of the immigrants' dilemma come from analysts who are themselves immigrants. Eva Hoffman (2016, p. 211), writing of herself as both an immigrant and an exile, said, "I feel myself to be shaped by the rupture of that uprooting as deeply as I do by my parents . . . or my historical background." Hoffman (p. 212) emphasized "how much we are creatures of culture . . . and how much incoherence we risk if we fall out of that culture." The exile may, however, "translate" herself to the new culture; approximately a half century after her immigration, Hoffman felt that she was "just as strongly" formed by her post-migration "cultures and experiences" (p. 213). "I have become inescapably hybrid," she elaborated. Accommodation to the new culture can occur. Yet to belong, the immigrant must be understood by others, said Boulanger (2004; 2016). "Belonging is the condition of being understood" (Boulanger, 2016, p. 66).[20] Without that, the immigrant bears the pain and psychological scars of being a chronic other.

MISSING THE OLD COUNTRY: LIFE STORIES

Many immigrants had the support of family in America. But the Eastern European Jewish migration was generally one of young people (e.g., Howe, 1976, p. 58), and half my interviewees' parents had no parent in the U.S. when they arrived. Indeed, a great many young immigrants found themselves in a new and confusing world without the support and guidance of the parental generation.

How does the human being fare psychologically when torn from his roots (Boulanger, 2004)? This is an underlying question of this chapter; among my interviewees' parents, adjustment to America seemed most difficult for those who came alone. Immigrants' experiences of missing either Eastern Europe itself or the people left behind varied widely, depending in part upon whom a person migrated with or joined here in the U.S.[21]

Interestingly, only a few parents, all mothers, talked to their children in any depth about the loss of their families or previous homes. A couple of children were aware that their fathers missed their families, although they rarely or never actually mentioned this.

I found that two categories of intensity characterized those who talked about missing life in what had previously been home. Some missed either family or the place they had left so acutely and for so long that their migrations were traumatic. I distinguish these individuals from others who were homesick only temporarily; this was normal. Also normal was nostalgia, a regretful but tolerable yearning for the past; this might be long-standing.

Of my interviewees, it was only these seven for whom a parent's separation from family, nostalgia, or homesickness was a major theme. Because we know from secondary sources that homesickness was widespread, it seems that often these important feelings were not passed on to immigrants' children.

Arriving in America Alone: Two Daughters' Stories

Two mothers, Elaine's and Helen's, came to America alone, and both found the separation from family to be traumatic. Helen's mother missed not just family but home. Although their stories bear similar outlines, they actually differ; Elaine's mother lived with loving extended family when first in the U.S. and, partly because of circumstances, this overall secure woman was years later able to significantly recover from her loneliness. Helen's mother lived with a depressed aunt after arrival, and she remained vulnerable and insecure throughout her life.

Elaine

The reader will remember Elaine's mother, Chaya, from the previous chapter: she cried herself to sleep for years after she emigrated because she missed her family. Elaine herself was pleasant, social, soft-spoken, and contained; she spoke slowly, quietly, and in detail, and her account was open, thoughtful, and intelligent. A retired educator in her seventies, she and her husband had done well financially and currently enjoyed an active and social life; they participated in Jewish cultural activities. Elaine was an only child, but she and her husband had raised three daughters with whom they were close. Elaine's mother's story was complex, encompassing both her hatred of Eastern Europe and her feelings of traumatic loss. That Chaya was permanently separated from her family was an extremely important part of the trauma she endured and passed on to her daughter.

Chaya's own mother had a huge extended family, and her many older first cousins emigrated to the U.S. prior to her own arrival. Chaya was able to emigrate to the U.S. in 1928, after the restrictive immigration laws had been passed, only because a cousin already living in the U.S. returned to their city and married her for that reason; the marriage was later annulled. Chaya lived with cousins in the Bronx who were relatively comfortable economically, and she even had her own room. Elaine said her mother was "surrounded by family." These family members "were wonderful to her," affectionately calling her the "*grine kuzine*" (newcomer cousin) and telling her how pretty she was. After Chaya arrived, a good friend from home also emigrated; thus she had a friend as well as family to help her bridge the gap from the Old Country. Chaya was also close throughout her life to a cousin in Brooklyn who had similarly come to the U.S. alone.

Nevertheless, Chaya for years after her arrival was heartbroken about missing her mother, sisters, and brothers. She believed for a couple of years after she emigrated that her family would be able to join her, and she was traumatized at that time in part because those expectations were dashed.[22] Elaine did not mention that New York must have felt alien to her unhappy mother, that everything around her was unfamiliar. Yet the inevitable dislocation of a life in which everything had changed must have added to Chaya's inconsolable feelings about the loss of her family.

Chaya had adamantly wanted to leave Poland behind, hating it because of the traumatic anti-Semitism to which she had been exposed. Born in about 1908, she was a child during World War I and its aftermath. According to Elaine, Chaya "couldn't stand" to think about the pogrom she had witnessed. Elaine said "hooligans" had "pulled" the beard of one of her brothers; otherwise, her mother was vague about the traumatic events that occurred—"probably a couple of people in the family [were] beat up or maybe killed." Chaya stated: "I was born there and I never wanted to go back." She said she "disliked everything Polish" and she refused to speak Polish in the U.S; thus Chaya adamantly denied the loss of her former home.

Apart from anti-Semitic violence, Elaine characterized her mother's life as a child and adolescent as hard but not unhappy. Chaya was the middle child in a large Orthodox family; according to Elaine, her mother had left behind a generally happy home in which she was her father's favorite. Chaya's father was in the book business, and the family was middle-class before his death from cancer when Chaya was eleven. Chaya, her father's favorite, was chosen to sit by his bedside during his final illness. It is possible that Chaya idealized the happy years before her father's death as a sort of golden age. After his death, the family struggled economically, and each child worked. Another trauma, which Elaine did not emphasize, was that an older brother died of disease as a teenager. The cumulative trauma of war, violence, death of a family member, migration, and separation from family must have subjected Chaya to immense psychological strain.

Several years after Chaya's arrival, she met her husband-to-be, Frank. According to Elaine, he filled the vacuum of her mother's neediness and emptiness. Although his silence about his past made him like a "closed book" to Elaine, later on he told a grandson something about it. Frank's Orthodox father wanted him to become a rabbi; he, however, wanted to play the violin, and because of this conflict, he ran away from home three times. Finally, he was allowed to study the violin in an Eastern European city. Frank had two older sisters who brought him to New York, and neither talked about their difficult family. After Frank came to the U.S., economic constraints meant that his musical career was ruined, and he became extremely frustrated. He was able to work at night as a musician before talking movies became popular, but his factory job made him "miserable," and he had to work at two jobs during Elaine's childhood. Yet Frank was an intelligent, cultured man, and Elaine guessed she received her own love of books and theater from him.

Elaine had a number of interesting insights about the stresses in her mother's life as an immigrant. In addition to financial problems, not knowing the English language was particularly difficult. Also, because Elaine was born during the Depression, Chaya needed to leave her young daughter to work in a factory. Elaine was profoundly affected by her mother's need to work; she cried when her mother left the house and resented that Chaya left her with a babysitter. She was too young to understand that her mother worked out of necessity. By the time Elaine was twelve, World War II had ended, bringing an improvement in the economy, and her mother was able to stop working in the factory. Her family was able to purchase a rooming house, and Chaya's new job was to manage it. Elaine felt better about herself after her mother stopped working.

When Elaine was twelve, Chaya's mother, who had emigrated to South America some years earlier, visited them in New York. Chaya's reunion with her mother may have been a turning point for her; I believe she felt more secure afterward. After this first visit, the extended family occasionally traveled to see one another.

Chaya was a strict disciplinarian, which sometimes made Elaine angry, but she emphasized that she had also felt loved. Despite the family's financial problems, which meant that Elaine slept in the living room as a child, she had toys and birthday parties.

When Elaine finished high school, her father expected her to get a job. But Chaya, like many other immigrant mothers, was determined that her daughter would have a better life than she did.[23] Chaya told her daughter, "You'll go to college if I have to scrub other people's floors." Elaine, in turn, felt she needed "to make something better for herself." She worked hard, becoming chairman of her department because she wanted her parents to be proud of her. Elaine repaid them for their sacrifices with her own success. She married and had three sons; although their first few years of marriage were difficult economically, the couple bought a suburban house, Elaine's husband's career flourished, and they gave their children many advantages.

The trauma of Chaya's separation from her family and consequent loneliness remained an important part of both mother's and daughter's lives. As we saw in chapter 2, Elaine felt overwhelmed by her mother's feelings when she was young. She stated that, although her mother "recovered" from her "sadness," it was nevertheless always a "factor" in Chaya's life. Elaine as an adult seemed to still feel the trauma of her mother's losses. Elaine would also have felt her father's silent suffering. How did Elaine have an overall satisfying and full life given the effects of her mother's trauma and her father's difficulties? Although I cannot answer this question with certainty, my thoughts about it follow.

Elaine stated that, overall, her mother did not feel like a sad person. She had a good marriage, she was very social, and most people found her sweet and loving. At one point, Elaine said she herself "made up for" her mother's earlier loneliness by having made many friends throughout her life. Mother's and daughter's capacity to be social was one indication of secure attachment that may have characterized Chaya, as it almost surely did Elaine. Chaya and

Frank, from Elaine's description, were generally responsive to Elaine's needs as a child. Although Chaya was to some degree as a young mother distracted from her daughter by her mourning for her family, she was able to connect with Elaine in the ways that mattered (Boulanger, 2016). This connection argues for Elaine's secure attachment status, and the clinical evidence during her interview also argues for her secure attachment. Furthermore, Elaine's balanced and thoughtful statements—she was able to see both positive and negative aspects of her parents' personalities, rather than idealizing them as many of my interviewees did—argue for her ability to mentalize, which is associated with secure attachment (Fonagy et al., 2002).

Chaya suffered from both historical and familial trauma; the early death of her father, traumatic anti-Semitism, and migration trauma, affected her. She had emigrated without any members of her immediate family, and she forever lived far away from those she depended on during her early life. Living in the U.S. without any nuclear family members was less usual among the Eastern European immigrants. When Chaya as a recent immigrant realized she would never again live with her loving family, she felt not only sad but perhaps also helpless. Meeting her husband was healing, as was the limited contact she had with her family beginning after World War II. Moreover, Chaya's ability to be social helped her to feel less like an outsider and to heal the damage from her loneliness. Thus Chaya proved in the end to be resilient.

Helen

Helen was a gracious, pleasant woman in her eighties and a people-pleaser; she loved to talk but also had a somewhat formal manner. A retired professional, she was an intelligent, cultured, social woman who was active in her community. She lived in a beautiful apartment with her second husband, whom she married shortly after the death of her first husband in middle age.

Helen's mother, Rivka, arrived in the U.S. alone at age sixteen and missed her family intensely. The "devastating cutoff," as Helen called her mother's migration, was a traumatic separation that had an ongoing destabilizing influence on Rivka and affected her ability to be a responsive mother.

Rivka's emigration in 1913 was unintended, according to Helen. Rivka, born in 1897 in a Russian shtetl, was the third daughter in a large, middle-class family. Originally, it was her older sister, rather than the more timid Rivka, who had wanted to travel to America. By the time the ticket arrived, however, her sister was already attending a university in Warsaw. The girls' mother chose Rivka to use the ticket, expecting that Rivka would return home after a few years.

Shortly after Rivka arrived in the U.S., World War I began, and Rivka was cut off from her family. The war made communication impossible, and she could neither contact her family nor return to live with them. Rivka was reportedly "distraught beyond words" and felt "trapped" many thousands of miles from home. This adolescent had been "happy at home," according to Helen; she had been neither ready nor eager to emigrate. The deteriorating situation in Eastern Europe after the war's end prevented her from returning.

Helen said her mother told "colorful stories" about her life at home in Eastern Europe. Rivka's father was in the textile business, and in her family, Judaism was a "way of life"; rabbis were often consulted on day-to-day matters, for instance, to determine whether a blemished chicken was unkosher. Notwithstanding this, a photograph shows the family dressed in secular clothes, and Rivka was taught Russian in addition to Yiddish.

A tragedy had occurred in Rivka's shtetl, however. During a pogrom, Russian Cossacks repeatedly raped Rivka's young cousin in her home, forcing the cousin's parents to watch. One week later, her cousin committed suicide. Helen mentioned this traumatic event when I asked her about anti-Semitism, but she communicated nothing more about it and never referred to it again. My feeling was that Helen embraced her mother's picture of her previous life in a joyous, warm, humor-filled family in a traditional town. Although Helen was very much aware of the Holocaust and did allude to this pogrom when asked, I felt she did not want to allow more than passing thoughts of danger into her own pleasant view of her mother's pre-emigration life.

Rivka's life after she departed from home was very difficult, and her journey to the U.S. presaged her challenging early years in this country. She traveled to New York with a married man from her shtetl, who "made a mild pass at her" during the journey. Reportedly "horrified," this insecure and timid teenager must have been deeply upset by what was a betrayal of trust. In New York City, Rivka lived with her uncle and his family in a Lower East Side tenement. Her uncle's wife was clinically depressed, and consequently their household was "cheerless and drab." Though economically, according to Helen, her uncle's family was not extremely poor, the household was characterized by a "poverty of spirit"; her aunt cooked without salt, making Rivka's food tasteless. Fortunately for Rivka, the eldest son was bright and cultured, and he introduced Rivka to cultural events and literature.

When Rivka first arrived, she was not only lonely and homesick but also afraid, which was common for immigrants. She feared getting lost, and—having enrolled in evening high school but unable to read the signs as she walked to school—she devised a mnemonic song system to guide herself. She found a factory job during the day and persevered with her studies, earning a high school diploma.

Rivka lacked confidence in her own self-worth. Apparently, her inability to assert herself amounted to a significant handicap, and a vacation that she took with a friend a few years after arriving provides an example of this. The

Rivka's family in Eastern Europe in 1913. *Courtesy of the family of anonymous interviewee Helen.*

two young women went for a week to a farm, where her friend's brother, in whom she was not interested, proposed to her. Her "horrified" reaction was to pack up and run away. Helen explained her mother's low self-esteem in part by saying Rivka had always compared herself to her older sister who was "beautiful" and "eager for education," the "shining light." Consequently, Rivka always thought "someone else could do it better." Yet Helen described Rivka as being talented; she felt her mother failed to recognize her own gifts in language and humor.

Rivka's unintended and traumatic separation from her family, coupled with the dislocations of immigration, seemed to have an adverse psychological effect on her. As an involuntary immigrant, her feelings of helplessness, uprootedness, inner upheaval, and isolation must have been intense. Migration by its very nature tends to be psychologically challenging. According to Grinberg and Grinberg (1989, p. 90), for the immigrant, who is known by no one, "feeling anonymous increases his inner insecurity." Moreover, loneliness and isolation make it more difficult for the immigrant to cope with the loss of his former life. The person who comes alone has no family or community to depend on for support in processing this loss. Rivka talked about missing her family in Eastern Europe rather than missing the place itself. Yet the insecurity she felt in her early years in America was due both to the loss of her parents, siblings, and friends, upon whom she depended, and the loss of the comfort of the place in which she had grown up. Her story hints at the inevitable anxieties of a life in which everything around her has changed. Rivka must have felt anonymous in New York City and, in addition, unsupported by her aunt and uncle. She had no one to depend on for support in coping with or processing the loss of her previous life.

Helen believed her mother was insecure and needy when she first arrived from Eastern Europe and would likely have been somewhat unconfident had she remained with her family. She was probably even lonelier than a more resilient immigrant might have been. I hypothesize that, because this already uncertain adolescent had to endure the painful separation from the family she loved—and that could have supported her—and because she had no one to depend on in America, Rivka's inner turmoil and sense of isolation must have been extremely painful and difficult. Helen's description of her mother as "distraught beyond words" when so far from her family rings true. Moreover, Rivka's enduring insecurity suggests that she never fully recovered from the loss of her family and former world.

Helen's description leads me to believe that her mother had some narcissistic traits that affected her ability to be responsive as a mother. Rivka "needed to attach herself to a strong person who could give to her," according to her daughter. Helen also stated that Rivka never forgot a slight, which hints at her low self-esteem. Helen described the family her mother left behind in Europe in an idealized way, as warm and affectionate, full of humor, laughter, and joy. Helen must have received this idealized description from her mother. (Idealization often suggests narcissism.) Rivka also idealized her shtetl, seemingly overlooking a pogrom that affected extended family members.

Helen's father, Ray, had a life and accomplishments that were unusual for an immigrant. Ray came from an extremely Orthodox family in a shtetl near Rivka's. In 1911, at age seventeen, he emigrated to avoid the Russian army. According to Helen, Ray as a young man rebelled against his father's orthodoxy and rejected the narrow, closed life of very Orthodox Jews. As an adult he wanted to forget the difficulties of life in Eastern Europe, and Helen said he had "no interest in his past." Unlike his wife, he did not miss the Old Country.

Ray worked with a traveling carnival and then at the admissions booth of a traveling circus after his arrival in the U.S. An excellent salesman, he later "sold himself" as a suitor to Rivka. During the first couple of years of their marriage, Helen's parents struggled economically. Soon, however, her father started a retail business that became very successful.

Ray's success was related to his self-assurance, Helen said. Although he was uneducated and always retained a strong foreign accent, he was never self-conscious, and he "always seemed to know what he wanted." A "risk taker," he "forged ahead with confidence," according to his daughter. Yet Ray's success also meant he worked so hard in the store that he was not much of a presence at home. Helen was not close to him, and she felt there had been no time to confide in her father. Her mother, who enjoyed getting out of the house, also worked in the family business. Helen said that, during busy seasons at the store, her parents worked so many hours that "you didn't have parents." (The family always employed live-in help.)

Helen's family was well-off, and Ray was able to build a large house during her childhood. Later in life, her father on many occasions took his wife first class by boat to Europe and Palestine. Moreover, Ray was a fervent Zionist, and the family hosted Zionist meetings. According to Helen, in the late 1930s and early 1940s, her father smuggled guns to the *Haganah* (a paramilitary organization in Palestine).

Returning now to my understanding of Rivka's psychology and the consequences of her traumatic separation on her ability to be a nurturing mother to Helen, I note that Helen stated the following: when, as a young married woman of twenty-four, Rivka learned she was pregnant with Helen, she was "horrified."[24] The couple had little money, and new motherhood proved to be very difficult for Rivka. Furthermore, Helen said she did not get affection from her needy mother and that her mother did not meet her needs. As a child, Helen was never able to come home from school and tell Rivka what had happened to her there. Rather, her mother required that her children listen to *her* when they arrived home. This emotionally needy and narcissistic mother was unable to be empathically attuned to her daughter.

Ray's very Orthodox family in Eastern Europe. His father looks like a stern disciplinarian. In contrast to the photograph of Rivka's family, in which people are touching and the children are held, family members are stiff and do not touch one another. *Courtesy of the family of anonymous interviewee Helen.*

It appeared that, just as Rivka felt alone as a young woman living in New York City with extended family, so Helen felt alone as a child and adolescent living with her compromised mother and a father who was too busy. Rivka's inability to respond to the psychological needs of her own daughter led to a conflictual relationship with Helen, who said she fought with her mother "all the time" when she was growing up.[25] By the time Helen was fifteen, the dissension was so intense that her father took her to Palestine, where he had set up a household for his own parents. Helen stayed in Palestine for a year attending a boarding school.

Helen as an adult seemed to me to be insecurely attached, probably a result of her mother's difficulty with empathic attunement. Moreover, Helen, like her mother, seemed to have narcissistic traits. A discrepancy between the attractive surface she presented and reality, which was darker, characterized Helen's descriptions; from Helen's depiction, we assume that her mother communicated in a similar way. Examples of Helen's idealizations abounded in her interview. She repeatedly described her parents and her life growing up with them in a glowing manner. When asked about her earliest memories of childhood, Helen responded that she was "always surrounded by love"— she explained that she spent much time with a neighboring Portuguese family who adored her—and that she had a "very secure home."[26] These responses, of course, generally belie her statement that she did not get affection from her needy mother.

Helen repeatedly studded her descriptions of her mother with hyperbole. Her mother had "an incredible facility for language," "remarkable assets," "enormous energy," and "such ingenuity"; she also was a "wonderful story-teller." Thus Helen attempted to cover up the severe conflicts with her mother with a patina of graciousness. Describing holidays in her parents' home, she said, "Ours was a house so full of hospitality." Helen portrayed her father as "extremely generous," "extremely rapid at arithmetic," and, as mentioned above, a man who "forged ahead with confidence."

Helen presented herself as a charming woman who lived in a home full of beautiful objects, thus emphasizing the attractive exterior. Analogously— although she was raised by a woman damaged by her traumatic separation from her own family—Helen attempted to compensate for the deficiencies of her childhood by painting her parents and her early years in lovely tones.

An Unwilling Immigrant: A Daughter's Story

Like Elaine's and Helen's mothers, Frances's mother, although she arrived with her husband, also suffered a traumatic migration. Frances's mother moved to a German city several years before emigration; she deeply missed her sophisticated former life there. She seemed narcissistically vulnerable and never recovered from the intense pain of her losses. Her daughter suffered from her mother's lack of responsiveness.

Frances

Frances's parents, originally from Eastern Europe, emigrated from a large German city in 1921, and her mother, Anna, was lonely and miserable in New York. Moving to the U.S. was a wrenching transition for Anna. Frances herself was a "great disappointment" to her, and she received little nurturance from her homesick mother. During her interview, Frances, then in her eighties and retired from a career in the helping professions, was modestly dressed, task-focused, and detailed. Frances and her husband lived in a large downtown Brooklyn apartment; Frances had raised three children while working. Psychologically aware in many ways, she was sardonic and sometimes still angry in telling me the story of her unaffectionate mother.

Frances's parents, Anna and Louis, differed in social status, family backgrounds, and personality; they were mismatched from the beginning. Anna was beautiful, ambitious, and snobbish, while Louis, though intelligent, was an ordinary working man. Anna's family was secular and educated. Her mother was a medical professional and her father was learned, while Louis's father was an Orthodox grocer. They were from the same large Eastern European city, although Anna's family lived in a higher-status neighborhood.[27]

Louis intensely disliked his father's religiosity and rebelled against it; when young, he smoked on the Sabbath to annoy his father. After repeatedly running away from home as an adolescent, he made his way to a large German city, where he made a life as a skilled needle-worker. Anna spent time in Paris in her late teens and, when she returned home, opened a millinery shop. She met Louis later, when she traveled to his German city to buy millinery supplies. After they married and had a son, Anna joined Louis in Germany.

Frances saw her mother as "self-involved" and "pretentious." Anna boasted that her family had the first bathtub in their Eastern European city. She also had sophisticated friends there. Anti-Semitism was a darker side of her life in Eastern Europe. The gentiles hated the Jews there, said Frances, and both Anna and Anna's own mother found the anti-Semitism frightening and perhaps traumatic.

According to Frances, in Germany, which Anna saw as modern and sophisticated, she lived a "gay, cosmopolitan life," made friends, was happy, and had "great aspirations to the intelligentsia." She was also a successful businesswoman during her two years there. In 1921, however, Louis decided to follow his sister to the U.S. Anna, already almost thirty years old, did not want to emigrate. Not only was she frightened of going to America, about which she knew little, but she had close relationships with her sisters, who had remained in Eastern Europe. Moreover, she would not be joining any close relatives in the U.S., as Louis was. Unlike Anna, Louis saw emigration as an adventure; leaving Germany was a choice for Louis rather than the necessity that it was for most of the immigrants discussed here.[28] Anna, Louis, and their son lived briefly in the Midwestern city where Louis's sister lived, then proceeded to New York, where Louis had a better future in the needle-working industry.

Once they had immigrated, the easy-going and venturesome Louis did not look back on his past; he had left Europe behind, and whatever he achieved in America was fine with him. Anna, however, was miserable and depressed and, according to Frances, cried for five years after arriving. She missed her sisters and felt alienated and displaced. She experienced her new life in America as a loss, and she may have seen leaving Germany as a narcissistic blow. She felt that, in comparison to Germany, New York City was dirty and inferior culturally. Anna also found the Yiddish language spoken in the city to be "lower-class" and beneath her. She did not make friends, probably because her neighbors in New York were working-class individuals on whom she looked down. Also, according to Frances, Anna had "multiple complaints" about her husband, including that he was "satisfied with so little."

Frances noted that in reality Anna would have had more friends and higher social status had she remained in Germany; her parents' learning would have given her the status that she lacked in the U.S. She added, however, that her mother would have been unhappy anywhere, and Frances was probably correct in this assessment. Frances felt that her mother's "aggrieved sense of loss" was part of her self-involvement. But the difficult reality was that by immigrating, Anna lost the place she loved, her friends, proximity to family, and her middle-class status.

Anna's pronounced difficulty in adjusting to the U.S. may have been due to several factors (Lieblich, 1993). I hypothesize that she felt so deprived by the loss of the cultural and social sophistication of her adopted German home that she was neither able to give up her attachment to it, nor to find anything similar in the U.S. (Akhtar, 2011; Hoffman, 1999). The loss of her sophisticated European home entailed a very difficult-to-mend split between who she felt she was in Europe and who she felt she had become in New York. She could no longer be the "cosmopolite" aspiring to the "intelligentsia," and the consequent disruption to her self-continuity must have caused severe psychic stress. Anna mourned everything, not just her family and friends, but also, for instance, the attitudes toward artistic and intellectual culture she had left behind in Europe. In this context, Anna's prolonged depression is understandable; her loneliness and isolation would only have increased her desolation at what she had lost. Moreover, the fact that Anna's move to the U.S.

was not motivated by persecution gave her less motivation to adjust. Her apparent underlying narcissistic vulnerability and what Frances saw as a tendency toward depression left her even more susceptible to debilitating homesickness than other immigrants. It took Anna a very long time to accept that she would indeed be living in the U.S. and to bridge the split between her European and American identities.

In New York City, Anna and Louis struggled to make a living. Louis's needle-working business failed during the Depression, and the family did not recover economically until after the war, when they bought a "specialty" retail shop. Anna and Louis sacrificed economically to help both their children become professionals. Frances believed that her mother wanted her children to have a high social status.

Frances was born three years after her parents' arrival. When she was young, the family lived in an apartment in Brooklyn with her maternal grandmother—who came to America to care for Frances so her mother could work—and her mother's cousin Sarah.[29] Anna began working when Frances was three, and Frances felt her mother was "gone"; Anna worked six days a week and was in no hurry to come home. Frances described herself as the "original latchkey child" when she was in grade school, as her grandmother had begun to travel frequently then.

Frances felt largely ignored as a child; she stated that no one cared whether she was happy or unhappy. She received no hugs, kisses, or physical affection. In contrast to her blond, blue-eyed, attractive, and considerably older brother, not only was Frances plain looking, with "bad hair" that her mother disliked, but she was also so severely cross-eyed that she appeared impaired. She also resembled her father, which would have been one more reason for what, according to Frances, was her mother's "great disappointment" in her.

Frances experienced family relationships as painful. As a child, she viewed her beautiful working mother as a "fairy princess" and as inaccessible. Frances felt her brother was more important to and worshipped by the entire family. Frances also felt Anna used her for her own purposes. For example, she read precociously at age four, which gratified Anna, but she remembered being "smacked" when she made a mistake while reading. Anna later had Frances take piano lessons, which Frances viewed as an example of her mother's "phony values" and pretentiousness. Frances's father was generally fonder and more accepting of her; Louis "in a way favored her" rather than her brother.

Eventually, by writing a letter to a hospital clinic, Frances arranged on her own for surgery to correct her eyes. The clinic had a social worker help Frances, and she had the surgery as a charity case. Her father accompanied her for appointments about the surgery. Frances remarked that she was surprised that she was not at this point angry at her father for not having taken the initiative with her eyes.

When Frances was college-aged, her parents both lost siblings during the Holocaust; her mother's three adored sisters were all killed, as well as some young nieces or nephews. Although Anna did not talk to Frances about this, Frances imagined that her mother was "horrified."

My sense is that Frances was deeply wounded and probably quite damaged by her mother's disappointment in her and her appearance. Perhaps just as important is that, from Frances's description, it appears her mother was completely and strikingly unable to be empathic to her daughter. Even in Frances's adulthood, Anna remained critical. When Frances and her husband purchased a home, her mother was "horrified" and "aghast" that this was an old home. Anna, Frances said, had "no insight," and perhaps her mother was unable to even understand her effects on her daughter. Anna's conspicuous lack of empathy suggests her extreme narcissism.

Anna did not want to emigrate; however, because she was married, she had no choice but to follow her husband to America. Her feelings of uprootedness and loneliness must have been profoundly painful, and she must have seen her husband as the cause of her unwanted upheaval rather than as a support. Thus she would have had no one to turn to in processing her traumatic loss. Anna's narcissistic vulnerability might have made the normally deep insecurity associated with immigration almost unbearably destabilizing.

When Frances was born, Anna's underlying psychological difficulties and continuing preoccupation with her migration trauma would have compromised the attachment bond with her daughter. Like Helen's mother, Anna was unable to be nurturing. She seemed to have been interested in only what her child could do for her. As mentioned, Frances described her mother as having been "gone" when she was three years old and Anna began working; Anna, however, may have been emotionally unavailable to her daughter much earlier.

Anna's effect on Frances's development may have been somewhat offset by her father's accepting attitude and by the presence of her grandmother and her mother's cousin. As an adult, Frances was able to lead a life with some fulfillment. To some degree, she seemed able to recover psychologically. She married a man who was also her friend and had a career and three children. Though she stated that she did not make friends readily, she did have a few. She and her husband had done well economically.

Nevertheless, the profound and lasting effects of this damaged and wounding mother on Frances's personality are suggested by the fact that, so many years later, Frances continued to harbor what she recognized as very "negative feelings" toward her mother. Though she was aware of her mother's losses, and at some points during the interview she seemed to understand her mother's point of view, at other times she implied that her mother's unhappiness about immigration was an expression of her self-involvement. Frances remained understandably angry at her. Frances's inability to identify with her mother's experiences speaks in turn to her mother's marked lack of empathy for her.

Frances's interview was unusual because of her negative feelings about her mother. I both completely believed Frances and felt that I was able to understand the traumatic effects of Anna's migration. I also now wonder how others perceived this damaged and seemingly haughty woman.

In reality, Anna suffered a traumatic loss in migrating. Although she also had a significant underlying psychological vulnerability, the intense pain of immigration and loneliness, of losing her middle-class status, her family, and all that she loved, was real. Most likely, Frances was correct in saying her mother would have been unhappy anywhere. Moreover, the effects of Anna's traumatic migration were passed on intergenerationally to her daughter, Frances. Anna would have been more responsive to Frances, and Frances would have had a more satisfactory childhood, had Anna not had to leave everything she knew.

Nostalgia and Normal Homesickness: Two Daughters' Stories

Two other mothers, Susan's and Miriam's, missed the places from which they emigrated but were able to adjust normally to life in America. Susan's mother, who came with family as a child, was nostalgic about the shtetl life she had left; she escaped pogroms by emigrating. Miriam's mother emigrated from a Russian city as an adolescent; she came without close family members and was homesick and lonely when she first arrived. Both arrived before World War I, the first in 1907 and the second in 1911. I hypothesize that this is significant because—unlike for those who disavowed any sense of loss in the face of the inescapable trauma of the World War I years—it seems that their lives in the Old Country held something positive that they then lost.

Susan

Susan's mother, Raisa, emigrated with other family members. Her family's understandable nostalgia contrasts with Elaine's and Helen's mothers' traumatic loneliness, as well as Frances's mother's lasting misery. Susan was a widow in her eighties, a retired civil servant who was active and interested in culture. She was deferential and nervous about whether she could perform well enough during the interview, and she stated that she usually did not do this sort of thing. Despite this, she shared a great deal of information about her family's history; "I'm the repository" of all the family information, she explained. She dressed up for the interviews. Susan saw herself as unassertive. Although she participated in various cultural activities, she did not have many friends.

Susan's mother and aunt—who came from a background "a notch above poor"—lived in a farming village in Russia, where their family owned an inn. Susan's grandmother worked in the family's inn, her grandfather went to synagogue several times a day, and all family members helped in earning a living. The area was replete with anti-Semitism; this was encouraged by tales about the blood libel (see glossary), the accusation that Jews murdered Christian children to use their blood for ritual purposes. Local peasants routinely bullied the family and "roughed them up." Much worse, pogroms occurred. During one pogrom, Susan's aunt was seized and forced to dig trenches. Susan and her now deceased husband suspected that, during this pogrom, her aunt might have been raped. A second trauma was that, when Susan's mother was eight or nine, she survived a catastrophic cholera epidemic.

Despite all this, Susan's mother and aunt spoke about how their apples, bread, and potatoes tasted better in the "alte heim" (the old home). Susan associated her mother's and aunt's feelings of sadness and nostalgia with their longing for their youth when their parents were alive. Susan pointed out that, although conditions were indeed dire in Europe, there, in contrast to the tenements of New York City, they had space, fresh air, and food they had grown. Susan's mother and aunt also missed the closeness of family, who were able to spend so much more time together in Europe. There the members of the extended family lived in one small community, while in New York, they were scattered, some, for example, in Brooklyn and others in Washington Heights. Family members had to work six-and-one-half days per week.

According to Susan, her mother and aunt remembered "nothing joyous" about their childhoods in Eastern Europe. Life was pure drudgery, particularly for their mother's own mother, who was "so worn out." The family had included the children from two marriages, so many children that Susan did not know the exact number. During the cholera epidemic, eight or nine of the children perished, an unspeakable trauma.

Overall, Raisa did not speak much about her life as a child in the Old Country. She spoke about her reverence for her father, and sometimes, when helping to care for Susan's children, she described how a task was done back home.

The mild longing for home that Susan's mother and aunt felt may be seen as normal. This nostalgia for an idealized home, such a contrast to its actual drudgery and trauma, can be seen perhaps as a defense in the face of the hardship of life in America (Hoffman, 1999). Of course, idealizing one's former country is part of the immigrant's normal process of mourning. Susan's family saw the past as being radically different from the present and preserved it by making it mythically good. Interestingly, Susan and her sister reacted to this fantasy version of the past by becoming exasperated or angry when their mother and aunt spoke nostalgically about it. She pointed out that her mother remembered nothing joyous from her childhood, so why would she long for it? She wanted her mother to sever her ties to the Old Country, to become more American.

Susan's feelings demonstrate that immigrants' children were often unable to understand that their parents' sense of loss could coexist with their having survived pogroms, epidemics, and near-starvation. They wanted their parents to look forward, to forget the past with its brutality and loss.

Susan's parents had a marriage of convenience, and Susan felt sorry because of the hardship they endured in the U.S. Her parents ran a store and worked constantly, from morning to night. Raisa was timid, kind, always either caring for family or working in the store; even cooking for the family had to be done in the store. Her clothes, her manners, and her poor English marked her as very Old World, and she was uninterested in Americanizing— she did not read newspapers or vote.

Susan's father, Milt, was a lonely man, who came to the U.S. at age seventeen from a middle- or upper-middle-class family; they lived in a cosmopolitan Russian city. He was forced at first to do manual labor. More acculturated than Raisa before his arrival and more Americanized in later years, he loved opera, though he could not afford to hear it in the theater. A frustrated man and sometimes irritable, Milt was not close to his own family and had in fact been excluded from the family of his wealthier sister. He neither talked much in general nor talked to Susan. In his sixties and a heavy smoker, Milt became sick and was forced to close his store; he needed care in the Jewish Home for the Aged.

Susan's family worked so hard that they never sat down for a meal together; their apartment was just across the courtyard from their store, and they would constantly come and go from the apartment to the store. There was no time to attend synagogue. Their apartment was small, with the kitchen serving as a bedroom. The family had many hard times; Raisa endured both a stillbirth and the death of a child at age two. A son was born eight years before Susan and a daughter three years later. Susan's brother was not able to have a Bar Mitzvah celebration because Milt was then ill with pleurisy.

Susan's parents' marriage was conflictual. Her parents fought, and the two had different ideas. On Sunday afternoons and evenings, their only time off from working in their store, each went their separate ways, Milt often going to the movies and Raisa spending time with extended family.

Susan's story, rather than featuring migration trauma, demonstrates normal nostalgia for home. During childhood, however, Raisa witnessed devastating deaths during an epidemic; pogroms and persecution deeply affected her family. Yet, because Susan was not psychologically oriented, I could not assess whether the effects of her mother's evident trauma had been passed on. Susan *did* share with her mother an unassertive personality, but the fact that in her late eighties she was active and interested suggests her adaptability.

Susan's story highlights the journey of many immigrant families from Old World to America. Whatever energy her parents had left after meeting basic needs was focused on launching their children so that they could partake of the American Dream. Her parents prioritized education. While other families might have put Susan to work in the store—Susan and her sister only helped with deliveries—often her mother would tell Susan to read a book instead. It was a hardship to send Susan to college, even the free New York City college Susan attended, but sacrifices were made so that she could get a degree.

Susan did indeed succeed at being part of the American world. She married a lawyer after the war, and in 1950 gave birth to the first of two sons. When her older son was ten years old, she began a career in the public sector and retired thirty years later. She was a member of several Jewish organizations, and while not a member of a synagogue, she did attend services at times with family. She and her husband "were steeped in literature." At the time of her interview, Susan contributed to liberal organizations (organizations that "combat hate"); took courses, including some about opera and the Old Testament; and had traveled to various European destinations. Susan had moved light years away from her parents' Old World way of life; she was educated, culturally modern, and middle-class. While her mother longed for the slower life of the Old Country, Susan herself embraced New York life and fulfilled her parents' dream of success in America.

Miriam

Miriam's mother, Trudy, came to the U.S. in 1911 from a Russian city. Only sixteen, she traveled with a distant cousin, but once in New York City, she was alone. Miriam said her mother felt very lonely, unhappy, and homesick at first; she was also frightened and "probably isolated." Trudy had experienced middle-class life in Europe, and she felt life in the U.S. was primitive and very disappointing.

While Trudy's loneliness, homesickness, and fear were serious, they were temporary; Miriam's story about her mother is, in part, one of normal homesickness. Miriam's narrative also stood out because she portrayed Trudy as a determined and indomitable entrepreneur.

Miriam herself was an intelligent woman in her early eighties, a Yiddishist and a socialist who dressed plainly for the interview. She lived with her husband in a modest New Jersey house and had two successful children and several grandchildren. Although retired from her position in the public sector, she was still actively involved with her profession. She idealized others, particularly her mother, and spoke somewhat naively, without the perspective of what I might be thinking about how she portrayed herself and others. At the time of her first interview, Miriam was understandably upset because of a serious illness in her family. She also seemed disconnected from her feelings, which made it difficult to understand both her as a person and her relationship with her unusual mother. I wondered later whether her detachment might have masked unconscious negative feelings about her mother.

Miriam's mother was born into a poor family in a Russian shtetl. When Trudy was ten or eleven, she was sent because of economic necessity to live with a middle-class uncle in a cosmopolitan city; there she apprenticed as a seamstress.[30] Miriam reported that her mother loved her happy life in the city. She was befriended by one of her uncle's four sons, who took her to the opera and for walks down the grand boulevard. They rode sleighs in the snow, and later in life, she remembered the sounds of sleds traveling over snow. This beautiful though industrialized city had a sizable Jewish community, much of it assimilated, and a thriving cultural life. Trudy considered herself sophisticated, no mere shtetl girl; it upset her that a brother-in-law could not be convinced that she had known about opera houses and elevators before coming to New York.

Trudy often spoke about how she had enjoyed her life as a teenager in her Russian city. She also talked about her early life in a Russian shtetl. The family were very poor and dreaded pogroms; they were terrified of being taken from their homes. They also feared gypsies, who were thought to snatch small children.

When Trudy arrived in New York, she found a life of hardship. The Lower East Side was "dirty" and "filthy," and she did not like the "standard of living." She longed for her previous cultured life in Russia, and "she wanted to go home." In New York she worked in a sweatshop for a penny a piece and was forced to carry her own sewing machine to her job. Miriam emphasized the difficulty of her mother's life in New York. During her first months in the U.S., she was not only homesick but also very frightened and anxious. While riding the subway, she saw people moving their mouths; she was afraid to be near them as she thought they were sick, but found out later that they were in fact only chewing gum. When asked to wait in the lobby when first meeting the French woman with whom she later boarded, Trudy feared she would be sold to gypsies. Despite her difficulties, she did not go home but instead moved to Harlem, where living conditions were better than on the Lower East Side; she proved her adaptability.

After Trudy's initial homesickness and fear, she worked hard and had many friends. She attended dances and socialized in Central Park. Miriam reported that her mother was self-assured and competent; she was elected chairwoman of her union in the 1920s.

Miriam's account emphasized both Trudy's temporary homesickness and her lifelong nostalgia for her previous life in a sophisticated city. I noted, however, that while Miriam mentioned the loneliness that accompanied her homesickness, she did not specifically mention that Trudy missed family members from Eastern Europe. Thinking about this omission, I realized that, in fact, immigration to New York was her mother's second big move. She had left her own family behind in the shtetl several years before her departure for the U.S. I wondered whether, since Trudy probably had to suppress missing her parents and siblings as a child, she continued to do so after immigration to New York. In the book *Homesickness*, Matt (2011) wrote that the "ability to sever ties was often considered a prerequisite for success." Trudy was indeed a success. Some years after her arrival, Trudy brought her brother and sister to the U.S.; perhaps this was one reason that missing family members was omitted from Miriam's narrative.

Although homesick, Trudy had ambition and grit. She came to the U.S. to "make something of herself," to be rich, not just to escape anti-Semitism and pogroms. Trudy's enterprising nature, her reliance on her own wits, and her ability to subsume everything to her ambition made me see her as a venturer, a go-getter. As a young and middle-aged woman, Trudy worked extremely hard; she managed to earn enough that she was able to lend money to relatives who wanted to start businesses. She also set her husband up in business.[31] In fact, this domineering woman, who clearly "wore the pants" in the household, was disappointed that her husband did not "fulfill" her financial "dreams." As a middle-aged widow, Trudy bought a rooming house, and she employed her older daughter, six years Miriam's senior, as her bookkeeper; her two sons-in-law ran it. When she sold the rooming house, she bought an apartment house, and her sons-in-law both rented the apartments to others and completed all repairs. Although Trudy did eventually attain a middle-class life in the U.S.—recovering the middle-class life she had left in Eastern Europe—Miriam emphasized the continuing hardships of her mother's life.

Trudy had many ongoing worries, including caring for several family members whom she brought to the U.S. She assumed the role of mother to her brother, whom she referred to as "my Jake" and who was just sixteen when he arrived. Soon Jake was drafted into the army to fight in World War I. Later, in about 1931, Trudy brought her own mother and a niece to America and made sure they were fed when work was unavailable.

Miriam described her father, who like Trudy arrived in the U.S. as a teenager in about 1912, as sweet, gentle, and loving. He came from a very poor family in a small city in the Russian Empire. Miriam's father rarely spoke about his experiences in Eastern Europe. He worked variously as a locksmith, a draftsman, and an auto mechanic. Miriam said that, although her father worked hard, he was not aggressive about finding work.

During the Depression, Trudy worked, but her husband did not. Her parents' relationship was one of *Sturm und Drang*, according to Miriam. Trudy tended to dominate her husband; she was "the boss" who called the shots. Money was a primary source of conflict. Her mother yelled when she was worried about money, but her father did not yell back; he tried to keep the peace. Tragically, Miriam's father was hit by a trolley car and died when she was sixteen. Miriam said that she herself "fell apart" when her father was killed, while her mother "carried on."

Trudy was a woman of "extraordinary energy" and determination, according to Miriam. Despite Miriam's idealization of her mother, I believed her portrayal of Trudy as unique in her indefatigable drive to make money. She learned to drive a car when her husband worked in the auto repair business, highly unusual for a female immigrant. So that Miriam would be unashamed of her Jewish identity, despite the anti-Semitism of the times, Trudy enrolled her in a Yiddish program after school.

Miriam's account of Trudy as the "boss" mother suggests she used people in her game plan of making money and creating an American life. Miriam said her mother "used her" and her sister "differently." Trudy chose Miriam to become a professional, but her considerably older sister was not given the same advantages. Her sister remained working-class, employed by their mother as her bookkeeper. She neither went to college nor had the same amount of money as an adult that Miriam did. Indeed, her sister envied Miriam.

Trudy's attitude toward motherhood seemed to be one of duty rather than warmth. She did not hug or kiss Miriam as a child and, as a mother of young children, came home from work and reluctantly cooked, boiled diapers, and cleaned. As Miriam grew up, Trudy did not teach her how to cook or sew, as she wanted Miriam instead to "have a profession." Both mother and daughter preferred the world of work to the role of nurturer.

Although Miriam talked about how her mother "used her" seemingly without resentment, underneath I believed her attitude toward Trudy was ambivalent. Her mixed feelings and her mother's high-handedness are evident in an incident from Miriam's adolescence. When she was fifteen and a half, her high school graduation coincided with the approach of her sister's wedding, and because of the wedding, Miriam's graduation was treated as of no importance. Miriam said she felt ignored and angry.

Trudy used relationships to fulfill the purposes of economic necessity because of her history and also because of her anxious determination never again to be poor. At the age of ten or eleven, as a matter of economic necessity, Trudy was sent to the city as an apprentice, and she perhaps suppressed her feelings toward the family she left in the shtetl. From Miriam's description of her mother's migration to the U.S.—when her mother expressed homesickness for the place rather than the people she had left—it is possible that she may have again valued economic needs over attachments to others. For Trudy, there was no choice but to subordinate attachment needs to economic necessity, to her need and desire to make money, to be ambitious. Yet economic necessity had its own psychological consequences. It appears that Trudy's husband and her daughters suffered emotionally because of the actions of this domineering and economically successful immigrant.

Despite the way Trudy bossed others around, this family was not without affection. They were affected by the traumas of poverty, fear, and migration and by the reality of having to "make it" economically. This meant that familial love came along with ideas about how each family member should be "utilized," which was not unusual. What seemed out of the ordinary, however, was Miriam's way of talking about it. When she said that her mother "used us differently" (referring to her and her sister), she did so without comment.

Trudy was a determined and dominant entrepreneur, who, in Miriam's words, "made it here for everybody." Miriam idealized her mother as a "pioneer woman" and stated that she didn't know that she could have accomplished what her mother did. She also sympathized with Trudy. When the "going was tough," her mother was "frustrated," and Miriam added that Trudy "carried a heavy load," never had security, and worked very hard even in later life. But I believe that, although during the interview Miriam rarely expressed negative feelings toward Trudy, she also resented the mother who bossed others around with little regard for their feelings.

Trudy was lonely, homesick, and sometimes frightened when she first arrived in New York; she suffered from normal homesickness. Although she was alone in the U.S., she was able to adapt. This unusual woman worked hard, giving her younger daughter a ticket to a successful American middle-class life.

Normal Homesickness or Nostalgia

A couple of other interviewees knew that a parent had feelings about missing their homes or families in Eastern Europe (for these people, loss was not a major theme). These parents, for instance David's and Dorothy's mothers, seemed to have eventually adjusted well to life in America; both of them experienced real trauma in Eastern Europe. As we know, immigration inevitably entails mourning, and the solution to a migrant's pain is in reaching the point at which ambivalence is tolerable and normal. It appears that these interviewees' parents in their own ways were able to tolerate ambivalent emotions about home. While I believe doing this was not unusual, the integration of such feelings was not usually described by my interviewees.

FATHERS WHO ARRIVED ALONE:
A DAUGHTER'S AND A SON'S STORIES

The fathers of my interviewees rarely spoke directly about their emotions, and consequently, the narratives of loss and homesickness presented above have been mothers' stories. Nevertheless, some immigrants' children were aware of their fathers' feelings of loss. Seymour, for example, discussed in chapter 2, believed that his father very much missed his family. Two additional interviewees knew that their fathers suffered profoundly after leaving their entire families in Europe. Norman's father had an unusual history, and Louise's father's story of the loss of his family was both traumatic and heartbreaking. I will write briefly about these two interviewees and their fathers; fuller versions of their stories will be presented in the next chapter.

Louise

The tragic story of Beryl and his family, as told by his daughter Louise, combines that of his emigration in 1921 or 1922 with a Holocaust narrative. Louise herself was an intelligent, energetic, and sensitive professional in her seventies who had a successful career and an advanced degree. Louise had, over the course of her life, devoted significant energy to healing her parents, both of whom passed on their trauma to her. She was insightful about the psychological impact they had had on her. Louise inferred that her father, Beryl, missed his family profoundly after he emigrated from a Russian shtetl, although he did not speak directly about his loneliness.

Beryl was the oldest child and the only son in a poor family of six children; he was the only one to emigrate, and he did so to avoid the draft. He traveled alone at about age nineteen to New York, where an uncle and other extended family members lived. Before arriving at the boat that took him to the U.S., Beryl experienced loneliness that turned unbearable, according to Louise. He decided to kill himself and thought he could do so by failing to follow the Jewish commandment to put on *tefillin*, the prayer-filled black boxes with which all religious Jewish males pray each morning. Of course, his suicide attempt did not succeed, but the incident suggests both the depth of his ties to his family and his lack of readiness to leave his relatives.

Part of Beryl's migration history is that his own father had emigrated to Boston when Beryl was a boy of two (in about 1904). However, by the time his father sent for the rest of the family, one of Beryl's sisters had developed trachoma, and consequently, the family was unable to join their father.[32] Subsequently, Beryl's father returned home to his family in Eastern Europe.

According to Louise, Beryl rarely spoke about his life at home in Eastern Europe for fear he would cry. Two stories he did tell suggest that his own father was quite strict, perhaps even punitive. Beryl was very musical, and his mother somehow obtained a violin for him; his father then proceeded to break the instrument, as "a Yeshiva boy shouldn't have a violin." The second story contains his father's reaction to secularization. One day, Beryl was studying at home from a large Talmud (the collection of Jewish law and tradition), while hidden inside the Talmud was a book by the Russian author Turgenev. When his father discovered the Turgenev, he beat Beryl.[33] Despite his father's seeming strictness, Louise said that when Beryl spoke about his family in Eastern Europe, he did so with "enormous love and yearning." She believed that, because he was a loving man, he was probably loved as a child and had a loving family. It is likely that Louise's unambiguous view of her father's family was her own idealization.

Beryl corresponded with family members until the late 1930s, sending them a photograph of Louise as a baby in 1936. In the late 1930s, he sent them money to pay for a photograph of themselves, and sadly the image he received from them in return was one of "starving people." The tragedy of Beryl's story is that not a single member of his family survived the Holocaust.

Louise was five years old at the start of World War II, and she remembered that every Sunday her father took her along to see newsreels of the Russian army. He scanned each one hoping to see pictures of his family. "He was always looking and looking for his family," she said. Moreover, Louise remembered that one year at a Passover Seder her father said to her and her mother, "You're all I have." Her father's sense of loss "overshadowed everything" during her childhood. Louise noted that on her father's side "it was as though she was the child of Holocaust survivors."

Louise said her father lived with a "palpable" depression. He functioned well and was "never a sad sack," however; he was tender toward Louise and composed funny poems for her and her cousins. Louise speculated about whether her father's depression was due to the traumatic separation from his family or, alternatively, was related to a genetic predisposition. My assumption is that both were contributing factors. It is possible that the influence of the severe form of Judaism favored by Beryl's father aggravated any underlying depression.[34] The trauma of losing his family in the Holocaust surely also added to his depression.

Although Beryl was intelligent, he lacked self-confidence. He was a store-keeper and provided well for his family, but he would rather have had a different career; his attitude toward this was one of resignation, not frustration. His wife was more severely traumatized than he, and he behaved protectively toward her. Louise dealt with her parents' legacy of loss and trauma in several ways. She said many aspects of her life concerned healing them; one way in which she did so was to become a successful, high-achieving professional, an option not open to her immigrant parents. She also tried to entertain and enliven her parents. We cannot know whether Beryl would have recovered from missing his family had they not been killed in the Holocaust. We can surmise, however, that being cut off from family by an involuntary immigration would have had profound effects for this probably vulnerable man.

Norman

Norman's father's story, like Beryl's, is about a man who came to the U.S. alone, deeply missed his family, and suffered from depression. He only occasionally spoke directly about missing his family, yet his emotional instability had a profound effect on the family he formed in the U.S. Norman himself was an intelligent, talkative, active, working professional in his eighties who seemed generous and open. His interview had an obsessional style, which suggested underlying anxiety. Norman seemed emotionally out of touch with the difficulties of his own life as a child.

Norman's father, Abe, came to the U.S. in 1907 from a very isolated, tiny village in Russia containing only a few families. Abe, born in 1885, was one of five or six children from a very poor family; one of his brothers was blind. His family farmed, and Abe talked to Norman about having enjoyed farm work such as milking cows. Abe recalled that as a boy he had been caught on a road in a blizzard and had huddled together with his big dog, whom he credited with saving his life. The family lived in this isolated village because Abe's own father had been asked, due to his unconventional religious ideas, to leave his Eastern European shtetl. He was a freethinker (dissenter).

Because he did not like the constricted way of life in his village, at age sixteen or seventeen Abe ran away from home, landing in England; he had "wanted to see the world." After a year away, he returned to Russia because his family "implored" him to do so. He could not remain, however, because of the Russian draft, and after several years, he immigrated to America. Unbeknownst to Abe, the boat he took from Bremerhaven was not bound for New York, and he must have been astounded when it docked in Galveston, Texas.[35] There, someone said, "Hey, Sam, can you ride a horse?" (he indeed knew how to ride from his farming childhood). Thus Abe became a cowboy called Sam, and for eight years he herded cattle, mended fences, and worked as a day laborer in winter. Norman believed his father was homesick and lonely during these years, although Abe did not say so directly. Abe knew no Jews in Texas, and he finally decided to move east, where he had wealthy relatives in New Jersey. These relatives, however, rejected Abe, who was uneducated and perhaps unmannered. Abe then developed his own business, using a horse and wagon to deliver eggs, cheese, and butter to small groceries and individuals.

Soon Abe, who was secular, married a more traditional Jewish woman; both were in their thirties and lonely people. After two miscarriages and a stillbirth, Norman's mother gave birth to a son who tragically died at age eleven months. Abe became so distraught and depressed after the baby's death that his wife had to accompany him on his delivery rounds; she was afraid he might kill himself. The baby's death triggered a collapse from which Abe seemed never to recover; he sold his delivery route as his depression continued, and afterward he always struggled to make a living. Abe and his wife had two more children who survived, Norman and—three-and-a-half years later—a daughter. Abe worked at various jobs to earn money, including painting houses.

Abe's depression seemed connected to loss. The death of his baby son was a traumatic loss, which must have been all the more painful because his wife had already suffered a stillbirth. The baby's death also echoed the loss of Abe's family, whom he had had to leave behind so many years before. Abe spoke about his family occasionally, and each time he did so was "with sadness"; "he always longed to see them." Norman added that when talking about his family, Abe would "get into a longing to see them again." Maybe he would go back to see them, or they would come to America, he would say. Abe and his family in Russia exchanged letters, but they did so infrequently; because he functioned so poorly, he could only afford the price of postage for a letter perhaps once a year. Abe occasionally sent his family money, but he did not have much to send them.

Abe suffered a second loss in the mid-1930s, when Norman and his sister were still children. Abe received a letter informing him of his father's death, and he was "uncontrollable with grief." At that time, Norman, his sister, and his mother spent days trying to stop Abe from crying.

The story of the rest of Abe's family ended tragically. After World War II, Abe received no news from his siblings, and he never found out how they died, although the family made attempts to do so. They assumed that Abe's siblings and their families died from starvation. It is more likely, however, that they were killed in the Holocaust.

Abe's family truly suffered because of his inability to make a living. His wife gave birth to his daughter at home and unassisted. This daughter, Norman's sister, never saw a doctor until she was thirteen years old. Moreover, Norman and his sister attended school when they were sick with fevers because their home was unheated in winter. For two years, the family lived without electricity because they didn't have the twelve dollars it would have cost to have it turned back on. By the time he was fourteen, Norman was supporting the family.

From Norman's description, I gathered that Abe was not continually depressed. He enjoyed spending time with family and friends and "loved to talk" about being a cowboy. That Abe was consistently unable to make a living well before the Depression began, however, suggests that his economic difficulties were associated with his emotional instability. Norman's de-

scriptions led me to believe that his father, Abe, was at times very psychologically compromised. He may have had a genetic predisposition to major
depression. Like Helen's and Elaine's mothers and Louise's father, Abe
arrived in the U.S. alone, and like them, he seemed to have been deeply
affected by having been cut off from his family. Immigration increases the
risk of psychological illness and—although we cannot know with certainty
the roots of Abe's depression—we can assume that being cut off from home
and family deeply influenced this vulnerable man.

Norman seemed out of touch with his own needs. Interestingly, although
his childhood was truly deprived, he said he had felt loved and secure when
young; this will be discussed in the following chapter. As an adolescent and
young adult, Norman attempted to repair his parents by giving them financially what they had been unable to provide for themselves.

CONCLUSIONS: THE GRIEF AND TRAUMA OF IMMIGRATION—ITS EFFECTS ON PARENTS AND ADULT CHILDREN

Because of persecution, poverty, and pogroms, a "stunning one third" of
Eastern European Jews migrated between the 1880s and 1924; most chose
America as their destination (Sorin, 1992, p. xv). Whether an individual felt
that emigration was a choice or a necessity, making the transition to life in
America was very difficult and migration generally involved massive loss.
Because many Jews believed that there was no future for them in Eastern
Europe, this "great migration" (Zahra, 2016) was necessary; it meant not
only loss but also grief and, in many cases, trauma for individuals.

Each of the immigrants weathered the "staggering" psychological experience of adjusting to America, of reconciling his European identity with his
new American ideals and culture (Ravage, 1917). So many aspects of life
were different in the United States. As we have seen, new immigrants were
often confused and frightened, and it was common to feel displaced and
homesick in the new and alien environment. In America, not only was there a
new language to learn, but there were also new values to which one must
adjust. The Old World of tradition and religion seemed turned on its head.
Living conditions were often deplorable, and immigrants felt deprived of
light, air, and the natural world. Most immigrants were young, and many felt
the lack of anyone who could guide them. Many people were even poorer in
America than they had been in Eastern Europe. Feeling homesick and displaced in an alien environment was psychologically destabilizing; psychological suffering was a frequent companion during the transition from Eastern Europe to America.

Homesickness was real and potent for many Eastern European Jewish
immigrants, and its miseries could be all encompassing. Even those who

hated many aspects of life in the Old Country might experience powerful homesickness, and we know that some who were well aware of renewed anti-Semitic violence at home might, nevertheless, try to return (Matt, 2011; Sarna, 1981). Several mothers expressed nostalgia (less intense than homesickness) for the Old Country despite having suffered terribly there. Susan's mother lost many siblings in a cholera epidemic and remembered life in Eastern Europe as full of drudgery, yet she missed the food and the closeness of family life there.

Homesickness for most was temporary (Matt, 2011). For instance, Miriam's mother, who missed the cosmopolitan life she shared with cousins in a Russian city, adapted after an intensely unhappy period. Yet sometimes the longing to see one's home might persist throughout one's life. The magnitude of loneliness and loss seemed to differ between those who came to the U.S. alone and those who came with or to join close family members already here. As the accounts of Elaine, Helen, Louise, and Norman show us, those who came alone might have experienced persistent loneliness and loss from which they were unable to recover.

People seemed truly pained as they adjusted to incomprehensible American values. My maternal grandmother, reunited with her father in America after many years, was crestfallen to find that he had shaved off his beard. Not only was she very disappointed to feel that he was unrecognizable, but a beardless man was no longer religious, and seeing that was a terrible shock to her and to many new arrivals. To feel that you had come to a world in which everybody was for himself, that the old framework of mutual aid had collapsed, must have provoked insecurity and anxiety in new immigrants. In Eastern Europe, status was extremely important, and a central aspect of status was religious learning; to realize, as the character in Asch's "Alone in a Strange World" did, that he was a respected scholar at home but a tailor to be pitied in America, must have been painful indeed. Probably many were truly chagrined to find themselves working in sweatshops. The shame and desperation of poverty drove a few to suicide.

Boulanger likens the psychological distress of migration to the "violence of being torn up by the roots" (2004, p. 354). An important perspective on why migration is so destabilizing is provided by the research of van Ecke, Chope, and Emmelkamp (2005). They remind us that migration couples major separation and permanent loss with a period of time during which all relationships and life structures change simultaneously. Moreover, immigrants must cope with the "loss of familiar ways, sounds, and faces" and, in addition, with the problem of "not knowing quite how to belong, connect, and get support" in the new environment (van Ecke, 2007, p. 22). Because these pose radical challenges to the psyche, immigration increases the individual's risk of psychological disorder and, in particular, of depression (Angel, Buckley, & Sakamoto, 2001; Grinberg, 1978, as cited in Akhtar, 2011; Hollander, 2006).

As mentioned, the Eastern European Jewish migration more often included families who emigrated together than did other European groups (e.g., Howe, 1976, p. 58). Indeed, about 30 percent of the parents of those I interviewed emigrated with their own parents when they were older children or teenagers.[36] Nevertheless, this migration was also overwhelmingly a movement of young people. Many of these young people, including half of my interviewees' parents, had left their own parents in Eastern Europe (e.g., Howe, 1976, p. 58). Both because so many of the immigrants were separated permanently from their parents and also because—of the parents of my interviewees who migrated alone—many were deeply affected by having done so, I began to ask: what are the effects on the immigrant psyche of permanent separation from parents and others on whom the individual depends?

A study of the effects of contemporary immigration to the U.S. on attachment status suggests that being cut off from one's home environment and family of origin in itself "constitute[s] an attachment-related risk" (van Ecke et al., 2005, p. 671). Specifically, it is the ongoing loss and separation inherent in immigration that prove problematic. Compared to a control group of non-immigrants, a significantly higher proportion of middle-class, largely Caucasian immigrants who had been in the U.S. for many years were classified as unresolved for attachment.[37] Unresolved attachment is the adult version of childhood disorganized attachment.

Immigration eventually entails "grief and even trauma," whether it is voluntary or not, wrote van Ecke et al. (2005). In the course of speaking professionally and personally with many contemporary immigrants, van Ecke herself (2007, pp. 16–17) realized that even many of those who had wanted to move to the U.S. felt years after immigration that they had "not adequately considered the emotional consequences" of living "out their lives" far away from their families at home. She noted the longing that immigrants felt when births occurred in their absence and the grief they endured when family members died and they had been unable to say goodbye. Many years after their arrivals, these voluntary immigrants found it difficult to live far away from family and friends, even with the ability to e-mail, telephone, and travel to the home country. In contrast, except for the occasional letter, neither voluntary nor involuntary immigrants of one hundred years ago could have regular contact with home; consequently, many must have experienced immense loss. As we have seen, Helen's mother, whose migration was involuntary, seemed permanently psychologically distressed by the separation from her family. How might Seymour's father—who left without really having had a chance to say goodbye because he feared the retaliation of the Cossacks—have felt many years later?[38]

The permanent separation from their own parents and other attachment figures was one of the losses faced by many Eastern European Jewish immigrants. As mentioned, about half of the parents of those I interviewed were separated from their own parents by emigration; a few were able to bring family members to the U.S. years after they themselves arrived. We need to remember that all humans need relationships with those whom they can lean upon, look up to, or admire. If the parental and grandparental generations cannot be easily contacted, the individual will suffer. Moreover, one parental function is to hold and keep in mind representations of their children, and even adult children need to be held in mind in this way. What happens to the immigrant when he knows that he will never again see the parent who holds him in mind? Van Ecke et al.'s (2005) research suggests that, for many people, the permanent separation from and loss of parents, siblings, and spouses is very painful and may lead to lack of trust, feelings of abandonment, or a degree of helplessness.

Because I did not interview the immigrants themselves, I can only speculate about how lack of trust, abandonment, or helplessness might have affected the parents of my interviewees. I suggest that Louise's and Norman's fathers' depressions were in part associated with the damage caused by their separation from parents and siblings. To experience chronic helplessness after immigration—as Elaine's, Helen's, and Frances's mothers and Louise's and Norman's fathers may have—is surely debilitating.

Experiences of loss, grief, and trauma varied widely among immigrants. Those who were separated from their own parents constitute one category of immigrants. Another category among the parents of my interviewees were those who came as older children or young adolescents with their mothers and siblings; most often they joined their fathers who were already in America. Despite the trauma that most of them experienced in Eastern Europe, many of these young immigrants—like Barbara's parents and David's father—seemed happy to be in America. In general, in many ways immigration proved easier for the young than it did for those whose lives were already established in Eastern Europe.

For those who experienced the losses of migration itself as traumatic—Elaine's, Helen's, and Frances's mothers and probably also Louise's and Norman's fathers—the trauma was passed on intergenerationally. Frances's and Helen's mothers were too preoccupied with their own losses to be emotionally present for their daughters, and Elaine was burdened with her mother's profound sadness and loneliness. Just as migration trauma differs in type from the trauma caused by violence, persecution, or extreme poverty, so the quality of what was passed on intergenerationally in the two types of trauma differs. A parent's ability to be empathically attuned to her child is affected in both types of trauma; however, uncanny repetitions seem absent from transmitted migration trauma.

According to van Ecke et al.'s (2005) study, immigrants more often have unresolved attachment styles. While individual parent-child relationships varied between my interviewees and their parents, parents with unresolved attachment styles would probably have been unable to help their children to fully trust others. These parents remained preoccupied with their own losses. In addition, they had to cope with the difficult tasks of economic survival in America, and therefore they were doubly unable to optimally respond to the needs of their children as individuals.

Several of my interviewees were aware of their parents' pervasive sense of loss and grief around immigration. What must it have been like for Elaine's mother to realize that she would never again live near the family which she once thought would join her? Louise's father had no choice but to emigrate to avoid conscription, and he felt suicidally depressed shortly after leaving his shtetl. Many of the parents described in this chapter probably had pre-existing psychological vulnerabilities, and they experienced the enforced separation of emigration as traumatic.

As mentioned, of my interviewees' parents, those who came alone had a more difficult time than those who came with or to join family. Five of the seven immigrant parents described in depth in this chapter emigrated alone. Elaine's, Helen's and Frances's mothers experienced debilitating loss or homesickness. Moreover, Louise's and Norman's fathers, who seemed to miss their families tremendously, suffered from depression. It appears that, as men, it was more difficult for them to speak directly about missing their families. As we have seen, the permanent separation and loss of immigration can have lasting psychological consequences.

Social status may have played a role in immigrants' adjustment. Helen's, Frances's, and Miriam's mothers had been middle class in Eastern Europe and were working class when they arrived in America. As status was very important in Eastern Europe, a loss in status might be destabilizing. In addition, those who were more financially comfortable in the Old Country, in contrast to those who were extremely poor, gave up something significant in coming to America, where they struggled economically.

An important distinction here is the experience of World War I. It separates many of the parents of those profiled in this chapter from most of those who were discussed in chapters 1 and 2. The parents of Helen, Susan, Miriam, and Norman, who missed the Old Country or their families, arrived before the trauma of World War I and its aftermath. For some immigrants who arrived before World War I—for example, Helen's and Miriam's mothers—they left an existing culture that they could miss. Much of the Eastern European Jewish world was in ruins and chaos after World War I. Importantly, one aspect of this historical phenomenon is related to the children's perceptions. The children of those who arrived after World War I and its after-math reacted to the trauma of their parents' pre-emigration lives and very often said, "They left it all behind." Rarely could my interviewees accept that their parents were homesick if they came after the horror of World War I. Thus the children's perceptions of their parents' trauma and loss were an important factor in how they interpreted the losses of immigration.

We know from secondary sources, as well as from letters to the "Bintel Brief," that homesickness was both normal and widespread among the Eastern European Jewish immigrants. Nevertheless, as discussed in chapter 1, the denial of loss was an important phenomenon. Here, as we now understand the losses better, we can discuss the denial of loss from a somewhat different perspective.

In the early years after arrival, the "business at hand" for the immigrant was fitting into the new culture (Boulanger, 2004, p. 355). This was one reason why immigrants themselves could not allow themselves to feel home-sick. They feared being overwhelmed and, therefore, unable to "forge ahead" on the difficult road to success in America. Parents' own denial of loss—frequent in the families of my interviewees—was, of course, an important phenomenon. Another reason why the losses of immigration were so often unacknowledged was, I believe, that migration was so common.[39] That is, as the experience was not unusual, many people would have felt that coping with migration should be a matter of course.

Only some of my interviewees knew about their parents' homesickness or nostalgia. Why was so much information about missing family and the Old Country itself lost between the generations? As we saw in Susan's story, the immigrant's children often found it difficult to understand that parents might have missed Eastern Europe when many had also survived pogroms, perse-cution, epidemics, or near-starvation. Consequently, it was natural for the children to deny parents' losses and instead to assert that they had lost little in leaving the Old Country.

Underneath children's belief that their parents missed little was the knowledge that immigration of necessity involves a complex web of gains and losses. Thus one of the difficult and painful psychological realities that immigrants' children must have experienced was the ambiguity of their par-ents' losses. Many immigrants felt the pain of leaving their families but had to do so for survival. Others missed the countryside, where they had light and air, but hated the persecution of life in Eastern Europe. The economic real-ities of life in Eastern Europe were such that, even in the absence of danger-ous anti-Semitism, most of the immigrants felt that they had to leave their homes.

Specifically, Elaine's mother missed her family intensely, but in actuality she needed to leave behind the anti-Semitism and hated economic struggle of life in Eastern Europe. Susan's mother's experience was somewhat different.

She was nostalgic for her previous life, but her daughter reflected that the reality of that life—with its drudgery, epidemics, and pogroms—was indeed terrible. Miriam's mother mourned her middle-class life in Eastern Europe, but there was little future for her in the Old Country; her losses were essential for her to build a new life for herself and her family in America.

Fathers often had to leave Eastern Europe to avoid conscription—Jews were brutally treated in the Russian army. The ambiguity of Helen's mother's loss, as Helen told it, was particularly poignant: she missed the family she was cut off from and whom she expected to rejoin. Had she returned, however, she would have died in the Holocaust along with all those members of her family who had not moved to Israel.

Because the losses of immigration were painful, it served a defensive function for the immigrants' children to deny their parents' losses. Moreover, because so many aspects of the Eastern European Jewish immigration were involuntary, it served a defensive function for the immigrants themselves to deny a feeling of loss. Because they *needed* to leave, it was less painful to devalue the Old Country, to say metaphorically, "I don't want to go home again."

Another related way of looking at the children's denial of their parents' losses involves their inability to see their parents' ambivalence toward the Old Country. To be able to tolerate ambivalence about the country one left is both normal and a developmental achievement. Parents left not only persecution but also friends, family, language, and cherished foods. I suspect that many of the immigrants themselves were aware of their own ambivalence toward their old homes. This actually complex attitude, however, may not have been passed on by immigrants to their children. Those parents who articulated to themselves their destabilizing feelings of confusion, disorganization, or pain may have wished to keep such feelings to themselves. Yet there were a small number, for instance, Susan's and David's mothers, who communicated their feelings of nostalgia to their children.

One final reason that parents did not pass on their feelings of loss to their children was the language barrier. Yiddish was a very different language from English, and emotions formed in Yiddish might not have translated easily into English. Often immigrants' children did not speak their parents' Yiddish, sometimes because their parents deliberately spoke English to them.

Immigrant parents' emotions about migration tended to be in reality mixed and complex. They might feel nostalgia at one moment yet hate the Old Country the next. And, as we have seen, even some who had experienced significant trauma might at times feel nostalgia or ambivalence. My maternal grandmother was one of these. Her nostalgia is illustrated in a story she told me about ten years before her death. My grandmother, then a teenager, had been forced to leave her Russian city during World War I, and she experienced serious trauma at that time, including the deaths of several family members. At the time in her life that she told me this story, my grandmother, a good cook, consistently burned small desserts; she called them cheese-cakes. One day, while serving the desserts, she said:

> There is a reason that I burn the cheesecakes. When we [she and other family members] returned to our city after World War I, much of the city was rubble, and when we were lucky enough to have food, we were forced to cook over an open fire. The burnt flavor of the cheesecakes reminds me of that time.

She meant both that she was reminded of being able to eat after having been hungry and that she had a bit of fondness for that time. My grandmother had never once spoken of missing Eastern Europe. Yet this story illustrates nostalgia for a time of overall devastation. The denial of loss was wide-spread, and there was good reason for it; yet underneath this disavowal, complex and ambivalent emotions were common.

NOTES

1. The folk song, which is translated from Yiddish, continues:

Now my parents plead with me to come home,
And I am ashamed to return.
A fire burns in my heart,
As I long for my beloved mother.

2. "Homesick Russian Jews: Refugees Who Yearn for the Land of Persecution," *Dallas Morning News*, March 10, 1906. The United Hebrew Charities organization, among other charities, actually paid Eastern European Jews' return tickets so that immigrants would not become a financial burden for the Jewish community (Matt, 2011; Sarna, 1981).

3. Men weren't allowed to be homesick, whereas women were (Matt, 2011).

4. Sholem Asch arrived in the U.S. in 1909.

5. As noted by historians and sociologists, because stories such as Asch's were written by immigrants themselves, the information they provide about subjective perceptions of immigrant life are valuable (Cohen, 1972). Gittleman, however, notes that Asch's stories tend to be "deliberately overdrawn" (1978, p. 136). Because it is likely that literary impressions of displacement and homesickness draw on immigrant authors' own experiences, I provide the authors' dates of migration in endnotes. Moreover, in writing about the transition to life in America, I use sources that detail economic and living conditions for Jews new to America in the years 1880 to 1920; these sources are sometimes vague about precisely to which years during this forty-year span they refer. Therefore, I attempt, where possible, to be more specific about dates, and I usually include this information in endnotes.

6. Sarna's (1981, p. 265) carefully researched article, which lists a prime cause of return migration as the "inability to find work," uses the inclusive dates 1881 to 1914.

7. Matt (2011, p. 152) wrote, "To many, it was a shock that they might have enjoyed a higher standard of living in their homelands than in the United States, reputed to be so wealthy." This was true for Jewish and non-Jewish immigrants alike.

8. According to Howe (1976), poverty among the immigrant Jews was at its worst in the depression of 1893. Because economic conditions in America generally began to slowly im-

prove between 1898 and 1904, immigrants "found it easier to get work" (p. 120). "In the years between 1890 and 1914, there was a very slow rise in standards of living" (p. 145).

9. Marcus Ravage, an immigrant from Rumania who arrived in the U.S. in December 1900, wrote a 1917 memoir from which this quoatation was taken. He became a successful writer and public intellectual.

10. Leon Kobrin, author of "The Tenement House," arrived in the U.S. in 1892.

11. Fictional depictions of the tenements are supported by such well-researched historical accounts as Rischin's (1970, p. 82), which refers to their "foul smells" and darkness, and Sorin's (1992). In 1901, additional construction of the dark, unventilated "dumbell" tenements (so called because of the shape of their floorplans) was prohibited (Rischin, 1970). Landlords were slow to apply this new law, however, and as late as 1908, "300,000 dark, unventiliated interior rooms" remained on the Lower East Side (Sorin, 1992, p. 73).

12. Crowding on the Lower East Side was a very serious problem. In 1910, the Lower East Side reached its peak level of congestion (Rischin, 1970, p. 93); however, immigrant Jews had earlier begun to move to other parts of the ctiy, and by 1916 only 23 percent of the city's Jews lived there: they had moved to Harlem, the Bronx, Williamsburg, or Brownsville in Brooklyn (Moore, 1981).

13. Some authors would qualify this statement. Rischin (1970, p. 175) writes that in Eastern Europe "economic individualism" coexisted with "social and religious cooperation." In addition, Cowan & Cowan (1996) write about the entrepreneurial skills that some Jews developed in nineteenth-century Europe.

14. The author Chaver Paver arrived in the U.S. in 1923.

15. The poverty in Eastern Europe caused many Jews to move to cities in the hope of finding work. Young Jewish people were most likely to do so. (For example, my grandmother was told by her father to move to Vienna; she had to lie to her father because he wanted her to have a white glove job, and she was only able to find factory work. She was able to move with her much loved sister.) As we know from Sholem Aleichem's story about Tevye the Dairyman, however, even in the shtetl, new ideas had begun to infiltrate that affected behavior and family life.

16. The "historical, anecdotal, and memoir literature supports the conclusion that in the years between 1890 and 1914 there occurred among immigrant Jewish workers a modest rise in the standard of living" (Howe, 1976, p. 145).

17. Acccording to Weinberg (1988, p. 91), before 1925, at least $800 a year was needed to support a family of five, while in 1915 the averge yearly wage was only $670. Consequently, more than half of working families were forced to rely on wives' and children's additions to family income.

18. Eva Hoffman describes this rift in *Lost in Translation* (1989).

19. Although Hollander's (2006) article only refers to the female migrants fleeing Latin America in the late twentieth and early twenty-first centuries, it can be applied to the Eastern European Jewish immigrants who arrived before 1924.

20. Boulanger is here borrowing from one of Isaiah Berlin's essays, which is quoted in Ignatieff (1998, p. 292).

21. In my small sample of twenty-two interviewees, each of whom had two immigrant parents, family status upon arrival was as follows. Several arrived in the U.S. alone and had no first-degree relatives here. Quite a number either joined siblings or a spouse already here or arrived with a sibling or spouse but had no parent in this country; a few had no parent but both a sibling *and* a spouse here.

22. Because of changed U.S. immigration laws, her family were unable to emigrate to the U.S. The Immigration Act of 1924 (also called the Johnson-Reed Act) greatly limited the number of immigrants allowed into the U.S. through a quota based on nation of origin. Chaya's family eventually immigrated to Argentina.

23. It was not uncommon for immigrant mothers to champion their daughters' desires to go to college so that they could have better lives than they had (Gay, 1996; Weinberg, 1988).

24. It is interesting that Helen used the word "horrified" three times in describing her mother's reactions to her difficult experiences. Rivka was overwhelmed by what she was forced to contend with in America.

25. Helen quickly tried to take this back, averring that she did not know when the fighting started and that she did not remember fighting.

26. Helen elaborated on her secure home by saying that dinner was always at 6 and that she had eight best friends, played outdoors a lot, and lived in a safe neighborhood.

27. In Eastern European Jewish society, social status, or social class, was an important issue. Religious scholarship was the most important marker of social status. Money was important but secondary to religious knowledge in determining social status, or *yikhes*. The social classes did not mix, and *yikhes* was traditionally very important in choosing a marriage partner (Weinberg, 1988).

28. In Frances's narrative, no mention was made of the effect of World War I on her parents' lives. The German economy was in ruins after World War I, and there was great political unrest.

29. Anna's mother arrived in 1924, three years after Anna emigrated. Thus Anna had three years in the U.S. with no close relative except her husband to help ease her misery.

30. Miriam mentioned that her mother's family feared pogroms in the shtetl. Interestingly, however, Miriam did not refer to a dreadful pogrom that occurred in the city her mother so much loved (this city was located in what is now the eastern Ukraine). This pogrom, which took place in 1905, was well known and is mentioned in a "Bintel Brief" letter.

31. In the U.S., the norm for the immigrant Jewish female was that, after marrying, she stayed home to care for her children rather than becoming an ambitious figure, although many women worked in the family business. In Eastern Europe, however, women were at least as competent and worldly and often more so than were men.

32. Trachoma is a contagious eye disease that can cause blindness. A diagnosis of trachoma during the medical inspection that occurred at Ellis Island meant that the prospective immigrant would be sent back to the old country.

33. Louise said about this story, "For every hit he got from his father, he knew his father was proud of him." This twist on the story sounds improbable.

34. Beryl as an adolescent attended a Yeshiva that was influenced by the Musar movement. Musar emphasized the study of moral texts and can be seen as ascetic. Thus I believe that the Judaism practiced by this family was moralistic and strict.

35. Because of objections to the increasing numbers of impoverished Eastern European Jews flooding eastern U.S. cities, the banker Jacob Schiff promoted the Galveston Plan. Jews embarking at the German port of Bremen were transported to Galveston, Texas, and from there they were helped to find employment in other places in the American West.

36. Here and below I talk about proportions of my interviewees' parents who emigrated with particular family constellations, and I am referring only to this group of immigrants. These proportions are not meant to refer to any larger group of immigrants.

37. The authors of this study acknowledge that its results are limited by the lack of data on pre-immigration attachment classification of those in the immigrant group.

38. Cases like Seymour's father were not, I think, infrequent. For example, the father of Rose Cohen—she wrote an immigrant memoir—was forced to emigrate suddenly when the Russian authorities denied him the proper papers (Cohen, 1995).

39. Howe (1976, p. 95) quotes the memoir of Abraham Cahan on the collective nature of the Eastern European Jewish immigration:

> Each new wanderer, ruined by a pogrom or seeking to improve his lot or caught up in the excitement of the exodus, thought that he was coming to better his own condition only. . . . But soon every emigrating Jew moving westward realized he was involved in something more than a personal expedition. Every Jew . . . came to feel he was part of an historical event in the life of the Jewish people. (Ellipses in text; Cahan's memoir was unpublished.)

Chapter Four

Childhood

Growing Up in America

DRAMATIS PERSONAE

In order of appearance:

Norman: His father, who missed his family terribly, was at first a cowboy in the U.S. Norman grew up in abject poverty, but he denied his childhood of deprivation.
   Mother: Gitel
   Father: Abe

Louise: Louise was like a child of Holocaust survivors because of her father's experience. Her mother, because of World War I trauma, was "terrified as a person." Louise felt that her job was to repair her damaged parents.
   Mother: Edith
   Father: Beryl

Aaron: His mother as an adolescent discovered the body of her own father, who had been murdered in a pogrom. Growing up, he was expected to be "the best, the first."
   Mother: Estelle
   Father: Max

Barbara: Her parents experienced terrible poverty in Eastern Europe; as adults, all talking was fighting. Barbara felt unloved and neglected as a child.
   Mother: Bella

Father: Joe

Dorothy: Her happy household turned unhappy when her father became ill and later died. Her mother, who had suffered trauma in Eastern Europe, could not provide for her emotional needs.
Mother: Dina
Father: Harold

> It was not for myself alone that I was expected to shine, but for [my parents]— to redeem the constant anxiety of their existence. —Kazin, 1951, p. 21

Whether their parents missed what had once been home or disavowed any connection to the places they had left, my interviewees felt the hardships, trauma, and loss of their parents' pasts, as well as the anxieties of their parents' day-to-day lives. In trying to understand what it was like to be the child of immigrants, I will look at how the "anxiety of their [parents'] existence" influenced them. Often parents were preoccupied with the struggle to make ends meet and sometimes also with their own trauma. Yet for most of my interviewees, childhood was not bleak; many were able to enjoy friends, and even traumatized parents might be nurturing in some ways.

The Depression was a potent economic factor and an ongoing daily stressor during the childhoods of many of my interviewees. Many of their mothers worked in the family store, while others stayed home trying to make do with very little money. Usually fathers worked very long hours. Many parents did not have their own parents to turn to for help or guidance with childrearing, as they were thousands of miles away. For the parents who had experienced trauma in Eastern Europe or for whom coming to America involved devastating losses, these factors affected day-to-day interactions with their children.

In the attachment relationship between parent and child, there is a constant interchange around mood and affects (Salberg, 2017a). Very traumatized parents are in some way emotionally compromised and therefore inaccessible to a child for emotional regulation, self-soothing, and cognitive growth. Parents may have moments of emotional dysregulation or even dissociation; consequently, they may either flood the child with too much affect or transmit the opposite, a deadened or absent state. Thus attunement with their children is difficult, and parental trauma influences the attachment relationship with the child. But when a parent who has experienced trauma remains emotionally alive, infrequent moments of dysregulated affect are bearable for the child, and the parent may pass on resilience to the child.

We will see that Barbara and Aaron, both of whom had at least one very traumatized parent, were affected sometimes by too much parental affect and sometimes by too little. Louise's father, however, at times remained "resilient and alive" (Salberg, 2017a, p. 90). Yet this chapter is not just about the effects of trauma and the resilience that accompanies it. In a broader sense, it is about what it was like to be a child of these particular immigrants. How did the children play? How, as young people, did my interviewees make the first steps toward moving beyond their parents' lives? The children wanted to be Americans, and many or most knew that they wanted to have lives different from those of their parents. The ability to have a better life was perhaps the redemption of parents' losses and suffering. A brief historical background will help us to put this in context.

In addition to the intergenerational transmission of trauma that affected many families, there were the feelings about parents' sacrifice and children's debt that the passage from Kazin reflects. Irving Howe, himself the son of Eastern European Jewish immigrants, wrote: "It was the unspoken hope of the immigrants that their visions and ambitions, the collective dream of Jewish fulfillment and the personal wish to improve the lot of sons and daughters, could be satisfied at the same time" (Howe, 1976, p. 251; also cited in Moore, 1981, p. 9). The immigrants realized that neither their visions, which grew out of their socialist ideals, nor their personal ambitions for success could be satisfied in their own generation. They were burdened by their poverty, limited skills, poor education, awkward grasp of English, and alien manners. Moreover, the immigrants could not feel "at ease in the new world" (Howe, 1976, p. 251). Thus they were a "transitional generation," and they felt themselves to be "personally doomed," unable to fully enjoy the pleasures of America (p. 250). Because of this, they would instead stoically work hard and sacrifice for their children, so that their sons and daughters could attain the goals they "could not reach themselves" (p. 251).

The immigrants' children in turn received their parents' vision as their "Jewish inheritance" (Moore, 1981, p. 9). Howe contrasted the immigrants' socialist vision, inseparable from their ideals, with the ambition for making money; this theme recurred in immigrant memoirs. Living in America meant participating in a materialistic society, and therefore, of necessity ambition won out over socialist or religious visions. The immigrants were determined that "my son shall not work in the shop" (the sweatshop). Consequently, fathers labored and mothers skimped and sacrificed so that their sons, and sometimes their daughters, could become educated and, as a result, achieve business or professional success. The children indeed became successful, but in the process, they not only discarded "much of their immigrant background as 'foreign'" (Moore, 1981, p. 11) but also experienced the conflict between their parents' immigrant ways and the American lifestyles to which they aspired.

The author's paternal grandfather, left, and two of his brothers, who appear to have been malnourished, circa 1958. The immigrants were limited by their awkward grasp of English and alien manners. They stoically worked so that their children could prosper. *Courtesy of Dora Hahn.*

Parents' sacrifices and children's psychological debt to them, which sometimes felt like a burden, has a foundation within the "Jewish religious world view" (Weinberg, 1988; Silberman, 1985, p. 137). Parents' sacrifices made sense within the Jewish world view because Jews believe that redemption occurs in this world rather than in the afterlife. Consequently, Judaism "encourages a belief in the future and lends itself to the willingness of parents to sacrifice their well-being to advance their children's prospects" (Silberman, 1985, pp. 137; also cited in Weinberg, 1988, p. 288, n. 41). Children gave their parents "honor and fulfillment," and thus Jewish children, especially sons, were viewed as "extensions" of their parents and were loved for their attainments (Silberman, 1985, p. 138; Weinberg, 1988).

Weinberg (1988) discussed the gender differences in how sons and daughters were expected to fulfill their parents' ambitions. Although some mothers encouraged their daughters to attend college and to perhaps become teachers or social workers, more often than not Jewish daughters could make their mothers happy by "marrying and having children" (p. 163). Later on, they were expected to care for their elderly parents, very often by having parents live with them. Sons, on the other hand, were expected to fulfill more impressive expectations. "Mothers often pushed them to study and work to 'make it' in the American system by becoming successful businessmen, or possibly professionals—a way of justifying the sacrifices made by the family" (p. 163). Weinberg contrasts the "physical demands" placed on daughters as caretakers or breadwinners with the psychological burdens sons carried; the pressure for sons to achieve was indeed high. More often a daughter might flourish "within the context of her parents' value system," while a son, in order to achieve the hoped-for success, might have to forsake his parents' values (p. 163). When their parents were elderly or widowed, sons were expected to visit them and help financially rather than having them move into their homes. "Sons were often raised to believe that their interests were paramount" (p. 164).

Alfred Kazin, writing about shining *in order to* redeem the anxiety of his parents' existence, continued: "I was the first American child, their offering to the strange new God; I was to be the monument of their liberation from the shame of being—what they were" (Kazin, 1951, pp. 21–22). In the following pages, we will look at some of the forces that encouraged the immigrants' children to feel ashamed of their parents. The children, who "no longer fully" belonged to the "immigrant culture, yet somehow" bore "its stamp," embodied the tension of living in two worlds (Feingold, 1992, p. 36). As a consequence, they were not only ashamed but also conflicted. Interestingly, the children I interviewed denied many of the conflicts they must have experienced with their parents over issues of Americanization. The feelings about the debt they owed their parents will be explicated both in this chapter and the next, which treats the children's lives as adults.

The immigrants' children were taught in public schools to "substitute American manners and morals for those of their parents" (Ewen, 1985, p. 88). Americanization was taught along with academic subjects. In the 1910s and 1920s, schools "made a deliberate effort to wean American children away from the cultures of their parents" (Cowan & Cowan, 1996, p. 99). The school system was actively used by progressive Protestant reformers, who hoped to preserve the way of life of a prosperous, rural, middle-class America. Such values as privacy and serenity, which differed from immigrant life, were taught. The immigrants were resolved that their children do well in school, but in school the values of the "reformers reigned supreme" (p. 73). Thus, to gratify their parents by "doing well in school," "Jewish children were forced to reject the other traditions that their parents prized" (Howe, 1976).[1] Wrote David Blaustein, the superintendent of the Educational Alliance, "The children are imbued with the idea that all that is not American is something to be ashamed of" (Howe, 1976, p. 275).[2]

It was not only in schools but also in what they read in the library, in civics books, and in newspapers, as well as what they saw in the movies, that Jewish children encountered powerful messages encouraging assimilation (Cowan & Cowan, 1996, p. 43). Moreover, the settlement houses, which provided educational and social services to the immigrants, were staffed by Protestant reformers. Some settlement social workers, like Jane Addams of Hull House, *did* recognize that teachers' efforts at Americanization could be harmful, as it drove a wedge between parents and their children (Cowan & Cowan, 1996, p. 104). The push to become American widened the gap. Wrote Blaustein, "The child attends the public school, and within a few months may come to despise that which he formerly held sacred" (as cited in Ewen, 1985, p. 88). Children were unable to look to their parents as role models, and young people felt "unable to talk to parents about what had come to matter" to them (Feingold, 1992, p. 36). Children might be reluctant to hurt their parents' feelings, yet they might feel caught between the American world and the world of their parents. A traditional father, unable to speak English, "lost parental authority in the eyes of his children," who emulated assimilated friends from the block (p. 38). Children had to help their parents with the American bureaucracy, and neither parents nor children felt good when parents seemed like children and children were "unwillingly" pressured into parental roles (p. 38).

In the 1920s, these stresses were accompanied by the weakening influence of communal associations and the extended family. "People no longer thought in terms of community" (Feingold, 1992, p. 37). The American way of life required independence and freedom, which meant rejecting the collective way of life of the community (Ewen, 1985). Upward mobility prized winning and taking over generosity and sharing. An additional source of conflict between immigrant parents and their children was religious observance. "As secular America increasingly beckoned to the young," traditional orthodoxy proved uninspiring (Sorin, 1997, p. 80).

The New York City public schools were the site of a battle over language. Yiddish, the "language of poverty and oppression," was denigrated, as it was associated with lower-class, "un-American" immigrant culture (Moore, 1981, p. 107). In Lower East Side schools during the early twentieth century, the Yiddish language was barred in the halls, bathrooms, lunchrooms, and schoolyards; this was enforced by Julia Richman, a German-Jewish district school superintendent, and teachers were told to give pupils demerits for speaking the language (Moore, 1981; Weinberg, 1988).[3] When they spoke

English, Jewish pupils might do so colloquially or with an accent. Alfred Kazin wrote about this:

> Our families and teachers seemed tacitly agreed that we were somehow to be a little ashamed of what we were. . . . It was certainly not because we were Jews, or simply because we spoke another language at home. . . . It was rather that a "refined," "correct," "nice" English was required of us at school that we did not naturally speak. . . . This English was peculiarly the ladder of advancement. . . . We were expected to show it off like a new pair of shoes. (Kazin, 1951, p. 22; also cited in Weinberg, 1988, pp. 114–115)

The pain this caused parents and children was immense. The children were ashamed of their parents' foreign accents, of their mothers dressed in old-fashioned clothes, of their fathers who "shuffled" around the house in bedroom "slippers and suspenders" (Howe, 1976, p. 262). For a peddler father to work so hard, only to be perceived by his son as Americans did, "as an old sheeny peddler," was painful to both father and son (p. 254). Anzia Yezierska's story "The Fat of the Land" tells of a daughter's shame about her mother: "God knows how I tried to civilize her. I dressed her in the most stylish Paris models, but Delancey Street sticks out from every inch of her" (quoted in Ewen, 1985, p. 202). Howe (1976, p. 255) wrote that the immigrant "fathers had borne intolerable burdens and now the sons did too." The children understood the magnitude of the debt they owed to their parents. Nevertheless, "the distance between generations came to be like a chasm of silence which neither affection nor good will could bridge."

Tensions over Americanization and language began to abate in the New York City schools in the 1930s (Moore, 1981). A somewhat successful movement to teach Hebrew in some public high schools began, with the intent of mitigating the estrangement of parents and children and correcting past injustices. As it turned out, however, the teaching of Hebrew was "largely a symbolic" victory (Moore, 1981, p. 114). It was taught in only a few schools, and in 1940 only 4 percent of New York City Jewish high school students were enrolled in Hebrew classes.

Despite the conflicts between the generations, in many ways the immigrants too wanted to become Americans. Because Eastern Europe had been at best inhospitable to them, Jews intended from the beginning to remain permanently in America (Sorin, 1997, p. 88). My interviewees confirmed that most of their parents wanted to become Americans, even though a few held onto Old World values and styles of dress. Jews worked toward American living standards particularly vigorously (Sorin, 1997, p. 88). Moreover, the children of the immigrants were "eager to assimilate" (Cowan & Cowan, 1996, p. 71). Second-generation Jews eagerly embraced American values and ideals; this was a "headlong rush to Americanization," noted Charles Bernheimer, a founder of Jewish social work (Feingold, 1992, p. 36).

They took on American styles, deeming much of their immigrant background to be "foreign."

That the immigrants' children were expected to shine, to be the "best," is amply reflected in my interview data. Louise pursued an advanced degree and a professional career not just to repay the debt she owed her parents but as part of her desire to psychologically "repair" her traumatized parents. She knew that doing so would gratify her parents and, more specifically, that her mother, who was unable to formally pursue her own education, would vicariously enjoy her daughter's success. Aaron and his brother knew family values required them to be "the best, the first," which meant attending medical school. And Sarah, herself an immigrant—and who had lived some of her mother's hardships along with her—knew as a child that "college was in her future" (Sarah is described in chapter 5).

Doing your best was reinforced within the Jewish family. "In high school we used to think that if you got less than ninety on a math test, you had disgraced God, Country, and Home," stated a man interviewed by Neil and Ruth Cowan (1996, p. 91). Parents "instilled" the "passion for learning" in their children, and they continued to encourage their children throughout their school years (Sorin, 1997, p. 87). Jews had come to the U.S. with a very high literacy rate, approximately 74 percent, and they were familiar from traditional religious schools with the patterns of "drill, recitation and rote learning" necessary for school success (p. 160). The immigrants' children "had internalized the drive to achieve" and to fulfill their parents' hopes (pp. 160–161).

Jewish boys were encouraged to remain in school and indeed most went to college; even if they did not attend college, they tended to pursue white-collar jobs (Cowan & Cowan, 1996). Many girls went to commercial high schools so they too could obtain white-collar jobs, but as secretaries, stenographers, bookkeepers, or retail clerks. Some mothers stood up to their husbands and insisted that daughters as well as sons attend college. Elaine's mother, described above, said: "You'll go to college if I have to scrub other people's floors." The passion for education women as well as men possessed was very much directed toward attaining middle-class status (Feingold, 1992, p. 42).

The children of the immigrants became successful by pursuing careers both in business and the professions "with a fervor their ancestors had reserved for religion" (Feingold, 1992, p. 58). Jews gave to professionals, such as doctors and lawyers, the status once accorded rabbis (Feingold, 1992). Furthermore, Jews also became successful in small businesses, and this played an extremely important role in the rapid social mobility of immigrants and their children (Sorin, 1997). One additional career choice favored by many of the immigrants' children was the helping professions, such as teaching and social work. Because many children had been raised in "politically progressive communities" and had grown up with Jewish mutual aid institutions, they were attracted to professions working toward social action (p. 164). Many of my female interviewees and a few of the men were successful as teachers or social workers. With their drive to succeed fueled by the sometimes unconscious wish to redeem their parents' suffering, Jews who had spent their childhoods in cold water flats moved as adults to ranch houses in the suburbs or apartment buildings in upper-middle-class neighborhoods in Manhattan (Cowan & Cowan, 1996). As we will see in the next chapter, in one or two generations, Eastern European Jews ascended from the working class to the middle class.

Before beginning the life stories, it will be helpful to understand more about trauma and its transmission in the attachment relationship. Jill Salberg (2017a) explained in detail how parents who have been traumatized can pass on further trauma or in some cases resilience.

Salberg (2017a, p. 94) states that when trauma is passed on, it very often is "less a discrete event"—expressed as a repetition or "ghost"—than what we call relational trauma; she refers to it as the texture of traumatic attachment. Rather than being a "clear transmission of something," the intergenerational transmission of trauma can instead be thought of as the consequence of the traumatized parent's "dysregulated affect states" or "fragmented states of mind." The parent who has "self-states that are dysregulated or even dissociative" will be to some extent emotionally impaired "and thus at times inaccessible to the child to help with self-regulation, self-soothing, and mentalization of feelings and thoughts" (p. 87). In other words, because the traumatized parent cannot provide a containing, empathic holding environment, the child's developing psyche is damaged.

When parents who have experienced trauma are in states of "internal disorganization," they can pass on this disorganization to their children "not only by directing their anger, punitiveness, and unpredictability towards the child but also by exposing" the child to chaotic situations in daily life that the child must "helplessly" experience (Lieberman, 2014, p. 278; as cited in Salberg, 2017a, p. 90). "Fear states" associated with "unrecognized experiences of disrupted safety" in the parental generation may "terrorize" the children, "often in nonverbal and early unmetabolized forms" (Harris, 2014, p. 270; as cited in Salberg, 2017a, p. 90). On the other hand, writes Salberg, the "traumatized parent" may remain resilient and "emotionally alive," and when this happens, frozen moments of "fragmentation" may be "fleeting" and "tolerable" for the child (p. 90). In the role reversals that occur when children attempt to affectively regulate their traumatized parents rather than vice versa, the child may develop a "kind of resilience," as the child is required to be the "more affectively regulated one" (p. 91). For example, if the child soothes the parent, she precociously learns, though perhaps not in an optimal manner, to soothe herself.

Responsive parenting, the ability to be in tune with children's needs, is affected by parental trauma. In addition, parents who have little time or emotional energy because of the struggle to make ends meet might be too preoccupied to be responsive to their children's needs.

LIFE STORIES AND VIGNETTE

The context above gives us a taste of the broad trends during this period of tumult. Now let's explore the stories of five individuals who grew up during this period and who both confirm and complicate the general portrait of the era. Four are portrayed in longer life stories, while one, Barbara, is described in a shorter vignette.

Two of my most interesting interviewees had parents who had experienced great difficulties, but they nevertheless remembered happy aspects of their childhoods. Both in different ways needed to "shine" in order to redeem or repair their parents' suffering. Norman grew up poverty-stricken and deprived. Louise, in contrast, was more middle-class and had more than enough food and many advantages; both her parents were self-educated and intellectually interested. Because Louise's narrative was not only rich and detailed but also full of extraordinary psychological insights, her narrative is the book's longest.

Norman

Norman, born in 1924, was a very intelligent, active, working professional in his eighties when we met. His immigrant father, Abe, described in chapter 3 as missing his own family, was a cowboy for eight years and an animal lover. Unlike almost every other family described here, Norman's family treated education as unimportant. Nevertheless, by going to night school, Norman completed a master's degree in a practical field and then a professional degree.

Norman spoke in great detail and, though very kind, seemed cut off from his emotions. As we have seen, his father had emotional problems and lost his family during the Holocaust. Norman's mother, Gitel, came to the U.S. from a tiny Russian village, where her family hated the tsar and feared pogroms. Both parents arrived before World War I, his father in 1907 and his mother in 1913.

Norman grew up in abject poverty, and as his wife said, he "glamorized" his childhood of deprivation so that it seemed interesting and colorful. His many memories of childhood divorce the miseries of poverty from the reality. Many children have the capacity to do this, as they need to find the good in their lives and to hold onto that good (M. O'Loughlin, personal communication, September 16, 2016). Although Norman seemed to have been successful after some difficult times during the first half of his life, he seemed obsessional and out of touch with his emotions.

When he was young, Norman's family was so poor that they were evicted several times. Their rented quarters had no hot water or toilet; the house was cold except for the kitchen, where there was a coal stove. In order to take a bath, they were forced to heat water on the stove. "What did it matter to me" that we were evicted, said Norman; the next living quarters would have no hot water anyway.

Family members never went to a doctor or dentist, and Norman said his sister never saw a doctor until she was thirteen years old; at that time Norman himself was already supporting the family. The family had little to eat—sometimes dinner was bread soaked in egg, and a couple of times his parents ate only after the children had finished, presumably so they would not take food that the children wanted. Moreover, the family ate pigeon when they were hungry, and Norman's parents bought only damaged fruits and vegetables. "Once," said Norman, "I ate salami at a friend's house, but my parents couldn't afford that." Not only did he and his sister never have ice cream, they never went anywhere because of their poverty. Yet Norman said his parents were devoted to their children, and he recalled "being loved" and "well-taken care of" by his parents; "they spoke lovingly" to him, he added.

Perhaps the most strikingly discordant note in Norman's conception of his loving but poverty-stricken upbringing was this: he and his sister always went to school when they had a fever because home was unheated. At school at least it was warm. Furthermore, although their kitchen had only one light bulb, for years they had no electricity—it would have cost $12 to get the electricity restored, but a candle cost only one cent.

Norman's mother, Gitel, came to the U.S. at age twenty-seven. The second oldest of six children, her siblings married before she did and immigrated to America, leaving the tiny village where there were no opportunities. Gitel was left behind to care for her parents. Their village was surrounded by non-Jewish peasants. The Jews never knew when a pogrom might occur, although Norman believed that his mother's family had not themselves experienced a pogrom. Gitel spoke about how much the gentiles there hated the Jews. Her family was very poor, and she was uneducated; the Jewish families of the village pooled their money to hire a teacher only for its boys. Norman's grandmother ran a grocery store, while his grandfather studied but did not work, and each child took whatever job he or she could.

Norman said his parents and his mother's extended family hated Russia. They spoke among themselves about their hate for the tsar, whom they referred to using various epithets, such as one that meant "dirty pig." When asked about his mother's feelings about being uprooted, Norman said he couldn't imagine that she missed anything about her former home. His own judgment of his mother's connection to her village, that she disavowed any connection to her past, went something like this: it was all bad and there was nothing to miss. "They didn't think of it as home," he said. After all, his mother had been reunited with her siblings when she arrived in the U.S. with her parents. Notably, it was Norman's own denial that made him unable to balance Gitel's connection to the past with its traumatic associations.

I imagine that Gitel was damaged by her early life in Eastern Europe. Certainly the fear of pogroms and her family's poverty—along with the responsibility of guaranteeing her parents' safety during the difficult journey to America—may have amounted to cumulative trauma. Moreover, Norman depicted his mother's early years in New York City as a narrow extension of her Eastern European life; as the unmarried daughter, she continued to care for her parents. "All she saw [here] was a more crowded way of life."

Perhaps one result of Gitel's trauma was that she never Americanized. She wore old-fashioned clothes, never learned more than a few words of English, and rarely went to the movies. Her insistence on using outdated methods of housekeeping suggests an almost pathological refusal to modernize. Norman reported that, until her death in 1959, she continued to wash clothing using a scrubbing board and ironed clothes with an iron heated on the stove. The cumulative difficulties of her life may have contributed to an inability or a refusal to adapt.

Gitel had had two miscarriages and a stillbirth before Norman's birth; tragically, she also lost a baby son at age eleven months. "Therefore," said Norman, "I was her fifth pregnancy and oldest child" (his sister was three-and-one-half years younger). His father had owned a small business delivering milk, cheese, eggs, and butter in their Long Island small city before the death of the baby, but afterward was depressed; he then sold his delivery route and was never again able to make a living. Gitel, after so many losses, was probably psychologically compromised herself. Fearing that her husband would commit suicide after the baby's death and then watching as he was unable to recover psychologically must have engendered deep feelings of helplessness. She understandably seemed not to recognize the family's dire economic situation and did not find a way to bring in income.

The first story Norman related about his childhood had to do with being called a Christ killer; he told this to me with no trace of resentment at the anti-Semitism behind it. Norman was walking home from school at age eight or nine with a good friend who asked, "Why did you kill Christ?"

Norman answered, "I didn't."

"My priest said you did."

"I never killed anybody."

"If you didn't, your parents did."

Norman continued, "I asked my mother, 'Did you kill Mr. Christ?'" His parents then started speaking Ukrainian; they were so upset. Because they were speaking in a language that was secret from their children, Norman was at first suspicious that perhaps they *had* killed someone. Probably, Norman told me, they were saying, "We thought we got away from that." Eventually, his parents spoke to him and explained his friend's question. Norman stated that his school buddy "was my good friend" and that he, Norman, wasn't upset.

One of Norman's earliest memories was of his mother giving birth to his sister unattended at home. He then remembered the visit of his mother's sister when he was four; she died a year later in childbirth (this was his only memory of this aunt). Although he consciously expressed no distress around the memory of his mother giving birth, that he followed it with the memory of his aunt dying in childbirth suggests that he knew his mother was at risk. Moreover, it must be upsetting to a toddler to hear the sounds of his mother in the throes of childbirth. Norman immediately banished such feelings during the interview by saying he felt well taken care of; to me he seemed to be showing his good will toward his parents by absolving them of any inadequacies. Next Norman mentioned the "joy of being in school." He was intelligent, and therefore he skipped both second and fourth grades. Yet his teachers held spelling bees on Jewish holidays—they knew he would be absent on these days—because he won all the spelling bees. Again he did not acknowledge that he may have been affected by anti-Semitism.

Norman's family survived in part because his father created a sort of semi-urban farm, where he raised chickens, ducks, geese, and pigeons; he also grew potatoes, onions, garlic, radishes, sunflowers, and corn (all this was only for the family's consumption). Consequently, the family was able to eat a chicken each Sabbath. It was Norman's job as a boy to find a Jewish ritual slaughterer to properly kill the chicken. Norman's father trained dogs to protect the chickens; Norman also said it was his job, if the chickens "sounded endangered," to run outside and discover what the problem was.

Norman described such details colorfully, mentioning not only that his father built a chicken coop, but also that he constructed a pond for the ducks. Abe taught their Italian neighbors to farm as he did. "A Jew knows how to raise ducks?" Norman said, echoing the thoughts of their neighbors; and Norman seemed proud that his father could do this. Occasionally Norman's elementary school teachers brought class members to his house to see the chickens and ducks, and his father would tell the children how to raise them. In addition, Abe spoke at Norman's school about being a cowboy; he told stories of fighting off wolves that attacked the cattle.

Norman's social life was a positive part of his childhood. "We had a corner where me and every one of my friends went," he said. He and his friends played games, "hung out, and talked." Norman valued this, wishing that his own children could have enjoyed a similar social life. A few years ago, he reported, his childhood Jewish neighborhood had organized a reunion that three hundred people, rather than the expected seventy-five, attended. Norman's social life continued to be one of his strengths all his life, and at the time of the interview he had many friends.

At age fourteen, Norman shouldered the burden of supporting his family, and he did so seemingly without resentment. He first retrieved bowling pins at a bowling alley, then began to work in a factory, all the time attending high school; he made 60 cents an hour at the factory and handed his paycheck to his father. For the first time, his family could pay the rent and they had enough food. Abe then called the family together and announced that he would open a bank account. At some point, Abe had saved $70 from Norman's pay, and Norman said his father had "never seen that kind of money."

Strikingly, education meant nothing to this family; with such an incredibly bright son, most Jewish families would have moved heaven and earth to further his education. Their attitude suggests that Norman's mother's limitations and his father's depression and emotional instability affected their ability to envision a better life for their son. His teachers had been certain that Norman would be his class's valedictorian, but because he was working, he never wrote any English compositions, and consequently he almost flunked sophomore English. He did, however, graduate third in his class.

Norman said that in his part of town, all the teenagers were poor. However, his high school included students from the entire town, and many had new clothes and some money. He described being amazed when one day a classmate spent a quarter for lunch and then paid an additional nickel for a second dessert.

When World War II began, Norman was almost fifteen, and his mother cried because she feared he would be drafted. Little did she know then that Norman would not wait to be drafted; he entered the army at seventeen, as he himself "wanted to kill Hitler." Norman explained this somewhat grandiose wish by saying, "I was an idealist." In fact, in the army he earned four stripes as a marksman.

When the war ended, Norman returned to his factory job. Because of the G.I. Bill, he was able to attend college, but he took evening classes, as he continued to have to support his family. He interrupted his studies for a stint in Israel. Ever resourceful, Norman had, before leaving, established a messenger business. He earned a bachelor's and a master's in practical fields and finally a professional degree, completing all his studies at night.

One of the most interesting parts of Norman's narrative was the good cheer with which he reported a childhood and adolescence so full of deprivation and difficulty. He used denial, dissociation, and splitting so that he would not experience appropriate emotion. While on one hand these defenses were useful in helping him to enjoy his life, they resulted in him seeming out of touch with himself and in many ways out of touch emotionally with others. Norman was unable to admit to negative feelings about his parents. When I remarked during the interview that he now seemed to be very sad about the hardships endured by his parents, he replied that his family had had enough to eat and immediately spoke about enjoying his corner childhood friends. I asked Norman about the effects of his father's depression on him, and he stated that he didn't think he was affected by it. "I tried to be good to him. I gave him all my paychecks," said Norman. Yet it is impossible that he was unaffected by Abe's periods of severe depression and consequent inability to support his family.

Norman's dissociative defenses allowed him to make his childhood of miserable poverty into a colorful narrative during which he described himself as "well taken care of." He did not see, for example, the anti-Semitism of his schoolteachers who held spelling bees when he was absent for Jewish holidays. Norman had a childhood that he felt was normal, and I feel that he indeed felt loved and enjoyed his social life. From a psychological point of view, however, Abe's depression and emotional instability—as well as both parents' passivity in the face of their economic hardship—had consequences, contributing to Norman's denial, dissociation, and splitting.

Norman continued to care for both his mother and his father well into adulthood. When, in his thirties, he began to make money as a professional, his father had already passed away, but he tried to make his mother feel that she had money. "I tried to give her a feeling of affluence. I dropped a $10 bill on the floor to give her that feeling." He did so habitually, and he added, "She had a happy life because of this." Norman sacrificed *for* his parents, who had themselves endured so much, and in doing so he not only symbolically repaired them but also fulfilled the debt incurred by their losses and misery. Norman also said that, when his mother needed a ride home from somewhere, he and his sister's husband vied for the privilege of driving her.

Norman made a poor choice of a first wife, suggesting that he was out of touch with his own needs. In his late thirties, he married a woman who seemed both narcissistic and immature, and because they had a baby, he remained in this unacceptable marriage for thirteen years. When he was about fifty, he met and married an intelligent and accomplished professional woman ten years his junior. The marriage was satisfying. In addition, his career was a fulfilling one that utilized his intellectual talents.

Norman's childhood seemed to have had both positive and negative consequences for him. The psychological difficulties that led him into a disastrous first marriage—his naivete and desire to take care of others, even to his own detriment—originated in his early years. As an adolescent he cared for his own parents, and he must have learned as a child to excuse his parents'

inadequacies. Moreover, I believe the extraordinary effort and personal sacrifice required to become the sole support of his family at age fourteen was his
own response to his parents' trauma. In supporting them financially, he acted
as a parentified child.

Because his mother and father had suffered so much, Norman could not
allow himself to see his parents realistically as having failed him in important
ways. Instead, he idealized them, viewing his parents, their marriage, and
their extended families in an exclusively positive light. For example, he said
his mother's family was a happy one with "virtually no arguments," but
then—without realizing that he was contradicting himself—he described a
family feud. After describing his mother's difficulty having a child, he stated,
"She was always upbeat" and was possessed of "a sterling character." "She
never complained . . . about their poverty." A bit later he added, she "never
said negative things about people." When talking about his father, he was
firm in saying that he didn't think of his father as depressed. Rather, he said
his father was just sometimes depressed, which was understandable because
his father missed his family. His description of his parents as all good suggests a defensive use of splitting—his mother was the self-sacrificing house-
wife, rather than a rigid and old-fashioned woman, and his father was the
dreamer and good-natured raconteur who farmed for his family.

Norman dissociated or denied his parents' negative qualities. The black-
and-white thinking that made it impossible for him so see them as realistic
individuals also made it difficult for him to evaluate others astutely. He could
not foresee, before he married his first wife, what would probably befall him.
He was well-intentioned but misjudged people, and he presented as out of
touch with others.

Norman's desire to care for and repair his parents was extreme. He stated,
"Many times I wished I could retroactively do what my parents wanted or
needed." Talking about the family's lack of electricity for two years, he said,
"How often I wish I could retroactively pay" the $12 so that their electricity
could be restored.

There was much that I did not understand about Norman's parents'
psychological limitations. Both had arrived before World War I, and thus
they may not have experienced the same degree of trauma in Eastern Europe
that some other parents did. Certainly, both parents suffered profoundly
when they lost their baby son. Moreover, Abe probably had a biological
predisposition to depression. Because there is much that I don't know, the
following formulations about Norman are hypothetical.

Norman's splitting, denial, and dissociation may have originated in his
attachment to his traumatized parents. His father was surely often emotionally dysregulated due to his depression; furthermore, during Norman's infancy,
he must often have felt terrified that he would lose this child as he had lost
his first son. Similarly, Gitel may have experienced periods of panic and

moments of dissociation during Norman's infancy. It is also possible that fleeting fear states might have been a legacy of her earlier terror of pogroms. And probably the trauma of her cumulative pregnancy losses, the death of her baby son, and her anxieties about her once-suicidal husband led to frequent dysregulated affective states.

Moreover, Norman's dissociation and denial may have originated also with his parents' historical trauma and therefore may have had intergenerational value (N. G. Pisano, personal communication, February 10, 2018). Just as Norman denied his childhood poverty and the impact on him of his father's depression, Abe might have denied the intense loneliness of his eight years as a Texan cowboy, and his mother might have dissociated from the fear and hunger of her early life in Eastern Europe. These defenses seem to have had survival value for Norman's parents, and therefore they were passed on intergenerationally.

Norman's parents, as he said, very much loved him, and I believe he felt this love. He had a cheerful disposition and was very social, both important assets, and his firm knowledge of his parents' love must have contributed to these qualities. Another very positive quality was his perseverance; his hard work throughout his life paid off. Had he not felt loved and persevered he would not have been able to marry his second wife. Despite his childhood of deprivation, and despite the necessity of dissociating the many negative aspects of his early life, Norman was able to achieve the American dream.

Louise

Louise's is the rich and complex story of the daughter of two very traumatized parents; despite their trauma, from her point of view she was a very lucky child with good parents. Her unusual and detailed narrative forms an interesting counterpoint of lovely comments about her parents and painful memories. Louise's father, Beryl, discussed previously, missed his family profoundly, and after they perished during World War II, his sense of loss overshadowed everything.

Louise was a lively, intelligent, and very energetic professional in her seventies who had a great deal of insight. Attractive, very intellectual, and in some ways unconventional, she admitted that, because of her background, she had to present a perfect exterior impression to others. She was anxious but also generous and warm, and she worked very hard over the course of our interviews to present a very detailed description of her parents and herself. That she had two homes suggested that she and her husband—a professional who was still working well into his eighties—had done well economically. Each had been married previously, and they had one daughter and a granddaughter with whom they spent as much time as possible. Part of Louise's intellectual energy had in recent years been focused on a second degree in a subject related to her Jewish heritage.

Toward the end of her interview, Louise stated that it was her "job" to "repair" her parents because of their trauma; indeed by "repairing" them, she was making up for their losses. To understand her need to repair, I will examine in more depth the evidence of her parents' traumatic experiences.

Louise's mother, Edith, had come from a small town in Eastern Europe at age fifteen or sixteen in 1922, and she was the youngest child of at least five who lived to adulthood. Edith remembered her home in Eastern Europe with fear; indeed, she "spoke of having been frightened all the time" there. Born in 1906, and therefore a child during World War I, she was not only constantly afraid but also hungry and cold. Louise said that Edith's family had only one potato to use in cooking soup for the family of five children. During World War I, Edith saw her father cut his leg because he did not want to be drafted. Edith did not want to speak about a pogrom that occurred during her childhood. Actually, she rarely spoke about her life in Eastern Europe, and given her unspeakably traumatic experiences, this is hardly surprising.

Louise felt that Edith suffered from "interpersonal trauma," as well as the trauma of war. Edith's older sister Sarah (at least five years older) was among the group of young people with whom Edith traveled when she emigrated in 1921. Not only was the trip "fraught with fear" (there was a very frightening and cold river crossing), but Sarah abandoned her during part of the journey. Louise added that Sarah was the meanest person that she, Louise, had ever known. Furthermore, Louise stated that both her mother's parents were cold. Edith's mother, who came to the U.S. in 1929, was "self-involved" and apparently self-important—she would "hold forth" on whatever topics she felt knowledgeable about; moreover, she was not nurturing and never cooked for anyone.

When Edith arrived in New York City, she lived with a middle-class aunt, as did her sister. She found a job and, already having received a significant secular education in her Eastern European town, proceeded to educate herself in the U.S. She attended not only night school to learn English but also many seminars. By doing so, she continued her secular education and also studied Hebrew and Yiddish. When Louise was born, fourteen years after Edith's arrival, Edith "knew the entire children's literature"; in addition, she was the president of a Hadassah chapter (a Jewish women's volunteer organization) and a "great public speaker." As Louise described her, Edith was pretty, charming, popular, and successful. In fact, she was the more successful and dominant of Louise's parents.

Louise honestly described her mother's psychological disturbance. She was extremely easily wounded: if Louise or her father even slightly misunderstood her, Edith would withdraw for a long time, and she would not speak to them for days or weeks if she felt they hurt her. If someone at

Hadassah were "slightly snippy," Edith would become "*very* hurt and with-drawn" (emphasis Louise's). During the interview, making up for this assess-ment of her mother, Louise added that Edith would have been psychologically more "compromised" had she not been so intelligent. But when Louise would say to her father (presumably as a teenager), "My mother is crazy," he would reply, "It's all right; she's very sensitive." Imagine how confusing her father's glossing over her mother's illness must have been to the young Louise, who herself must have been vulnerable.

In general, Louise said, Edith was "terrified as a person." She was also largely silent about what had befallen her in Eastern Europe. The persistence of her terror throughout her life testifies to the unsayable nature of her trau-ma. For example, she did not want anyone to wear a yarmulke in public lest that person be hurt for being Jewish. Moreover, Edith's traumatic memories took over in 1973, when Louise, then an adult, planned to visit the region her mother had emigrated from. Edith reacted with fear and anger, saying: "Why do you want to go back?" "You don't go back to a war zone." "It was a terrible place!" Louise added that Edith "imagined it haunted." That her mother collapsed time and imagined that the area continued to be a war zone after sixty years indicates the uncanny effects of Edith's trauma.

Louise's father, Beryl, suffered the traumatic loss of his family during the Holocaust, and he seemed to learn about it in the company of his daughter. Louise was born in 1935, and she said that this knowledge was part of her reality as she began to attain consciousness during her early childhood. "Eve-ry Sunday we went to see Russian army movies [most probably newsreels]. He looked at every person trying to see his family. He was always trying to see his family." As Louise watched her father scanning the movie screen, she must have read his facial expressions. We can assume that—as he absorbed the terrible realization that his family had been slaughtered—she, in turn, assimilated this traumatic knowledge. Thus Louise as a very small child was unprotected from her father's dawning realization of his traumatic loss. Trag-ically, this was the culmination of the loss that Beryl endured when, as a young man, he was forced to leave his family behind in Eastern Europe. The reader may remember that, during his journey from his shtetl to the port, Beryl was so sad that he hoped to die by God's wrath when he no longer followed the commandment to pray with *tefilliln*.

Louise described her father as warm, gentle, and very often humorous; he was sweet and also composed funny poems for her and her cousins. The family sang during car trips, and I imagine the songs being initiated by Beryl. Beryl offered her friends rides to school in his van (for a time their car was the van he used for his business). Like her mother, Beryl was extremely well-educated in Hebrew and Yiddish, and both parents were proud of their knowledge of secular Jewish culture.

Very early in Louise's interview, a profoundly painful memory about her mother emerged; it was, notably, the first thing Louise told me about her childhood. When Louise was a member of a Brownie troop, perhaps seven years old, her troop held a cake sale for which each member's mother was to bake something. Edith was afraid to show she wasn't a good cook, and therefore she contributed cupcakes she had purchased, first removing the cupcake paper and intending to pass them off as her own. The troop leader, however, rejected Edith's cupcakes when she realized they were not home-made. Edith was "caught and embarrassed," said Louise. Louise herself felt "embarrassed" but also felt "bad" for her mother, since Edith felt badly about herself. As an adult looking back on this, Louise realized that this incident had been damaging for her as a child.

Louise's painful memory of the cupcakes—which she told me spontaneously, without being specifically asked—contrasted markedly with most of what she said when I asked her much later about her earliest memories of childhood. She remembered her father bending over her in her crib and picking her up, perhaps singing a song; she believed this occurred when she was less than one year old. In addition, she remembered being in her baby carriage, and someone had laid pussy willow across the carriage; Louise was feeling the pussy willow. Louise added honestly that these memories could have been either real or reconstructed. Another memory, from when she was two or three, was about a friend of Beryl's; Louise and he took a walk together, and the two of them made up a secret handshake. The idealized quality of these memories is apparent. Next, however, Louise presented an incident during which she was unprotected and must have been frightened.

At about age five, Louise was left with her aunt Sarah and her family overnight, and she was distressed because all the members of her aunt's household were fighting. Louise, consequently, stole money from her aunt, left the house to find a phone booth, and called home. An hour later, Beryl appeared to pick her up. On the way home, said Louise, her father both taught her a song and told her a biblical story. Louise thus ends this memory with her father comforting her. Yet this was surely an instance in which she was temporarily unprotected and, therefore, forced precociously to take care of herself. Louise followed this difficult recollection with another positive memory. She remembered her first day of school, and she wore a new outfit for the occasion; moreover, she added that she loved school and began to talk about her "wonderful" seventh-grade teacher, who was "the best."

Beryl owned a small business by the time Louise was born, and until she was thirteen the family lived above its storefront; the family was happy to finally move into a house. In their middle-class neighborhood, Jews were a minority. Although Beryl earned an adequate amount of money, and his business did not suffer during the Depression, the family had less money than most nearby, and Louise felt different as a Jew. She remembered being called a "dirty Jew" as a six-year-old, and she had a lower status with other children because she was Jewish. Louise also was different in Hebrew School, where everyone else had American-born parents. During the interview, she undid the import of this sentiment by saying that she "loved" Hebrew School.

Louise stated that there was a "synergy between" her parents "that allowed them to be very good parents." She also said, "Except for not having a sibling, I thought I was very lucky." Although she *was* lucky in some ways— for example, she went to a well-known and wonderful secular Yiddish camp—she followed this by saying, "I was too important to my parents"; she meant that they were too narcissistically invested in her. Because her parents did not have to spend every moment working, they had time to be excited for her, for instance, when she received her first library card. And her parents made sure that she took part in the usual American activities, such as the Girl Scouts. School came easily to her, and Louise was the valedictorian of her eighth-grade class. I understand the basis for Louise's feeling that she was a lucky child; she was an only child and the focus of much parental attention. In addition, her parents, unlike many immigrants who were consumed with the struggle for economic survival, had time to spend with her. Yet she must have been overscheduled, as she went not only to Hebrew School and to public school but also to Yiddish School.

Although she did not actually say this, adolescence must have been very difficult for Louise, and interactions with her mother would, I think, have been painful, contentious, and wounding for both of them. Louise did mention that she and her mother fought in part because Edith was extremely anxious about Louise's budding sexuality. When a boyfriend called Louise "vivacious," her mother thought that "vivacious" was a bad word. "I was difficult and willful," Louise explained (although this sounds like an expectable and not unhealthy reaction to such a mother). Indeed, Louise married at age eighteen to get away from home, and this relationship lasted only for a year.

In trying to understand Louise, perhaps from a darker point of view than her own interpretations represent, I attempt to shed light on the part of Louise that was scarred by having to care for damaged parents, while also acknowledging the healthy aspects of her personality. Louise's childhood recollections seesaw between positive memories and descriptions of life with two traumatized parents. Louise's memory of being unprotected and frightened at her aunt's house was followed immediately by those of loving school, having a new outfit, and having "the best" seventh-grade teacher. Louise soothed herself during the interview: after revealing a presumably traumatic memory, she comforted herself by convincing herself and me that her childhood was not terrible but wonderful. Similarly, she preceded her revelation of the store-bought cupcakes—a demonstration of her mother's damaging behavior due to what Louise would have agreed were Edith's narcissistic needs—with the recollection that when her intellectual parents visited the Yiddish theater, they saw Shakespeare in Yiddish rather than the common low-brow comedies.

That Louise's childhood memories oscillate between the positive and the unintentionally damaging parallels her movement between being a child forced to play an adult role (parentified child) and being a child who is allowed to be a child. Louise told the cupcake story as though as a child she understood and seemed to forgive Edith for her poor self-esteem. That is, she, the parentified child, was empathic with her suffering mother. Similarly, in the story about her turbulent visit to her aunt's house, from which she rescued herself by stealing money and going outdoors to find a pay phone, she was forced to take a parentified role. As an aside, I find myself incredulous that Louise's parents left her alone with her aunt's family, as Edith believed her sister was an extremely mean woman. This makes more sense when we realize that Edith, who probably made the decision to leave Louise with her sister, was often unconsciously preoccupied with her own trauma; she would, consequently, frequently have been unable to be empathically attuned to her daughter's emotional needs (e.g., Davoine & Gaudillière, 2004; Kaplan, 1995).

Louise's childhood and her life story were complex and therefore difficult to understand, and I found myself as a clinician wanting to believe that her childhood included many happy and positive times. Part of the complexity is that, despite Beryl's obvious wounds, he was, as Louise stated repeatedly, a loving man; I believe Louise felt very much loved by her father. She correctly stated that her father was better put together psychologically than was her mother. That Beryl was not only warm and sweet but that he also composed funny poems and sang songs truly suggests some happy times.

A second part of the complexity in understanding Louise—and which made me believe her childhood was in some ways a good one—is that she was well-related. In other words, she felt emotionally present and responsive with me during the interviews. It is possible that this characteristic was developed later in her life through her self-healing activities; it may also have resulted from her father's frequent, though not constant, capacity to be emotionally available.

Louise realized that, though she was treasured by her parents, in fact both her parents were narcissistically invested in her: she was "too important" to them. She stated that her father's narcissistic investment in her sometimes got in the way of his understanding her. And her mother, a poet who published a Yiddish poem, pasted the following poem on Louise's baby picture:

> You are the pearls I cannot buy
> You are the trip I cannot take
> You are my blue Italian lake.

Louise explained that her mother meant, "You are my everything." In other words, she was her mother's "compensation." To feel "too important" to one's parents, to represent "everything" to one's mother, is a weighty burden for a child.

Louise was forced to navigate a very confusing relationship with her parents. I picture this relationship as often very problematic, as she probably bounced from one parent to the other as their capacities for empathy varied. At any time, Edith might become wounded by an interaction with Louise; when this happened, she would not speak to Louise for days or weeks, and Louise must have turned to Beryl. There were times, however, when Beryl was unable to understand Louise because of his own needs; Louise also mentioned a time when her mother understood what her father did not.

Louise was the recipient of intergenerational transmission from both her parents. As an adult, Louise, almost the child of Holocaust survivors, was involved not only personally but also professionally in thinking about the Holocaust. One hypothesis is that, when she was a child, as a way of coping with the unspeakable traumatic legacy she received from both parents, Louise became a caretaker to them. Louise described her mother's "inside terror," which often would have preoccupied her during Louise's infancy; because of this pervasive terror, Louise probably experienced Edith's momentary dissociations, or absences, as representations of overwhelming emotional states (Halasz, 2012, p. 153). Louise's response to this would have been a need to protect herself and, in order to survive, a need also to protect her mother. She would have attempted to empathize with and care for her mother, to become her mother's "bridge to life" (Kaplan, 1995, p. 225). As an infant she would have begun to serve as her mother's caretaker. In addition, as an older child, Louise might have seen Edith's terror on the street; something could have reminded her mother of the anti-Semitism of her childhood (Kaplan, 1995). In such a situation, Louise would have realized that "something" was wrong, that "existence" was "precarious," and that—in order to provide calm for her mother and for herself—she would have to provide the soothing (p. 231).

One of Louise's most perceptive interpretations of her own life came toward the end of her interview; she stated then that it was her "job" to "repair" her parents. Louise, in fact, said that she was "in every way repairing" her parents: in her "vitality," in her "humor," in her effort to get an advanced degree (her parents were not able to obtain formal educations), and in taking care of her parents when they were older. And I recognized that Louise repaired her parents by portraying them as good parents and herself as their lucky child. Louise was a caretaker to her traumatized parents, and she cared for them at the deepest level by devoting so many aspects of her life to repairing them; she was making up for their losses.

Another of Louise's interpretations of her own life was that she needed, and continues to need, to present a perfect exterior to the world. Louise's understanding of this was that she would make up for her mother's fragility and narcissistic vulnerability by appearing perfect. As a child, Louise literally tried to look perfect; her parents would help to ensure that her clothing had no obvious flaws. During her interview, Louise tried to present a perfect exterior to me by depicting her parents as more benign and less disturbed than they often were; she showed me an idealized version of her mother and father. I believe that, in the moment that she said her mother was charming and articulate or that her father was warm, gentle, and funny, she believed that these idealized characterizations were accurate. Indeed, others must have seen her parents this way. Yet at other moments, Louise's position would shift, and she would describe, for instance, her mother's emotional disturbance with clinical accuracy. Reflecting on what she told me, Louise observed toward the interview's end, "Maybe I've 'whitewashed' my childhood." Louise herself must on some level have felt shame associated with the trauma passed on by her parents. That she, both during her childhood and continuing into the present, presents a perfect exterior to the world may be related to shame she unconsciously felt about having damaged parents.

Although her father's psychological makeup differed from her mother's, Louise's role as caretaker to him was in some ways similar to her role with Edith. As Louise accompanied Beryl to the Russian army movies, I can imagine her as his willing companion, on some level feeling proud that she could help cushion her father's anguish. Beryl may have enlisted his young daughter as his partner in this sad undertaking because it was paramount that he not be alone (Auerhahn & Prelinger, 1983).

Louise, by lessening her mother's anxiety and buffering her father's torment, was thereby also taking care of and protecting herself (Garon, 2004). Louise probably received little soothing from her jittery and apprehensive mother, who was unable to provide adequate affect regulation; consequently, it fell to Louise even as an infant to be the "more affectively related one" (Salberg, 2017a, p. 91). Moreover, Louise's parents would likely have been internally disorganized due to trauma. They were preoccupied with the past and therefore unavailable for effective parenting (Auerhahn & Prelinger, 1983). One aspect of Louise's precocious soothing capacities would have been in organizing and conceptualizing the disorganized parts of her parents. Furthermore, Louise may have unconsciously hoped that, if she could heal her parents, they in turn would be able to refrain from using her as a narcissistic self-object. They would then be able to be better parents.

I suggest that, even as a toddler and nursery-school-aged child, Louise precociously soothed and contained both her parents when they were distressed. She used her mind to cope with and contain their affects (Corrigan & Gordon, 1995).[4] Traumatic for Louise, I believe, was not only what she knew about her mother's fear-filled childhood and her father's loss and loneliness, but what she did not know (Auerhahn & Prelinger, 1983). She might have had unconscious ideas about the terrible suffering her mother underwent as a child during World War I. Furthermore, she consciously experienced *with* her father the discovery of his own family's murder. I believe that Louise's understanding of her parents' suffering created not only a desire to parent or heal them but also high levels of anxiety about the horror she imagined.

I will turn for a moment to the effects of Louise's childhood on her adult psychological life. In someone who otherwise seemed very self-aware, the examples of how Edith's trauma was transmitted intergenerationally to Louise were stunning. Louise, in a statement reminiscent of her mother, noted, "I don't like when [my husband] wears a yarmulke on the street." She said that his wearing a yarmulke made her feel that he was like a "sitting duck." Louise then continued to talk about associating Judaism with hiding because of danger. Next Louise explained that when her own daughter was a small child, her Jewish nursery school faced the street. Louise so much feared that something terrible could befall these Jewish children that it was all that she could do to refrain from telling the school's administrators to move the school. Louise, in explaining her fear, said that she actually had a fear of aggression and that anti-Semitic incidents had occurred in a town not far from her daughter's nursery school. Notwithstanding these anti-Semitic incidents, Louise's fears are not the rational result of an incident during her adult life. They represent the unconscious transmission of her mother's terror, as well as her understandable identification with Holocaust victims.

Louise needed to reconcile her memories of herself as the lucky girl with new clothes for the first day of school and the girl who lived with her parents' darkness and trauma. How did she put together her idealized childhood picture of her charming, articulate Hadassah leader mother and her "other" mother who could turn on a dime, becoming enraged at and refusing to speak to her daughter for a week or more at a time? How did she reconcile the gentle and empathic father with the father who chose her as a companion as he searched newsreels for probably murdered family members?

Louise seemed confused between the irreconcilable parts of her parents. The balancing act was conspicuous. Louise seesawed between painful portrayals of her parents and attempts to downplay anything negative. She appeared unable to truly integrate the positive and negative—the parents who together were "very good" parents with the sometimes duplicitous, "crazy" mother and the depressed, needy father. Louise seemed to have two different solutions. One was to "whitewash" the negative, to attempt to present a perfect exterior, thus covering up the shame associated with having damaged parents. A second was to show me everything: in an attempt to be truthful despite her inner confusion, Louise worked very hard to present an extremely detailed portrait. Thus I would have all the facts.

Because Louise needed to repair her parents and make up for their losses, she felt compelled to be very careful in how she presented them to me; telling the truth might hurt her parents. Her very speech, her benign descriptions, cared for them. Yet because she was in many ways self-aware, she tried very hard to tell me whatever truth she could.

The truth was, I think, complex: as a child Louise often had fun, and she believed, I think correctly, that both parents treasured her; yet she *had* been damaged by her traumatized, often disturbed, parents. It seemed that Louise had received enough nurturance from her parents that, much later, as an adult, she was able to heal significantly.

In order to survive psychologically, children need to find the good in their lives and to hold onto that good. Even children who lived through the Holocaust formed positive fantasies that sustained them (M. O'Loughlin, personal communication, September 16, 2016). As we saw with Norman, parents who seem to be harmful to their children may be turned by the children into "good people"; otherwise the children feel that they are living in a "bad" world. And children's capacity to pretend serves them well in developing positive fantasies about their lives with their parents. [5]

To Louise's great credit, over the course of her adulthood, she had put her formidable energies into self-healing. Given the depths of the terror passed on to her, Louise's attempts at self-repair had resulted in admirable growth. She had worked hard to understand her parents and herself, and she had created a full and satisfying life for herself. Her professional life was fulfilling, her second marriage was to a man who both admired and loved her, and she fostered a good relationship with her daughter and granddaughter. Furthermore, her study of Jewish subjects in recent years suggested that an aspect of her growth was studying her Jewish past as a way to work through the legacy of trauma passed on by her parents.

Aaron's life story and the vignette about Barbara are darker than Norman's and Louise's, without the joys of play, and neither features childhood happiness. The effects of parental trauma—and, also for Barbara, her mother's mental illness—often prevailed at home. In both their families, talking was fighting and thus, at least for Barbara, life as a child must frequently have been frightening. The mothers of both took up a great deal of space in their children's psyches. Aaron needed to "shine" in order to make up for his parents' sacrifices.

Aaron

Aaron's story, as we glimpsed in chapter 2, combined family trauma, painful childhood memories, and a portrait of family life marred by constant fighting and economic stress. His mother's father was murdered in a pogrom, and his father had been a commissar in the Red Army; in the U.S. his father felt "diminished." Aaron was an intelligent, well-spoken ophthalmologist in his eighties who, during our interview, seemed not entirely at ease with himself. Although he noted that his stories were well-rehearsed, he nevertheless seemed hungry to talk, speaking at great length. I surmised that anxiety and an inability to deal with his painful feelings motivated his obsessional need to talk. Aaron was flattering and courtly yet formidable and imposing in his need to be in control. Over the course of three interviews, he guarded his time carefully, ending each one after a set time period. The information he presented was detailed and rich.

Aaron's childhood seemed emotionally bleak and with little nurture. As we have seen, his earliest memory was of getting lost during a trip to the beach with only his mother, Estelle. He was then less than five years old and "scared to death." He emphasized that he was still to this day affected by this experience, which contributed to his anxiety about "screwing up." His mother, he said, was "*not* overprotective"—"she was burdened with other things" (his emphasis). A second early memory was of his mother's failure to protect him; he was hit by a motorcycle when he ran across the street and, as a result, suffered a broken clavicle. "She shouldn't have let me get out," Aaron said of his mother, acknowledging that he was hurt because she was not caring for him. In an additional early memory, his mother took him to a clinic because he was very bow-legged. She changed her mind, however, and ran out of the clinic with him because she became afraid that the doctor would "do something." Her fear got the better of her desire to take care of Aaron's medical problem. As discussed in chapter 2, Aaron's mother was disengaged and misattuned because she was unconsciously preoccupied with the trauma of her father's murder.

Aaron was born in 1929, seven years after his parents emigrated to the U.S. Aaron was the second of two sons—his older brother had been born in about 1925—and his parents demanded that both boys be "the best, the first." Aaron was the "non-preferred son," and his brother was held up as a role model; Aaron resented that his mother treated him badly. Yet Aaron's attitude toward his mother was contradictory. He in part excused her derogatory attitude toward him, noting that "she was preoccupied with keeping the family together." This mother—who because of her own trauma seemed to be unable to feel—could, Aaron said, perceive that she was favoring his older brother, but his mother did not understand that he was "hurt" and let down by her treatment of him. Aaron was, needless to say, envious of his older brother, who, he said, never taught him anything, and the two were "intensely competitive."

Excluded within his own family, Aaron felt alone and lonely as a child. He and his mother ate dinner together every night (his brother and father ate separately later on), and Estelle talked about whom she had spoken with that day, rather than asking Aaron about himself. Aaron's father, Max, who worked all the time, was distant, "very self-centered," and "not interpersonally sensitive." Aaron felt "on the outside looking in," and he "never felt comfortable forming friendships." These painful feelings persisted all his life. That his family moved almost every year must have exacerbated Aaron's feelings of being excluded. Probably some portion of this feeling was related to his being Jewish, although Aaron grew up in Jewish neighborhoods; Aaron felt peripheral, however, even with Jews. "I'm not part of them," he felt with everyone. Feeling like the "other," Aaron perceived "anti-Semitism behind every bush," and he described the "intense feeling that they hate us."

As we remember, Aaron's parents were married as a "business arrangement" during the chaos following World War I in their Eastern European shtetl. His upper-middle-class mother married his father—who was lower class but had a high rank in the Red Army—for protection for her and her family. In the U.S., the combination of Aaron's parents' unhappy marriage and their "ever-present" economic strain caused constant fighting. His parents were "totally preoccupied" with the struggle of how to economically just "make things work." Because they were "dirt poor," the constant issue was, "how are we going to keep this [family] together?" "Fighting is talking," Aaron said. His parents' arguments, usually about money, were in his words "background noise." Estelle found Max's earning inadequate, and she consequently looked down on him. About his parents' relationship, Aaron said, "If my father said it was Tuesday, my mother knew it wasn't. If my father deviated one little bit from my mother's version of the truth, she would be on his back." We can imagine that the continual family strife would have been anxiety-provoking for Aaron and contributed to the bleakness of his childhood.

Aaron was born just as the Depression began, and his father, Max, always had a minimum of two jobs at a time. Although the family owned a small storefront business, Max worked in the garment industry, while Estelle worked at the store. When Max came home at night, he did deliveries for the family business. Much of the time, Max also worked in his brother-in-law's store on weekends. Estelle was extremely independent, and for a time she worked during the day at still another job, keeping this a secret from her husband.

The family usually lived in the back of their store, allowing them to pay only one rent; they moved nineteen times in twenty-one years, presumably because they could not afford rent raises. Moreover, moving ensured a clean and freshly painted apartment. When the family finally was able to afford the rent for an apartment separate from the store, "it was a big deal," noted Aaron. Only when he was sixteen did his parents have their own bedroom.

Furthermore, Aaron always, even when in medical school, slept on a Murphy bed in the living room.

Appearances were important in Aaron's family, and he was "dressed as nicely or better than anyone in his class." Consequently, Aaron did not realize how poor the family was. When the family was doing a bit better economically, Aaron asked for a used bike, but his parents did not buy him one for six months. That they waited so long was "shitty," Aaron commented. They just "didn't get around to it."

Aaron was expected to work as a child. Even at age seven he delivered newspapers; later he stocked shelves and delivered cleaning. He was in high school during World War II, and because all the men were at war, stores needed salespeople; Aaron worked long hours on Saturdays. By that time, Aaron's family must have been better-off financially, as he kept his earnings, using the money to play pool and to pay for dates with girls.

Both of Aaron's parents were critical, and his father, Max, like his brother, was competitive. Max, he said, worked hard and "he expected that you would work hard, too." When Aaron's high school performance was not stellar, Max was unkind: "What's wrong with you" that you're not in the top ten percent of your class? he asked. Both Aaron's parents behaved hurtfully to him.

Being "the best, the first" meant that both Aaron and his brother became doctors. Aaron had "to be the best within our family value system." Although he had done everything possible to "fulfill" his parents' "dreams," his mother nevertheless treated Aaron as the "second son," the lesser one. Estelle's seemingly deliberate cruelty seemed related to the trauma that left her with an inability to feel. [6]

Not just Aaron's loneliness but also his sense of exclusion and his anxiety about "screwing up" persisted into adulthood. He continued to feel that he was the "other," and as a young doctor, he felt "awkward" and embarrassed that he had not yet "learned" American culture adequately. "Not knowing is not OK," he commented; "it's not something you take in stride." To illustrate this, he related an anecdote about giving a paper in London for the first time—he was told before joining the receiving line, "Doctor, you don't go on a receiving line with a coat on your arm."

Aaron wanted a different life from that of his parents, although he agreed with their values. Becoming a doctor would bring him "major material success"—it would give him the "Packard view of life"; Packards were "what doctors drove" (the Packard was a luxury car aspired to until the mid-1950s). But Aaron emphasized that "being the best," rather than prosperity, was his "motivation" in becoming a physician.

In Aaron's family, "the children are the name of the game, not yourself." Aaron was happy about his career choice, but by becoming a doctor, Aaron was not just responding to his parents' sacrifices; for him it was much more complex. He stated that becoming a doctor was a way of fulfilling his parents' dreams. "You'll be proud of me," he said, referring to his parents; he very much needed his critical parents' approval. I suggest that in his career choice he was simultaneously also repairing his parents and responding to the sacrifices they had made for him. He seemed to need to repair both his mother, who had been so badly damaged when her father was killed in a pogrom, and his father, whose life was never the same after he came to the U.S. For these parents, "education was the be all and end all." Max implied that he would "support" Aaron "endlessly" if he went to school. Getting into medical school was for Aaron almost a requirement.

No play, spontaneity, or warm feelings were mentioned in Aaron's account of his childhood, and I suggest that this was associated with growing up with a traumatized mother who had no capacity for empathy. Moreover, Aaron lived in the midst of criticism, as well as constant and probably noisy fighting. I speculated that Aaron's hunger to talk during our interview could have been related not just to anxiety but also to never having been listened to as a child; his intense sense of aloneness meant that he needed attention from me.

Aaron's attitude toward his parents was complex, combining "gratefulness," admiration, and idealization with occasional anger. The following brief anecdote demonstrated Aaron's anger. Once when he was in medical school and studying late at night, his father admonished him to "go to sleep"; Aaron retorted, "My studying is your fault."

Aaron said he was obsessed with the mother who demanded so much from him. Even now, he was still the boy trying to please her: "I want her to be happy with me," Aaron said, using the present tense. Aaron's obsession with his mother seemed related to the intergenerational transmission of trauma. Perhaps trying to please Estelle, to keep her in his mind daily thirty years after her death, was a kind of transposition. She took up an inordinate amount of space in his psyche, and he had to live *for* her in order to repair her (Kaplan, 1995).[7] He felt that, no matter what he did, nothing was good enough for his unfeeling and critical mother. Aaron seemed to dissociate from or split off the terrible hurt that he felt as a result of his mother's sometimes derogatory treatment. He called her "my heroine," and he said, in addition, "I have a very good opinion of my mother, of what made me." In what seemed like a glaring instance of denial, he said, "My mother had so much interest in caring for others." Aaron, like his mother, seemed to split off or deny what he could not think about in the moment.

Estelle's trauma about her father's murder was unsayable; as the magnitude of this horror was impossible to capture in words, she was silent about it. I imagine that during Aaron's infancy, Estelle had frozen moments, periods of dissociation or fragmentation during which she was unavailable to soothe him. Indeed, her misattunement was evident throughout Aaron's narrative; one striking instance was her allowing him to get lost at the beach.

Because of her chronic misattunement, Estelle was unable to perceive that she ignored and badly treated her younger son. Moreover, the constant criticism and the competition with Aaron's father and brother suggest a painful and anxiety-provoking home environment. Consequently, even as an older adult, Aaron said that he was anxious about "screwing up," preoccupied with the constant task of living up to his critical parents.

My sense was that Aaron lived with the impossible dilemma of needing to repair the parents who behaved hurtfully to him but had nevertheless sacrificed for him. He needed to perform mental gymnastics: he split off the anger he felt at his mother's cruelty and his father's nastiness. As a result, he was, for example, able to conceive of his mother as "my heroine."

Yet the reality must have been even more complex. Despite the many difficulties and the loneliness of his childhood, Aaron nevertheless felt "fortunate." He elaborated that earning parental approval became the basis for his many "professional accomplishments"; he was "very highly published," he said. Aaron admired his parents' "struggles," noting that they "made it possible for me to do what I did." "They were there for me and I knew it." Thus alongside the psychological dilemmas that seem paramount to my formulation of him were Aaron's own complicated, occasionally positive, feelings. Despite Aaron's adult anxieties and occasional depression and self-hatred, the evidence of his fulfilling career and his relationship with his four children suggests he had found avenues to healing. I surmised that as a professional, he had discovered the means to talk through the extremely painful circumstances of his childhood.

Barbara

Barbara was one of my interviewees most pervasively affected during childhood by her parents' trauma. "I was an unloved child," she said, and she seemed in some ways to have been truly neglected both by her tired, overburdened father and depleted, depressed mother. We know Barbara from chapters 1 and 2, in part for the extreme poverty of her parents' early lives. As a child, she seemed to have been overwhelmed by her parents' traumatic communications, and I could almost feel tangible echoes of this trauma during Barbara's interview.

During her childhood, Barbara felt not just different from children with American-born parents but "stigmatized" and "disadvantaged." She stood out like a sore thumb because her parents ignored her ordinary needs. They "didn't seem to know things that other parents knew." She was laughed at because, for example, her knee socks always fell down—their elastic had worn out. Other parents, she said, knew "the trick" of holding up socks with rubber bands. In school she was "reprimanded" because papers fell out of her loose-leaf notebook; other children's American-born and sometimes college-educated parents bought their children reinforcements for loose-leaf papers so this wouldn't happen. Barbara's parents never purchased Scotch tape or a ruler for her to use for projects. Barbara said, "They had no use for Scotch tape," so she instead used Band-Aids. Barbara's parents cruelly laughed at her when she explained that she had learned at school that zero times zero equaled zero.

Barbara's traumatized parents seemed incapable of empathy. Barbara recalled saying to her mother, "Mommy, I'm bored," and her mother answering: "I have an idea. Why don't you go bang your head against the wall?" In truth this was something that mid-century mothers sometimes said, but I imagine that Barbara's mother said this with a deadened expression that might have been deeply frightening to her daughter. Because her parents had been traumatized—and, in addition, because of her mother's mental illness—they neglected their youngest daughter. As Barbara grew older, these unempathic parents even attempted to quash her artistic ambitions: "You can't be an artist; you'll never be an artist," they said. They wanted her to marry and become a mother; perhaps she could also become a teacher.

It seemed to me that for Barbara, like for Louise, the mechanism of repair was all-encompassing. Barbara seemed to be aware of her parents' suffering in every pore of her body and to take it in with her mother's milk. Indeed, I believe that Barbara was likely subject to transposition (Kaplan,1995)—when she was an adolescent and young adult, she experienced a severe illness; this seemed to me a repetition of her mother's devastating depression some years earlier. She may have in effect taken on this illness as a way to herself live out her mother's dreadful previous illness. This was a manifestation of her need to repair her parents and, particularly, her mother. Both as a child and as an adult, Barbara took on her parents' suffering, spending time with them and "egging them on" to tell their traumatic stories. She was drawn to their psychic pain. This out-of-place, deprived child became an adult instilled with her parents' pain.

Dorothy, like Barbara, was expected to marry and become a mother rather than to "shine" intellectually or in her career. Nevertheless, when she was a child, her father encouraged her to become educated. Similarly to Norman and Louise, Dorothy's childhood included both happy times and the influence of trauma.

Dorothy

Dorothy grew up in a happy household that abruptly turned sad when her father became ill with cancer. She was then ten years old, and her father died about three years later; this was traumatic for both Dorothy and her mother. The very bleak years after Dorothy's father's death, when both she and her mother were depressed and depleted, formed one theme of her interview. "Emotional needs were not seen as important" during her childhood; "Only physical needs were met," she said repeatedly. Like Louise, Norman, Aaron, and Barbara as children—all were affected by the difficult circumstances faced by their immigrant parents—Dorothy as a child lacked responsive parenting. Her family was affected by both individual trauma and by the historical trauma that Dorothy's mother suffered as a young person in Eastern Europe.

Dorothy was a small woman in her late seventies who was retired from a career as an educator. She seemed to find it somewhat difficult to share herself and her time with me. During her first interview, she was polite, reserved, and respectful of me as the authority. For this interview, she was very well-dressed and wore noticeable but not flashy jewelry, as if to reveal that she led a good life. During her second interview, Dorothy was more relaxed both in manner and in dress, but she did not seem to be quite at ease and was more difficult to read psychologically than some of my other interviewees. She often seemed sad when talking about her parents. Dorothy had retired more than twenty years earlier, immediately after her mother's death, and it seemed to me that she stopped working because of the emotional impact of losing her mother. In middle age she married a man several years her senior with whom she lived in downtown Brooklyn, and she had a sister who was three years older.

So that we can better understand the psychological tragedy of Dorothy's father's death, I will introduce her parents' lives and the contrast between the two of them. Dorothy's father, Harold, was a more sophisticated and outgoing person than was her mother, and in Dorothy's memory he was also gentler and more nurturing. Born in a shtetl in 1898, he had spent several years in Vienna, where he lived with an uncle before moving to America in 1922; he was sent to Vienna in order to avoid conscription. Dorothy knew nothing about her father's early life, but she knew that in Vienna he had enjoyed himself. He snuck into the Vienna opera house and learned to dance, and he and a sister won a dance contest there. During Dorothy's childhood, he was "good-natured," a "charmer" who liked to tease people and tell jokes (sometimes dirty jokes); he was more Americanized than his wife. Although he read the *New York Times* from cover to cover, he felt embarrassed about his lack of education, refraining from signing Dorothy's report card because he felt his signature wasn't good enough.

Dorothy's mother, Dina, suffered trauma as a child in Eastern Europe, as well as distress as a young immigrant in New York City. Dina arrived in 1921 at age seventeen with a younger sister, leaving her parents and four or five other siblings in Eastern Europe. In their shtetl, Dina's very poor family feared encountering the gentile peasants on market days. Furthermore, the family experienced pogroms, and during pogroms her father hid his older daughters to protect them from rape. (Dorothy believed that her mother was not one of those who was hidden, although she did not know this with certainty.) My sense was that this family experienced very devastating pogroms. Once, terrorized when fleeing a pogrom, they inadvertently left one of their children behind when they turned at a fork in the road. The horror and consequent trauma of this are barely imaginable. Dina's experiences of pogroms such as this one very likely left her with gaps or absences that would necessarily have affected her as a mother. Dorothy and her sister must, consequently, have experienced moments of frozen affect or "not-there-ness" in the relationship with their mother; in this way, Dina's trauma would have been transmitted to her daughters (Gerson, 2009, p. 1347; as cited in Salberg, 2017a, p. 85).

Despite the pogroms, Dina missed her family and had fond memories of her life in Eastern Europe. She remembered her mother baking bread, and she recalled holidays and Sabbath dinners. A piece of Dina's childhood was conveyed in a Yiddish folk tale, a legacy of Dina's own mother, which Dorothy volunteered toward the beginning of her interview. The folk tale concerned a grandmother whose many children were eaten by a wolf after she left them alone in order to gather wood. The story ended happily with dinner, however, specifically a Sabbath dinner.

The benevolence and affection with which Dorothy recounted this tale were at odds with her usual manner, and that she told it in its original Yiddish suggested that it replicated her mother's own affect in telling it to Dorothy. (Dorothy translated the story into English for me.) Moreover, Dorothy stated that her mother's family was loving, and my clinical judgment, based on Dorothy's warm delivery, suggested that this may have been true. My own reaction to this folk tale was that it paradoxically expressed both the love within Dina's family and the dangers of her shtetl childhood.

According to Dorothy, Dina had a poor self-image as a young person, which was associated with her family's poverty. The family was considered lower class, and her mother consequently "always felt less." Moreover, Dina and her sister were looked down on because they were Jews in the Eastern European school they attended, and the nuns in school would slap her wrists. When Dina and her sister arrived in the U.S., they were met by an uncle with whom they then lived. His children looked down on them as greenhorns, treating them unkindly. Dina's poor self-image must have been exacerbated by her cousins' disparaging treatment of her. Dorothy felt that her mother was lonely and homesick at first and, in addition, that she might have felt rejected because her family had sent her away to America. Dina continued throughout her life to suffer from a poor self-image—she "didn't give herself credit for much."

To add to her difficulties, Dina required mastoid surgery as a young woman in New York; Dorothy understood this to have been the result of typhoid fever that her mother had contracted as a child. Because she was poor, Dina was, in her daughter's words, "butchered" during the operation, and she had hearing loss afterward.

In introducing Dorothy's childhood, I note that the themes of physical care and food as nurturance were important ones. Dorothy's parents owned a small grocery store, and as immigrant parents, "they were so focused on working hard" there. Because her parents were in the grocery business, the family had enough food, and Dorothy mentioned food repeatedly in her early positive memories.

An anecdote about food and physical care reveals what appeared to have been an ambivalent relationship between Dina and her daughter since Dorothy's infancy. Dina would try to feed Dorothy, and when her baby daughter refused to eat, Dina would become frustrated and throw Dorothy's food dish in the sink. Thus there were times when Dina was unable to respond sensitively to the needs of her very young, and therefore vulnerable daughter.

Dorothy grew up in the Bronx near her father's family. Often sick in bed when she was small, she remembered that Dina would send Harold up from the store with tea for her. She also remembered that, on summer evenings when she played outdoors until late, Dina sometimes fed her pumpernickel bread with cream cheese from the store, adding a sour pickle right from the barrel. Harold, who had worked in a bakery in Vienna before emigrating, loved to bake, and theirs was the first family in their neighborhood to own an electric kitchen mixer; he baked Passover cakes, birthday cakes, and meringue cookies with walnuts made "in the French way." Dorothy remembered carrying these cakes to family and neighbors. Harold also drove a car and liked baseball, taking only boys who worked for him, rather than his daughters, to baseball games.

Harold enjoyed life and had a sense of humor, and he brought a sense of life to Dorothy's more serious and constrained mother. Her mother, however, contributed to physical care for Dorothy and for the family in general. She loved to cook, made meals for extended family on Sundays, and always ensured that their apartment was "festive" for holidays. Because their apartment was often cold in the winter, Dina would put her daughter's underwear in the oven and then dress her under the covers (Dorothy liked this). Sometimes Dorothy would spend the afternoon with her mother after going to the doctor, feeding the squirrels they saw, a novelty since there were no squirrels near their apartment. On the other hand, Dorothy wished her mother appeared more American. She wanted her to dress in a "more upscale" way and to remove her apron when she brought Dorothy's lunch to school on a rainy day.

Other childhood memories seem typical for children of this generation, including playing hopscotch on the street, being taught to crochet by a friend, and putting on a charity fund-raiser with other neighborhood children. The fund-raiser was held in the courtyard of their building, and a contest for the prettiest baby was part of the event. Sundays were spent with extended family. Dorothy became best friends with a cousin close to her age. During the summer, Harold drove everyone to the beach, where they would stay late into the evening, and the children would sometimes fall asleep on the sand.

All this changed when Harold became ill. Dorothy was left to her own devices; at age ten she was thought to be old enough to be on her own. Her mother had to manage the store alone and worked seven days a week. At some point Harold's family, who Dorothy believed had had a contentious relationship even in Eastern Europe, began to meddle. They accused Dina of not taking good enough care of her husband; she should have been caring for him rather than working, they argued. One happier experience of these diffi-cult years, which occurred during the last summer of his life, was a trip Dorothy and her father took to the Catskills. He would take Dorothy out to dinner, giving her the menu to read herself and treating her like a "young lady." He also taught her table manners, which she appreciated.

When Harold was dying at age fifty-two, he was bitter, regretting that he had not gotten enough out of life; this was extremely distressing to Dorothy. During one "devastating" experience from his final illness, her father's ex-tended family gathered in Dorothy's family's apartment, yelling while her father hemorrhaged; Dorothy was beside herself, hiding in a closet. Her father died when Dorothy was graduating from junior high school, and Doro-thy felt bereft that her graduation could not be properly celebrated; in fact, she still lamented this. Dorothy described the following terrible scene: in an attempt at a graduation celebration, she, her mother, and her sister had a graduation cake. The three laughed as they ate cake, while Harold was upset that they were laughing. On the day of her father's funeral, Dorothy felt lost, as her grieving mother was unable to think about her anguished daughter's emotions. No one could guide the thirteen-year-old even about how to dress for the funeral.

Dorothy's life and her mother's collapsed emotionally after Harold's death. Because of the long-term effects of her own trauma, Dina seemed never again to have the capacity to provide emotional nurturance for her daughter. Thus for Dorothy the family, or individual, trauma of her father's illness and death interacted with and exacerbated the effects of her mother's historical trauma.

After Harold's death, the warmth of the immigrant family was gone, Dorothy said. Her father's family "walked out" of their lives, and she lost her best-friend cousin. Her mother cried; she was depressed for years. Dina was, and remained, a deadened mother for her younger daughter. Dorothy, who described herself as "still a little girl at that time," felt "alone and lonely in a dreary household." Her sister was usually off with friends, and Dina was working hard so that they had enough money, but she was away from home. The house was no longer festive.

"I think I was a neglected kid," Dorothy said. She had lost the warmth her father provided; he was the one she could look up to and who wanted the best for her. Her high school years were bleak and depressing. She just sat in the back of the classroom, and there was no one to encourage her to join organizations or to "come into [her] own." Indeed, she said that because of her depression, she had very few memories of high school.

The effects of the Holocaust also influenced Dorothy's family during the years of her father's illness and death. Although Dorothy, born in 1935, was too young to remember exact events, most of her mother's family was then still living in Eastern Europe. Dorothy told me several times about her survivor uncle, who had been in the woods when the Nazis arrived. He returned to his village to try to save his mother, Dorothy's grandmother. Loaded onto a freight car with others, he slid its door off and jumped from it, rescuing others in the process. They then survived in a bunker under a German hospital and foraged for food at night. This uncle made his way to New York as Dorothy's father was dying and remained in New York to help her mother in the store. That Dina lost her own mother and some siblings in the Holocaust was an additional trauma that she bore and that must have drained her.

Because of Dina's unmetabolized trauma, during Dorothy's infancy, she was probably at times unable to provide containment and soothing for her daughter. Later, after her husband's death, Dina's maternal abilities broke down; she was psychically absent, drowning in her own understandable depression. Dina's continuing psychic collapse had long-standing consequences for Dorothy. The ghost of Dina's trauma was not visible as an explicit symptom for Dorothy. It survived, however, in Dorothy's lengthy depression after her father's death.

For children to achieve material success was one way of rising above the immigrants' struggles, and Dorothy emphasized the contrast with her parents' lives: "When you're an immigrant child, whatever you do is a success," she said several times.

Dorothy said that when she was young, "it was a given" that her life would be different from that of her parents. The road to the success that she wished for began with education and Americanization, and—rather than follow her mother's wishes that she be successful by marrying and having children—she instead followed her father's legacy: she chose to attend college. Dorothy was disappointed that she received little recognition from her mother for her educational accomplishments.

Dorothy chose a career as an educator, which allowed her to advance. She was proud of her success and of the success of the "immigrant generation." "We made it in America," she stated. Dorothy's career and her recovery from the prolonged depression of her early adult life form part of our story of adulthood in the next chapter.

CONCLUSIONS: PREOCCUPIED PARENTS AND FULFILLING PARENTAL DREAMS AND AMBITIONS

In writing about the childhoods of the immigrants' children, I could not help but notice that, overall, many of the children did not have parents who were responsive or attuned to their needs; ever the clinical psychologist, I could not help but see what we might think of as psychopathology. Conceiving of it in this way, however, is oversimplifying. In trying to digest this, we must remember first that parenting styles were very different in the 1920s through the 1950s, when my interviewees were children. Parents were not expected to attend to their child's every need or to spend what we call quality time with them. In addition, many of the immigrant parents had experienced trauma, and trauma, by its very definition, affects attachment relationships. These parents might at times have been in dysregulated or frozen states that made the attunement necessary for secure attachment and responsiveness impossible. Moreover, most of them were too preoccupied with the daily struggle of earning a living or running a household with little money to regularly respond to their children's emotional needs. Nevertheless, it is important to remember that parents who were at times or even often preoccupied or not attuned could still be, though inconsistently so, good parents. Their children, for example, might still be aware of parental support or love.

Salberg's (2017a) emphasis on the complex communication of both trauma and resilience through the attachment bond is extremely useful in thinking about the development of my interviewees. For example, Louise, whose parents were both traumatized, had the advantage of having a father who was empathic much of the time. I imagine this helped Louise to develop empathy, which was one of the most important and salient aspects of her adult personality. But Louise also needed to prematurely help her mother with affect regulation, and it is possible that parenting her mother might have been a mechanism that contributed to a precocious ability to soothe herself; this would have come with underlying psychological vulnerabilities, however.

Dorothy's life story illustrates both relational trauma and a hypothesis about resilience. During Dorothy's childhood, her traumatized mother sometimes directed her unpredictability toward her child, for instance, when in frustration she threw her infant's food in the sink. Dorothy imbibed relational trauma in the attachment bond with her mother, and we see this in the low self-esteem and depression that characterized the first half of her adult life; this will be illustrated in chapter 5. Nevertheless, Dorothy's traumatized mother, I thought, had a capacity for warmth, as did her father. As an adult, Dorothy was focused on treating herself well by, for example, attending the ballet and purchasing herself nice clothing and jewelry; I associated this to her family's emphasis on food as a means of nurture during her childhood. I wondered whether Dorothy absorbed this piece of adult resilience from her early life. Perhaps this early nurture was also taken in through the attachment bond and translated in adult life into a healthy self-repair. This might have helped Dorothy as an adult to recover from her depression.

Salberg's (2017a) theory—building on earlier work by, for example, Halasz (2012) and Kaplan (1995)—helps us to understand the mechanism by which trauma is transmitted to children in the attachment bond. When a parent caring for a child experiences a fleeting, perhaps unconscious memory of, for example, a pogrom, this is manifested in a momentary dissociation or absence. Thus the parent's overwhelming emotional state, a representation of "unrecognized experiences of disrupted safety," is felt by the child, who in turn is "terrorized by the parent's unmetabolized trauma" (Harris, 2014, p. 270, as cited in Salberg, 2017a, p. 90). Louise, Aaron, and Barbara were, I suggest, affected by this kind of unconscious communication of trauma from their mothers, and Norman and Dorothy may have also experienced something similar.

Most of the parents of my interviewees had to work extremely hard to make ends meet, and their necessary preoccupation with the struggle to earn a living was another factor that might have made them less responsive to their children. Parents might be anxious about finding rent money lest the family be evicted or about making nutritious meals with only pennies to spend; they might be exhausted from working long hours in their stores. Many children felt the loss of growing up with parents who simply had no energy for attunement to their children's needs. In this chapter, Norman's and Aaron's parents stand out in this context, as does Dorothy's mother after her husband's death. These parents were probably less empathically available to their children because of the anxiety of raising children in poverty.

If, in general, parents were unable to be attuned to their children's needs in the way we now expect parents to be, there was good reason for this. Nevertheless, many of the children were resilient, and memories of happy moments in the context of what seem to us to be difficult childhoods are plentiful in my interviewees' life stories. Norman relished his street corner social life, playing games with friends and developing the social skills that became one of his adult strengths. And Dorothy enjoyed playing hopscotch with friends, as well as family trips to the beach.

Not every family was poor. Louise's family, for example, was middle-class, and their financial cushion meant that her parents had time to spend with her. Two interviewees' families described in earlier chapters were well off. These were Stanley's, whose mother was traumatized by bullets whizzing by during World War I (chapter 2), and Helen's, whose mother intensely missed the family from whom she was separated by World War I (chapter 3).

To give the reader the flavor of a childhood free from economic anxiety, I will briefly present the middle-class early life of Elizabeth, a retired educator in her seventies.[8] Her father had been a grocer in a "suburban," somewhat genteel neighborhood of greater New York City, and he had prospered. Her parents had an "overriding" desire to be American, and social class was very important to them. Elizabeth described a "peaceful" and overprotected childhood. She "loved going to the library," as well as the library's smell. She read before she had a lot of friends. Because of the Lindbergh kidnapping, she was not allowed to ride a bike, and her parents did not want her to ice skate by herself. As a child, Elizabeth did everything her mother wanted her to: Girl Scouts, piano lessons, and Hebrew School. Her mother, she said, gave Elizabeth "a sense that the world was mine."

As a child, the desire to be American was important not just to her parents but to Elizabeth too. She was "ashamed" of her parents' foreign accents, though her mother's accent was slight, as well as of their immigrant status. She added, "If you were not American, you felt lower in the hierarchy." She herself didn't feel "as good as" the American kids, who had a "head start on me." Moreover, Elizabeth was self-conscious that she wasn't dressed in clothing from Saks, as were some classmates; her clothing came from Klein's, a bargain store. Elizabeth was one of my only interviewees to admit to feeling inferior to American children.

We began this chapter talking about those immigrants' children who were expected to "shine" in order to "redeem the anxiety of their [parents'] existence." Although this may have been more of a pattern for males, the ability to have a better life than that of one's parents, to make up for their parents' losses and sacrifices, certainly seemed to be an important theme in the lives of many of my interviewees. It was extremely important to move up, to become middle class, to do one's best. Aaron, Louise, and Norman did everything in their power to "be the best, the first," and success was a very important theme for Dorothy.

Most of my interviewees knew they wanted lives different from those of their parents, and many knew college was in their future; education was very important to the majority of their families. It was through education that the majority of my interviewees began the road to success. In discussing this, however, it is important to remember that my interviewees were a self-selected group. They volunteered to be interviewed, and perhaps those who were less materially successful might not have done so. Of course, there was a gender difference, and certainly many Jewish women of this generation were expected to marry right after high school. Yet of those I interviewed, every one, male and female, had graduated from college.[9] Often this involved great sacrifice by parents and, at least in Norman's case, his own sacrifice—in order to support his mother, he worked during the day and attended college and graduate school in the evening. The mothers of many of my female interviewees wanted their daughters to be educated, and the sacrifices of many parents to send their daughters to college stand out for me. Whether it was education itself or the security that it could bring that was the value, the vast majority of the parents wanted their children to have better lives, and children worked hard to repay this debt.

The theme of wanting to have a different life than that of their parents was important, and some interviewees discussed this in terms of Americanization. In order to fulfill their parents' and their own aspirations to have better lives, the children needed to become more Americanized than their parents. Parents wanted their children to be successful, but sometimes this could not come without some strain. When Dorothy moved out as a single adult, this was a new and shocking concept to her mother and a source of significant difficulty. A few interviewees described more minor conflicts with their parents about Americanization. For example, Stanley's parents, discussed in chapter 2, retained their European ways, continuing to speak Yiddish all their lives— they were just "geographic transplants" who happened to be living in America. But Stanley wanted a different life from theirs, an "American life." One of the conflicts around Americanization that occurred in his household was over his father's inability to understand Stanley's love of the American sport of baseball. Moreover, several of my interviewees spoke about feeling embarrassed about their parents' foreign accents.[10]

Seymour, whose mother had seen nightmares around her during World War I (chapters 1, 2, and 5), described wanting a different life, a "freer life," than his parents. Discussing this in intellectual terms, he said he wanted to be free to read Jack Kerouac and Allen Ginsberg. His ideal life would be open to exploration rather than "predetermined" by a "bunch of rules," like those by which his modern Orthodox parents were constrained. Benjamin (chapter 1) said his parents *expected* him to go his own way (my emphasis), that they wanted him to have wider interests than they had, and he described his ability to decide on his own career in this context: "I felt that this was a great country, that one could make one's way here. We had little money. I was a child of immigrants. I had to see what I could do."

Americanization, education, and middle-class status were at the same time things parents wanted for their children and things that might cause conflict. Louise wanted to repair her parents in every way, and she gratified them by getting an advanced degree. But her parents did not understand her choice of a very new world profession, and for a number of years objected to it; this upset her. Moreover, David, discussed in the next chapter, was in

direct conflict with his father, who wanted him to take over the family business rather than go to college; his mother intervened so that he could continue his education. Having a better life than one's parents might at the same
time make up for parents' losses and be difficult for parents and children.

In choosing education, the immigrants' children began to move beyond
their parents' lives; they began to enter the American world in ways that their
parents could not. The contrast with immigrant parents' lives and the themes
of hard work, education, and Americanization will be elucidated further in
the life stories of the interviewees as adults.

NOTES

1. Howe, however, believed that the schools made an honest effort to do what was best for
the students.

2. The Educational Alliance, founded in 1905 by German Jews as a settlement house for
the poor, taught new Americans English, as well as such subjects as cooking and sewing,
history, music, and art.

3. German-Jewish Americans—who preceded the Eastern European Jews in immigrating
to America—looked down on the more recent immigrants. They tended to be wealthier and to
believe that their culture was more refined. Uncomfortable feelings between the two groups can
sometimes exist to this day.

4. The concept of the mind object (Corrigan & Gordon, 1995; Impert, 1999), a defensive
posture involving an "overly developed sense of self-sufficiency" and the use of the mind to
cope with disruptive emotions or self-states, seems to fit Louise's adult personality and how I
imagine her as a child (Impert, 1999, p. 648). I would imagine that as a toddler, Louise, like
others who use the mind-object constellation, was especially well-related, charming, and talkative. From what she told me, Louise's parents would have prized her precocious intellectual
abilities. The mind object involves a posture of pseudo-maturity; the mind is used to cope with
disruptive emotions or self-states. "Strong affects" and "certain bodily experiences" are com-
partmentalized in order to "insure stability" (Impert, 1999, p. 648). Those who depend on the
mind object as a defense, however, are in some ways fragile: for example, anxiety, depression,
"somatic concerns," despair, or emptiness can break through their equilibrium (pp. 647, 648). I
imagine that Louise "precociously" learned "not only to read her mother's moods, but also to
defensively adapt to them by compliance" (p. 650). I picture her extremely well-adapted to the
mother-child dyad, "shrewdly anticipating the experience of impingement itself." As part of the
"vigilance" associated with the mind-object constellation, she would have dissociated "states of
distress, appearing 'super adjusted'" (Krystal, 1988, p. 247, cited by Impert, 1999, p. 650).

5. This defense functioned for both Norman and Louise.

6. That she was narcissistically gratified by her older son's accomplishments does not
mean that she behaved empathically toward him either.

7. The concept of transposition was originally developed by Judith Kestenberg. It is explained in the theory of the intergenerational transmission of trauma section in chapter 2.

8. It was Elizabeth who reported that her father "wanted to leave it all behind." Her mother
had been traumatized during World War I, and Elizabeth stated that "both parents agreed that
they would never set foot in Europe again. They had had it."

9. Many of my interviewees grew up in New York City, and because of this, they were able
to attend the free city colleges. Without these free colleges, many of them would have been
unable to attend college. In addition, the G.I. Bill was helpful in paying for the educations of
those who had served in the armed forces.

10. That only a small number of interviewees described conflicts with their parents while
growing up—and some denied that any such conflict took place—was surprising, as the literature described conflict between the generations as widespread, and I believed that my inter-

viewees generally minimized this. I also felt that my interviewees minimized embarrassment or shame around their parents' foreign accents. I was interviewing them toward the ends of their own lives, and I believed that at that point, many wanted to idealize their relationships with their parents rather than acknowledge past conflicts. But it is also possible that, since so many had grown up in immigrant neighborhoods, having parents with foreign accents was not unusual. Diner (2004, p. 287) wrote that by the late 1960s, "immigrant origins lay so far in the past that [descendants] no longer had any reason to be embarrassed by them." It is possible that many of those with whom I spoke would have been upset by parents' immigrant demeanor and accents when younger but now no longer saw this as an issue.

Chapter Five

The First Generation

Adulthood

DRAMATIS PERSONAE

In order of appearance:

Irene: Irene called Eastern Europe a "bad place with bad memories for the Jews." Her mother was mentally ill and physically abusive. Building Jewish community was important to Irene as an adult.
    Mother: Letty
    Father: Leo

David: He "grew up in the shadow of the shtetl." Although he deeply felt the pain of his mother's childhood of fear and starvation, he as an adult seemed determined to enjoy his life.
    Mother: Pearl
    Father: Philip

Seymour: His mother saw nightmares around her as a child during World War I. His father's entire family were killed in the Holocaust, and Seymour repeatedly re-experienced this event as a repetition of the past.
    Mother: Sadie
    Father: Amos

Dorothy: Her happy household turned unhappy when her father became ill and later died. Her mother, who had suffered trauma in Eastern Europe, could not provide for her emotional needs.

Mother: Dina
Father: Harold

Sarah: Sarah immigrated at age six with her mother. She minimized her mother's losses, saying: she "took it in stride. This is how it was." She herself lost her father as a young adult.
Mother: Blume
Father: Avram

My mother's second cousin Fay smoked herself to death. A lifelong smoker, cigarettes were, I believe, the only reliable way she could soothe herself. She smoked even after developing lung cancer (she "told off" the doctor who suggested she stop). Fay had difficulty with self-soothing for good reason. The youngest by far in her family, her Eastern European immigrant parents fought constantly and loudly, and her sister and brother joined in their parents' fighting. As a child, Fay found the yelling and the flying furniture terrifying. The violence was one manifestation of the unprocessed trauma that permeated Fay's family. As a young child, she was afraid of everything.

In adulthood, Fay married, had two children, and became a teacher, following a typical trajectory for women of her generation. Yet she could escape neither the legacy of her parents' trauma nor her own. When I spoke to Fay about her experiences, late in her life, she seemed to use dissociative defenses. Her dissociation, her inability to connect what she referred to as her "too many lives," made it difficult for her to formulate a narrative that would help her heal from the trauma of her childhood.

I knew both Fay and her parents, and although I spoke to Fay when I was conducting research interviews, she was not a research participant, and I had not originally planned to write about her. I did not ask her the same questions as I did my interviewees. Consequently, in various ways I knew both more and less about Fay than I did about my research participants.

In this chapter about the adulthoods of my interviewees, I will speak again about trauma, but also about resilience. To me, resilience has to do with the ability to rebound or spring back (Merriam-Webster's dictionary), with "patterns of positive adaptation in the context of significant risk or adversity" (Rutter, 2012, as cited in Holmes, 2017). The idea of narrative is one lens we can use to look at the relationship between trauma and resilience. This vignette about Fay will introduce us to the concept of how narrative and its ability to create inner meaning can initiate a pathway to healing from transgenerational trauma.

Fay's mother, Becky, was a tiny woman, intelligent, sometimes stern and even steely, who was traumatized as a teenager during World War I. She was forced to flee her Eastern European city, then saw her mother die because of Russian cruelty, and at age fourteen, still a war refugee, was left to care for her three younger brothers. Her heroic action in 1920 meant she and her brothers could immigrate to America before the Bolshevik army cut off their escape route. The first half of her life was full of deprivation, as well as both discrete and ongoing trauma.

Shortly after she arrived in the U.S., Becky married Sam, by her own account in order to create a home for her brothers. Sam had emigrated with his family at about age twelve, and his verbally abusive, uncaring father told Sam he would amount to nothing. The marriage was difficult from the beginning, and the couple fought continually. Becky both looked down on Sam and suspected him—probably without grounds—of looking at other women. Fay's older sister was born in 1923, and her brother joined the family three years later. Her parents struggled financially, and during the Depression, when there was no work to be had, were often "on the dole." Running a house with little money was at best a strain, and Becky was often tired and ill. Fay, the unplanned youngest child, was born in 1934 during the depths of the Depression, and she experienced her older sister as a better mother to her than her own mother. Both Fay and her brother described Becky as cold. Life in this family became even more difficult when, in about 1936, Sam contracted spinal meningitis and was hospitalized for a year. In 1942, when Fay was only eight years old, her brother, still underage, enlisted in the navy; because he was in active combat, Becky was beside herself with anxiety.

Fay's mother was always too strained to soothe her, and her father, Sam, was either sick or working. As a young child, Fay found the shouting and violent fighting by the four much larger people in her household to be absolutely terrifying. Fay as an adult told me that she had always been afraid of everything, but she wasn't sure of what. Maybe, she said, she feared being abandoned, and she had good reason to fear this; as a child she was hospitalized two or three times for ten days at a time for eye surgery, which was traumatic. Moreover, during visits to her extended family, Fay was teased mercilessly by older cousins and chased by one abusive cousin who carried an axe. As a child Fay was, she said, "bratty." (Her older sister and brother nicknamed her "Poison.") Angry and destructive, she tore the heads off her dolls.

Because of her eye problems—she wore glasses and sometimes an eye patch—Fay looked different from other girls. She suffered greatly from feeling that she wasn't as smart as her older sister, although she too was extremely bright and consequently skipped grades in school. In contrast to her, her older sister was perceived not only as the smart one but also as the "good one." At seventeen, Fay married a bright working-class boy in order to escape her mother. She had two children, and in her thirties became a teacher, eventually working with disabled children. Fay had an irreverent sense of fun; she was down-to-earth, forthright, and direct. She also was often truly generous.

Yet there were aspects of her personality that carried the terror of her childhood, the unhappiness and unmetabolized rage of her parents, and also, I propose, the unprocessed terror of her mother's adolescence. The fear that she was unable to explain to me may have had undertones of her mother's adolescent terror; it may well also have resulted from those childhood incidents when she was surrounded by the terrifying rage of the four much bigger people in her family.

Fay's life was affected by her mother's trauma in several ways. Because Becky was traumatized as a teenager and exhausted by the time of Fay's birth, she did not have the internal resources necessary to lessen the trauma of her young child's repeated hospitalizations and surgery. Fay probably feared abandonment in the hospital. She learned that she would have to soothe herself, and as a young adult, she found that cigarettes provided more reliable soothing than did people. Furthermore, her mother, Becky, was both unhappy and angry during Fay's childhood. Fay, who had received too little nurturance, in turn was not only angry but also, I believe, felt empty as an adult. She could withdraw, and she sometimes had screaming rages; at these times she wanted contact with no one.

As I mentioned earlier, when I spoke to Fay about her childhood, she revealed what seemed to be dissociative defenses. She at one point stated, "I don't know the person we're talking about. There are too many lives. There's not always a connection." Thus she seemed to be saying that she felt she was separate people at different times and that often these people did not feel connected. Fay dealt with her fear of her family's violent rages and her fear of abandonment by defensive splitting and as an adult sometimes did not feel a sense of continuity.

I do not mean to imply that Fay was always miserable or that she developed no resilience. During middle age, she and her husband began to travel widely, which they very much enjoyed. She was a voracious reader and loved art. Furthermore, she offered to move her elderly parents into her home; they instead decided to live with her older sister, the "good one" in the family. Because of Fay's and her family's history of terror, however, she found that only smoking could reliably soothe her, and she was unable to give up smoking even when it was killing her. I propose that Fay was not able to fully speak about, to symbolize, her own and her family's trauma history. Thus she could not adequately develop a narrative that she could use to explain it, and the trauma remained undigested and destructive inside her. Perhaps she did not trust any one person enough to talk through the trauma with him or her. The story of her in adulthood smoking herself to death is indeed striking.

That Fay as an adult felt fragmented suggests she had been unable to heal from the trauma that resulted from ducking tables thrown by her parents, sister, and brother (a legacy of her parents' earlier trauma) and from being left alone in the hospital as a young child. Salberg (2017b, p. 246) wrote: "As we now know, massive trauma disrupts the normal processes of mind by flooding us with affects and experiences that cannot be contained and turned easily into memory stories. To protect ourselves we fragment, dissociate, disavow so as to function and exist." Fay's trauma left her unable to form a memory story, a narrative, that would help her begin to heal. She was unable to integrate the painful stories of her childhood into a narrative that would lead to inner meaning and inner dialogue, thus forming the "basis of self-hood" (Salberg, 2017b, p. 247). In other words, over the course of her life, she had not been able to use her knowledge about her childhood to connect the fragments of herself. Her childhood left her with overwhelming affects that surfaced in her own rages. Because no one had been able to soothe her, she dissociated and then smoked to continue to function. This symptom of smoking was, at least in part, the result of intergenerational transmission passed on by her parents.

For a person to heal from trauma, it must be worked through and given meaning so that it becomes something "speakable, analysable, and ultimately symbolisable" (O'Loughlin, 2018, p. 2). When this occurs, the individual "can make use" of it rather than disavowing it. Until it is worked through, the person relates what happened as a "flat record of events," a chronicle, "which does not reflect the internal experience or world of the person" (Salberg, 2017b, p. 247). In contrast, a healing or true narrative is complex, reflective, nuanced, "*authored* by an agentic self," and "constructed in relationship to the inner and outer worlds" (Grand, 2009, p. 16; as cited in Salberg, 2017b, p. 247; emphasis is Grand's). Usually a healing narrative is co-constructed with an empathic listener, but it is sometimes formulated in the narrator's own imagination, as he or she tells the story to a "virtual listener" (Cyrulnik, 2007, p. 27; as cited in Pisano, 2012). According to Salberg (2017b, p. 247), intergenerational transmission of trauma proceeds through flat records or chronicles. "True narrative," on the other hand, "reflects the repair and resilience that the internal work of deep healing has done." Because of this deep healing, those with true narratives are able to break the cycle of "re-experiencing and re-enacting" the trauma.

In understanding the adult lives of my interviewees, I ask whether their stories are more like Fay's, relying on such defenses as disavowal, denial, dissociation, or repression; or, on the other hand, do they reflect an actual beginning of healing from the legacy of their parents? I will not have precise answers to this question as, of course, my interviews were limited in scope. As they spoke to me, most of those I interviewed grappled with the legacy of their parents' pasts. In some way, the interview of each person I spoke with reflects his or her parents' suffering. I will discuss how the immigrants' children psychologically managed the reality of their parents' losses and suffering. Notably, I believe that each interviewee demonstrated resilience along with the effects of their parents' losses or trauma. Before turning to the stories of some of my interviewees as adults, we will look briefly at some influences on them and the history of the period during which they came of age.

HISTORICAL INTRODUCTION

In only one generation, the children of the immigrants moved from their parents' largely Yiddish-speaking ethnic world into the secular American world. As adults they participated in an America in which they found themselves to be largely secure and successful (Diner, 2004, p. 320). This was a huge leap. In this section, I will both speculate about how this might have felt to the immigrants' adult children and consider the historical factors that enabled this transformation. (Because all my interviewees except one grew up in the New York City metropolitan area, I will sometimes speak about New York City.)

In order to succeed in secular America, which enticed them, the second generation would need to become Americans. Indeed, they "rejected much" of their parents' immigrant pasts as "'foreign' and adopted American styles instead," although they did not reject their Jewishness (Moore, 1981, p. 11). Their Jewish identities were very important to almost all those I interviewed. Although most immigrant children understood Yiddish, most left it behind (Moore, 1981). For example, Yiddish was my mother's only language until she entered public school at age five, but both my parents chose not to teach Yiddish to me and very rarely used Yiddish words at home. In their eagerness to be accepted as educated Americans, they even jettisoned any trace of a New York working-class accent, and doing this had been, I believe, encouraged during their educations in the best of the New York City public schools. What might it have been like to have had Old World parents who were not comfortable in gentile America and to then integrate into the larger American world? This was not one of the questions I asked my interviewees, so we can only speculate about this. For my parents, who were not, in general, socially comfortable and who chose, perhaps inadvertently, to move to a gentile suburb in which they were indeed different, doing so did not seem easy.

As the first generation to integrate into secular America, the immigrants' children were in a sense pioneers. I remember watching as my parents discovered the delights of non-kosher seafood. It must have been strange for them to grow up with uneducated parents and to then move into an educated, highly cultured world; in this, too, they were pioneers. The immigrants' children had in one generation made a huge leap—their world was radically different from their parents', and they must have had many feelings about this difference. Berman (1978, pp. 193–194) wrote that this generation were "very much on their own, conscious of the loss of original belief with little to replace it." Berman continued, "It may be heretical, but I think this generation was never at ease in America, although it has been supposed to have been assimilated."

As the immigrants' children integrated into America, most gained prosperity. This was possible because of the many rapid changes that made postwar American society a completely different world for Jews from the one in which the immigrants' children had grown up (Silberman, 1985). The troubling years of the Depression—as well as the anti-Semitism of the 1920s, 1930s, and 1940s and the horrors of Nazism—were now in the past. The Depression had constituted a serious trial in the lives of the immigrant Jews (Wenger, 1996). The many in the garment industry and those owners of already marginal businesses were extremely hard-hit, and many of my interviewees, including Elaine, Frances, David, and Benjamin, spoke about this (Sachar, 1992). The Depression also contributed to an already "disintegrating parental authority" (Berman, 1978, p. 194). Anti-Semitism increased in the 1930s with the rise of Charles Coughlin, a priest, whose radio influence reached its height in 1939 (Sachar, 1992).

Between 1946 and 1973, "affluence and embourgeoisement steadily took hold of American Jewry" (Joselit, 2007, p. 213). Jews felt confident (Joselit, 2007, p. 214); more and more Jews, "having fought in World War II, put their faith in America." Philip Roth wrote that after the war, American Jews had "that wonderful feeling that one was entitled to no less than anyone else, that one could do anything and could be excluded from nothing"; this "came from our belief in the boundlessness of the democracy in which we lived and to which we belonged" (Roth, 1988, pp. 122–123, as cited in Joselit, 2007). By 1985, American Jews, as well as others from various ethnic and religious backgrounds, could choose from an "extraordinary range of options" that they had "assumed never would (or could) be open" to them (Silberman, 1985, p. 22).

The postwar period, until roughly 1967, was characterized by prosperity, liberalism, and the beginnings of "unlimited possibilities" (Diner, 2004, p. 259). During these years, Jews continued to mediate between their status as a minority and the development of "new opportunities" (p. 259). Diner (2004, p. 280) described how Jews worked to counter the anti-Semitism that many felt was quiescent but not laid to rest. Because Jews felt that they would be most secure only when Americans of all races and religions experienced full equality, Jews participated enthusiastically in the fight for civil rights. Indeed, in 1961, Jews comprised about two-thirds of the "white freedom riders who challenged racial discrimination in public accommodations" (p. 268).

During the postwar period, Jews also had to work to convince Americans that they should not be thought of as Communist or even sympathetic to Communist ideas (Diner, 2004, pp. 276, 279). These were years when anti-Communist hysteria spread across America. Because Jews had, over the course of many years, been politically liberal, many non-Jewish Americans considered their points of view to be suspect. Indeed, the American public associated anti-Semitism with anti-Communist sentiment (Diner, 2004, pp. 276–281). Therefore, Jewish organizations actively worked to demonstrate that, as Jews were, in fact, working toward increased opportunities for all, they were actually in the mainstream of an America that was becoming increasingly liberal and tolerant of differences. In addition, some Jewish organizations purged themselves of Communists.

Moreover, Jewish organizations worked actively to bring about an end to educational quotas, housing restrictions, and discriminatory employment practices (Diner, 2004, p. 282: see also Moore, 1981). By the early 1960s, twenty states and forty cities had passed some kind of legislation outlawing employment discrimination (Diner, 2003, p. 110). Jews indeed were gaining more acceptance and increased opportunities. During the Kennedy and Lyndon Johnson presidencies, Jews held notable positions in government (Diner, 2003). Jewish writers, including Arthur Miller, Norman Mailer, and Philip Roth, were enormously successful beginning in the 1950s and 1960s. Although in the 1950s Jews made up less than 5 percent of the American population, public ceremonies already "included Judaism right next to Protestantism and Catholicism" (Diner, 2003, p. 104).

Many Jews eagerly flocked to the suburbs after World War II (Sorin, 1997; Diner, 2003, 2004). The housing shortages and financial constraints of the 1930s and 1940s had forced many young couples to double up with parents; Sarah, described below, and my mother's relative Fay were among these. With the assistance of the G.I. Bill, however, Jews may have suburbanized more quickly than did other Americans (Diner, 2003, p. 94). Moreover, the relative affluence of Jews meant many could more readily afford to move to suburbs than members of other ethnic groups (Diner, 2004, p. 285). Although in some towns "gentlemen's agreements" kept Jews out of certain neighborhoods, very often it was by choice that young Jewish couples chose to move to largely Jewish communities. Nevertheless, overall suburban Jews had much more contact with non-Jews than they had had in cities. Jewish and non-Jewish children played together in playgrounds, and their mothers worked with one another in PTAs. Many suburban Jewish women, who tended to be well-educated, had "worked as teachers, social workers, and librarians" before having children, and many returned to these careers when their children became older (Diner, 2004, p. 301). But when their children were young, they often volunteered in Jewish charities, and they worked as secretaries and librarians in synagogue schools. Because I gathered interviewees through New York City sources, a lower proportion of those I spoke with had raised families in typical suburbs; many had lived within the five boroughs of New York.

The careers of those I interviewed had been extraordinary. Of the men with whom I spoke, two were PhD-level scientists; two were medical doctors; one was an engineer; three were attorneys (two of these went to Ivy League law schools); and two were educators, one of these at the college level. Of the women, one was a PhD-level social scientist; three were social workers; seven were educators; one was an artist; and one held prominent volunteer positions in Jewish charities.

From the end of the 1940s through the 1960s, because of the events of recent decades, American Jews were understandably anxious about anti-Semitism; however, polls demonstrated that between 1940 and 1962, there was a sharp decrease in anti-Semitic attitudes (Sorin, 1997, p. 218). The increase in black anti-Semitism in the U.S. in the late 1960s and early 1970s was an upsetting phenomenon, although the Jewish community managed to recover from it (e.g., Joselit, 2007). Yet even in 1989, "most Jews continued to feel that anti-Semitism" was a real "problem in the United States" (Sorin, 1997, p. 220). Fears related to earlier anti-Semitism persisted.

Nevertheless, Jews came to feel increasingly at home in an affluent, increasingly democratic America.[1] Throughout the 1970s to the 1990s, during the time in which most of those I interviewed were middle-aged and at the peak of their careers, Jews attained prominence in many fields that had previously excluded them. Now options were no longer restricted, and no neighborhoods or schools were off limits.

To be sure, the losses during both the postwar period and the following decades were immense. English conclusively replaced Yiddish as the Jewish vernacular, and the traditional culture that accompanied Yiddish was almost completely eradicated. Joselit writes about the "dramatic" sense of loss: "loss of life, loss of language, [and] loss of patrimony" (2007, p. 215). The old ways of life were replaced by a sense of nostalgia, represented by the 1964 musical *Fiddler on the Roof* (Diner, 2004). That the shtetl was remembered with wistful affection suggests that it was no longer a place from which to flee, either literally or culturally (p. 287).

The children of the immigrants themselves felt that they were in some ways between two worlds (e.g., Feingold, 1992); they became integrated into American society while remaining Jewish-Americans. The experiences of individual Jews during this period were complex and varied, and it was not always easy for individual Jews to feel comfortable with new realities, and still is not for some. For example, Seymour, discussed in chapter 1 and below, felt that he was not a "normal American," and Aaron, about whom I talked in chapters 3 and 4, always felt like he was the "other." Yet by the time they reached middle age, the immigrants' children had unprecedented opportunities in America. They had come so far from their parents' lives.

LIFE STORIES

As we move into life stories about adulthood, we will see that my interviewees, were, in one way or another, successful in America. In becoming successful Americans, they moved on from their parents' immigrant pasts. Nevertheless, all were in one way or another of course influenced by their parents' histories. Because I asked many questions about their immigrant parents, the interviews elicited their feelings about mothers and fathers. How were my interviewees connected to their parents' pasts? Many idealized their parents, perhaps because of guilt about their parents' sacrifices. A few were able to depict their parents realistically. Were they able to use narrative to heal from any trauma passed on by parents or did they need to use defenses such as disavowal or splitting in order to function? As a psychoanalyst, an important part of understanding their adult lives was to make sense, in whatever way I could, of how they managed the connection to their parents' pasts.

Irene

Irene was a lovely, warm, animated, social, and lively woman in her eighties. Described briefly in chapter 1, she characterized Eastern Europe as a "bad place with bad memories for the Jews." During her interview, Irene was welcoming and self-possessed, and she lived in an attractive house on Long Island. She had two children and several grandchildren with whom she was close; they seemed to have caring relationships. Irene and her husband appeared to enjoy the good things in life, and although she did not seem materialistic, she and her husband had not been afraid to spend their money to make their lives more pleasant.

Irene grew up with a mentally ill and physically abusive mother, Letty, and because of her mother's illness, her parents divorced when she was eight. Irene's history with her mother had been traumatic, and although she admitted that this had caused her "lots of psychological issues," her demeanor suggested that she wanted to project the appearance of having overcome the difficulties caused by her terrible history. Knowing Irene's history made me feel somewhat in awe of her and the good life she presented to me. Although she was not overtly distancing or evasive, I believe that my reaction to this genuine and forthright woman may have been due in some part to an unconscious reluctance to truly show me the degree of damage she had suffered as a child. Irene may have been hiding some painful feelings about herself behind her warm, engaged persona. Nevertheless, she was resilient, and her interview suggests both real healing and a desire to have a better life than the one bequeathed to her by her disturbed mother.

Irene's parents fought violently with one another when she was a young child, and she was often frightened during these "scary" altercations: these were among her earliest recollections. In one early memory, her father, Leo, was on the floor; her "gigantic, sturdy" mother had probably hit her "weak-looking, impotent" father, knocking him down. There were nights when her parents, mostly her mother, would be screaming, and these fights often awakened Irene. As a consequence, Irene's "primary goal" as an adult was to be "the mother and wife in a real family of people who cared for one another." In other words, she wanted to create a life and a family that was the opposite of the one in which she had grown up. A second key element of Irene's adult life was belonging and contributing to the Jewish community, and doing so may also have been a way to compensate for what she had not had as a child.

Irene's mother hit not just her father but her too, and she did so until Irene left home to get married. One moment Irene was the "best and most beautiful," and the next moment Letty would "get really mad" at her and hit her. We might say that Irene was assailed by her mother's insanity. Irene said, however, that her life after age eight, when her father left and the "terrible fights" with him stopped, was "not as awful" as her life before that. Her grandmother, who was "kind" but not a "sweet" person, lived with Irene and her mother after her parents separated, and Irene then was old enough to escape the household to play with friends. Yet Irene was in no way protected from misery. She was young during the Depression, and because her family was very poor, she was frequently sent alone to her maternal uncle's house to ask for money. Although her uncle was a "sweet guy" whom she liked, asking for money "felt bad." Later on, her mother, because of her mental illness, developed a violent hatred of Irene's father. Ready to graduate high school at age sixteen, Irene invited both her parents to the ceremony, and her mother responded by throwing Irene out of her house. Only months later was Irene allowed to return.

Perhaps most psychologically difficult about Irene's childhood was that, in order to feel psychologically "safe," she could not be close to her mother. Even when things were good, she never knew when the "peace of the moment" "would turn to chaos." Also very difficult psychologically was that Irene could not rely on her mother to tell her about childhood events that she herself did not remember.

One key to understanding Irene's resilience was in her relationship with her father, Leo. When her parents' arguments woke Irene up, her father would enter her room, tell her not to worry, and lie down on her bed with her. In one memory, Irene's father took her for a walk in the park after one of the fights. Leo's presence must have helped to reassure and soothe the young Irene and also helped her to recognize that the arguments were not her fault.

Irene specifically spoke about her desire for a loving family as a "legacy" of her parents' scary fights. "I chose to marry somebody who was basically healthy psychologically. I wanted to have a big family," Irene said. An only child herself, Irene originally had wanted six kids. She wanted to repair not her parents but herself by having what she did not as a child, a close-knit family. At another point in the interview, Irene said the "adversity" and violent discord of her early life gave her a "strong sense of wanting and needing a loving relationship"; she also fiercely wanted a family in which there would be "acceptance, love, and respect." Her aim in having the kind of life that she missed as a child hinted at her resilience.

The primary reason for the trauma in Irene's life was her mother's severe psychological illness. Although Letty may have been constitutionally vulnerable to mental illness, it is likely that the trauma of her life as a child from a poor family in Eastern Europe—in addition to the significant stresses of immigration—exacerbated her disturbance. As mentioned in chapter 1, Letty had been one of seventeen children, two of whom had wandered away and drowned during childhood. The trauma of such a life is clear-cut, and it could certainly have made her illness considerably more severe. Irene may differ from other interviewees because the difficulties of her childhood—and their implications for her adult life—were only indirectly related to being a child of immigrants.

Irene's father experienced severe trauma as a teenager during World War I; he spoke only occasionally about it, however. Irene learned in detail about Leo's brave but painful adolescent experiences only when she was an adult and transcribed her father's tape-recorded Yiddish memoir. Leo and his family had been war refugees, often extremely hungry and in peril; furthermore, a sister died because of lack of medical care. Afterward, Leo spent three intensely difficult years in Palestine. Leo then immigrated to America to join his family; because he was so ill then, he expected that he would die shortly thereafter. I was able to read Leo's memoir, and both the love that he felt for his family of seven and the affection he held for his shtetl shined through his narrative.

While Irene did not live with her father after age eight, she did spend time with his extended family, listening to them debate politics, world affairs, and Zionism, and her father remained an important presence in her life. I hypothesize that one factor in Irene's ability to envision and build a caring family was the example of her father's extended family—they had stuck together and remained affectionate despite the trauma they suffered in Eastern Europe. "They were wonderful people," said Irene.

As mentioned above, Irene's adult desire to build and contribute to the Jewish community, like her wish for a loving and stable family, was a way to compensate for what she had not had as a child. She was a child of divorce when divorce was very uncommon, and she felt both different from others and badly about herself because of this. Moreover, due to her mother's illness, Irene felt that they "didn't have a home like others." As an adult, Irene and her husband moved to their suburban town just as it was beginning to accept Jews. She and her husband became "very active" in the local synagogue in order to strengthen the Jewish community there. Her need was to create a place where she and her children "would belong" and "feel part of something." Indeed, Irene and her family were close to three other Jewish families with whom they formed almost a "family unit." Her husband eventually became the synagogue president, and she became the chair of its social action committee.

Irene's father had been active in the Jewish Zionist community and had also been connected to New Yorkers from his shtetl. Thus community had been important for him. Moreover, Irene herself was knowledgeable about the crucial role of community both for the Eastern European shtetl Jews and later for the immigrant generation as they adjusted to life in the U.S. Irene asserted that, when she and her husband first moved to the suburbs, they were trying to "replicate" the Jewish community that had in the past been so crucial to Jewish survival, and "to some extent" they were able to do so.

Leo's extended family, like many Jews, had been keenly interested in socialism and social justice, and when Irene herself began her career, she carried this interest into her professional life. "It was a common thread in my family," she said. Irene went back to school after her youngest child was in high school and completed a degree that allowed her to advocate and "pave the way for the have-nots." She worked for various Jewish charitable institutions that helped new immigrants and for organizations that advocated for the needs of Jews all over the world.

When Irene talked about the "interest in social justice" that led to her career, she added that individuals must have a sense of responsibility for one another. Thus in both her professional life and her activities in her local Jewish community, she was influenced both by the ideals held by her father's family and by her knowledge of the organized social welfare networks maintained by Eastern European Jews. Even in retirement, Irene and her husband continued to build and to benefit from their community. At the time of her interview, Irene volunteered teaching English to new immigrants. Because of her parents' experiences, she wanted to help people who "don't have the language" to "find their way." Moreover, she and her husband continued to spend Jewish holidays with the group of three other couples and their extended families whom they had befriended so many years earlier.

Irene's rich social life and successful career were particularly admirable for someone whose early life had been so difficult. Yet Irene as a child and as an adult had been deeply affected in myriad ways by life with her mentally ill and physically abusive mother and by the trauma of witnessing her parents' violence. "Lots of psychological issues" had complicated her life, Irene said; some of these problems continued into her adult life. As a child, Irene seemed to have had painful feelings about herself; she said that she felt badly about herself because her parents were separated, adding later that her family "wasn't normal." She may have felt in some ways unacceptable both because her mother was mentally ill and because her mother had repeatedly hit her. Moreover, because of her mother's unpredictability, Irene said that it was "threatening to live in that home." As a child she had to remain psychologically detached from her mother to feel safe; needless to say, she could not turn to her mother for nurturance. Because Irene lacked the responsive home environment that would have allowed her to depend on adults outside the home, she lacked confidence in school. She said she was unable to speak up in class, and as a young adult, she lacked the confidence to pursue a teaching career. Irene's confidence did improve as she became a mother, however.

One persisting "legacy" of Irene's childhood, she said, was a difficulty in asking for help. Because she had been sent to ask her uncle for money as a child, getting help from others continued to be difficult. "I like to take care of things by myself," she explained. Even now her children admonish her to ask for help if she needs something.

Irene was at times ambivalent or understandably in denial about the lasting effects of the psychological problems she carried from childhood. For example, she said that her psychological issues "*basically*" affected her "in a positive way," reasoning that she had "learned to compensate for" her problems "in many ways" (Irene's emphasis). Also positive for her was that she was now "aware of the psychological issues" that influence both her personality and her "reactions to things." It certainly made sense to me that, in constructing a narrative about her own life, she wanted to present herself as successful in overcoming her psychological problems. A similar desire to present herself positively was evident in her description of her decision to marry. Once she said that a positive "legacy" of her parents' fights was that she chose to marry someone "basically healthy psychologically." At another point in the interview, she realistically said that both she and her husband married to escape difficult home lives, and she acknowledged that this was problematic enough that it had legitimately caused her father significant concern.

How my interviewees spoke about their parents was important in understanding them psychologically. Irene had "little empathy" for her mother, she mentioned as an aside. For me as a psychologist, lack of empathy toward an abusive mother makes sense. I found it interesting, however, that Irene did not admit to anger at her mother. Later in the interview, Irene seemed to rationalize her mother's treatment of her as a child, perhaps trying to show me that she understood that her mother could not have done better. "My mother cared for me to the greatest extent that she could. She couldn't care *about* me," about "who I was as a person. She didn't have any perspective on how she could make life more secure or less threatening for me because her problems were so overwhelming" (Irene's emphasis). Irene seemed unwilling or unable to admit to the more difficult feelings about her mother that I assume she experienced. In telling me the traumatic story of her life with her ill mother, Irene was matter of fact: she detached herself from the horror of the story.

Irene clearly admired her father, who—while being less of a presence after her parents' divorce—nevertheless was a very positive influence on her development. Although he was frequently sick and physically weak, Irene not only admired but idealized her father. About her father's "wonderful command" of the English language, she said, "I'm amazed at that. I don't know how he did it." Speaking about how he was able to work, learn English, and keep up with world events, she said that she thought that he had made a "remarkable adjustment" to the U.S. He was "caring" and "nonjudgmental," "considered by friends and his second wife to be a wise man." I thought that Irene, like many of my interviewees, idealized her father as a way to manage her emotions about the terrible suffering he had endured during his adolescence and early adulthood. If he had been so wise and had adjusted so well to America, perhaps she needn't feel so guilty about his suffering. Irene also spoke about her father in some other contexts. "I learned a lot about parenting from him," she said, elaborating that during a very difficult patch with a teenaged daughter, it had been Irene's father who had been able to maintain communications with the child. Moreover, Irene had taken the opportunity to become closer to her father when he was an older man, helping him to move near her when he developed health problems.

Over the course of her life, Irene had to the best of her ability developed a narrative that would help her to begin to heal after the trauma of her childhood. Her story reflects both resilience and, additionally, the difficult psychological aftereffects of her childhood. Irene was, however, unable to construct the "true narrative" described by Salberg (2017b), which reflects the integration of inner and outer worlds. She did not have a clear picture of her troubled childhood. As mentioned previously, some of Irene's childhood was a blank because her mother did not recount to Irene stories of what happened when she was very young; she was missing information she might have used in understanding her childhood. Moreover, perhaps because of the effects of trauma on memory, Irene's memories of her life with her grandmother were all "topsy-turvy"; she had distorted the chronology of the years when her grandmother had lived in their household. There had been chaos at home with her grandmother and mother, and Irene felt guilty about how she had treated her grandmother during those childhood years.

Despite the roadblocks, not of her own making, to understanding her early life, Irene's story overall was rich and complex. Moreover, her knowledge of Jewish history, reflecting her connection to her father's family, suggests a desire to grapple with her own personal history. Irene wanted to carry forward her father's family's concerns for the world beyond their family, as well as their desire to better that world. This may be seen as integral to her constructing her own identity and thus knitting together her own story.

Throughout her adult life, despite the psychological problems resulting from her childhood, Irene demonstrated resilience in her capacity for connection with family and community. I wondered whether, in order to connect, Irene needed to suppress or overcome a feeling of unacceptability associated with both having a mentally ill mother and having been repeatedly hit by her. She very successfully found a way to make herself acceptable. But it is possible that some leftover feelings of difference and lack of acceptability accounted for the slight feeling of distance that I experienced during the interview. In telling me the traumatic story of her life with her mother, Irene detached herself from the horror of the story. Perhaps she needed to do so in order both to keep this horror from herself and to preserve her own feeling of acceptability.

Over the course of her life, Irene worked hard to build both Jewish community and a caring family, and she needed to work toward self-healing in order to do so. She had the inner strength to persist with these two goals and she was indeed able to connect with family and community. Irene constructed both a good family and a rich life of helping others in her community.

David

David was the sprightly, courteous, educated, and knowledgeable man who "grew up in the shadow of the shtetl" (his life story appears in chapter 2). Although he was deeply empathic with his mother's childhood trauma, his energy and immense "joie de vivre" suggested his considerable resilience. During David's extremely rich and detailed interview, he imparted both copious information and nuanced emotion to me, and he integrated past and present; he also seemed to have the inner resources to make sense of his family's painful past. His energetic involvement in fulfilling intellectual activities led us to agree in the interview that he was "self-actualized." Nevertheless, as mentioned, he felt deeply burdened as an adult by the pain of his mother's life.

David had relationships with friends, coworkers, and people in his synagogue, and these were sources of resilience. He described an easy social life—he had "lots of friends" in high school and in college, and indeed, he was "always very social." In middle age, this quality allowed him to love being president of his Brooklyn synagogue.

David also loved his career as an educator, working with children and adults. His energy and interest in the world were evident both during his career and after his retirement. David's job had required stamina and the ability to deal with bureaucracy; his career was "fun" even as he served in several different positions. He was "very compatible" with one of his supervisors, and the two "grew to respect" one another." David enrolled in two Jewish studies programs while continuing to work in his career full time; he was then a father in his forties. When he was ready to retire, he worked part time as a consultant in the same department in which he had spent many years; he did this in order "to help out" while trying to "figure out what to do next." David's activities in later life had been prodigious; while working part time as a consultant, he also worked with "historical papers" and, in addition, was a docent at both a historical museum and a historic Jewish synagogue. Now, in his seventies, he guides tours of Jewish sites and of New York City; he also lectures on Jewish themes.

As an adult, David continued to feel the distress of his mother's "too painful" childhood. He repeated during his interview that his mother's childhood had been racked by "illness and poverty," and he wondered aloud, about ninety years after his mother's arrival in the U.S., whether she had felt "deserted" by her father while waiting for him to send for the family. At that time, her father had already been in America for some years, and he might have sent for his family years earlier than he did. David was haunted by his family's traumatic past, and yet I believed that he was also trying to work through his feelings about it. He asked out loud why he was "attracted to the field" of his Jewish past, even though what his mother transmitted to him had been "more negative." And then he answered his own question: he and his older sisters had been "imbued" with the "nostalgia" that their mother felt for her past. In other words, the attraction was because his mother also missed her old home. Although David spoke during his interview in a calm manner, his obsessional presentation of detail seemed to reflect an undercurrent of deep anxiety, perhaps a legacy of his mother's own trauma.

David's late adolescence and early adult life were marked by some conflict and by his father's tragic illness. His mother "expected" that he would attend college and "become a professional." Interestingly, in this family college was not in the plans for David's two older sisters, and one sister resented that she was not able to continue her education past high school. She was told that what was "important" was that she "go to work." David's father's desire was that his only son carry on the family business. "As I got older," David said, "I realized . . . that our goals were different. I realized I was not going to do it." Thus David was one of the minority of my interviewees who admitted to generational conflict. He also realized that he wanted a different life from that of his parents. "I knew that I wanted to be better educated . . . to be more worldly, and to not be so concerned with money," he said. David's education and career choice were complicated by his father's illness; his father was diagnosed with a brain tumor at age fifty, when David was eighteen. This was a "horrific time," said David. His father's symptoms were "so awful": they "diminished him" because he "lost sharpness." David's mother was "hysterical" over her husband's illness, as she had so many economic fears. With the Depression behind her, her "worst fear"—of having no income—was now "becoming true." Since his sisters were then married and out of the house, it would have fallen to David to forsake his education and become the breadwinner, and he must have keenly felt this to be a dilemma. But in the end David's mother returned to work. David experienced his mother's "building resentment" over the thirteen years of his father's illness and also his father's feelings of "emasculation." Moreover, during his father's illness, it became even more important to him that David take over his business. David commented that he was "angry" at his father about this, but denied that he felt "guilty" about his decision to become a professional instead. He clarified his feelings by saying, "I loved my father very much, but it was the issue that made me angry." Eventually, David obtained two master's degrees. About his father's reaction, he said, "once the die was cast," his parents attended one of his master's graduation ceremonies, and his father was "very proud." David's father's illness was one trauma affecting this part of David's adult life; a second was the early death of a sister.

It was originally important to David that he marry someone with whom he had "a lot in common." Although he and his wife chose careers in liberal helping professions, as the marriage developed, the couple shared less than David would have wished. In particular, as his wife's Communist-leaning family had "disavowed" Judaism, she did not share David's strong "identification" with it. When, at age thirty, David married her, this caused a minor family conflict—David's father was angry that the couple's Jewish wedding was not an Orthodox one. Currently, David and his wife continue to "disagree" about religious "observance," although one encouraging development is that David's wife has now happily "embraced" every Passover custom. Nevertheless, David, though not a believing Jew, spends every Saturday morning in synagogue, while his wife never attends.

David's generally calm approach to life contrasted with his undertone of anxiety. His father had passed on to David an attitude of calm acceptance, a sense that "no matter how terrible things" were, they would "work out." David's anxiety came from his mother who, though a strong and tenacious woman, never recovered from either the trauma of her childhood in Eastern Europe or of trying to raise her two older children in the U.S. during the Depression. Overall, however, I believe that David as an adult was securely attached, as suggested by his resilience, ability to reach out to others, self-awareness, and his easy relationship with me during the interview. Secure attachment is also associated with a capacity for emotional regulation. Although David's mother had been traumatized, it is likely that she had been able to remain resilient and alive during his infancy (Salberg, 2017a); David had been born in 1938, after the worst of the Depression was over, and I expect that the situation in his family was better by then. Moreover, David's considerably older sisters were perhaps able to calm him when his mother was preoccupied. About his childhood, David said that both he and his sisters lived in a "very safe, secure environment," and he stated that he "never doubted his parents' love." David also said that his considerably older sisters were "exceedingly protective" of him.

Those children and adults who are securely attached are believed by psychologists and psychoanalysts to have the capacity for mentalization. They are able to understand both their own and others' thoughts, feelings, and motivations. This makes "others' behavior meaningful and predictable" to them, and in addition, they are able to find their own experiences to be meaningful; in other words, they are able to think reflectively (Fonagy, 2001, p. 165).[2] Individuals with these capacities are thought to be better able to regulate their emotions. David was one of just a small number of my interviewees who I believe was securely attached, and thus he was better able to reflect on his own experiences; I believe that this contributed to his ability to form a meaningful narrative about his family's past. In other words, because David was securely attached, he was "more capable of drawing on inner psychological resources" in his search for his own narrative (Meyers, 2012, p. 291). This narrative was, in turn, an important factor in David's resilience.

David was able to speak about his parents in a nuanced way, describing both the positive and the negative. He mentioned both his father's overall satisfaction with his ability to provide for his family and his fear of making necessary changes in his business practices. And he could talk admiringly about his mother's strong feelings about herself as a woman but also could say that he was "annoyed" that she did not make a better attempt to read English. Furthermore, he was able to admit that his parents' marriage suffered during his father's long illness.

That David was able to speak about both positive and negative aspects of his childhood suggests his ability to reflect objectively on his own life. For example, he described his father driving up to their house in a truck carrying a bicycle for him, but then followed it with two negative memories. In the first, David was four or five years old, and two men came to his house to notify the family that David's aunt had just died; this was two weeks before this aunt's son was to die of leukemia. In the second memory, David was in front of an aunt's house and he crossed the street without listening to his mother, who told him to wait before doing so. A car driving by slowly knocked him down, and he was bruised but not badly hurt. That David was able to relate these positive and negative experiences without idealization of his parents' responses and without a deadening of his own affect suggests his flexibility, a quality of secure attachment.

David had over the course of many years done fascinating research into Judaism and the Jewish past. The trauma in his family—which constituted part of his inner identity—was specifically related to being Jewish, and I believe his studies were a way of working through the painful feelings passed on to him. For his two doctoral-level programs, one of which covered the "ethnicity and social history of the Jews," David had interviewed a Satmar Hasidic man.[3] I wondered if, in doing this interview, he was able to sift through his feelings about his own Orthodox forebears. David also wrote about a Brooklyn Reform Jewish congregation in the "throes of disintegration" and in the process learned "so much about Judaism in Brooklyn." Furthermore, he wrote a scholarly paper about preparations for the High Holy Days, drawing in part on his mother's preparatory activities; she would spend weeks cleaning and menu planning, believing that a "spotless" home was imperative for the holidays.[4] David said he enjoyed "every minute" of his studies, and I believe that in doing this research he was also integrating his parents' considerable Jewish beliefs and practices into his own identity as a secular American Jew.

David's Jewish studies were part of his search for continuity and connection with the past, a way of finding whatever meaning he could in his family's suffering. It was also part of his development of a narrative that could foster resilience (Pisano, 2012). That David could narrate his family's story to himself and to others, that he could look at his own suffering intergenerationally, was helpful in integrating his "thoughts and emotions in a coherent structure" (Pisano, 2012, p. 181). Doing so seemed to be a work in progress for David. Though David remained pained by this mother's past, his studies, his work on Jewish fields during his retirement, and indeed his detailed narrative with me were a way to loosen his obsession with the traumatic past.

David's energy and zest for learning meant that he had lived, and continues to live, a fascinating life. His ability to enjoy both socializing and career contrasts with the burden of his mother's pain, which he still continues in some way to carry. His inner drive to succeed was a positive one, fueled not only by his knowledge of his parents' sacrifices but by his father's perspective that life would "work out." David's considerable resilience, seemingly unmitigated by evident psychological difficulties, seemed unusual among my interviewees. He was able to successfully develop a narrative that helped him talk about the pain of the past and to integrate his inner psychological reality with the real world. Nevertheless, the past had been traumatic, and for David the pain of "knowing too much" persisted.

Seymour

Seymour was a remarkably intelligent, brightly cheerful man whose intense manner and intellectualism made him seem at times not quite in tune with others. Described in chapter 1, his mother, who "saw nightmares" as a child in Poland, wanted to leave it all behind. Seymour was also mentioned in the trauma chapter: his weekly "vision" of his grandmother's (and possibly his own) death at the hands of the Nazis suggested that the terror of the past remained alive inside him. In his vision, he seemed to be retrospectively trying to help his dead father.

Seymour's adult life can be seen as a study in contradiction and complexity. He carried a lifelong sense of anger, alienation, and estrangement. Yet he also had good friends and a loving family and seemed to be a truly caring person; in addition, he lived his work life with remarkable integrity and accomplishment. In adulthood, he manifested some degree of resilience alongside the damage both from what had been passed on from his parents and from childhood events.

To find out more about Seymour's adult life, I re-interviewed him after the passage of several years. In this later interview, Seymour's style was extremely detailed and more reflective. I think that he trusted me more at this time, and, moreover, he seemed to have thought about his life during the intervening years. He also had become ill during this time, which had probably encouraged reflection. Furthermore, my sense was that it was not only between the first set of interviews and the second but also in the process of talking to me during the later interview that Seymour developed a narrative that could help him make sense of his own life.

Some background about Seymour's childhood and adolescence will help us to understand the anger and isolation of his adult life. After his birth mother died, Seymour lived with his "saintly" aunt, his uncle, and the couple's three daughters, with whom he was very close; he stated that he was "surrounded by love." Yet he saw very little of his father, who could come to visit only late at night. When Seymour was three-and-a half years old, his father remarried, and he brought Seymour home from his aunt's and uncle's apartment in the Bronx to Brooklyn. This was the "first clear trauma" of his life, said Seymour. No one had emotionally prepared him for the staggering fact that the woman he was about to meet was not his own mother. Seymour told me that in moving from his aunt's house back to his father's, he was "uprooted again" and brought back to an "alien world." "This isn't my world," he had felt at the time. He had "lost" his girl cousin, with whom he had felt a sense of "twin-ship." In addition, after meeting his stepmother, he had to "adjust to [the idea that] this is my mother and it's a different woman." "Sociologically," too, Seymour felt that his new world in a "rough" Brooklyn neighborhood was an alien one, and he often felt estranged there. The Jewish kids in his new neighborhood did not mix with the Irish and Italians. By the time he was in the first grade, Seymour experienced violence in his neighborhood; a Jewish friend was "jumped" by Catholic kids outside their school, and Seymour fought off the attackers. "That's not right," he felt at the time. This was the first of many such encounters. Seymour described the beginning of an inner split. He had been "a very sweet little boy" who now became angry and violent, while, simultaneously, the sweet boy remained inside. Moreover, Seymour feared abandonment. Because his birth mother had died and because his stepmother was hospitalized twice during his childhood, "I knew that the world could disappear."

When Seymour was ten, his father became permanently withdrawn after learning of the deaths of all of his family members in the Holocaust. With his father effectively gone as a guiding force in his life, Seymour had no one to talk to about the neighborhood violence he faced. Seymour was an angry adolescent who always fought back, was "determined not to be a victim," and was even rude to the customers on whom he waited in his father's store. Although he was highly accomplished and attended an elite public school, he was also very rebellious—he cut his Friday classes during his senior year to spend his time in bed with a girl. As an adolescent, Seymour knew that both his father and his stepmother had survived terrible trauma that was the result of anti-Semitism. In addition, he himself had suffered attacks in his often anti-Semitic neighborhood. Seymour said that his anger enabled him to "live in the world without fear," adding that "growing up in Brooklyn was more useful than a PhD in learning how to get along in life."

When Seymour as a young adult told his Orthodox Jewish father that he intended to become a scientist, his father asked whether becoming a scientist would be "good for humanity." His father also taught him to "live simply and speak the truth." As we shall see, in many ways Seymour internalized this dictum. But Seymour had begun his adult life "estranged from the normal world." This slight man engaged in many terrible fights, and he, consequently, did not "expect to live past age twenty-one." He excelled in his New York City college but continued to have a "horrible temper." Once when "grabbed" on the street, he "spontaneously" and "without thinking" "growled" at his attackers "like a dog." And like an animal, after "immobilizing" another man in a fight, he "didn't care about" that person anymore—his temper would end and he would be "fine." The intensity and immediacy with which Seymour became frighteningly enraged and then could in turn calm down—while at the same time excelling in his academic and professional life—suggests that his Jewish and idealistic side was split off from his traumatized and therefore enraged side. The sweet little boy he had been was now represented by the idealistic man. When threatened, however, he could still turn violent.

Seymour traveled to the West Coast to study for his PhD. There, at age twenty-eight, he carried his switch blade inside his suit pocket during his dissertation defense. He also married a non-Jewish woman from New York who had a mentally ill mother, and she converted to Judaism for him. Seymour described the following from that period of his life as an example of the "distance that I felt from others," his "estrangement from the normal world": he became involved with the "hidden world," the "underside of society," "crazies," "drug addicts," and "criminals," and he brought his wife along when he "hung out" with them. He explained that he thought that, because he "enjoyed" these people, his wife also would like them. Later Seymour realized that "these people scared her" and that he had been insensitive in expecting that she would be comfortable with them. "Why aren't you feeling what other people feel?" he asked himself, referring to his inability to be empathic toward his wife.

After receiving his doctorate, Seymour returned to New York. He had obtained a prestigious post-doc position researching a cutting-edge question in biological science, and he continued to successfully conduct studies at the same institution for ten years. He and his wife separated, reconciled, and finally divorced. For at least some time, Seymour continued to be involved with, in his words, the "underside of society." For example, he would visit Harlem with a friend who needed to "score heroin," and Seymour himself tried heroin several times. His reasoning for accompanying his friend seems, in a way, noble and will help us in trying to understand the disparate parts of himself that Seymour was attempting to hold together. He "really" wanted to "connect" with his drug-abusing friend. Furthermore, he wanted to "know all the varieties of being human"; rather than just observing his friend, he could truly understand him by doing what his friend did. Seymour's own feeling of difference, of not being normal, led him to act this out.

Seymour had a moral justification for his dangerous activity, yet, as he did something antisocial, his angry feelings seem embedded in his actions; we can see the strands of the sweet or moral person versus the angry individual in them. Since childhood, when the "sweet" little boy was confronted with anti-Semitic violence, he had felt it was him and his "real tight buddies" versus "the rest of the world," and he habitually tried to help his friends who were "in trouble." "How do you live in a world where people want to hurt you?" he asked rhetorically. "Some people will do really bad things, and it's up to you to do something about it." This was intimately connected to both the "nightmares" his stepmother saw in Eastern Europe—and about which she spoke to Seymour when he was a boy—and to the slaughter of his father's family during the Holocaust. Seymour must have seen these as horrendous injustices. After Seymour's father learned about the deaths of his family members, his father had nightmares during which he actually struck out; his father was defending his family. This piece of his father's life still lives within Seymour; as we recall, every week he relives his "vision" of his grandmother's slaughter. Seymour takes on his father's role in this vision. Thus Seymour took inside himself the anger at what had damaged his parents. His internalized anger caused him to fight what he perceived as injustice with his own violence.

Currently, Seymour feels not just that he needs to be responsible for righting injustices, but also that he must be "responsible for what's going on around" him. He associated this during the interview with the feeling that he is "different from normal people." In explaining his concept of being responsible, he said, "Whatever you rely on, you learn it." For example, he learned how to fix his own car and to repair electrical appliances at home; unfortunately, doing so had caused conflicts at home, as his second wife became anxious when he took on home repairs. Furthermore, during the complex treatment of his current illness, he had educated himself about and participated in all the details of his medical care; this, he said, had delighted his doctors. Seymour's sense that his exaggerated need to do things for himself was not "normal" suggests to me his sense of separateness from others.

Seymour's desire to right injustices was reflected in his lifelong involvement in leftist politics, and it was when speaking out against the Vietnam War on street corners that he met his second wife. The couple married when Seymour was forty-two. Like his first wife, his second too was not Jewish, and, in addition, she was from a very different background from his own; because of this, her family did not accept Seymour for many years. When their first child was born, the two had begun to grow apart, but it took some time for Seymour to understand that there were some marital issues. The distance between them, which Seymour said resulted from his feelings about how his wife's family treated him, led to angry outbursts from Seymour. When his temper flared, Seymour said, he had the "good sense to leave" the house so his child would be less directly affected. Eventually, Seymour and his wife worked on their problems, her family came to accept him, and the couple had two more children.

Throughout his career, Seymour sought to behave with integrity. This, he believed, was directly related to his Jewish upbringing and to his father's injunction that his career be "good for humanity." For example, when federal grant money began to dwindle for his biological research, Seymour decided to leave the field, as he feared that his idealism would be compromised: "I didn't want to run around making nice to people to get [grant] money," he said. Consequently, at about the time of his second marriage, he obtained a degree that would allow him to combine his scientific abilities with managerial skills. He then worked in a series of positions involving research and the public sector. Seymour told me that he never sought Civil Service status because he believed that it would be important to tell superiors, "If you don't like me, fire me." When, during the interview, I commented on Seymour's idealism, he responded idiosyncratically, "If it's not impossible, it's not worth doing," adding, "I love human intelligence." Seymour's own exceptional intelligence stood out to me as he recounted the various professional positions he had held. The genuine gratification he received from his work was striking.

Seymour described various professional situations during which he believed that his integrity was on the line. In one instance, he challenged a city commissioner over a proposed action that could negatively affect the health of New York City residents: "You're free to sign this bill, but I won't," Seymour told the commissioner, who eventually backed down. There were additional instances in which he insisted successfully on healthy outcomes for New York City communities. Seymour was actually fired from one consulting position, however, when he insisted on his ideals about helping individuals whose health had been damaged. Losing this job affected Seymour's family economically.

Currently, Seymour continues to be split between the "sweet little boy" he once was and the angry person he eventually became. He has good friends and cares deeply about his family, and he also radiates warmth and involvement. He participates actively in two synagogues and several leftist political groups. Yet, although Seymour does not become as enraged as he once did, he can still quickly become intensely angry, and he continues to feel that he is "different from normal people." Perhaps most troubling is that, despite good friendships, Seymour continues to feel a sense of alienation that interferes with his sense of connection. He elaborated on this, saying, "My alienation doesn't deprive me of human warmth, but it interferes with it." Therefore, he finds it extremely difficult to ask for help when he needs it. "I don't feel like we're humans who have a bond." In other words, he cannot rely easily on others.

Just as Seymour himself tried to live with integrity, splitting off his own "bad" and angry impulses, so he idealized his tough stepmother and her relationship with his father. As mentioned in chapter 1, he emphasized his stepmother's "moral attributes and positive disposition" and said that she and his father absolutely never fought. I suggest that psychologically Seymour needed to see his parents as conforming to his view of how people should be; Seymour protected himself by keeping his parents in such high regard. Idealizing them also protected his internal representations of these people who had indeed endured so much from any damage that could result from his negative feelings.

Seymour's extraordinary career and his warm relationships with friends and family suggested that he was in some ways resilient. His resilience derived from several sources: the love he experienced from his aunt and cousins as a small motherless boy, his father's emotional involvement with him when he was young, and the "bond" he eventually enjoyed with his stepmother after he became used to her.

Seymour was an admirable and complex man, full of energy, geniality, intelligence, drive, and determination. Although he had experienced love as a child, he had also lost his mother at age two. The love he undoubtedly took in was not enough to make up for his mother's death, for his identification with the deadened parts of his father, or for the trauma he absorbed in the relationship with his stepmother. Seymour experienced too little affect from his withdrawn father; on the other hand, he was probably flooded with affect from his stepmother's description of her childhood trauma during World War I. He may have dissociated some of the devastating realities that confronted him during his early years. I suggest that Seymour also utilized splitting in processing some of the overwhelming knowledge that he took in from other people. Despite the reflection evident during his later interview, Seymour had been unable to develop a true healing narrative that could have prevented him from "re-experiencing or re-enacting the trauma" passed on by his father and stepmother (Salberg, 2017b, p. 247). He continued to experience the weekly intrusion of the terror of his father's family's deaths at the hands of the Nazis.

Seymour's caring relationships and his career devoted to integrity and doing good existed alongside his tangible fear that "people want to hurt you." Despite his ties with friends and family, he continued to experience anger and alienation that, in his words, interfered with his ability to connect with others. Seymour remained split between the man who wanted to combat injustice and benefit humanity and the person who had been repeatedly attacked and therefore needed to ferociously fight back. Nevertheless, he had made every attempt to live an exemplary life, and in most ways he had succeeded in doing so.

Dorothy

Dorothy (described in chapter 4), in her late seventies when I interviewed her, had grown up in a happy household that quickly turned bleak in the years after her father's illness and death. A naturally private person, her diffidence during the interview process may have been related to the difficult nature of her life; perhaps she did not want to devote much time to talking about it. Moreover, I guessed that, overall, she was not quite at ease socially. Now long retired, Dorothy had worked as an educator, often in very rough areas of the Bronx. She had married in middle age, and her husband, who was several years her senior, had done well economically in a retail business.

Several things stood out about Dorothy's adult life. She commented that she "came into [her] own much later in life." In addition, she had conflictual feelings about her mother, Dina, and she seemed to be quite pained when thinking about her mother's life and their relationship. Furthermore, Dorothy seemed to enjoy treating herself well materially, which was both a contrast to her mother's self-sacrificing life as an immigrant and Dorothy's means of healthy self-repair. Dorothy's resilience is suggested both in her career and in her increasing fulfillment over the course of her adulthood.

Dorothy's career as a high school teacher required that she often work with students who had learning or family problems, and it spanned a time of tense racial conflict; it was sometimes dangerous. "We were the system they [the neighborhood residents] were fighting," she stated.[5] At times, because of her point of view, she was at odds with colleagues and, therefore, isolated. Understandably, she sometimes liked her job, but at other times she did not. It is admirable that Dorothy taught such a difficult population and continued to teach through the years of crisis. Dorothy honestly stated that she was "finding herself" during this period of her life.

Dorothy's mother wanted her two daughters to marry and have children. Dorothy, however, married only in middle age and was childless. Because of this, Dorothy said that she "didn't meet her [mother's] needs." As a young adult, after Dorothy began her career, she lived with her mother, Dina, but she was unhappy living at home. Consequently, at age thirty she moved to Manhattan on her own, and to Dina that Dorothy had done so as a single woman was a *shande* (a scandal or a shame in Yiddish). Even after some time, her mother could not accept her single lifestyle, Dorothy said. Not only was Dina judgmental about her moving out, but also Dina believed that a "woman without a man has no value." To add insult to injury, she didn't give Dorothy much "recognition" for her education. My hypothesis was that Dorothy felt to some degree rejected by Dina, as her mother was unable to accept her for who she was as a person.

I surmised that Dorothy's feelings of rejection by Dina are reflected in her unique interpretations of Dina's emigration. Dorothy rhetorically asked more than once in her interview how her grandmother could have sent her two daughters off to America alone. Indeed, she had asked her mother's brother, "How could a mother send her two daughters away, knowing that [she would] never see them again?"[6] Her uncle replied that they were sent away "because there wasn't enough bread." Dorothy said that she "assumed" it had been her grandmother's decision (rather than her grandfather's) to send her two daughters to America, and she felt that Dina "probably" "felt rejected because of this." Dorothy was my only interviewee who talked about a parent's emigration in this way.

Dorothy's older sister had married and borne two children, and Dorothy compared her sister's good relationship with Dina and her difficult one. This may have been particularly hurtful to Dorothy. In speaking about her relationship with her mother, Dorothy said, "We were just different people." In contrast to her sister, Dorothy "couldn't share" or "open up" to Dina; Dorothy mentioned that she herself was "more private." Neither Dorothy nor Dina was outgoing, while Dorothy's sister was more sociable. Probably one reason that Dorothy was unable to be open with Dina was that she felt Dina did not approve of her. Nevertheless, Dorothy made an effort to spend time with Dina as an adult.

When I interviewed her, Dorothy seemed to be quite pained when thinking about her mother's life and their relationship. I noted to myself that Dorothy looked sad when talking about Dina in her later life. Not only was she "sad thinking that [her] mother had a hard life," but she added, "Looking back, there were probably things that I would have done differently." Dorothy was distressed that she and Dina had been "fighting" when her elderly mother became ill. Indeed, Dorothy believed that she had failed to realize that, during one fight, Dina "probably" had already suffered a "mini-stroke." In general, during this difficult period, Dorothy, "more passive in my aggression," was not "talking very much" to Dina. Dorothy, during Dina's final illness, visited her in a nursing home daily after work; then in her midfifties, Dorothy felt terribly strained by this routine, and I think also by the emotional pain of her guilt. Prominent in her memory was that immediately after sitting *shiva* (mourning) for her mother, she retired from her job. She added that, had she remained in her job for several more months, she would have received significantly more money, but she decided not to; she was then married and consequently financially able to retire. But I believe that the emotional pain of her relationship with her mother, in addition to her job, were more than she could bear. "It was just enough," Dorothy stated.

Dina's lack of empathy with her daughter was most probably related to the trauma she had experienced as a child in Eastern Europe. Perhaps the terror that Dina had experienced left her at times dissociated or frozen and thus unable to be available to her daughter (Halasz, 2012; Salberg, 2017a). Dorothy realized too late that she, in turn, had understandably not been as empathic as she wished with Dina. When talking about this, Dorothy mentioned the extreme poverty her mother had suffered as a child, but she did not at this point discuss either the trauma of pogroms or that her mother lost a sibling during the terror of fleeing a pogrom. Perhaps because this was unthinkable, Dorothy was unable to understand how she herself had been affected by her mother's trauma; thus this was perhaps not integrated into her own narrative about herself.

As mentioned in the previous chapter, I believe that ghosts of her mother's trauma, passed on in the relationship between the two, were Dorothy's long depression after her father's death and her low self-esteem, which slowly receded over the course of her adult life. Because of Dina's own trauma, she did not recover from the death of her husband for many years; thus she was depressed and absent, and Dorothy was, in effect, psychologically abandoned by her withdrawn mother when she was an adolescent (Salberg,

2017a). Even years later, said Dorothy, her widowed mother as a "woman without a man" continued to suffer the low self-esteem that had begun when she, an immigrant, felt that her American cousins looked down on her. For example, Dorothy mentioned that though others admired Dina's ability to run a business on her own after her father's death, Dina herself was unable to take in their compliments.

Dorothy likely internalized her mother's low self-esteem. As a depressed adolescent, Dorothy probably did not think well of herself, and her low self-esteem was suggested by her feeling that she was not "capable" in high school. (Years later, perhaps regretting her own withdrawal as a young person, she wrote to her nieces that they "should try new things.") Other possible indications of her low self-esteem were her diffidence and slight difficulty in sharing herself with me during the interview and "that she did not do well with dating." However, Dorothy's long but ultimately successful struggle to "come into her own" suggested her resilience.

During Dorothy's adulthood, her mother—who had believed that it was important to wait until her daughters were on their own before she began bringing "strange men into the house"—had relationships with suitors and later married. Dorothy felt that Dina's admiration for her very ordinary second husband reflected her low self-esteem. Dina's husband died after a marriage of only five years, and his grown children treated Dina badly. Dorothy mentioned that, in contrast to her own adult life, her mother had not cared about dressing nicely or wearing makeup.

Dorothy expected that her life would be different from that of her parents, that she would be "getting away from the neighborhood, doing more things, and traveling more." As an adult, she indeed participated in activities that interested her, such as going to the ballet and opera. I believe that the fact that Dorothy felt she could enjoy herself—and that she liked having nice clothes and jewelry—was a legacy of the physical nurture that she had received as a child before her father's death. The food and festive occasions that her family had enjoyed may have allowed Dorothy to feel that in later life she could nurture herself. Dorothy stated that, as an adult, she had a "whole world of single friends," and many of them enjoyed activities such as travel and higher culture. She even purchased a subscription to the Metropolitan Opera; her father had been an opera lover but could not afford the tickets. Indeed, said Dorothy, she introduced her mother to ballet and opera, and she invited her mother to spend time in the city when the two attended events together.

After her mother died, Dorothy's husband also retired and the two moved to New Jersey, where they purchased a house. Later on, they moved to downtown Brooklyn. As an older woman, Dorothy was fortunate to enjoy luxurious activities because of the largesse of her husband's son, who had become wealthy.

"My lifestyle was always better than my mother's," said Dorothy, and she enjoyed that she was so successful materially in comparison to her parents. For her it felt natural that she would have a life enriched by travel and material goods; it also may have been a source of guilt. During the interview, immediately after stating that her lifestyle was so much better than her mother's, Dorothy added, "I wasn't very close to her," and she was suggesting that this, in retrospect, was upsetting. Dorothy attempted to repay the debt she owed her parents by paying to commemoratively place their names on a plaque at Ellis Island. In addition, she hoped in the future to put their names on seats at the Metropolitan Opera.

Dorothy's resilience was suggested in how much she enjoyed both the good things in life and her overall pleasure in how far she had been able to travel from her parents' poverty and her immigrant mother's foreign ways. (As mentioned in the childhood chapter, Dorothy was proud that "we made it in America," thus identifying herself with the immigrant generation, which "accomplished a lot.") Yet the distance she herself had come from the immigrant life had created a rift with her mother. The disapproval she encountered in moving away from home as a young adult was surely a conflict over Americanization.

In later life, Dorothy continued to develop. Although her husband—in his mideighties when I interviewed Dorothy—no longer wanted to participate in the same activities she did, Dorothy had become an active member of the community at her Manhattan synagogue, and she felt enriched by the Jewish and Yiddish cultural life she found there, including Yiddish theater and a trip to Eastern Europe with fellow congregants; she was now considering adult Bat Mitzvah classes. Dorothy contrasted her shyness as a child with the "new world of friends" she had met at the synagogue, suggesting her increasing ease socially. Indeed, she had spoken at a conference there, and she was happy with the "recognition" she had received for her work on it. That she enjoyed learning about the Yiddish culture of the immigrant generation suggests that she was able to integrate her early life with her current life.

Dorothy was, I believe, continuing to develop a narrative that would help her to heal from the trauma of her father's death and her very painful feelings about her relationship with her mother. Because Dorothy could not remember much about her adolescence, when she was extremely depressed, she could not construct a complete narrative, and her narrative lacked nuance. Thus Dorothy's story did not yet reflect "deep healing" (Salberg, 2017b, p. 247). But she was able both to freely talk about the pain of her father's death and, at this point in her life, to speak empathically about her mother. That she could do so, even though her mother had hurt her by failing to understand her, was impressive. Dorothy now understood how hard her mother had worked to support the family after her father's death; in addition, she was able to speak about her mother's poor opinion of herself without looking down on her. I suggest that both Dorothy's current interest in immigrant life and indeed her interview with me were ways of continuing to work on constructing a healing narrative.

Sarah

Sarah was a pleasant, round, outgoing, direct, and assertive woman in her eighties who had retired twenty years previously from a career as a high school teacher. She lived in a small Long Island house full of photographs. Although her husband had died perhaps ten years prior to our interview and she walked with some difficulty, she described herself as an optimist: "If you act miserable, you make yourself miserable." One of her three children, a daughter, lived within an easy drive of her home, and she was happy to be able to have enjoyed the company of her daughter's two children. Sarah was very social, and she and her neighbors in their adults-only community depended on one another for help. Unlike the majority of my interviewees, her husband's and her own combined income meant that her family was middle-class rather than upper-middle-class.

Sarah was the only one of my interviewees who was herself an immigrant, and this added a layer of complexity to her story. She came to the United States with her mother, Blume, in 1930, when she was six-and-a-half; her father had then been here for six years. Several of her mother's siblings and their families were also here. Sarah's was a fascinating story: she had an extraordinary number of memories of her life as a young child in Europe, but during the interview, her flood of memories abated after she described her arrival in the U.S. Her narrative brings us back to the disavowal of loss. During her interview, Sarah repeatedly minimized her mother's losses in leaving what had once been home, and she often denied her mother's suffering. Throughout the interview, Sarah spoke about her mother's difficult life as an immigrant using phrases like these: she "took it in stride. This is how it was." Or "this would be her life and she faced it." Sarah's defenses interested me. What I did not take into account at first in thinking about Sarah was that she had shared many of her mother's experiences. I now wonder whether—as her mother's "companion" both in Europe and then in America—she absorbed her mother's inevitable anxieties and needed to defend against them.

Sarah's earliest years were spent in a Western European city, where she and Blume waited until the immigration quota imposed in 1924 allowed them to join Sarah's father in New York. Each summer until they emigrated, Sarah and her mother returned to the tiny, "primitive" village in Poland in which both Blume and Sarah's father, Avram, had been born.[7] Sarah's early memories of her summers with her grandparents on the farm were particularly compelling. Her grandparents were very caring and loving, and her grandfather, in particular, "doted" on her. One childhood memory from the village involved falling into a well. A man rescued her, and afterward her grandfather went to synagogue and Sarah was given a new name to fool the "evil eye." Sarah's recollections included imaginary play in the shrubs near her grandparents' cottage; she would "play house," pretending that one shrub was her kitchen and another was her living room.

Sarah also had many childhood memories of her life in Western Europe, which she happily described to me. There she and her mother lived in a major city and cultural center, in a room which had a two-burner stove; they had "all the conveniences." At least in comparison to life in her grandparents' *dorf*, this was indeed a "good life." Blume's sister-in-law lived nearby, but the two women were not close. Sarah said she was her mother's "companion" in Western Europe, and she must have enjoyed their close relationship.

The quality of Sarah's memories changed when she told me about life after she and her mother joined her father, Avram, in New York. After six years apart, her parents were "almost like strangers." In addition, one of Blume's brothers living in the U.S. suffered his wife's death. Blume then spent four years caring for her brother's sons in a distant area of Queens, while her husband commuted to Manhattan to work long hours as a waiter; his time with Blume and Sarah was very limited. This was a difficult time for Blume, and Sarah had to share her mother's attentions with her cousins. Sarah stated that her father could be short-tempered and her mother was strict. Blume, like many women of that time, believed in "corporal punishment," and she once hit Sarah with a "scrolled carpet beater." "I got spankings and I was stubborn," she said. Sarah also had to navigate life as a greenhorn—"I decided to speak only English," she said, "to fit in and be Americanized."

When, at the height of the Depression, Blume and Avram were finally able to get their own apartment in the Bronx, Avram lost his job, and the family endured serious financial worries for a couple of years. Sarah had only two dresses, one of which she wore while her mother washed the other. Blume then became pregnant with a second child, who was born when Sarah was eleven. Sarah was put to work after school caring for her baby sister, which allowed her mother to complete her housework; her father doted on her "spoiled" baby sister. Sarah never portrayed herself as having been unkindly treated, but she must have suffered along with her stoical mother.

After the birth of Sarah's sister, the family finally began to enjoy ten years of stability. Sarah knew early on that she was destined to attend college: this would make her a real American. Born in 1923, she began college in the early 1940s, about the time that Jewish Americans were aware that family members remaining in Eastern Europe were being killed. Sarah's family, however, had "no way of finding out where" those in Eastern Europe were or "what had happened to them," although they "knew it was not a good outcome, not to expect anything." Sadly, they received one letter written from a concentration camp by Sarah's cousin. Indeed, the only survivor was one of Avram's nephews. Sarah was the only one of my interviewees who herself intimately had known family members killed during World War II. Sarah's knowledge of what would only later come to be called the Holocaust must have been formative for her. Because she and mother had been given the opportunity to emigrate, she commented, "When Hitler came, we realized how lucky we had been."

Sarah's father, Avram, became ill when Sarah was a young adult, and his early death was traumatic for her. Not only was Sarah very upset by her father's illness, but after one-and-one-half years of full-time college attendance, she now needed to attend school at night. It was her responsibility to support her family, and she returned home on weeknights only at 11 p.m. Avram was bed-ridden at home, where Blume cared for him. Sarah described Avram's death at home when she was twenty-four as "heart wrenching" and a "terrible blow"; "he left a large void in our lives." Because her father died about two years after World War II ended, during which Sarah lost many family members, his death added to her existing feelings of loss; she had been "envious of children who had their grandparents."

When she was twenty-five, Sarah married a man who was distantly related and "a little rough around the edges." Meir had been pursuing her for several years; eventually, she said, "He wore me down." Before they married, Sarah informed Meir that he would be helping to support her mother and her much younger sister. Her decision to marry may have been a practical one, as she perhaps feared that she would have no other marriage offers. Meir always worked in garages or gas stations owned by his cousins.

For a year and a half, Sarah and Meir lived in a small room in his parents' house; Sarah worked as a bookkeeper, quitting only when she became pregnant. The couple lived in an apartment in a semi-urban area of Long Island until their second child was school age. Then they moved to a developing community on Long Island, where Sarah, despite her husband's wishes, learned to drive. Because she "had to get out" of the house, she joined the Jewish women's organization Hadassah. To do this, she needed Meir to babysit, and he at first was not "happy" to do so. Sarah also developed an active social life in their town, becoming friends with all the neighbors, playing mahjong, and becoming more active in the women's group at their synagogue. When the couple's second child started school, Sarah, then in her early forties, obtained additional college credits and went back to work. Although she had never wanted to teach "others' kids," she had decided that the "best thing for a mother was to be a teacher." "If I had my druthers, I would have preferred being in the office," she said. Teaching was "all right." Sarah as a teacher surpassed her husband, Meir, both in income and in social status.[8]

Blume's oldest sister and her husband, who remained in Eastern Europe. They and their children died during the Holocaust. *Courtesy of the anonymous interviewee Sarah.*

After twenty years of work, Sarah retired, and Meir followed, announcing, "You're retiring; so am I." The couple soon moved to a "55+" adult community. For years after they relocated, Sarah "refused" to sell one of their two cars, presumably so she could retain her independence. Sarah enjoyed her social life in this setting also, saying that her neighbors there were "wonderful people." They helped one another with shopping and doctors' visits.

To better understand Sarah psychologically, I will explore her minimization and denial of her mother's hardships. First, however, it will be helpful to know more about her mother's early life. Blume was the second-youngest of eight or nine children. This was a "rough life"—on winter nights the family brought their animals inside their dirt-floored cottage, and there was no running water. Blume was probably hungry as a child. When she was about twelve, her oldest brother's wife died, and Blume then spent several years caring for his children.

Sarah told me horrifying stories about what happened to Blume's family during World War I, which began when Blume was a teenager. Blume feared pogroms. The Cossacks (or "maybe just Russians") "aggravated" and "stole" from them, and they once threatened to kill her father. Blume herself narrowly missed being snatched by Cossacks, which might have resulted in rape or even death. As Sarah told this story, when "they came for" Blume, Blume's mother said, "Run," and she somehow managed to escape.[9] Moreover, she and her family were displaced during part of World War I and lived in a truly deprived manner, surviving in the woods on wild potatoes. Their lives, without "security or comfort," were "mind-boggling," said Sarah. At that moment in the interview, Sarah, defending herself against fully experiencing the trauma of her mother's life, said: "They existed. They took it in stride. This is how it was." Sarah's mother's life was traumatic during World War I, but Sarah herself, minimizing her mother's trauma, said, "This is how it was."

At the conclusion of my interview with Sarah, I was aware of an undercurrent of palpable suffering in her portrayal of her mother's life. Yet Sarah could only sometimes acknowledge the great difficulties that Blume had faced, and I was surprised at her defenses. She not only minimized, but she was sometimes vague and talked about Blume's life in black-and-white terms (although she occasionally qualified her words by saying "probably"). It was important to Sarah that she paint her immigration with her mother as a linear upward progression: she described it as "looking up towards better." Rather than sacrificing, her parents had "improved their lot."[10] For Sarah herself, it was important that she was "away from where we started."

While Sarah herself was aware of how much it meant for her to have known her grandparents and their village, she had trouble admitting that her mother might have missed her life in the Old Country. She herself had loved visiting her grandparents in Poland, and "it meant so much" to "feel their love," "to see the area, the landscape, what it was like." But because she believed that for Blume coming to America represented "an improvement" and also because "it was a relief to come here . . . probably," Sarah felt that her mother "probably" was not lonely or homesick when she arrived in America. Later she said that her mother was "happy to leave Poland. They had nothing there." She added—to bolster her own feelings about her mother's adjustment to America—that her mother "took things in stride." Sarah *was* able to admit that her mother missed family; she might have felt "a longing to see [her] family, but not for the geographical area." She might have longed for her "youth," but "[she] felt much better off" in America. In the following passage, Sarah at first admits her mother's loss, but, unable to remain with this feeling, she begins to split: "Leaving there was very hard. But leaving [Western Europe] was different. Coming to her husband and siblings was looking up toward better. You have to think of priorities. You couldn't have both. . . . She knew that she wouldn't see them again." And, she said, emigration itself was like "two sides of a coin. One was good and one was bad."

As noted, when Sarah and her mother initially arrived in America, they lived with Sarah's uncle so that her mother could care for his children. Although Sarah could admit that not being in her own home probably disappointed her mother, her initial assessment of this situation was that her mother was a "stoic" and a "realist." She added that her mother "faced . . . reality. She was a strong woman. This would be her life and she faced it." Sarah at that time had to share her mother's attention with her cousins, after enjoying being her mother's "companion" in Western Europe. Sarah's initial denial of any negative feelings her mother had about this might have been hiding her *own* real disappointment that she no longer had her mother's attention to herself.

When talking about her mother, Sarah was sometimes vague or even psychologically opaque. She said she had "no picture" of her mother "psychologically." In addition, in talking about her parents' relationship, she said that it was a "normal good relationship. They didn't fight much." It was "the way it should be." Indeed, Blume may have been strong and uncomplaining. Nevertheless, I suggest that Sarah might have described her mother as "stoical" in order to defend herself from knowing too deeply about her mother's very real anxieties. She at one point elaborated on Blume's stoicism by saying she "never talked about her feelings. [I] don't know if she had words for them."[11]

One point at which Sarah did speak with genuine feeling about her mother was when we discussed her parents' severe financial difficulties during the Depression. Sarah elaborated, saying that Blume had a "physically hard life" and was so often separated from her husband. "She had a really hard time, but you never heard her complain. I lived it with her, I was there. So she didn't talk about it." It was at this point in the interview that I asked Sarah whether she was her mother's companion, and she answered yes, "especially" in Western Europe. Sarah may have been very identified with her mother, experiencing her mother's inevitable difficulties as her own.

Sarah's vagueness and psychological opacity gave her story a flat quality; I felt that her denial showed a determination to avoid psychological pain. Because she experienced and was affected by the many anxieties of her mother's life, she needed to defend against them. As Sarah herself said, "I lived it with her. I was there." A second possibility is that Sarah needed to defend against knowledge of the trauma her mother experienced as a young person during World War I. Sarah's denial, minimization, and vagueness during the interview served to protect her from being overwhelmed by these feelings. These defenses seemed to serve her well; indeed, like her mother, Sarah was able to successfully face reality.

Blume's life and Sarah's own were extremely difficult both in Europe and America. Nevertheless, I felt that Sarah was able to make what she considered to be a good life for herself. She brushed away or denied her mother's losses and put aside her own suffering, and from a psychoanalytic point of view, that she did so rather than weaving them into a narrative that took them into account would not be considered ideal. Sarah did not have much reflective capacity, and, therefore, we cannot consider her story to be a true healing narrative. Sarah, however, seemed to me to be resilient, and this is important; she struck me as strong rather than brittle.

In trying to understand Sarah, I wondered whether perhaps there might have been psychological aspects of her life that she did not reveal. It is possible that the warmth that Sarah absorbed from her grandparents during summers in Poland and the attention that she received from her mother before their move to the U.S. were protective and contributed to her resilience. That Blume never talked about her own feelings may have made it easier for Sarah to maintain her stance of protective denial.[12] The strength of Sarah's defenses, however, make it difficult for me to determine to what extent she was negatively affected by her mother's anxieties, losses, and trauma.

Sarah was very social and temperamentally a pleasant person, and this seemed to be one source of her resilience. Even as a child on the ship journeying to America she had been the "belle of the ball." She described her optimism in social terms and in reference to herself: "If I'm nice outwardly, I'm being good to you and myself." Sarah seemed able to maintain a positive outlook, and even her rationalizations demonstrated her ability to see things positively. After talking about having been poor during the Depression, she said, "We may not have had much money, but we had a good life."

For me, the key to Sarah's interview came toward its end, when I asked her about World War II and its effects on her family. At that point, she spoke about her own losses, stating that "even before the war, my grandparents were so far away." She had as a young adult lost her father, her grandparents, and her cousins, and she admitted that this was very painful. Her mother, however, lost even more; immigration meant that Blume lost her home, her parents, a brother, and, temporarily, her husband. Sarah had such difficulty admitting to her mother's painful feelings, probably because her mother had lost so much. And yet, because as her mother's companion she identified with her, Sarah had to defend herself against this knowledge to maintain her own strength.

Sarah, like her mother, had made many compromises. When her father became ill, she was forced to give up full-time college, and her choice of husband and career came with trade-offs. Yet like Blume, she faced reality and made the best of what life brought her. I wondered whether, perhaps because she herself was an immigrant, she had observed so many others who had made peace with compromise. But surely her immigrant status was only one factor in what seemed to me to be her healthy attitude. Sarah's life, in comparison to that of her parents, was successful economically. Although as a woman she had not herself been expected to "shine," she responded to her parents' sacrifices with her own version of success.

Sarah's life returns us to the disavowal of loss with which I began this book and to the ambiguity of loss. Although Sarah could acknowledge how much it meant to her to know her grandparents and the landscape of her family's home, she could not talk about what Blume might have lost or how difficult immigration might have been for her. Sarah's and her mother's losses help us to define the ambiguity of loss. After all, Blume and her family had suffered in so many ways and had endured trauma at home. And Sarah intimately knew how lucky she and her mother had been to be able to leave Eastern Europe before they were killed at the hands of the Nazis. Only through loss were they saved.

CONCLUSIONS

A central theme of this research is the attempt to understand the influence of history on the individual. Both migration trauma and the trauma of violence, persecution, or poverty affected the parents of many of my interviewees; this trauma was passed on intergenerationally to varying degrees. However, my interviewees generally would not have seen this as a defining factor in their lives, nor did I myself think that their parents' trauma or loss described their identities. But because one of the discoveries of my research is that many of the pre-war immigrants were affected by trauma and that this trauma was passed on intergenerationally, it is central to my purposes to continue to discuss trauma's psychological implications. It is remarkable that events that occurred in 1915 influenced those I interviewed in 2010.

The immigrants' children flourished in American society in ways that would have seemed unimaginable to their parents. As we have seen, every-one I interviewed was materially successful. Much of this success was made possible by the changes in postwar America, by both American affluence and by the decline in anti-Semitism. The Jewish emphasis on education was also a factor in individual success. Each had felt it important to strive toward "generational upward progress" (Lederhendler, 2001, p. 40).[13] The reader may remember that every person I spoke with, both male and female, had at least a college education. Many of the men and one woman became high-earning professionals or academics, and many of the women became social workers or educators. They also fulfilled their immigrant parents' ambitions that they move to American middle-class neighborhoods. (Ruth Bader Gins-burg, herself a child of immigrants, termed the opportunities open to mem-bers of her generation and their resulting successes as the "classic American dream" [Eisner, 2018]).

In their careers, financial successes, educations, cultural interests, and intellectual lives, the immigrants' children left their parents' pasts behind them. Each person described in this chapter worked hard to succeed, follow-ing the examples of their own parents. But the differences between their parents' lives and their own were striking. Irene's mother and father, neither with a formal education, did garment industry piece work during the Depres-sion and were extremely anxious about economic survival; in contrast, Irene herself had an active cultural life and a beautiful suburban home and pursued postgraduate studies after her children were in high school.

The process of transition from their parents' largely Jewish immigrant worlds to full participation in an American milieu involved many emotions. Some, like Aaron (chapter 4), felt self-conscious when they did not under-stand the manners expected by their American peers. Moreover, the contrasts to parents' lives must have entailed complex feelings. Immigrant parents' lives were bounded by necessity and often by Old World ways; but their children each had available to them a much greater range of choices, and some were able to actively think about and select a career.

What can it have felt like for my interviewees to compare their adult lives with their parents'? For example, Seymour's father had received an educa-tion in Russia, but in New York he needed to toil in a small grocery, which involved long hours and physical labor. Seymour might have felt guilty that he was able to obtain a PhD and to live in a beautiful, middle-class neighbor-hood. David's mother had experienced malnutrition as a child; as an adult she suffered through the Depression and forever afterward feared she might again fall back into poverty. But David was able to decide on his own way of life, refusing to enter his father's business. His mother sacrificed, returning to work in middle age so that David could attend college and thus make his own choices. David enjoyed the cosmopolitan, self-actualized life that his education made possible, but he also felt pained that his mother had never recovered from the Depression. The second generation was transitional, belonging neither fully in the immigrant nor in the American world (Howe, 1976); at times individuals felt both "growing pains" and guilt at the contrast between their adult lives and their parents'.

Despite their successes, and despite the advantages and opportunities of living in the affluent and democratic America of the 1960s and 1970s, second-generation Jews "found their assumptions about humanity in modern societies profoundly challenged by the implications of the Holocaust" (Lederhendler, 2001, p. 205). For example, Lederhendler (p. 44) wrote that 1950s and 1960s literature on modern mass society and racial and ethnic prejudice written by Jews "was pervaded by an awareness of the Holocaust." Social psychology studies such as Milgram's on obedience to authority and Asch's on conformity grappled with an understanding of the roots of Nazism. Notwithstanding public perception that American Jews refused to think or talk about the Holocaust in the 1950s and 1960s, Jewish communities held Warsaw Ghetto memorial evenings each April (Diner, 2004).

The Holocaust in so many ways influenced my interviewees. Several had Holocaust survivor relatives who contacted their families, and thus these individuals were deeply aware of the horror that befell European Jews. For example, Dorothy's survivor uncle helped her mother run her store for several years. Norman, who enlisted to fight in World War II, himself "wanted to be the one to kill Hitler." As we have seen, the Holocaust profoundly affected Louise's (chapter 4) and Seymour's lives (chapters 1, 2, and 5). It would have been a disturbing undercurrent for many others to whom I spoke.

My intention in writing about resilience is to recognize the psychological achievements of each individual in the face of the "wounds of history" (Salberg & Grand, 2017).[14] Each found a way to be successful, and resilience is one way of discussing the various psychological mechanisms by which each was able to overcome what had been passed on by parents. For each individual mentioned in the chapter, what stands out in thinking about resilience versus trauma and loss? Resilience is not a "one size fits all" strategy, and I will examine several different paths to resilience. Some of these are individual sense of agency, the ability to "create meaningful lives for themselves and their families," and the presence of sustaining relationships with friends (Holmes, 2017; Richman, 2012, p. 115).

Irene, whose mother was physically abusive because she was mentally ill, must have experienced terror as a child when her mother was violent. Unlike

The author's already college-educated father in his World War I army uniform with his parents, before he left to fight in the Battle of the Bulge. His parents seem proud of their accomplished son. *Hahn family photo.*

Fay, who as an adult did not understand her terrible childhood fear, Irene was able to explain to herself later in life that she had been terrified because of her mother's mental illness. Irene's narrative had discrete gaps because she was missing facts about her very early life. In addition, Irene seemed to be in denial about aspects of her psychological life, at least as she reported them to me. Nevertheless, Irene's narrative, as well as her overall competence and warmth when I interviewed her, suggested that she had to some degree been able to work through the impact of her mother's mental illness and the resultant trauma on her development.

In Irene's story, several aspects of resilience stand out. Her strong sense of agency is suggested by her drive to build a life different from her mother's as well as her success in both creating a strong family and a place in her community. Irene seemed to be determined to repair the damage done by the trauma of her early life with her mother. Although she often had trouble relying on others, Irene also had the capacity to foster real relationships. Resilience and trauma seem balanced in Irene's story.

Dorothy felt lost at age ten when her father became ill. Moreover, she described feeling terrified by family fighting shortly before her father's traumatic death. When her father died, Dorothy experienced a traumatic absence—her mother's withdrawal, which added to the tragedy of her father's death; there was no one present to empathically witness the impact on Dorothy of her father's death (Salberg, 2017a). The depression and low self-esteem that affected Dorothy for so many years was, I think, in part a result of these years of collapse.

Although Dorothy displayed no overt denial, splitting, or dissociation, significant aspects of her difficult life had not yet been worked through (I felt that she was still working on a healing narrative). For example, she was not able to understand or integrate the effects of her mother's trauma on her psyche. Because she could not remember much about her adolescence, when she was extremely depressed, she could not construct a narrative that would help her to make sense of this traumatic period of her life.

Nevertheless, Dorothy was in many ways resilient. Her approximately thirty-year career as an educator under difficult circumstances suggests her persistence and commitment. Her persistence as an adult was also evident in her personal life: she continued to work through interpersonal difficulties, and she eventually developed very fulfilling relationships. Moreover, I hypothesized in chapter 4 that Dorothy's adult ability to treat herself well materially was a means of healthy self-repair. Finally, Dorothy's ability to develop new capacities as an older adult—for example, enjoying a leadership role at her synagogue and becoming comfortable socially—point to her capacity for growth.

In order to broaden my discussion of adulthood, it is important to look at psychological aspects of adulthood across all those I interviewed. Despite their real resilience and although, as mentioned, their outward lives were not defined by their parents' losses or trauma, the immigrants' children were profoundly affected by this. An infant being raised by a traumatized parent

must attach to a caretaker who has moments of dysregulation and dissociation. Thus the "parents' trauma story enters the child's cellular makeup before there are words" (Salberg, 2017a, p. 91). One example is Fay, whose
mother witnessed her own mother's death as a teenager and who must have
had periods of dissociation during Fay's infancy. As a child, Fay was ignored
and also terrified by the shouting and physical fighting in her household;
even when she was an adult, her mother favored Fay's older sister. The
trauma of Fay's childhood remained undigested during her adulthood, and
her screaming rages, dissociation, and smoking were a result.

Even those parents who missed their former homes or families deeply—
but had not experienced violent trauma—might as a result damage their
children. For example, Frances's mother, who cried bitterly for five years
after her emigration, was unable to nurture her daughter. She was continually
disappointed in her cross-eyed, awkward-looking daughter, and as an adult
Frances remained both troubled by and angry at her mother's treatment of
her.

Certainly, not every parent suffered from intense trauma or loss, and even
parents deeply influenced by trauma or loss might be excellent caretakers;
many were able to put their children's emotional needs ahead of their own.
Elaine (chapters 2 and 3), whose mother missed her own family immeasur-
ably, was well-taken care of; in her adult life she was fulfilled and well-
adjusted. In general, those whose parents suffered from World War I and its
aftermath tended to be more deeply traumatized than those whose parents
arrived before World War I.

Psychologically, fifteen of my twenty-two interviewees experienced
intergenerational effects of parents' trauma or loss;[15] for thirteen of these
fifteen, I believed that the effect on adult life was significant.[16] Intergenerational effects might be evidenced either in repetitions or reenactments of
trauma, such as Seymour's repeated "vision," or in less specific manifesta-
tions passed on in the attachment bond (Salberg, 2017a). More specifically, I
can sum up the effects of intergenerational trauma or traumatic loss on those
I interviewed as follows: parents' unspeakable horror affected a few people
enough that they bore definite scars. Parents' traumatic experiences or long-
lasting homesickness negatively (although less markedly) shaped the lives of
quite a number of others. A third group were those who knew something
about their parents' traumatic experiences or loss and as a result felt some
effects; because of their own and their parents' resilience, however, those in
this least-affected group went on to have particularly fulfilling lives.

As adults, those affected by intergenerational trauma needed to psychologically manage the reality of what their parents endured, and there were
many different ways of doing so. We spoke in chapter 1 about the disavowal
of loss ("they left it all behind") as a defense that helped the immigrants'
children to avoid thinking or knowing too much about their parents' traumat-

ic histories or the losses of migration. If an adult child said, "My father left it all behind," he might imply that, because of trauma, his father's home was a terrible place; consequently, he was disavowing his father's connection to what had once been home. A second way of coping with the reality of immigrant parents' lives was idealization, and this seemed relatively frequent for those whose parents had experienced more clear-cut trauma or loss; in a less extreme form, adult children might put a parent "on a pedestal." Denial was still another way of coping with immigrant parents' trauma or loss.

Idealization, related to splitting, is a defense that protects the ego from conflict by keeping contradictory negative experiences out of awareness (McWilliams, 1999). My interviewees who idealized parents saw them as having lived through something extremely difficult: they themselves bore the enormous burden of bearing witness to their parents' histories (Pisano, 2012). Some consciously or unconsciously attempted to parent their own parents. The immigrants' children often had difficulty processing their parents' suffering because they themselves were too intimately connected with it. Indeed, it is generally thought that the children of trauma survivors may not have much perspective on the dynamics of its impact on them (e.g., Pisano, 2012; Valverde & Martin-Cabrera, 2015).

Idealization may have served several functions for my interviewees. Because they needed to protect their own images of their damaged parents, they did not want to view them as less than perfect (Pisano, 2012). In addition, they often felt enormous gratitude toward their parents, who had sacrificed so that they themselves could succeed. Adult children might have very complex feelings toward their parents. For example, a parent who sacrificed for her child might also let down that child in various ways; the child consequently might have unconscious negative feelings toward that parent that idealization would disguise.

There might be additional functions for idealization. We should remember that the adult children wanted to present themselves to me as good people, and painting their traumatized parents as wholly positive in the interview with me served this purpose. In addition, most of my interviewees' parents were long dead, and, therefore, they were no longer confronted by parents' negative qualities; it may be easier to see a dead parent than a flesh-and-blood one as perfect. The death of a parent can even intensify idealization: if conflicting feelings toward a parent persist after death, adult children may be left with guilt, sadness, or distress that cannot be worked through (N. G. Pisano, personal communication, April 24, 2018). The resulting painful affects may then be disavowed and dealt with through idealization.

Throughout this book, I have highlighted idealization in the life stories of various interviewees who told me about the enormity of their parents' suffering; examples are Seymour, Benjamin, Helen, and Miriam. Each recognized parents' trauma or loss, and each responded with gratitude. Aaron and Norman are examples of adult children who idealized their parents and also seemed to need to parent them. Aaron, whose then-teenaged mother found her own father dead after a pogrom (chapters 2 and 4), seemed to split off the terrible hurt that he felt from his mother's sometimes derogatory treatment of him: in fact, he called her "my heroine." I suggest that he parented his mother by living *for* her, by becoming a doctor for her; he idealized this unempathic woman as admirable, "charismatic," and "strikingly good-looking." Indeed, Aaron kept his mother alive in his mind; the reader may remember that not a day passed in Aaron's life during which his thoughts were not occupied by his mother.

Norman's (chapters 3 and 4) description of his parents was one-dimensional, and his idealization suggested splitting, dissociation, and denial. He said that he and his sister "think of our mother with such fondness," referring to their mother, who had died so very many years before, in the present tense. Their mother, moreover, had a "sterling character" and was "always upbeat." Norman said that his depressed father was "devoted to his family." Both of Norman's parents had suffered intensely; his mother—who lost so many pregnancies and was coping with an emotionally distressed husband and true poverty in America—could not actually have been always cheerful. Norman parented his parents by taking over the family financial responsibility at age fourteen, sometimes to the detriment of his studies. I hypothesize that, by idealizing his parents, Norman was trying to protect the very damaged beings whom he had to parent. He must have felt very grateful to them; he also realized the enormity of their suffering.

Denial was one additional response to the overwhelming suffering in immigrant parents' lives, and both Ruth and Sarah used denial in their narratives. As the reader may remember, Ruth acted out for me her mother's family's procedure for hiding her younger sister during pogroms (chapter 2). Because the trauma passed on by Ruth's mother was unsymbolized, Ruth was unable to put feelings into words; instead she would reply to my interview questions about her childhood with vague responses like "It was a difficult life; I didn't give it much thought." Sarah was better able than Ruth to put feelings into words, but during her interview, she needed to protect herself from being overwhelmed by emotions, both about her own losses and about her mother's. One aspect of Sarah's denial reflected the disavowal of her mother's losses in leaving Eastern Europe. Despite her many defenses, Sarah's determination to avoid psychological pain seemed to work for her, and she seemed overall able to enjoy her life.

Studying the intergenerational transmission of trauma in descendants of immigrants has implications for psychotherapists. Because the displacement and losses of immigration can at times be traumatic and, in addition, because trauma often precedes immigration, unresolved psychological issues may be present among immigrants. Often it is the children or grandchildren of these survivors of trauma who "take up the task of healing," and they may seek therapy along the way, although they may not do so explicitly for this purpose (Salberg, 2017b, p. 248). Because trauma floods people with emotions and experiences that are difficult to turn into coherent stories, it may fall to the second or third generation to create a narrative or story about the trauma that is not fragmented and that, therefore, has the potential for healing (Pisano, 2012; Salberg, 2017a). In psychodynamic psychotherapy, "story-making is a deliberate and active process between patient and therapist, a tool" by which the "understanding of past" and present are explicated and "expanded" (Hauser, Golden, & Allen, 2006, p. 211). In other words, psychotherapy helps patients to develop meaningful narratives, and this can lead to deep insight, to psychological change, and to increased resilience. Thus co-constructed narratives that help our patients to make meaning from historical trauma will, we hope, be positive for our patients. When patients whose parents, grandparents, or even great-grandparents were immigrants come to our offices, we need to be alert to their immigration histories. We can think *with* our patients about their families' immigration histories and any associated trauma and see where this leads for them. We can help them to make sense of the origins of unexplained feelings in the intergenerational transmission of trauma in their own families.

NOTES

1. Diner (2004) noted that it was specifically after 1967 that Jews felt secure.
2. Research on secure attachment and the ability to mentalize was originally done with children, but has also been applied extensively to adults. See Fonagy et al., 2002.
3. The Satmar are an ultra-conservative, anti-Zionist Hasidic sect.
4. In Jewish practice, the home is scoured clean in preparation for Sabbath and holidays (see, for example, Zborowski & Herzog, 1952)
5. Jewish American history sources (e.g., Diner, 2004) describe the African American–Jewish tensions in the New York City public schools, which began in the late 1960s, as a turning point in African American–Jewish relations, after Jews had worked assiduously in the civil rights movement.
6. The expectation had originally been that Dorothy's mother, Dina, and her sister would save enough money in America to bring the rest of the family over from Eastern Europe.
7. The part of Poland that Sarah's family came from had then been part of Austria-Hungary, and Jews there did not experience a great deal of persecution until World War I.
8. That, in becoming a teacher, Sarah surpassed her husband is my comment. She herself probably would not have said this to me.
9. The full story that Sarah told me—which seems implausible—was that, when the Cossacks or Russians came to snatch Blume, she was told: "Get your things together; I'm going to get somebody next door." Blume escaped when her mother told her to run. (It seems implausible to me that the persecutors would have given her time to escape.)
10. Sarah said this in reply to an interview question about immigrant parents' struggles and sacrifices.

11. Sarah then tried to clarify this: "You knew that she had words for feelings, but she didn't verbalize them."

12. One very striking example of Sarah's denial was this: she stated that in Western Europe her mother was "footloose and fancy free," as she then only had to care for Sarah rather than a household. A woman alone in a strange city waiting until she could legally emigrate can hardly be called "fancy free."

13. Lederhendler (2001, p. 40) alludes to the "personal shame of failure" that immigrants' children might suffer if they disappointed their families by not moving up the ladder of success.

14. *Wounds of History* is the title of Salberg and Grand's (2017) book.

15. I describe the numbers of my interviewees who I believe were affected intergenerationally. However, in doing so, I do not mean to imply that these numbers have any statistical relevance to any larger group in the second generation.

16. For several others, at least one parent had lived through traumatic events, but I was not sure about how trauma had been communicated to and in turn manifested itself in the children. Because the interviews were limited in scope, not everyone provided enough psychological depth for me to ascertain this.

Conclusions

From Silence to Connection: Memory, History, Trauma, and Loss

One of our injunctions as Jews is to remember, to witness the past; indeed, it is a biblical command (Blair, 2004; Yerushalmi, 1986; see also Aron, 2011). The biblical command to remember has an ethical meaning, and we can think of the contemporary Jewish need to bear witness as a response to repeated exile, persecution both ancient and modern, pogroms, and the Holocaust (Blair, 2004; Yerushalmi, 1986). The directive to remember parallels my desire to re-create the memories that many of our families lost because of the silence of the immigrants. Yet remembering and witnessing the past of the pre-1924 Eastern European Jewish immigrants may be problematic. Since there was much that was too difficult or painful to speak about, many of us know only bits and pieces of our own family histories.

The need to remember the past, and thus the place of memory, is primary not just for Judaism but also in psychoanalysis and psychodynamic therapy (Aron, 2011).[1] Psychoanalysis aims to understand the personal past at a deeper level. Past trauma, which can interfere with understanding and distort memory, is one reason that we as psychoanalysts work with individuals to recognize their pasts; we hope that doing so will help them to feel more integrated and whole. I have similarly tried to understand on a deeper level how those I interviewed were influenced by the legacy of the discrimination, poverty, and trauma they described. By witnessing and interpreting these stories, I hoped to help us look at how we all have been influenced by living with the repercussions of the past.

As I began the research that led to this book, I knew that much was missing in my understanding of my grandparents' lives as immigrants. They had been silent about how it felt to leave the places where they were born. Though my family was one in which people talked, when I was young my parents had not fleshed out for me their understanding of their own parents' experiences. With the isolated bits of information I knew about my grandparents, I originally conceived of their extraordinarily difficult lives as nothing but ordinary stories for Jews of their generation. As my work proceeded, what I had conceived of as "objective" research turned out also to be a personal journey. As I learned more about my grandparents' lives, I began to understand how I was personally influenced by living with their pasts. And I began to understand that, although perhaps not far from the norm for the pre-1924 Jewish immigrants, my grandparents' lives were far from ordinary.

Surely those currently immigrating to the U.S. from Latin America and other countries afflicted by violence and poverty also have lives that are far from ordinary. We expect that they and their descendants will suffer from the sequelae of trauma and loss, perhaps in ways similar to the parents of my interviewees. I hope that my understanding of trauma and immigration can be useful in the future to those who will work psychotherapeutically with current immigrants and their children.

"Although as a young person I had received a good Hebrew School education, no one had ever taught me about the full extent of the traumatic discrimination, persecution, and poverty which were widespread for the prewar immigrant generation" (Hahn, 2015, p. 193). Indeed, the trauma suffered was obscured by the horror of the Holocaust; it paled in comparison. I realized that the parents of those I interviewed constituted a special subset of the 1881–1924 Eastern European Jewish immigration. The majority came to America after 1918, having survived the conflicts of 1914 to 1921 that afflicted Eastern Europe.

A number of the immigrant parents, like Benjamin's, lived through periods when the "risk of death was ever-present." Aaron's mother survived a pogrom during which her own father was murdered. Stanley's mother, forced to flee advancing troops during World War I with her young daughter in tow, could "feel the bullets whizzing by," and she was terrorized. And Irene's father lived for years as a war refugee. He and his family saw their shtetl burned down; they survived only by their wits and were often hungry. Irene's father also endured a sister's death due to lack of medical care.

Trauma was in many cases transmitted intergenerationally from the immigrants to their children. When trauma is too overwhelming to be processed, it is communicated unconsciously from parent to child. It lives on in the child as a wordless but visceral intrusion of the past, and in the process, trauma is repeated rather than worked through. Thus past becomes present in the form of a disguised reminder. Another way of thinking about the intergenerational transmission of trauma is this: trauma entails a breakdown in empathy, and living with a parent affected by past trauma means living with someone relationally damaged. Rather than involving a discrete repetition, the intergenerational transmission of trauma is the result of this difficulty in relationship, and it is this damaged attachment bond that is passed on (Salberg, 2017a).

Of the twenty-two people I interviewed, I believe that the intergenerational effect of trauma on their adult lives was noteworthy for thirteen. For this group of people, parental trauma had been significant enough to permanently affect their lives. The impact of this statement is striking, suggesting the widespread nature of the trauma affecting those caught up in World War I and its aftermath as well as the long-lasting effects of this trauma.

Poverty rather than pogroms motivated the immigration of many of the Eastern European Jews, in particular those who arrived before World War I (e.g., Alroey, 2011). For my interviewees whose parents arrived in this earlier period, overt anti-Semitic violence did not stand out in the majority of the stories (although two included accounts of pogroms).[2] Nevertheless, the wrenching poverty and extreme hunger took their toll, and the commonplace bullying to which many Jews were subject caused humiliation. The knowledge of persecution lurked in the background of everyday life.

Homesickness, as we know from the secondary literature, was widespread among Eastern European Jewish immigrants. Interestingly, while parents' migration trauma was described by a few immigrants' children, most often this involved missing family members rather than the place where parents were born or grew up. Only a couple of the children mentioned that their parents were truly homesick for the Old Country itself. America was thought to be a better place, and longing for the old life was considered unacceptable (Salberg, 2005, p. 436). Moreover, when my interviewees' parents arrived in America, Eastern Europe was a dangerous place for Jews, and they could not return. Consequently, during the interviews, the losses of migration were often disavowed; sometimes this originated with the immigrant parents and sometimes with the children. Yet migration trauma could be devastating, and it was particularly severe for those immigrants who came to America alone, without any immediate family. A few were unable to fully recover.

Immigration in itself can be traumatic, as suggested by the research of van Ecke, Chope, and Emmelkamp (2005), and it is the ongoing loss and separation inherent in immigration that prove problematic. For the immigrant, being cut off from one's home environment and family of origin "constitute an attachment-related risk" (van Ecke et al., 2005, p. 671). Van Ecke et al.'s study suggests that immigration in itself—in the absence of other risk factors such as poverty, discrimination, and language barriers—puts people at risk, corroborating previous assertions about the traumatic nature of immigration (Arredondo-Dowd, 1981; Levenback & Lewak, 1995; Marlin, 1992, 1994;

Mendlovic, Ratzoni, Doron, & Braham, 2001; as cited in van Ecke et al., 2005).

The separation and isolation of immigration may result in unresolved attachment, according to van Ecke et al. (2005); unresolved attachment is the adult variant of childhood disorganized attachment. Thus immigrants classified as unresolved for attachment have not psychologically recovered from the profound effects of being separated from the safety of a familiar life and from family. While in general the attachment style "developed in childhood . . . becomes more stable as we age," for some, changes in our perceptions of how we are treated later in life can cause our attachment organization to shift (van Ecke et al. 2005, p. 659, referring to Bowlby, 1988). That immigration is associated with unresolved attachment suggests that the loss of one's family, friends, physical surroundings, and cultural environment may permanently affect an individual's unconscious ideas about how interpersonal relationships work (van Ecke et al., 2005). Although in my own research, some immigrant parents who arrived alone were able to thrive, van Ecke et al.'s (2005) research suggests that the permanent loss of attachment figures puts many migrants at risk for emotional disorders. Indeed, among my interviewees' parents, Helen's and Frances's mothers, as well as Louise's and Norman's fathers, were permanently affected psychologically by their losses.[3] That immigration in itself constitutes a risk to psychological health must be kept in mind when thinking about current immigration to America.

For the parents of those I interviewed, life after immigration was often grueling: suffering did not end after the transition to America had been made. A large number of the parents of those I interviewed were deeply affected by the Depression, and for them significant economic strain did not end until after World War II (Wenger, 1996). Because many immigrants had left their own parents behind in Eastern Europe, they had no one to whom they might look up or turn for advice, and this created emotional stress. The vast strains immigrants felt in their lives meant family life was unhappy for some. Marriage partners were often chosen out of convenience. Both Barbara's and Aaron's parents were ill-suited, and for both couples fighting took the place of talking.

THE EFFECTS OF TRAUMA AND LOSS ON MEMORY AND HISTORY

Because I could not interview the immigrants themselves, what I know about their subjective lives was reflected through their adult children's eyes. Understanding the immigrants in this way provided the chance to consider the effects of trauma and loss on memory and history. How did trauma and loss affect what were passed on as memories and, by extension, what we know as our own histories? I expect that, if I had been able to interview the immigrants themselves instead of their children, many probably would have "expressed more nuanced points of view" about, for example, experiences of uprootedness and homesickness (Hahn, 2015, p. 194). Between immigrant parents and their children, much information and complexity of emotion were lost. This happened either in the "transmission of immigrants' stories" or in their "children's interpretation of them."

What interfered with the communication of "immigrants' memories to their children" (Hahn, 2015, p. 194)? For various reasons, many immigrants did not speak about what happened to them, and consequently, their histories are lost to us. One reason was trauma. As we know, massive trauma often causes dissociation, and what has been dissociated by definition cannot be remembered. We recall Aaron, whose mother found her father's body after he had been murdered in a pogrom (chapters 2 and 4). He said that he did not know how he found out about his grandfather's traumatic death: "he just knew." Aaron's account suggests dissociative elements in his mother's treatment of the past.

Because I did not interview the immigrant parents themselves, it was not possible for me to assess their use of dissociative defenses in response to trauma.[4] Hints of dissociation, however, appeared in some of the interview material. When Barbara (chapters 1, 2, and 4) asked her mother whether she had as a child seen women raped during pogroms, her mother refused to speak, suggesting trauma and a dissociative defense.

An immigrant memoir provides an insight into the effect of unsayable trauma on memory transmission. The immigrant Bertha Fox, who arrived in the U.S. in 1922, wrote that she omitted many traumatic incidents from her 1942 autobiography because she feared others would not consider her fully human had they known the extent of the harrowing experiences she had endured. She also wanted to save herself the immense pain of articulating hellish memories:

> I must add that I have left out many other episodes for two reasons. First, those who have been here in America for a long time will never be able to grasp that we who have experienced so much could still be full human beings like every-one else. Second, as I write, I relive these moments once again. I get terrible headaches and keep having to swallow aspirins. One example of this: Through the drawn shutters, we saw them leading a poor tailor by the name of Trotsky from Kriukov. He was walking with his hands pressed to his shrunken belly. The Cossack sat on his horse and drove him like a beast. There were many, many episodes like this. (Fox, 2006, p. 224)

Fox's omission of traumatic conscious memories shows that trauma limits our knowledge of the past and thus of history. When individuals are not able to speak about events, memory is not transmitted.

A remarkable example of disavowal or silence in the wake of trauma is provided in Michael Lewis's (2017) account of the life of Nobel Prize–winning cognitive psychologist Daniel Kahneman, who survived World War II as a child in Western Europe. Later in life he brushed off his traumatic memories, insisting that his past had little effect on either who he became or on his view of the world.

But it is clear that Kahneman's childhood was traumatic. As a seven-year-old living in Paris at the beginning of the war, Kahneman was forced to wear a yellow Star of David on his sweater. One day he was caught after curfew by a German S.S. officer. Because he had turned his sweater inside out, the officer did not notice the star and let the terrified boy go. Soon afterward, Kahneman's father was captured and jailed for weeks by the Nazis; he weighed only ninety-nine pounds when released. Kahneman's family then fled to the South of France, eventually living in a chicken coop; at that time the Nazis routinely hunted for Jews. Kahneman's diabetic father died when the child was ten; he had not sought treatment for his illness, since doing so was deemed too dangerous.

Lewis wrote that memory meant so little to Kahneman that "even to those he came to regard as friends he never mentioned his Holocaust experience" (p. 61). Indeed, it was not until after he had won the Nobel Prize and he was repeatedly questioned by journalists that these details were revealed. Kahneman's repudiation of the significance of memory—perhaps because of the immense pain and shame of what he had endured—amounts almost to a denial of psychic reality. Had he not received the Nobel Prize, the traumatic history of this renowned psychologist would have remained secret.

My interviews suggest that trauma, either because of anti-Semitic violence and deprivation in Eastern Europe or "because of migration, led to two different strategies for talking to children. Some parents spoke repetitively and in detail, flooding and overwhelming their children"; in these families, memories *were* passed down (Hahn, 2015, p. 194). Other parents "spoke very little about their pasts," and some were silent; more often these were fathers. There were many reasons for the silences that kept personal history a secret. Rose's father—who never once spoke about his experiences until Rose begged him—was traumatized as a child; he and his classmates were stoned daily while walking to school (chapter 2). For Rose's father, silence seemed to protect his children from memories that were too raw.

There were reasons other than trauma that made immigrant parents reticent about the past, impeding the transmission of memories to children. Many men both worked extremely long hours and tended not to speak about their feelings. Consequently, they told their children little about themselves and their experiences. In addition, some parents saw shtetl life in Eastern Europe as miserable and provincial, and these parents felt: "What was there to talk about?"

Reticence about the past often had to do with a need to look forward. "Both men and women may have felt that they had come to America to start anew, so why would they dwell on the past?" (Hahn, 2015, p. 194). They needed to forget in order to "pick themselves up and move on." Boulanger (2004) has a slightly different explanation. Immigrants in general experience a chronic but unacknowledged absence: "they fear being so overwhelmed by feelings of alienation and depression" that they will be "distracted" from the difficult "business" of fitting "into their adopted culture" (p. 355). The need to "stop identifying" with the Old World and "keep forging ahead" could cause immigrants to be reticent or silent about the past.

What I have called the disavowal of loss was an additional reason that immigrants were reticent about the past. Because of the anti-Semitic violence, discrimination, or acute poverty they had experienced in the Old Country, many immigrants had difficulty acknowledging that what had once been home also held positive memories. They could not acknowledge the loss of a place where they and those they loved were treated dreadfully. We can think of the resulting silence as a need to mute what was too difficult or painful to talk about.

Communication between the generations was sometimes difficult, and this affected the transmission of immigrants' memories. Children often "greatly exceeded parents in education," and this might mean that the differences between the generations were "too wide to be bridged by affection" (Weinberg, 1988, p. 249). For some parents, the language barrier made it difficult to pass on information about their lives (Cohen & Soyer, 2006, p. 8). Some immigrants never learned English well enough to communicate effectively in their adopted language. In addition, English and Yiddish are very different languages, and this meant that Jewish immigrants thought in dissimilar ways in Yiddish and English.

The differences in the Yiddish and American ways of life meant that, even if exact translations were found, it could still be difficult to communicate. Ruth Gay (1996, p. 11) wrote tellingly about the contrast between the Yiddish and the educated American sensibilities: "Alfred Kazin once . . . said about Yiddish that it was the sort of language where one smashed a chair through a window to let in a little air. By contrast, life in the world of the 'other' was so much calmer—where one only had to lift the sash." Gay (1996) was particularly eloquent in describing how the differences between Yiddish and English affected parent-child communication. From the children's perspective, she said:

> How were we to understand the meaning of the saying, "He is so poor that he doesn't even have money for the water over his kasha"? For us, water flowed

out of a faucet, free. We had to be told that water in the little villages of
Eastern Europe was bought by the bucket from the water carrier. (p. 62)

Similarly, translating from the American world into Yiddish could be nearly
impossible, and, consequently, the older generation was disadvantaged in
understanding American culture (Gay, 1996). These gaps in understanding
would surely have affected memory transmission.

What affected children's interpretations of what their parents said about
themselves? The adult children needed to "psychologically manage the reality of parents' losses or traumatic histories," and this "colored the way they
experienced and described their parents' experiences" (Hahn, 2015, p. 195).
Often the children of traumatized parents "tried to parent their own parents
and . . . cheer them up. They wanted to know but at the same time they did
not want to know" what their parents had endured (Valverde & Martin-
Cabrera, 2015, pp. 208–209). We must remember that—although they could
see from their parents' behaviors that they had suffered—generally the children were too intimately connected to their parents to have much perspective
on the dynamics of their parents' transmissions. Not every individual could
allow himself to consciously experience the "unthought known" of what his
parents had suffered (Bollas, 1987).

  "In many cases, 'they left it all behind' may have been the children's own
interpretation, a defense that helped them avoid thinking or knowing too
much about their parents' traumatic histories or the losses of migration"
(Hahn, 2015, p. 195). Often the children tended to minimize the complexity
of their parents' experiences. Because parents experienced trauma at home in
Eastern Europe, their children felt they couldn't possibly also have missed
the places where they once lived. Therefore, the children themselves disavowed their parents' losses and denied the pain of leaving everything their
parents had known.

  Children who disavowed their parents' losses in leaving the Old Country
were responding to what was, in fact, a complex phenomenon. Migration of
necessity involves a complex web of gains and losses, which I have termed
the ambiguity of loss; immigrant parents' losses were indeed ambiguous.
This was one of the difficult and painful psychological realities that immigrants' children were aware of in their parents. Some immigrants felt the pain
of leaving their families but had to do so for survival. Others missed the
countryside, where they had light and air, but hated the persecution of life in
Eastern Europe. The economic realities of life in Eastern Europe were such
that, even in the absence of dangerous anti-Semitism, most of the immigrants
felt that they had to leave their homes. Miriam's mother (chapter 3) mourned
her middle-class life in Eastern Europe, but there was little future for her in

the Old Country; the losses she suffered from immigration were essential for her to build a new life for herself and her family in America.

Because "parents' psychological losses were often massive," each immigrant's child needed to find a way to cope with her own knowledge of what parents had lost. For example, Sarah—who emigrated from Germany along with her mother (chapter 5)—experienced her family's economic struggles, which necessitated that her mother live apart from her husband for many years. When her mother's economic difficulties finally eased in middle age, her husband died and she was forced to go to work for the first time (Hahn, 2015). In her interview, Sarah "repeatedly denied and minimized the difficulty of her mother's life" (p. 195). She saw emigration as an improvement in her mother's life, denying that it might also have involved loss, and she described her mother as heroically stoical. Sarah "seemed to want to see her mother's life as better than it was." Her denial seemed to be in the service of her own determination to avoid psychological pain, as admitting her mother's losses would have been emotionally overwhelming. Sarah herself, "as a member of the middle class, had come so far, and she may not have wanted to think about her mother's sacrifices."

Sarah's story helps us see how the adult children needed to defend themselves from thinking or knowing too much about their parents' traumatic histories or the losses of migration. Parents' painful experiences could indeed be overwhelming to think about; they had worked so hard to build lives for their children in America, and their sacrifices were real. Children might feel guilty about their own successes compared to their parents, and they might feel pain when they allowed themselves to acknowledge their parents' wrenching histories. Yet they had to live their own lives, to enjoy their own successes, and this is what the immigrant parents wanted for them. Both immigrants' and adult children's emotions about this were complex. Children's emotions about these issues affected what they understood or remembered of their family histories.

Both going to school when they were young and achieving success as adults posed dilemmas for immigrants' children and their parents. In school children often learned that their Yiddish-speaking parents were to be looked down on, and thus school might alienate children from parents. For example, at New York City's Hunter High School in the 1930s, twelve-year-old girls were informed that their Yiddish-inflected English was a "lamentable habit" (Gay, 1996, p. 58). To advance in the world, they would have to learn to speak as their teachers, rather than their parents, did. Although parents most often urged their children to excel in school, attend college, and obtain white-collar professions, this very process was destined to drive a wedge between parents and children. Generally, expectations differed for girls and boys, but the intentions for both were similar; while girls, many of whom went to college too, were urged to marry and have children, the goal was to marry men who would bring them middle-class lives (Weinberg, 1988). As children, my interviewees generally started down a path toward futures that would separate them from their parents' lives. They would economically far exceed their parents' working-class status, and parents and children might then find it difficult to understand each other's ways of life.

Parents labored and sacrificed so their children and grandchildren could have better lives, and indeed the "economic or class differences between the children—most of whom had become middle- or upper-middle class—and their parents" were significant (Hahn, 2015, p. 195). My interviewees often expressed enormous gratitude toward their parents. But feelings were complex. Some children may not have wanted to think about their parents' sacrifices, that parents by immigrating had left everything familiar so their children could have better lives; alternatively, children may not have wanted to know that parents, because of financial necessity, had given up their own educations while they themselves reaped the benefit of their parents' hard work (Weinberg, 1988). Such feelings affected the children's interpretations of their parents' lives and, in turn, what they understood of parents' histories.

My personal connections to this research meant that, despite my distance of two generations from the experience of immigration, I too felt the pain of the past. Disavowal because of trauma sometimes played a role for me too, influencing what I probed further about during interviews. In retrospect, I realized that the Holocaust was not a topic about which I had fully come to grips, although in actuality I asked each interviewee about her family's response to World War II. For my own family and for many of those to whom I spoke, the Holocaust was, of course, a potent influence. My paternal grandmother lost her entire family during the Holocaust, and her story shows the sometimes intimate connections between the pre-1924 immigrants and the Holocaust. My grandmother emigrated alone to the U.S. in 1921 after working in a Vienna factory; she went to Vienna for two years after World War I, since the war had impoverished her family, which lived in a smaller Galician city. In America my grandmother lived with relatives until her marriage. During World War II, my grandmother received a note from her immediate family, which read, referring to her father: "Don't write to Mendel again; he doesn't live here anymore." She understood from this that he had been taken away by the Nazis (this oblique reference was a way of getting around the censor). Indeed, my grandmother never again heard from any member of her family.

For several of those I interviewed, the Holocaust had enormous psychological import. As the reader may remember, Louise (chapters 3 and 4) said she grew up like a child of Holocaust survivors, and as a very young girl, she coped with her father's disastrous loss of his entire family. Moreover, Seymour (chapters 1, 2, and 5) to this day endures a Holocaust "vision," which occurs every week during Sabbath services. In it he re-enacts his father's traumatic loss of his family, imagining that he can, in place of his father, at least comfort his grandmother while she is shot. For Sarah (chapter 5), who spent her early childhood in Europe, the Holocaust also was a powerful life influence; she was my only interviewee who personally had known cousins her own age who died in the Holocaust. She deeply knew how lucky she had been to escape that fate.

Toward the beginning of our second interview, Irene (chapter 5) confessed that, shortly after our first meeting, she dreamt twice that she herself was in the Holocaust, surely a powerful experience. She continued that speaking about family with me brought up "those who were murdered." Although I understood well the import of the Holocaust for Louise and Seymour, my disavowal meant that I missed opportunities for fuller exploration of what this meant to Irene. Furthermore, Aaron (chapters 2 and 4), Miriam (chapter 3), Dorothy (chapters 4 and 5), and Benjamin (chapter 1) had known family members who had survived the Holocaust and come to America; I might have talked about this more with them. What can it have been like for them to absorb the import of the Holocaust as young people? And there were those who fought in World War II—specifically Benjamin, my father, and Norman, who stated that he wanted to be the one to kill Hitler. What must it have felt like to do battle against a country dedicated to destroying your people?

IN SEARCH OF A BETTER LIFE

Just as Eastern European Jews did a century ago, people today fleeing violence, turmoil, poverty, and repression seek to immigrate to the U.S.; they hope for better lives for themselves and their children. But many of those trying to gain lawful admission to the U.S. in 2019 face very difficult barriers. Indeed, the U.S. grants visas only to family members of those already legally in the country and to those with "highly sought-after job skills," such as nurses and software engineers (Anbinder, 2016, p. 568). All others who seek to enter the U.S. legally must meet the criteria for refugee or political asylum status.

The percentage of U.S. residents who are immigrants is steadily rising (Lopez, Bialik, & Radford, 2018). In 2016 (the last year for which statistics were available), immigrants accounted for 13.5 percent of the U.S. population, nearly three times the proportion in 1970. Of the 1.18 million people admitted to the U.S. legally in 2016, 13 percent, or 153,400, were refugees and/or asylum seekers (U.S. Department of Homeland Security, 2017);[5] many of them were fleeing trauma. For them, gaining refugee or asylum status will be difficult. As I write in 2019, our harsh American immigration

policies mean that—for those trying to leave conditions of poverty or violence in developing countries—even the process of gaining admission to and
legal status in the U.S. may be traumatic. Psychotherapists and humanitarians
alike are faced with the fact that a huge number of immigrants living in the
U.S. are coping with the residue of terror; millions are dealing with feelings
of cultural exile and loss.

According to a 2018 report, at that time, New York City was the home of
3.1 million immigrants, constituting 38 percent of the city's population
(Mayor's Office of Immigrant Affairs, 2018). Thus a huge percentage of
New Yorkers have fled difficult conditions and dealt with the challenges of
dislocation. Currently, Trump administration policy causes increased anxiety
and stress for immigrants residing in the U.S. In 2017, immigration enforce-
ment had dramatically increased, which in New York City resulted in a 46
percent increase in arrests and caused widespread fear (Mayor's Office of
Immigrant Affairs, 2018).

As I write in 2019, thousands of people fleeing El Salvador, Guatemala,
and Honduras, which "offer no future but killing and being killed," hope to
enter the U.S. (Saviano, 2019, p. 15). In 2017, Honduras and El Salvador,
respectively, had the world's highest and second-highest murder rates (Cohn,
D., Passel, J., & Gonzalez-Barrera, A., 2017). Moreover, El Salvador, Guatemala, and Honduras were "among the poorest in Latin America." A December 2017 report stated that about 115,000 new immigrants arrived in the U.S.
from these countries in 2014, and those seeking entry to the U.S. were increasing. Because of violence, poverty, and harrowing immigration journeys,
those trying to immigrate are already traumatized. If they reach the U.S.,
their trauma is only increased, since U.S. immigration policy criminalizes
these immigrants and separates them from their families (Allen, 2019).

As we know, immigrants fleeing traumatic situations in their home countries suffer from the aftereffects of terror. Those who, like Central American
immigrants, leave extremely violent environments come to the U.S. with a
"legacy of social trauma" and psyches already under assault (Hollander,
2006, p. 63). They then must adjust to the "harsh living and working conditions" of the U.S. Often "immigration status" and limited work possibilities
beyond the most poorly paying jobs are "harsh obstacles to a successful
transition to a new life" (p. 66). Those refugees who suffer from trauma may
experience symptoms such as "disorientation, confusion . . . nightmares . . .
the inability to focus, depression, paranoia, and dissociation" (p. 65).

Because immigrants and immigrants' children will constitute an increasing percentage of our psychotherapy practices, we must keep our antennae
raised in order to hear the particular reverberations of loss and/or trauma
central to each person who seeks help. In my experience, issues such as
contextual discontinuity or the sequelae of trauma may not be the presenting
problems of immigrants or their children; however, often they will surface in

the course of treatment. I was surprised upon reflection to find a significant number of immigrants and their children in my own psychotherapy practice. Among immigrants' children, childhood backgrounds of verbal or physical abuse may be the result of trauma endured by their parents before migration; their own unprocessed anger may be associated with transmitted trauma. Moreover, families may suffer from generational conflict. It is important when working with immigrants or their children to be open to differences in cultural expectations—for instance, about relationships between parents and adult children.

Because our immigrant histories are commonly disavowed, we tend to be defensive in thinking about our country's current migration crisis. The stories of hardship, suffering, and loss that often accompany immigration are difficult to come to terms with; yet the fact that most Americans have forebears who once coped with the trauma of immigration is undeniable (J. M. Rosenberg, personal communication, February 19, 2019). We ourselves were once the outsiders. If we as Americans felt able to understand and accept our own psychological roots as immigrants, with all the hardships that entailed, we might be able to ease the current "climate of fear and suspicion" that feeds our migration crisis (Saviano, 2019, p. 16). It is "only from a soil of sympathy that's . . . personal" that a "sincere engagement" with the immigrant crisis can come (Heighton, 2019, p. 19).

FROM SILENCE TO CONNECTION

When I began my study, I knew some facts about my grandparents' lives, but there was much that I did not know. As I explored my twenty-two interviewees' stories, I also found myself in touch with extended family; I spoke about family history with members of my parents' generation whom I had not seen since childhood, and, in addition, I talked to close family members, putting together nuggets of family stories. Along the way, I discovered more about what had happened to my grandparents and their families. I began to understand Eastern European Jewish history from the inside, considering how it affected not only my parents but also my siblings and my cousins. In the process, Jewish history has become family memory.

Although the Eastern European Jewish immigrants, like all immigrants, "suffered enormous losses in leaving everything familiar, their children and grandchildren flourished as a result" (Hahn, 2015, p. 197).

> This concept of necessary loss reminds me of a memory my grandfather related to my father. As my grandfather was departing from his very poor Galician village, thinking that he would never again see his parents or his remaining siblings, *his* father accompanied him for part of the journey. His father said, "If

you remain here, you will not be a human being."[6] My great-grandfather meant that emigration was a necessity because in Galicia there was no way for my grandfather to make a living. Without that, my grandfather would be, in effect, less than human. Thus my grandfather's loss of his family, and his father's loss of a son, was necessary for economic survival. Indeed, though no one knew it at the time, this loss was necessary for my grandfather's physical survival. Those family members who remained were killed in the Holocaust. Thus this loss was profoundly ambiguous for the family. (Hahn, 2015, p. 197)

This story was one that my father told me in the course of my research. To learn about one's family in this way is indeed extremely meaningful.

My parents' generation were often too close to their own immigrant parents' suffering to truly understand the dynamics of its impact on them. Consequently, it falls to my own and successive generations to begin working through the effects of trauma and loss. If second-generation parents did not dissociate their immigrant parents' trauma, members of my generation could engage in understanding and working through what had happened to their grandparents. Sometimes, however, the trauma remained debilitating even to the grandchildren.

The cultural distance our families have traveled since the immigrants' arrival one hundred years ago is enormous. This was traversed in large part by the second generation, that of my parents and my interviewees, who had one foot in both the Yiddish and American worlds. Though for many there was strain involved in belonging entirely to neither world, as older adults, many enjoyed both the richness of the connection to the Yiddish culture and the benefits of being American.

The journey that I have traveled in researching and writing this book has been profoundly rewarding. In exploring my interviewees' family histories and subjective lives—in trying to understand what they told me on a deeper level—I learned about both what had been formative for them and what had molded my own family. My interviewees' stories deepened my understanding of my family's journey; in turn, my psychoanalytic lens helped me to understand their psychological lives.

In doing this work, I have come to a multigenerational perspective on my own identity (Pisano, 2012). While it has been painful to integrate the history of discrimination, poverty, and trauma into my understanding of my grandparents' lives, it has also helped me to feel grounded and connected. I routinely tell my own patients that we want to understand how they came to be the people they are today. I now have both a historical and a psychological perspective on what made my mother and father the people they became; in understanding the influence of history on our family's psychological issues, I better understand myself. And I feel deeply enriched by this process.

The immigrant experience is part of the history of many, or perhaps most, Americans. Indeed, the United States was populated by successive waves of immigrants, with the important exception of Native Americans. Thus the stories of hardship, suffering, and loss that often accompany immigration are part of many of our family histories. Often, however, families do not pass down the stories of the darker sides of their ancestors' lives: as I have shown, trauma and loss often impede the transmission of family history. For most of us, these painful narratives are difficult to come to terms with. But understanding these elements of our pasts may be helpful both personally and in being more empathic with the people who try to immigrate to America. "I hope that this exploration of the psychology of the immigrant experience will help all of us who are descendants of immigrants to more fully understand" ourselves (Hahn, 2015, p. 197).

Success in America! The author's paternal grandfather, circa 1960, visiting our family in our front yard in a largely Catholic neighborhood. Here my grandfather seems to be thinking, "Look how far I've come." *Hahn family photo.*

NOTES

1. The place of memory, of course, is very important not just in Judaism but also in many other religious and secular traditions (Aron, 2011).

2. The parents of seven of those I interviewed arrived before World War I began.

3. Frances's mother's own mother came to the U.S. after several years; thus the attachment figures whom Frances's mother lost in the long run were her beloved sisters, who were in fact killed in the Holocaust. Frances's mother also never recovered from missing the German city that she had so much enjoyed.

4. In order to participate in my research, informants needed to have learned about the past from at least one parent, thus that parent would have talked about his or her experiences; a parent who talked probably did not rely primarily on dissociative defenses.

5. Refugee or asylum status may be given to those who have been persecuted or fear they have been persecuted because of race, religion, nationality, and/or membership in a particular social or political group (U.S. Citizenship and Immigration Services, 2019).

6. The actual words his father said were: "Si fun dir nisht machen ah Leute." This appears to be an eastern dialect of German rather than Yiddish. This comment, to the extent that it foreshadowed the catastrophe to come, was more prophetic than my great-grandfather may have realized.

Appendix A

Questionnaire: Eastern European Jewish Immigrants and Their Children in America

[Note to interviewer: the following set of questions underlie much of the interview and can be posed at the beginning of the interview and referred to again. Alternatively, these may be asked after the first few interview questions.]

If you were going to imagine, or reconstruct, what your mother/father experienced subjectively when s/he came to this country, what would you say?
If you were able to put yourself in your mother's/father's shoes, what would s/he have experienced?

(Ask separately for mother and father:)

    What did they experience in their inner lives?
    Lonely?
    Homesick?
    Experiences of depression?
    Physical illnesses?
    What helped them to adjust? What was unhelpful?

I'd like to begin by asking you a little bit about your mother and father. Do you know when and where your parents were born?

    (Which country/city? Russian—Austrian—Polish? What was their sense of identity? Self-concept & self-esteem associated with this?)

Do you know anything about their lives in Europe before they immigrated? (Description of mother's and father's lives in Europe.)

Who was in the family?
Who came to the U.S. and who was left behind?

Social standing of the family?
What did your grandparents do for a living?

How did they locate themselves in terms of types of Judaism:

Orthodox—Misnagid—Chassid—Secularized
Bundist—Zionist—Mixed—Changing

Were you told myths or stories about the family?

Were you told about anti-Semitic incidents or atmosphere?

What year did your mother/father come to the U.S.?

How was the decision to leave made?
Who did they come with?
What do you know about the voyage and the journey through Europe to get to the boat? Any traumatic experiences?

What part of the U.S. did they go to and why?

(Did your family come right to the U.S.? If not, what was their journey and reasons for different stops?)
Was their name changed at Ellis Island?

Who greeted them here?

What do you know about any reunion that may have occurred?

What were their first experiences in the U.S.?

Parents' feelings about uprooting themselves?

How did they experience living conditions in the U.S.?

Making a living in the U.S.? (Any feelings about this?)

Any educational experiences in the U.S.?

What was your mother's experience creating a household/feeding the family, etc.?

Did your parents talk much about being Eastern European and immigrants?

Adapting to America . . .

> The process of Americanization? (Their experiences of and feelings about Americanization)
> Feelings about their Jewish identity here?
> Adapting their Jewish identity or practices in the U.S.? How did their religious practices change between Europe and America and over the course of their lives?
> Did they belong to *Landsmenschaften* or other groups?

When and where were you born?

> How many years were your parents here before you were born?
> What was the first language that was spoken to you (and why)?

Your parents marriage and relationship?

> Courtship? Why they married?
>
> Did they fight much?
> Reasons for their fights?
> Your understanding of the psychology of their relationship?
> Was this different from your mother's and father's perspective?
> How do you think that this might have been different under different circumstances?

What are your earliest memories of childhood?

> (Try to obtain a picture of the "texture" of the subject's life during early childhood. What did it feel like to be at home with his/her parents? What were the smells? The quality of interactions? If arguments, who argued and what was the quality of the arguments?)

Opportunities and obligations of various kinds for you and your parents in America?

> What were the struggles and sacrifices of making one's way here? (Ask for specifics)
> How did you/your parents feel about this?
> (For adult child): Did you have to work as a child?

Parents' sense of self?

> Self-confidence and self-esteem?
> Frustration?
> Independence and autonomy (women's roles)?

Education: parents' attitude toward education?

How was your parents' English when you were growing up and what were your feelings about this?

Differing experiences among you and your siblings re: the above issues (working as a child, education, feelings about parents' English)?

Did you feel that you were different from other American-Jewish or American kids?

What kinds of family conflict occurred around Americanization? (Around Jewish identity and practice?) Struggles growing up involving this?

Your feelings about wanting to have a different life from those of your parents? A different marriage?

Was your choice of occupation influenced by your parents' experiences? (For example, were you making up for their losses through your choices?)

How do you think your life might have been different overall had you been born of non-immigrant Jewish parents? Non-Jewish parents?

What happened in your family when World War II started?

> Talk about the war?
> People left behind?
> Did family members or others that you met survive the Holocaust?
> Were family members killed?

How do you think about your Jewish identity now? How do you identity yourself (re: both Jewish and national identity)? American? American-Jewish? Jewish-Hungarian or Jewish-Polish?

> How is that similar to or different from your parents?
> How have your religious practices changed over your lifetime?

Have you been back to where your parents came from?

The role of community?

> In your parents' lives in Europe?
> When they first came to the U.S.? In their adjustment to the U.S.? (mention the Jewish emphasis on community)
> Did they participate in the Jewish community?

In their lives overall?

In your life (ask about various periods of their lives)?

What Jewish or other communities do you belong to?
Religious? Social? Vocational? Political?

How would you formulate the psychological role of community?

Are there times when you are particularly proud/ashamed of your heritage?

Are there any remnants of European Jewish life in your home?

Food?
Jokes?
Objects?
Traditions?
Yiddish in the family?

Appendix B

Research Approach

RESEARCH PARTICIPANTS

Individuals interviewed had two parents who came to the U.S. during the wave of immigration that is usually dated between 1881 and 1924. Although this immigration formally ended with the restrictive Immigration Act of 1924, a few individuals belonging to this group arrived after 1924, particularly if close family members were already in the U.S. The parents of those I interviewed arrived no later than 1930.

Interviewees were located through synagogues, a Jewish senior service program, YIVO's (Institute for Jewish Research) online newsletter, a psychoanalytic institute's listserv, and acquaintances. All those interviewed were college educated. While the majority were in their eighties, one was in her fifties, one was in his sixties, five were in their seventies, one was in his nineties, and one was 104 years old. All were cognitively intact. Most were retired, and their former professions included medical doctors, lawyers, scientists, teachers, and social workers. Thus they were educated and articulate.

I chose interviewees after initial brief telephone conversations; I asked each whether their immigrant parents had told them about their pasts prior to coming to America or during the period of transition. My choice of interview subjects was, in fact, skewed against those whose families had told their children nothing about the past. Because—in order for me to understand the psychology of the immigrant experience—parents had to have communicated something about it to their children, my choice of interviewees included fewer subjects who stated that their parents had said very little about their pasts. (I used some individuals whose parents had said little but who had interesting experiences as children of immigrants.) In choosing interviewees, I also attempted to roughly balance the number of males and females.

RESEARCH INTERVIEW

For each participant, I conducted two detailed, semistructured psychohistory interviews; each interview lasted two to three hours. Several individuals' accounts were very detailed, and consequently they required three interview sessions. Thus I spent approximately five to six hours with each person and somewhat more with a few. Interviews consisted of both open-ended and specific questions, with the goal of understanding motivations and effects, in addition to gathering particular details about immigrants and adult children.

I asked the same set of questions of each participant, but people were able to elaborate on questions in their own ways. Analagously, I was free to follow up their responses based on what they said, and my freedom to respond this way is a hallmark of interpretive research (Addison, 1989). Interviews were recorded for backup purposes.

After each interview session, I recorded my psychological reactions to and "clinical" impressions of the individual: for example, what kind of person was he or she and how did each react to me and the interview questions? Was he or she open, or, alternatively, did the person use denial or evasion about certain types of questions? Although my clinical "antennae" were active during all interviews, they were intended to be more informal than psychotherapy sessions, and the interviewees—who possessed the information needed to help *me* with my research—were considered to be the authorities.

LIFE STORIES

In analyzing the interview information, I used my clinical skills and intuitions to understand the psychological influences on each participant. I then constructed what I called life stories based on my understanding of each. Interviewees varied greatly in their own level of psychological insight, and the psychological sophistication of the life story I formed varied in part because of this. My psychoanalytic theories of human development, as well as attachment theory, underlie the life story I formulated for each person.

Glossary

Yiddish Words and Other Terms

blood libel: An accusation that Jews kidnapped and murdered Christian children to use their blood in religious rituals; most often they were accused of using the blood in the preparation of Passover bread. This originated in the Middle Ages.

cheder: A school for boys, held in the teacher's house, where they were taught Hebrew and Jewish scripture. Teachers were typically badly paid and often ill-tempered; rote learning and reading out loud to one another were standard.

dorf: A village in Eastern Europe. Smaller than a shtetl.

freethinker: A person who forms his own ideas and opinions and rejects dogma, especially about religious beliefs. It is associated with secularism and atheism.

greenhorn: A newcomer unaccustomed to local customs and manners. It connotes someone naïve or gullible. Also refers to a novice or fledgling at a particular activity.

Hadassah: The Women's Zionist Organization of America. It is a volunteer organization whose goal is to strengthen a commitment to Israel and to enhance women's health and well-being.

Haganah: An underground Jewish paramilitary organization in Palestine.

haym: *Der haym* refers to home in Yiddish. Also transliterated as *der heym* or *der heim*. People also refer to Eastern Europe as the *alte haym*, literally the old home.

kehillah: The local Jewish community council in Eastern Europe, which dispensed charity and free loans and maintained orphanages and schools for the poor.

landsmanschaft: (Plural: *landsmanschaftn*). Hometown associations that helped Jewish immigrants to both assimilate and remain connected to home. Many immigrants were members of their shtetl's or region's *landsmanschaft*. They provided social structure, support, and help in learning English.

pogrom: A pogrom involves mass violence against a minority religious, ethnic, or social group. The word came into widespread use after the massacres of 1881–1884 against Jews in the Russian Empire. It usually indicates that the authorities at least passively encouraged violence and did not punish members of the violent mobs.

shtetl: A market town in Eastern Europe with a large Yiddish-speaking Jewish population. Although *shtetlekh* (plural of shtetl) varied in size, the shtetl was small enough, perhaps several thousand inhabitants, that members knew one another.

tefillin: A pair of small black leather boxes containing scrolls of parchment inscribed with Torah verses. Observant Jewish men (and today some women) wear them during prayer. Also called phylacteries.

treif: Any form of non-kosher food.

yeshiva: Traditionally, a school for the intensive study of religious texts. In Eastern Europe a boy attended a yeshiva after completing *cheder*. Currently, a yeshiva is usually an Orthodox Jewish school, college, or seminary.

References

Abraham, N., & Torok, M. (1994). *The shell and the kernel* (Vol. 1). Chicago, IL: University of Chicago Press.

Addison, R. B. (1989). Grounded interpretive research: An investigation of physician socialization. In M. J. Packer & R. B. Addison (Eds.), *Entering the circle: Hermeneutic investigation in psychology* (pp. 39–58). Albany, NY: State University of New York Press.

Ainslee, R. C., Harlem, A., Tummala-Narra, P., Barbanel, L., & Ruth, R. (2013). Contemporary psychoanalytic views on the experience of immigration. *Psychoanalytic Psychology, 30*(4), 663–679.

Akhtar, S. (1999a). *Immigration and identity: Turmoil, treatment, and transformation.* Lanham, MD: Rowman & Littlefield.

———. (1999b). The immigrant, the exile, and the experience of nostalgia. *Journal of Applied Psychoanalytic Studies, 1,* 123–130. doi: 10. 1023/A:1023029020496.

———. (2011). *Immigration and acculturation: Mourning, adaptation, and the next generation.* Lanham, MD: Jason Aronson.

Allen, R. (2019, Winter). Trump's war on immigrants. *ACLU Magazine.*

Alroey, G. (2011). *Bread to eat and clothes to wear: Letters from Jewish migrants in the early twentieth century.* Detroit, MI: Wayne State University Press.

Anbinder, T. (2016). *City of dreams: The 400-year epic history of immigrant New York.* Boston, MA: Houghton Mifflin Harcourt.

Angel, J. L., Buckley, C. J., & Sakamoto, A. (2001). Duration or disadvantage? Exploring nativity, ethnicity, and health in midlife. *The Journals of Gerontology: Series B: Psychological Sciences and Social Sciences*, 56(5), 275–284.http://dx.doi.org/10.1093/geronb/56.5.S275.

Antin, M. (1985). *From Plotzk to Boston.* New York: Markus Weiner.

Aron, L. (2011). Living memory: Discussion of Avishai Margalit's "Nostalgia." *Psychoanalytic Dialogues, 21,* 281–291. doi: 10.1080/10481885.2011.581110.

Arredongo-Dowd, P. M. (1981). Personal loss and grief as a result of immigration. *Personal and Guidance Journal, 59*(6), 376–378.

Asch, S. (1961). Alone in a strange world. In H. Goodman (Ed. and trans.), *The new country: Stories from the Yiddish about life in America* (pp. 36–49). New York: YKUF Publishers.

Auerhahn, N. C., & Prelinger, E. (1983). Repetition in the concentration camp survivor and her child. *International Review of Psychoanalysis, 10,* 31–46.

Bar-On, D., & Gilad, N. (1994). To rebuild life: A narrative analysis of three generations of an Israeli Holocaust survivor's family. In R. E. Josselson & A. Lieblich (Eds.), *The narrative study of lives: Vol. 2* (pp. 83–112). Newbury Park, CA: Sage.

Bartal, Y. (2005). *The Jews of Eastern Europe, 1772–1881*. Philadelphia: University of Pennsylvania Press.

Beebe, B., & Lachmann, F. (2002). *Infant research and adult treatment: Co-constructing interactions*. Hillsale, NJ: Analytic Press.

Beltsiou, J. (2016). Introduction. In J. Beltsiou (Ed.), *Immigration in psychoanalysis: Locating ourselves* (pp. 1–11). London: Routledge.

Benjamin, R. (1925–1929). *Essays by Jewish-American immigrant women*. Sponsored by the National Council of Jewish Women. First Impressions of America (box 1, folder 4). Princeton University Library Manuscripts Division, Princeton University, Princeton, NJ.

Benjamin, W. (1968). The storyteller: Reflections on Nikolai Leskóv. In Hannah Arendt (Ed.) and H. Zohn (Trans.), *Illuminations* (pp.192–251). New York: Schocken.

Berman, R. (1978). The American scene: Some notes from the third generation. In G. Rosen (Ed.), *Jewish life in America* (pp. 189–198). New York: KTAV Publishing House.

Blair, S. (2004). Jewish America through the lens. In S. Blair & J. Freedman (Eds.), *Jewish in America* (pp. 113–134). Ann Arbor: University of Michigan Press.

Blaustein, D. (1903). Oppression and freedom. *Charities and the Commons, 10*, 339.

Bodnar, S. (2004). Remember where you come from: Dissociative process in multicultural individuals. *Psychoanalytic Dialogues, 14*, 581–603.

Bollas, C. (1987). *The shadow of the object: Psychoanalysis of the unthought known*. New York: Columbia University Press.

Boulanger, G. (2004). Lot's wife, Cary Grant, and the American dream: Psychoanalysis with immigrants. *Contemporary Psychoanalysis*, 40, 353–372.

———. (2016). Seeing double, being double: Longing, belonging, recognition, and evasion in psychodynamic work with immigrants. In J. Beltsiou (Ed.), *Immigration in psychoanalysis: Locating ourselves* (pp. 53–68). London: Routledge.

Bowlby, J. (1988). *A secure base: Clinical applications of attachment theory*. London: Routledge.

Cahan, A. (1929). *Memoir of Abraham Cahan* [Unpublished].

Calof, R. (1995). *Rachel Calof's story: Jewish homesteader on the Northern Plains*. Bloomington: Indiana University Press. Originally written in 1936.

Chodorow, N. (1978). *The reproduction of mothering: Psychoanalysis and the sociology of gender*. Berkeley: University of California Press.

Cohen, B. (1972). *Sociocultural changes in American Jewish life as reflected in selected Jewish literature*. Madison, NJ: Fairleigh Dickinson University Press.

Cohen, J., & Soyer, D. (2006). Introduction: Yiddish social science and Jewish immigrant autobiography. In J. Cohen & D. Soyer (Eds. and trans.), *My future is in America: Autobiographies of Eastern European Jewish immigrants* (pp. 1–17). New York: New York University Press.

Cohen, R. (1995). *Out of the shadow: A Russian Jewish girlhood on the Lower East Side*. Ithaca, NY: Cornell University Press. Originally written in 1918.

Cohen, R. (2015). *The girl from human street: Ghosts of memory in a Jewish family*. New York: Knopf.

Cohn, D., Passel, J. S., & Gonzalez-Barrera, A. (2017, December 7). Rise in U.S. immigrants from El Salvador, Guatemala and Honduras outpaces growth from elsewhere: Lawful and unauthorized immigrants increase since recession. *Hispanic trends*. Pew Research Center. Retrieved February 23, 2019, from https://www.pewhispanic.org/2017/12/07/rise-in-u-s-immigrants-from-el-salvador-guatemala-and-honduras-outpaces-growth-from-elsewhere/.

Coles, P. (2011). *The uninvited guest from the unremembered past: An exploration of the unconscious transmission of trauma across the generations*. London: Karnac Books.

Corrigan, E. G., & Gordon, P. E. (1995). *The mind object: Precocity and pathology of self-sufficiency*. London: Karnac.

Cowan, N. M., & Cowan, R. S. (1996, rev. ed). *Our parents' lives: Jewish assimilation and everyday life*. New Brunswick, NJ: Rutgers University Press.

Cyrulnik, B. (2007). *Talking of love on the edge of a precipice*. (D. Macey, Trans.). London: Penguin.

Dallas Morning News. (1906, March 10). Homesick Russian Jews: Refugees who yearn for the land of persecution.

Davoine, F., & Gaudillière, J.-M. (2004). *History beyond trauma: Whereof one cannot speak, thereof one cannot stay silent*. (S. Fairfield, Trans.). New York: Other Press.

Dawidowicz, L. (1982). *On equal terms: Jews in America, 1881–1981*. New York: Holt, Rinehart, & Winston.

Derrida, J. (1986). *Fors*: The Anglish words of Nicholas Abraham and Maria Torok. Foreword to N. Abraham & N. Torok (1976), *The Wolf Man's magic word: A cryptonomy*. Minneapolis: University of Minnesota Press.

Dillingham, W. P. (1911). *Emigration conditions in Europe. Reports of the Immigration Commission*. 61st Congress, 3rd Session. Document no. 748, p. 279. Washington, DC: Government Printing Office.

Diner, H. R. (2003). *A new promised land: A history of Jews in America*. New York: Oxford University Press.

———. (2004). *The Jews of the United States, 1654 to 2000*. Berkeley: University of California Press.

———. (n.d.). German immigrant period in the United States. *Jewish Women's Archive Encyclopedia*. Retrieved February 9, 2019, from https://jwa.org/encyclopedia/article/german-immigrant-period-in-united-states.

Domnitz, A. (2006). Why I left my old home and what I have accomplished in America. In J. Cohen & D. Soyer (Eds. and trans.), *My future is in America: Autobiographies of Eastern European Jewish immigrants* (pp.124–159). New York: New York University Press. Originally written in 1942.

Ehrenberg, D. (2004). How I became a psychoanalyst. *Psychoanalytic Inquiry, 24*(4), pp. 490–516.

Eisner, J. (2018, March). Ruth Bader Ginsburg: Superhero of the Supreme Court. *Forward*, p. 33.

EMDR Institute—Eye Movement Desensitization & Reprocessing. (n.d.). Theory. Retrieved February 24, 2019, from http://www.emdr.com/theory/.

Engel, D. (2010, November 5). World War I. *YIVO Encyclopedia of Jews in Eastern Europe*. Retrieved October 31, 2015, from http://www.yivoencyclopedia.org/article.aspx/World_War_I.

Epstein, L. J. (2007). *At the edge of a dream: The story of Jewish immigrants on New York's Lower East Side, 1880–1920*. San Francisco, CA: Jossey-Bass.

Etkes, I. (2010, October 27). Haskalah. *YIVO Encyclopedia of Jews in Eastern Europe*. Retrieved November 12, 2015, from http://www.yivoencyclopedia.org/article.aspx/Haskalah.

Ewen, E. (1985). *Immigrant women in the land of dollars: Life and culture on the Lower East Side, 1890–1925*. New York: Monthly Review Press.

Faimberg, H. (2005). *The telescoping of generations: Listening to the narcissistic links between generations*. London: Routledge.

Feingold, H. L. (1992). *A time for searching: Entering the mainstream, 1920–1945*. (Vol. IV: The Jewish People in America). Baltimore, MD: Johns Hopkins University Press.

Fink, R. (1999). *A clinical introduction to Lacanian psychoanalysis: Theory and technique*. Cambridge, MA: Harvard University Press.

Fonagy, P. (2001). *Attachment theory and psychoanalysis*. New York: Other Press.

Fonagy, P., Gergely, G., Jurist, E., & Target, M. (2002). *Affect regulation, mentalization, and the development of the self*. New York: Other Press.

Foster, R. P. (2001). When immigration is trauma: Guidelines for the individual and family clinician. *American Journal of Orthopsychiatry, 71* (2), 153–162.

Fox, B. (2006). The movies pale in comparison. In J. Cohen & D. Soyer (Eds. and trans.), *My future is in America: Autobiographies of Eastern European Jewish immigrants* (pp. 204–232). New York: New York University Press. Originally written in 1942.

Fraiberg, S., Adelson, E., & Shapiro, V. (1975). Ghosts in the nursery: A psychoanalytic approach to the problem of impaired infant-mother relationships. *Journal of the American Academy of Child Psychiatry, 14*(3), 387–421.

Frosh, S. (2013). *Hauntings: Psychoanalysis and ghostly transmissions*. London: Palgrave Macmillan.

Garon, J. (2004). Skeletons in the closet. *International Forum of Psychoanalysis, 13*(1–2), 84–92. doi:10.1080/08037060410031142.

Garza-Guerrero, A. C. (1974). Culture shock: Its mourning and the vicissitudes of identity. *Journal of the American Psychoanalytic Association, 22,* 408–429.

Gay, R. (1996). *Unfinished people: Eastern European Jews encounter America*. New York: W.W. Norton.

Gelfand, M. (2018, September). After 9/11, Americans united to protect the country. Today, we're divided by threats that don't exist. *Time*. Retrieved January 12, 2019, from http://time.com/5392451/september-11-tightness-immigration-fears.

Gerson, S. (2009). When the third is dead: Memory, mourning, and witnessing in the aftermath of the Holocaust. *International Journal of Psychoanalysis, 90,* 1341–1357.

Gittleman, S. (1978). *From shtetl to suburbia: The family in Jewish literary imagination*. Boston, MA: Beacon Press.

Gonzalez, F. J. (2016). Only what is human can truly be foreign: The trope of immigration as a creative force in psychoanalysis. In J. Beltsiou (Ed.), *Immigration in psychoanalysis: Locating ourselves* (pp. 15–38). London: Routledge.

Goodman, N. (2012). The power of witnessing. In N. Goodman & M. Meyers (Eds.), *The power of witnessing: Reflections, reverberations, and traces of the Holocaust: Trauma, psychoanalysis, and the living mind* (pp. 4–26). New York: Routledge.

Grand, S. (2009). *The hero in the mirror: From fear to fortitude*. New York: Routledge.

Grinberg, L. (1978). The "razor's edge" in depression and mourning. *International Journal of Psychoanalysis, 59,* 245–254.

Grinberg, L., & Grinberg, R. (1989). *Psychoanalytic perspectives on migration and exile*. New Haven, CT: Yale University Press.

Hahn, H. (2015). They left it all behind. In M. O'Loughlin (Ed.), *The ethics of remembering and the consequences of forgetting*. Lanham, MD: Rowman & Littlefield.

Halasz, G. (2012). Psychological witnessing of my mother's Holocaust testimony. In N. Goodman & M. Meyers (Eds.), *The power of witnessing: Reflections, reverberations, and traces of the Holocaust: Trauma, psychoanalysis, and the living mind* (pp. 145–158). New York: Routledge.

Harlem, A. (2010). Exile as a dissociative state: When a self is "lost in transit." *Psychoanalytic Psychology, 27* (4), 460–474.

Harris, A. (2014). Discussion of Slade's "Imagining fear." *Psychoanalytic Dialogues, 24,* 267–276.

Hauser, S. T., Golden, E., & Allen, J. P. (2006). Narrative in the study of resilience. *Psychoanalytic Study of the Child, 61,* 205–227.

Heighton, S. (2019, February 24). Island of the lost. Review of *Notes on a shipwreck*, by D. Enia. *New York Times Book Review*, p. 14.

Hoffman, E. (1989). *Lost in translation: A life in a new language*. New York: Penguin.

———. (1999). The new nomads. In A. Aciman (Ed.), *Letters of transit* (pp. 35–64). New York: The New Press.

———. (2016). Out of exile: Some thoughts on exile as a dynamic condition. In J. Beltsiou (Ed.)., *Immigration in psychoanalysis: Locating ourselves* (pp. 211–215). London: Routledge.

Hollander, N. C. (2006). Negotiating trauma and loss in the migration experience: Roundtable on global woman. *Studies in Gender and Sexuality, 7*(1), 61–70.

Holmes, J. (1996). *Attachment, intimacy, autonomy: Using attachment theory in adult psychotherapy*. Northvale, NJ: Jason Aronson.

———. (2017, February). Roots and routes to resilience: Attachment/psychodynamic perspectives. *Psychoanalytic Discourse, 3,* 20–33. Retrieved from http://psychoanalyticdiscourse.com/index.php/psad/issue/view/3.

Howe, I. (1976). *World of our fathers*. New York: Harcourt Brace Jovanovich.

———. (1978). The East European Jews and American culture. In G. Rosen (Ed.), *Jewish life in America: Historical perspectives* (pp. 92–108). New York: KTAV Publishing House.

Ignatieff, M. (1998). *Isaiah Berlin: A life*. London: Chatto & Windus.

Impert, L. (1999). The body held hostage: The paradox of self-sufficiency. *Contemporary Psychoanalysis, 35,* 647–671.

Joselit, J. W. (2007). Upward into American life. In A. Newhouse (Ed), *A living lens* (pp. 213–239). New York: W.W. Norton.

Kaplan, L. (1995). *No voice is ever wholly lost: An exploration of the everlasting attachment between parent and child*. New York: Simon & Schuster.

Kassow, S. (2007a). Introduction. In S. Katz (Ed.), *The shtetl: New evaluations*. New York: New York University Press.

———. (2007b). The shtetl in interwar Poland. In S. Katz (Ed.), *The shtetl: New evaluations*. New York: New York University Press.

———. (2010, October 18). Shtetl. *YIVO Encyclopedia of Jews in Eastern Europe*. Retrieved April 29, 2018, from http://www.yivoencyclopedia.org/article.aspx/Shtetl.

Kazin, A. (1951). *A walker in the city*. Orlando, FL: Harcourt.

Khanin, V. (2010). Dnipropetrovs'k. *YIVO Encyclopedia of Jews in Eastern Europe*. Retrieved May 29, 2016, from http://www.yivoencyclopedia.org/article.aspx/Dnipropetrovsk.

Kirshenblatt-Gimblett, B. (1995). Introduction to *Life is with people: The culture of the shtetl*, by Mark Zborowski and Elizabeth Herzog (pp. ix–xlviii). New York: Schocken. Retrieved from https://www.nyu.edu/classes/bkg/web/liwp.pdf.

Kobrin, L. (1961). The tenement house. In H. Goodman (Ed. and trans.), *The new country: Stories from the Yiddish about life in America* (p. 27). New York: YKUF Publishers.

Krystal, H. (1988). *Integration and self-healing: Affect-trauma-alexithymia*. Hillside, NJ: Analytic Press.

Kusnetz, C. (2006). Why I left the Old Country and what I have accomplished in America. In J. Cohen & D. Soyer (Eds. and trans.), *My future is in America: Autobiographies of Eastern European Jewish immigrants* (pp. 233–287). New York: New York University Press. Originally written in 1942.

Langer, L. (1993). *Holocaust testimonies: The ruins of memory*. New Haven, CT: Yale University Press.

Laub, D. (1992). Bearing witness or the vicissitudes of listening. In S. Felman & D. Laub (Eds.), *Testimony: Crises of witnessing in literature, psychoanalysis, and history* (pp. 57–74). New York: Routledge.

Lederhendler, E. (1989). *The road to modern Jewish politics: Political tradition and political reconstruction in the Jewish community of tsarist Russia*. New York: Oxford University Press.

———. (2001). *New York Jews and the decline of urban ethnicity: 1950–1970*. Syracuse, NY: Syracuse University Press.

———. (2017). America. *YIVO Encyclopedia of Jews in Eastern Europe*. Retrieved January 27, 2019, from http://www.yivoencyclopedia.org/article.aspx/America.

Levenbach, D., & Lewak, B. (1995). Immigration: Going home or going to pieces. *Contemporary Family Therapy: An International Journal, 17*(4), 379–394.

Levitats, I. (1981). *The Jewish community in Russia, 1844–1917*. Jerusalem: Posner & Sons.

Lewis, M. (2017). *The undoing project: A friendship that changed our minds*. New York: W.W. Norton.

Libin, Z. (1961). A wall. In H. Goodman (Ed. and trans.), *The new country: Stories from the Yiddish about life in America* (p. 57). New York: YKUF Publishers.

Lieberman, A. F. (2014). Giving words to the unsayable: The healing power of describing what happened. *Psychoanalytic Dialogues, 24,* 277–281.

Lieblich, A. (1993). Looking at change: Natasha, 21—New immigrant from Russia to Israel. In R. E. Josselson & A. Lieblish (Eds.), *The narrative study of lives: Vol. 1* (pp. 92–129). Newbury Park, CA: Sage.

Livingston, E. (1986). *Tradition and modernism in the shtetl Aisheshuk, 1919–1939: An oral history*. Princeton, NJ: Princeton University Press.

Lobban, G. (2006). Immigration and dissociation. *Psychoanalytic Perspectives, 3* (2), 73–92.

————. (2016). The immigrant analyst: A journey from double consciousness towards hybridity. In J. Beltsiou (Ed.), *Immigration in psychoanalysis: Locating ourselves* (pp. 69–86). London: Routledge.

Lopez, G., Bialik, K., & Radford, J. (2018, November 30). Key findings about U.S. immigrants. *Fact Tank: News in the Numbers.* Pew Research Center. Retrieved February 20, 2019, from https://www.pewresearch.org/fact-tank/2018/11/30/key-findings-about-u-s-immigrants/.

Main, M., Kaplan, N., & Cassidy, J. (1985). Security in infancy, childhood, and adulthood: A move to the level of representation. In I. Bretherton & E. Waters (Eds.), *Growing points of attachment theory and research. Monographs of the Society for Research in Child Development, 50,* Serial No. 209, pp. 66–104.

Manekin, R. (2010, November 2). Galicia. *YIVO Encyclopedia of Jews in Eastern Europe.* Retrieved April 20, 2018, from http://www.yivoencyclopedia.org/article.aspx/Galicia.

Marich, J. (n.d.). What are adverse life experiences? Gracepoint Wellness. Retrieved February 24, 2019, from https://www.gracepointwellness.org/109-post-traumatic-stress-disorder/article/55727-what-are-adverse-life-experiences.

Markese, S. (2012). Dyadic trauma in infancy and early childhood: Review of the literature. In B. Beebe, P. Cohen, & S. Markese (Eds.), *Mothers, infants and young children of September 11, 2001.* New York: Routledge.

Marlin, O. (1992). Emigration: A psychoanalytic perspective. *Ceskoslovenska Psychologie, 36*(1), 41–48.

————. (1994). Special issues in the analytic treatment of immigrants and refugees. *Issues in Psychoanalytic Psychology, 16*(1), 7–16.

Masserman, P., & Baker, M. (1932). *The Jews come to America.* New York: Bloch Publishing.

Matt, S. J. (2011). *Homesickness: An American history.* New York: Oxford University Press.

Mayor's Office of Immigrant Affairs. (2018). *State of our immigrant city.* Retrieved January 6, 2019, from https://www1.nyc.gov/assets/immigrants/downloads/pdf/moia_annual_report_2018_final.pdf.

McWilliams, N. (1999). *Psychoanalytic case formulations.* New York: The Guilford Press.

Meltzer, M. (1974). *World of our fathers: The Jews of Eastern Europe.* New York: Farrar, Straus, & Giroux.

Menes, A. (1972). The East Side and the Jewish labor movement. In I. Howe & E. Greenberg (Eds. and trans.), *Voices from the Yiddish: Essays, memoirs, diaries* (pp. 49–72). New York : Peter Lang Publishing.

Mendlovic, S., Ratzoni, G., Doron, A., & Braham, P. (2001). Immigration, anomie, and psychopathology. *Journal for the Psychoanalysis of Culture & Society, 6*(2), 324.

Metzker, I. (1971). *A Bintel Brief: Sixty years of letters from the Lower East Side to the Jewish Daily Forward.* New York: Ballantine.

Meyers, M. (2012). Trauma therapy and witnessing. In N. Goodman & M. Meyers, (Eds.), *The power of witnessing: Reflections, reverberations, and traces of the Holocaust: Trauma, psychoanalysis, and the living mind* (pp.289–304). New York: Routledge.

Miller, N. K. (2011). *What they saved: Pieces of a Jewish past.* Lincoln: University of Nebraska Press.

Moore, D. D. (1981). *At home in America: Second generation New York Jews.* New York: Columbia University Press.

Naison, M. (2002). Crown Heights in the 1950s. In I. Abramovitch & S. Galvin, *Jews of Brooklyn* (pp. 143–152). Hanover, NH: Brandeis University Press

O'Loughlin, M. (2009). *The subject of childhood.* New York: Peter Lang Publishing.

————. (2013). Ghostly presences in children's lives: Toward a psychoanalysis of the social. In M. O'Loughlin & R. Johnson (Eds.), *Imagining children otherwise: Theoretical and critical perspectives on childhood subjectivity* (pp. 49–74). New York: Peter Lang Publishing.

————. (2018). Introduction: Bearing moral witness to South Africa's trauma. In L. Muofhe & P. Phaswana (Eds.), *And we forgave them: Life stories from apartheid South Africa* (pp. 1–14). Pretoria, South Africa: Unisa Press (University of South Africa Press).

Paver, C. (1961).The greenhorns. In H. Goodman (Ed. and trans.), *The new country: Stories from the Yiddish about life in America* (p. 92). New York: YKUF Publishers.

Pisano, N. G. (2012). *Granddaughters of the Holocaust: Never forgetting what they didn't experience.* Boston: Academic Studies Press.

Ravage, M. (1917). *An American in the making, the life story of an immigrant.* New York: Harper & Brothers.

Reisman, B. (2006). Why I came to America. In J. Cohen & D. Soyer (Eds. and trans.), *My future is in America: Autobiographies of Eastern European Jewish immigrants* (pp. 35–105). New York: New York University Press. Originally written in 1942.

Richman, S. (2012). "Too young to remember": Recovering and integrating the unacknowledged known. In N. R. Goodman & M. B. Meyers (Eds.), *The Power of witnessing: Reflections, reverberations, and traces of the Holocaust: Trauma, psychoanalysis, and the living mind* (pp. 105–118). New York: Routledge.

Rischin, M. (1962). *The promised city: New York's Jews, 1870–1914.* New York: Harper & Row.

Rogers, A. G. (2006). *The unsayable: The hidden language of trauma.* New York: Ballantine Books.

Roth, P. (1988). *The facts: A novelist's autobiography.* New York: Farrar, Straus, & Giroux.

Rubin, H. (1983). Workers on the land. In U. D. Herscher (Ed.), *The Eastern European Jewish experience in America: A century of memories, 1882–1982* (pp. 17–51). Cincinnati, OH: American Jewish Archives. Excerpted from H. Rubin's autobiography, trans. B. N. Schambelan, privately published in Philadelphia in the 1970s.

Rubin, R. (1979). *Voices of a people: The story of Yiddish folksong.* Philadelphia: Jewish Publication Society of America.

Rutter, M. (2012). Resilience as a dynamic concept. *Development and Psychopathology, 24,* 335–344. doi: 10.1017/S0954579412000028.

Sachar, H. M. (1992). *A history of the Jews in America.* New York: Random House.

———. (2005). *A history of Jews in the modern world.* New York: Alfred A. Knopf.

Salberg, J. (2005). Etudes on loss. *American Imago, 62*(4), 435–451. doi: 10.1353/aim.2006.0006.

———. (2017a). The texture of traumatic attachment: Presence and ghostly absence in trans-generational transmission. In J. Salberg & S. Grand (Eds.), *Wounds of history: Repair and resilience in the trans-generational transmission of trauma* (pp. 77–99). New York: Routledge.

———. (2017b). Introduction to Part IV: Fragmented legacies, healing narratives. In J. Salberg & S. Grand (Eds.), *Wounds of history: Repair and resilience in the trans-generational transmission of trauma* (pp. 245–249). New York: Routledge.

Salberg, J., & Grand, S. (Eds.). (2017). *Wounds of history: Repair and resilience in the trans-generational transmission of trauma.* New York: Routledge.

Sarna, J. D. (1981). The myth of no return: Jewish return migration to Eastern Europe, 1881–1914. *American Jewish History, 17,* 256–268.

Saviano, R. (2019, March 7). The migrant caravan: Made in America. *The New York Review of Books,* p. 16.

Shandler, J. (2014). *Shtetl: A vernacular intellectual history.* New Brunswick, NJ: Rutgers University Press.

Shapiro, E. S. (2008). Introduction. In E. S. Shapiro (Ed.), *Yiddish in America: Essays on Yiddish culture in the golden land* (pp. ix–xix). Scranton, PA: University of Scranton Press.

Shulman, A. (1976). *The new country.* New York: Charles Scribner's Sons.

Silberman, C. E. (1985). *A certain people: American Jews and their lives today.* New York: Summit.

Sorin, G. (1992). *A time for building: The third migration, 1880–1920* (Vol. III in The Jewish People in America). Baltimore, MD: Johns Hopkins University Press.

———. (1997). *Tradition transformed: The Jewish experience in America.* Baltimore, MD: Johns Hopkins University Press.

Soskin, R. (1976). The hungry child. In S. Kramer & J. Masur (Eds.), *Jewish grandmothers: A vibrant generation of women* (pp. 31–44). Boston, MA: Beacon.

Soyer, D. (1997). *Jewish immigrant associations and American identity in New York, 1880–1939.* Cambridge, MA: Harvard University Press.

Stern, D. (1985). *The interpersonal world of the infant: A view from psychoanalysis and developmental psychology.* New York, NY: Basic Books.

Stopper, C. (December, 1983). *The Stopper saga.* Unpublished manuscript.

U.S. Citizenship and Immigration Services. (2019). Refugees & Asylum. Retrieved from http://www.uscis.gov/humanitarian/refugees-asylum.

U.S. Department of Homeland Security. (2017, December 18). *2016 Yearbook of Immigration Statistics.* Table 7. Persons obtaining lawful permanent resident status by type and detailed class of admission: Fiscal year 2016. Retrieved February 21, 2019, from https://www.dhs.gov/immigration-statistics/yearbook/2016/table7.

Valverde, C., & Martin-Cabrera, L. (2015). The silence of the grandchildren of the war: Transgenerational trauma in Spain. In M. O'Loughlin (Ed.), *The ethics of remembering and the consequences of forgetting: Essays on trauma, history, and memory* (pp. 203–227). Lanham, MD: Rowman & Littlefield.

van der Kolk, B. (2000). Posttraumatic stress disorder and the nature of trauma. *Dialogues in Clinical Neuroscience, 2* (1), 7–22. Retrieved September 8, 2018, from https://www.ncbi.nlm.nih.gov/pmc/articles/PMC3181584/.

———. (2014). *The body keeps the score: Brain, mind, and body in the healing of trauma.* New York: Penguin Books.

van der Kolk, B., McFarlane, A. C., & Weisaeth, L. (1996). *Traumatic stress: The effects of overwhelming experience on mind, body, and society.* New York: Guilford.

van Ecke, Y. (2007). *Attachment and immigrants: Emotional security among Dutch and Belgian immigrants in California, U.S.A.* Amsterdam: Amsterdam University Press.

van Ecke, Y., Chope, R., & Emmelkamp, P. (2005). Immigrants and attachment status: Research findings with Dutch and Belgian immigrants in California. *Social Behavior and Personality: An international journal, 33,* 657–674. doi:10.2224/sbp.2005.33.7.657.

Volkan, V. D. (1997). *Bloodlines: From ethnic pride to ethnic terrorism.* New York: Farrar, Straus & Giroux.

———. (1998, August). Transgenerational transmissions and chosen traumas: An aspect of large-group identity. Presented at XIII International Congress International Association of Group Psychotherapy.

Volovici, L. (2010, November 19). Romania. *YIVO Encyclopedia of Jews in Eastern Europe.* Retrieved April 23, 2017, from http://www.yivoencyclopedia.org/article.aspx/Romania.

Weinberg, S. S. (1988). *The world of our mothers: The lives of Jewish immigrant women.* Chapel Hill: University of North Carolina Press.

Weisser, M. R. (1989). *A brotherhood of memory: Jewish landsmanshaftn in the New World.* New York: Basic Books.

Wenger, B. S. (1996). *New York Jews and the Great Depression: Uncertain promise.* New Haven, CT: Yale University Press.

Winnicott, D. W. (1967). The location of cultural experience. *International Journal of Psychoanalysis, 48,* 368–372.

Winter, J. (2015). The Great War and Jewish memory. *European Judaism, 48,* 3–22. doi:10.3167/ej.2015.48.01.02

Yerushalmi, Y. H. (1986, February 15). Interview by Bill Moyers. *Listening to America Heritage Conversations.* Retrieved April 11, 2019, from https://billmoyers.com/content/yosef-yerushalmi/.

———. (1996). *Zakhor: Jewish history and Jewish memory.* Seattle: University of Washington Press.

Yezierska, A. (1920a). How I found America. In *Hungry hearts: Stories of the Jewish-American immigrant experience* (pp. 250–298). Boston, MA: Houghton Mifflin.

———. (1920b). Hunger. In *Hungry hearts: Stories of the Jewish-American immigrant experience* (pp. 35–64). Boston, MA: Houghton Mifflin.

———. (1920c). The fat of the land. In *Hungry hearts: Stories of the Jewish-American immigrant experience* (pp. 178–223). Boston, MA: Houghton Mifflin.

Zahra, T. (2016). *The great departure: Mass migration from Eastern Europe and the making of the free world*. New York: W.W. Norton.

Zborowski, M., & Herzog, E. (1952). *Life is with people: The culture of the shtetl*. New York: Schocken Books.

Zipperstein, S. J. (2010, Summer). Underground man: The curious case of Mark Zborowski and the writing of a modern Jewish classic. *Jewish Review of Books*. Retrieved February 16, 2019, from https://jewishreviewofbooks.com/articles/275/underground-man-the-curious-case-of-mark-zborowski-and-the-writing-of-a-modern-jewish-classic/.

———. (2018). *Pogrom: Kishinev and the tilt of history*. New York: W.W. Norton.

Zollman, J. (n.d.). Jewish immigration to America: Three waves. My Jewish Learning. Retrieved February 9, 2010, from https://www.myjewishlearning.com/article/jewish-immigration-to-america-three-waves/.

Index

abuse: drugs, 197; physical, 1, 184–185, 187–188

Addams, Jane, 136

adult children, xxvii, 81; alienation and, 198, 199; with alienation and anger, 195–200; with anti-Semitism and poverty, xxi; with denial of trauma, 209–212; depression and, 14, 54, 59, 61, 216; with disavowal of loss, 205–212; empathy of, 188–189, 197; grief and migration trauma influencing, 121–128; with healing, 220; historical introduction and, 180–184; homesickness and, 94; integrity and, 198–199, 200; with intergenerational transmission of trauma, 48–71; interviews with, xxiii–xxiv, 4; with life and future, 190–194; with life stories, 8–19, 184–212; with life stories of home country, 94–121; loneliness and, 39, 41; memories and, 193–194; memory and history influencing, 231–232; with mental illness, life stories about, 184–190; with narcissism, 104; psychology of, xxiii, xxiv–xxv, 46, 48, 67, 216–219; resilience and, 200–205, 216; "they left it all behind" as viewed by, 6–7, 10, 35, 125, 217, 230; trauma and, xxii, 8, 41, 74

African American–Jewish tensions, 220n5

Ainslee, R. C., 91

Akhtar, S., 91

Aleichem, Sholem, 129n15

Alexander II (Tsar of Russia), 24

alienation: adult children and, 198, 199; anger and, 195–200; depression and, 229; fear of depression and, 90

"Alone in a Strange World" (Asch), 84–85, 122

Alroey, G., 28

ambiguity of loss: Boss and, 37n19; defined, 230; disavowal and, 92, 212; trauma and, 32–36

Ambiguous Loss (Boss), 37n19

Americanization, 135, 136, 166; community and, 179; education and, 167, 171; importance of, 171, 172, 204; inferiority and, 170; languages and, 136–137; trauma and, 142

anger: alienation and, 195–200; depression and, 48, 53, 55, 75; about unresponsive parents, 105, 107, 115; violence and, 196, 197–198, 199

anti-Communism, 182

Antin, Mary, 27

anti-Semitism: adult children with poverty, xxi; anti-Communism and, 182; children and, 142–143; decline in, 213, 220n1; in Eastern Europe, xix, 95, 105, 225; education and, 145; fear of, 155; influence of, xxi, 7; prevalence of, 6, 8,

families and, 93; fear and, xxvi, 22, 99,
157; of Great Depression, 58, 75, 76;
healing from, 179, 189, 204; history
with loss and, 179, 212–213, 226–233;
of Holocaust, 13–14, 72; idealization
and, 14, 104, 154; immigrants with
types of, xxvi; Judaism and, 155, 194;
large-T, xxvi, 43–44; "little t," 43, 44;
loss and, xxii, 7, 11, 15, 40, 42, 97, 118,
189, 211, 220n9, 237; mental illness
and, 156, 185, 186, 216; parents and,
xxv–xxvi, 162; the past with life stories
and, 48–71; poverty and, xxvi, 1, 58,
116, 128n8; psychological impact of,
xxii, 13; psychology of, 101, 102–104,
236–237; refugees with, 234; relational,
139, 168–169; secure attachment and
working through, 76; silence and, 29,
59, 64, 71, 149; small-t, xxvi, 8, 43–44;
suicide and, 142; transmission of, 139,
224; violence and, xxvi, 12, 63, 176,
217; of World War I, 7, 11, 13, 16–17,
29–31, 40, 59, 62, 125, 130n28, 148,
155, 172n1, 172n8, 186, 224; of World
War II, 1. *See also* intergenerational
trauma, transmission of; migration
trauma
Treaty of Brest-Litovsk (1918), 77n2
true narrative, 179, 189
Turgenev, Ivan, 117
typhoid fever, 56, 165

United Hebrew Charities, 34, 128n2
United States (US): as "Golden Land,"
xxvi, 34; immigrants in, 82, 237;
immigration to, 27–29, 234; with
immigration visas, 233; with Judaism in
public ceremonies, 182; life stories of
first generation in, 184–212; refugee or
asylum status in, 238n5; transition from
home country to, 81–88
unresolved (childhood disorganized)
attachment, 123, 125, 226
unthought knowns, 45, 77n3, 230
US. *See* United States

Van Ecke, Y., 122, 124, 225, 226
violence: anger and, 196, 197–198, 199;
fear and, 214; immigrants and, xxvii,

234; migration trauma and, 124, 212;
trauma and, xxvi, 12, 63, 176, 217. *See
also* anti-Semitism; Holocaust;
pogroms; rape
"virtual listener," 179
visas, immigration, 233

"A Wall" (Libin), 85
Warsaw Ghetto memorial evenings, 214
Weinberg, S. S., 129n17, 135
Weisser, M. R., 31, 43
Winnicott, D. W., 89
Winter, J., 29, 77n13
witnessing: of frozen states by children,
xxv, 45, 46, 139, 160, 163; Holocaust
with potency of, 73; the past, 223
women: brothels and, 87; employment and,
96–97, 107, 113, 114, 130n31, 158,
182–183, 192, 202, 207, 213, 220n6;
homesickness and, 84, 128n3; with men
deserting families, 86–87; with
mourning, 5; rape of, 24, 30, 31, 56
World War I: anti-Semitism after, 8, 12;
civil wars and, 9, 29–31; with
communication barriers, 98; families,
215; immigration before, 237n2; the
shtetl in, 16–17; trauma of, 7, 11, 13,
16–17, 29–31, 40, 59, 62, 125, 130n28,
148, 155, 172n1, 172n8, 186, 224
World War II: families and, 212; GI Bill
and, 10, 144, 172n10, 182; trauma of, 1
worth: gender and, 201, 203; lack of self-,
99, 188, 203
Wounds of History (Salberg and Grand),
221n14

Yekaterinaslav, 130n30
Yezierska, Anzia, 137
Yiddish language: assimilation and, 54, 72,
180, 229; community and, 20; English
and, 39, 127, 183, 229–230; with
negative connotations, 106, 136, 231
YIVO (online newsletter), xxiii
Yzierska, Anzia, 80, 81

Zangwill, Israel, 37n13
Zborowski, Mark, xxi, xxviiin3, 5
Zionism, 28, 102, 187
Zipperstein, S. J., xxviiin3

About the Author

Hannah Hahn maintains a full-time private practice as a psychologist and psychoanalyst in New York City. After graduate-level work in English literature, she obtained a master's degree in psychology from Harvard University, a PhD in clinical psychology from Columbia University, and psychoanalytic certification. She taught attachment at the New York Institute for Psychoanalytic Training in Infancy, Childhood, and Adolescence. Publications and presentations include "They Left It All Behind," in M. O'Loughlin (Ed.), *The Ethics of Remembering and the Consequences of Forgetting* (Rowman & Littlefield, 2015), and "A Safe Place to Stand: The Holding Environment with Child Patients and Their Parents," a paper presented for the Lecture Series of the Society for the Institute for Contemporary Psychotherapy in 2005.